CONFESSIONS OF A
HAPLESS HEDONIST

ERNEST KOLOWRAT

CONFESSIONS OF A HAPLESS HEDONIST

AN INCONVENIENT DISCOVERY
ABOUT THE MEANING OF PLEASURE

Library of Congress Number: 00-191744

COVER ILLUSTRATION:
From Michelangelo's Sistine Chapel Ceiling: *Fall of Man and Expulsion from the Garden of Eden*, after restoration.
Erich Lessing/Art Resource, New York.

AUTHOR'S NOTE

The generous blurb from Lewis H. Lapham on the cover dates back to 1986; the one from the late Stephen Birmingham to 1985. The mores of the world have changed in the intervening decades, and behavior that would have been excused with a smile is now likely to evoke a frown. In giving my prose a cosmetic once-over for this edition, I have consciously refrained from catering to the expectations of today – and heaven forbid, try to make myself look better than the past allows.

In this autobiographical tale, some names and details have been changed for reasons of privacy; other details have been modified to tell the story in an effective way within limited space, without compromising the essence of what took place.

My thanks to Natalie Chapman for introducing me to the finer elements of style, and to John Hersey for continuing that task in the final years of his life. My gratitude also to the late Oliver Swan, who had been my agent since discovering the initial version of this work in the early 1960s at a London book fair.

PROLOGUE

BOOK ONE
IN QUEST OF PLEASURE

BOOK TWO
IN QUEST OF REDEMPTION

EPILOGUE

If we are destined to wise up eventually, why not wise up now?

– *J. A. Comenius (1592-1670)*

PROLOGUE

"We take it for granted that our experience here on earth is supposed to be enjoyable, that it is our birthright to derive pleasure from daily life. Gentlemen, this assumption blithely ignores the evidence."

On the podium was Professor Franklin Le Van Baumer, delivering one of his three weekly lectures to our intellectual history class during my junior year at Yale. A tall, distinguished-looking scholar, Professor Baumer liked to gesticulate vehemently when his back wasn't hurting him. With his lumbago acting up, he was careful to make no untoward move. "There is no guarantee," he continued stiffly, "that our unexpected freak of history, when enjoyment of life is considered the norm, is assured any kind of a future. Virtually all of history, as well as the abject conditions in which most of humanity lives today, point strongly against it."

Our professor's prognosis resonated through the cavernous neo-Gothic hall but failed to strike a responsive chord. The unbounded optimism I held as an article of faith wasn't going to be affected by a few dire words. Most of my friends were sanguine about the future too, and not just because they were at Yale. Why, even in the blighted parts of the world people were leading better lives. Was Professor Baumer so isolated in his intellectual lair that he failed to understand the world in which he lived? Or was the professor's aching back more likely to blame? A permanent cure would surely brighten his views! And I wondered, why was it that so many of the great thinkers across the ages had some physical problem or mental quirk affecting the ideas with which they tried to saddle the world? Saint Augustine went around for years moaning, "God, make me chaste . . . but not yet!" – and then did his utmost to inflict the dubious blessings of his celibacy on everyone else. Was it because his personal ardor for intimate pleasures had waned? Having myself just turned twenty, this was a problem I could hardly understand. And I had an exciting thought. What if the world were to come under the sway of a philosophy formulated by someone who had a healthy appetite for life? I was the 175-pound intramural boxing champion, yet I had pretty good grades. Why couldn't I figure out a valid philosophical system for our times that would one day be taught in Professor Baumer's class – or at least be included on the optional reading list? It was a thought with which I occasionally liked to entertain myself, especially after a few beers at the Old Heidelberg bar.

It was also a thought that would remain with me to this day.

Book One

In Quest of Pleasure

I. Flaws

Call it a fortuitous twist, an improbable turn of a wheel a thousand years ago that would set me on an enviable path. The story has it that a sturdy young peasant was tilling a field in the highlands of Bohemia, when a chariot bearing the ruler of the realm hurtled by toward a deep ravine, the royal horses running wild. Dropping his hoe, this loyal subject rushed forth and with a surge of superhuman strength grabbed one of the chariot's wheels and began to turn it in the opposite direction. There was a swirl of dust and frantic neighing pierced the bucolic peace. When the air had cleared and the countryside was again still, there stood the chariot, halted at the edge of the precipice. For this heroic rescue of his sovereign, the young peasant was made a noble on the spot and endowed with our family name, which means *Turner-of-the-Wheel*.

How many genes of this progenitor of our line have been passed on to me? It would be pandering to fairy tales to pretend he had embodied only desirable traits. That sudden change of status merely placed his descendants in a privileged position to excel. And some indeed proved their mettle in subsequent centuries as military leaders and confidants to emperors and kings. Perhaps the most notable namesake was a wily Machiavellian type who, as interior minister to the Austro-Hungarian chancellor, Metternich, fomented a plot that ended the historic career of his durable boss.

More typical of our family annals were unusual affairs of the heart — presented herein with the caveat that some details derive from family lore, and more than one version may exist. Take the case of my great-grandfather that caused a scandal around the middle of the nineteenth century. A lieutenant field marshal in the Austro-Hungarian Empire with multiple tiers of medals, he was heir to some of the features I would inherit: the same gently sloping forehead, the distinctive nose with a little bump on the bridge and a suggestion of a cleft at the tip that gave his expression a hint of animalistic sensuality and zeal. As governor of Venice in 1850, a post he had received following his heroic deeds in military action the previous year, my 46-year-old forebear married an enchanting dancer half his age, without permission from the Hapsburg imperial court. This was a transgression that couldn't be ignored. He was stripped of his cushy Italian post and dispatched to Hungary to mop up the latest flare-up of Kossuth's rebellion. For some inexplicable reason the chastised field marshal decided to lug along an iron chest containing the bulk of his negotiable wealth in jewels and gold. Somewhere along the way this treasure chest was misplaced by his orderlies, alas, never to be located again. His mission against the rebels having fizzled and his military career now ended, my great-grandfather found himself virtually pauperized. The hereditary Turner-of-the-Wheel properties were in the hands of different branches of the family, and my hapless forebear was relegated to the charity of friends, while falling deeper and deeper into debt. The woman for whom he had risked everything died of tuberculosis still in her early thirties, and two years later, my ailing great-grandfather was headed for the *Schuldturm* — the debtors' tower — when he also died.

Their orphaned son, my grandfather Leopold, had the distinction of being the one left standing after the last fatal duel of the

Austro-Hungarian Empire. Brought up in relative poverty by well-meaning relatives, Leopold wasn't always regarded kindly by his noble peers. Displaying particular enmity was Prince Wilhelm von Auersperg, who cast aspersions on my grandfather's parentage, and accused him of having embezzled during their schooldays some student funds. These attacks turned especially venomous after both Auersperg and my grandfather became suitors of the same lovely Countess Waldstein, who apparently favored my more dashing grandfather. Reacting to Auersperg's public slights, my grandfather repeatedly challenged him to a duel, which Auersperg repeatedly declined, making it known he wouldn't lower himself by engaging with a mongrel – and one of questionable honor at that. Seeking to bring the situation to a head, my grandfather publicly accosted Auersperg at Prague's main railway station, slapping the prince's face as the prince and his retinue were boarding a special train to horse races in Slovakia. While Auersperg again sought to decline, the head of the Auersperg clan ordered him to uphold the family's honor and accept. The rumors at that time posited that this relative held a material interest in seeing his myopic nephew, sole heir to the vast family estate, removed from the scene. If so, was my grandfather wittingly or unwittingly complicit in such a plot? Whatever the case, on a sunny afternoon of May 6, 1876, in a quiet park on the outskirts of Prague, the twenty-two-year-old prince took his stand at fifteen paces from his adversary, a golden pince-nez perched on his nose, and in a show of bravado, smoking a cigar. The first two rounds resulted in misfires and misses on each side; however, when Auersperg missed on the third round, my grandfather's shot found its deadly mark. Struck in the stomach, Auersperg spent an agonizing night before expiring later that day. In the aftermath, my twenty-four-year-old grandfather retreated to Russia to avoid a trial in Vienna, while the young Countess Waldstein, over whom the duel had been ostensibly fought, retreated to a convent from which she would never emerge. Having eventually received a pardon from the Emperor, my grandfather returned to Vienna, where he incurred gambling debts in an effort to reestablish himself. He also happened to attend a glittering ball where he caught the eye of the daughter of an international tobacco mogul. The reason this wealthy entrepreneur and his wife had brought their daughter to Vienna at the height of the city's social season was precisely to catch the eye of a titled marital prospect; however, considering the dubious repute of the count involved, the parents did their utmost to disengage their strong-willed daughter from her bewitchment. She, nevertheless, prevailed, becoming my future grandmother at a society wedding in St. Patrick's Cathedral in New York.

The infusion of substantial negotiable wealth enabled the young couple to reclaim the hereditary Turner-of-the-Wheel properties in Bohemia. It would also allow their first born, my Uncle Sascha, to indulge an increasing array of appetites, talents and whims that would bring him fame in the capitals of much of Europe and in Hollywood. His most immediate distinction was to acquire remarkable girth already in his teens. It was said he could polish off an entire goose at a sitting when surrounded by his ever-present retinue cheering him on at some posh restaurant in Vienna or Prague. Sascha's status also enabled him to qualify for a pilot's license and acquire one of the first automobiles. Being mechanically inclined, Sascha soon became a familiar sight on the international racing circuit, his corpulent form magnified by the midget assistant next to him on the car's front seat. It was in Sascha's honor that Dr. Porsche named the *Saschawagen*, the forerunner of today's Porsche cars. But Sascha's greatest renown was as a pioneer of the European film industry. He produced the first version of *Ben Hur* and gave a start to the Korda brothers on their way to Hollywood (as was partially depicted by their relative, Michael Korda, in *Charmed Lives*). Sascha reveled in the intimacies involved in discovering some of the glamorous stars of the silent screen, as well as countless others who would never be publicly seen. Although struck down by pancreatic cancer at an early age, Sascha's last request ran true to form: that a promising young starlet from one of his films, who was already known for her shapely legs, come to his sanitarium room and lift up her skirts. And that's what Marlene Dietrich did, according to her own biography, giving my storied uncle one more lingering look on which to reflect during his passage to eternity.

With Sascha's death, responsibility for the family name devolved on Father, who harbored a morbid concern for the survival of his historic line. A set of twin brothers had died of diphtheria shortly after birth, another brother succumbed to cholera at two, and still another died at twenty-seven from unknown causes. The sole surviving sibling was an older sister married to an Austrian *Fürst,* whose noble line her sons would perpetuate.

Thus it was solely up to Father. No longer dependent on imperial approval in the democratic Czechoslovakia created after World War I, Father was on his own in picking a mate. He had read several books about the new science of eugenics – about heredity, recessive genes, and dominant characteristics – no doubt, some of the same books being perused by an obscure Austrian corporal, Adi Schickelgruber, whose conclusions a few years later as Adolph Hitler would forever change the world. But the conclusions Father drew had an altogether different thrust: Nobility was no longer suitable breeding stock. The titled families he knew had intermarried for too many generations and were weighted down with genetic debris. Practically all of those families had a daffy son or a relative whom they tried to keep out of sight, if not locked up in the proverbial castle tower. Also fresh on Father's mind was the fate of the Romanovs, whose predisposition to hemophilia had played such a crucial role in the collapse of their empire.

How ironic, then, that Father's most intriguing prospect was his deceased brother's seductive wife, an émigré princess from one of Russia's leading families. Married to Sascha for almost a decade, the princess attributed their failure to have a child to her husband's philandering, which had afflicted him with diseases that left his sperm impaired. But her most convincing ploy was to arouse Father in tantalizing ways and then stop in time.

Within moments after being released from his frustration on their wedding night, Father regained his senses. God, how could he have been so irresponsible and let pleasure overrule his mind! What if the princess's genes were irreparably flawed? What if she had lied about the reason for failing to produce an offspring with his brother? Even with Sascha's physical problems, how could any Turner-of-the-Wheel be infecund?

As it turned out, the princess couldn't have children and had known it all along. After several years of unrealized promises from fertility specialists, Father felt free to take corrective measures of his own. Lacking any scientific basis to evaluate a potential mother's genetic worth, Father decided to trust his instincts. If a woman he happened to spot had that something special which made him feel as if his genes were perking up, a follow-through was not only justified but obligatory. This meant he always had to keep his eyes open – in the streets, in offices, when traveling, when relaxing. For who could tell where the best prospect might turn up next?

That's how Father met Mother, an alluring nineteen-year-old in radiant health whom he had followed onto a tram she was taking to her home on the outskirts of Prague, where her parents owned a butcher shop. In the tram, this tall, mustachioed man with hair slicked back from a sloping forehead stood embarrassingly close, as he began to scrutinize her childbearing potential. How his eyes pressed on her until she felt herself blush, afraid he might topple onto her with each jerk and sway of the rickety car!

Reflecting on it later at home, Mother allowed that this admirer in his unpressed blue, pinstriped suit was attractive in a way

she couldn't quite figure out; yet he seemed a bit unkempt and noticeably slim, as if he couldn't afford to have enough to eat – not
at all like the strapping sons of her more prosperous neighbors.
Maybe he was an unemployed professor; hardly the type that she,
as the prettiest girl in Prague, had in mind to father the children
she wanted to bear. What nerve for him to have followed her
home!

It took another five years for Father to enlist Mother in his cause.
The problem was that he would make his impassioned plea and
then disappear for months into his privileged domain. This made
Mother dubious about the long-term parental guidance he would
provide. What finally instilled in Father the necessary persistence
was when his barren wife, the Russian princess, started to imply
that he was the one responsible for their failure to produce a child.

There was only one way to find out.

I was the second child. I came along a bit unexpectedly. Father was touring somewhere in Spain in his chauffeured car, and I
was born in a speeding taxi not far from Mother's home. The hospital where I was brought served one of the poorest sections in
Prague. So there we were, Mother and I, in a long, drab room
crowded with little metal beds occupied by women who had just
given birth. Even the younger mothers looked as if life had already passed them by. I wasn't especially pretty, and Mother worried that maybe I wasn't hers. Couldn't an overworked attendant
have made a mistake? Mother knew that the child sleeping at her
side would be well cared for. But what of her real child? What if he
were to end up with one of the destitute women in the ward?

For the first years of my life, I lived with Mother at her parents' home, a comfortable two-family house in a modest neighborhood not far from their butcher shop. Grandfather was a bar-
rel-chested man with a thick waist who could hoist entire sides of
fattened steers onto meat hooks in his store window. When I was

two years old, I remember him taking my older brother and me for a walk to a nearby square filled with chestnut trees. The chestnuts were ripening, but those that had fallen to the ground had already been picked over, leaving only the yellowing shells. Reaching up and swinging his walking stick against the lower branches of the trees, Grandfather loosened a torrent of the prickly crop. My brother and I started to gather the chestnuts, breaking them open and joyfully stuffing the brown cores in our pockets. Just then two older boys appeared who pounced on this treasure trove and tried to get their fill. Though I wouldn't have minded sharing the bounty, my hefty grandfather was already chasing off the intruders with his walking stick.

Grandfather often acted as if he were the custodian of some royal brood, ready to protect and uphold us with great pride. Our family situation, to be sure, was ideal for wagging tongues, not only in view of the mores of the thirties but because of who the father happened to be: an illustrious count with progressive views, an influential voice in politics, a generous patron of the arts. And Father wasn't about to disappoint curious neighbors by coming around on the sly. He was proud of his family-on-the-side, which he considered a symbol of his democratic ideals, a public rejection of the idle rich of his class. He would screech to a halt in a cloud of dust in front of the house in his racy eight-cylinder Tatra, loaded with presents. A play steam roller with a real, tiny boiler. A pedal automobile large enough to hold my older brother and me. All sorts of wind-up toys. The longer the interval between visits, the greater the load of presents. Of course, there were presents for Mother, too. A strand of pearls, a silver fox stole, French perfume. But Father always had to take those back. Mother didn't want it said she was consorting with a count for personal gain. Her primary motivation was to provide her children with the best opportunity in life, and we were her sole interest. She would begin to sulk if Father paid undue attention to the feisty Schnauzer he often brought along. "But everybody knows," Father would lightly protest, "until little children get to be bigger, little dogs are much more fun."

When I was three Father took us to Venice, where we stayed on the Lido at an ocean-side hotel that was pink and had brown shutters. The first evening, while having lobster in the chandeliered dining room, I noticed an elderly couple at a nearby table enjoying my struggles with the shell. How nicely they kept smiling at me! Eager to hold their attention, I tried spinning a piece of the empty shell on my fork. The paper-thin remnants unexpectedly took off and went sailing across the room. I was still basking in the old couple's smiles when I felt a sharp slap that surprised more than it hurt. "If this is the way you bring him up," I heard Father say to Mother, "he'll never amount to anything." Now crying, I was sent to bed.

By the time I reached my room, I could no longer feel the slap, and by the next day, my vanity had mended, too. I was quick to forget and even quicker to learn. Though neither of my parents was prone to mete out punishment, I found it easier and easier to avoid giving them cause (unlike my older brother, who sought to oppose Father at every turn). I came to know not only what was expected but also what type of behavior would bring me praise. This often meant I would have to dissimulate or pretend, but that was fine by me. The only reason I remember the slap is that it happened to be one of the last I would ever get.

As a three-year-old, I clung to a habit my mother was increasingly anxious for me to outgrow. I would unobtrusively slink around my sister Manya's crib, and the moment she fell asleep, snatch the pacifier from her mouth and stick it into mine. Sometimes, I would spring into action too soon or make too abrupt a move, which would wake up my baby sister and she would begin to bawl. With great alacrity, I would stuff the pacifier back into her mouth, hoping she would fall asleep before Mother responded to her cries.

What had me so hooked on the pacifier was not the sucking action but the plastic safety ring at the opposite end, through which I could stick my index finger and rotate it gently inside. There was just enough room for the plastic to glide over my skin and produce a deliciously tingling sensation. I never tired of this solitary game and preferred it to playing with my toys, which were usually commandeered by my older brother anyway.

It was this ability to amuse myself without fanfare that led to a momentous discovery. Although not exactly an accident, it wasn't anything I had purposely tried to do or consciously bring about. What I discovered was that by rubbing a certain part of my anatomy long enough, I could experience a feeling I had never known before.

The first time around, I was taken completely by surprise. I had no idea what was going on, but whatever it was, I recognized instantly as the most pleasurable thing that had happened to me yet. It certainly surpassed twirling my finger in the pacifier ring, or having my favorite meal of breaded calves' brains once each week. How overwhelming, I thought, already eager to be overwhelmed again.

With my ingenuity challenged more meaningfully than ever in the past, it didn't take long to reconstruct what I had done to bring about this glorious event. Before I knew it, like magic, there was that exquisite sensation again. I felt it coursing through my body, gathering momentum, then concentrating along the bottom of my spine and coming to its most intense, pulsating focus in the part I had rubbed.

What a discovery! It was like finding an Aladdin's lamp that nobody could take away. With the right kind of a repetitious rubbing, the genie would bring me pleasures I could never have imagined.

I started out twice a day, once in the morning and again at night, to keep the genie on his toes. When I caught a cold the following week and had to stay in bed, I tried to find out if I could keep the genie hopping throughout the day. What fun being sick might become! And indeed, several times the genie seemed to be right there, at my beck and call. Perhaps not as alert, not quite as quick, but ready to fulfill my wish. Only after responding again and again to my whims did his devotion begin to flag. It would take a more prolonged rub or shake to bring him forth, and his magic would be less likely to overwhelm. Eventually, there was no way to rouse him at all.

For a while, I was disappointed. Why couldn't the genie have more stamina and strength? I tried rubbing other parts of my anatomy that were similarly shaped, like the fingers of my hand, obviously, to no avail.

But I didn't despair. I was convinced this limitation was a temporary condition due to my age. I had no doubt that as I became older, I would find the genie easier to evoke, and he would bring me pleasures still more intense than now. Perhaps by the time I was fully grown, a single touch is all that it would take. Merely by walking down the street, the gentle action of my legs or friction of my underwear would bring the genie forth, and engulf me in a pleasure more intense than I could now conceive. I couldn't wait to grow up and find myself in such a perpetually blissful state.

2/

I had just turned four when I visited for the first time Father's residence in Prague, an unkempt Renaissance palace with a pastry shop on the ground floor. The Russian princess, Father's childless wife, had recently died from the lingering effects of an automobile accident, and I now came here occasionally with Mother to spend a few days.

Father didn't pretend to be in mourning. "I can only say I'm grateful I wasn't the one driving the car, " he would tell me in future years. Not long before the accident, the unhappy princess had sent a lucrative offer to Mother to adopt my brother and me, assuming that a butcher's daughter would have her price. When Father found out, he had been furious. "Typical trick of the indolent rich," he called it.

It was during one of these visits to the family palace that I met my father's older sister and her eldest son, Albrecht. The year was 1939, and while I had no idea about Neville Chamberlain and the Munich accords, or that Hitler's army was poised to march into the Czech capital, I understood even at my age that some calamity was about to occur. I could see people reinforcing their windows with tape, and there was an uneasy excitement in the air. My cousin Albrecht had made the risky journey from neighboring Austria to meet with his mother before the borders were sealed. She, in turn, had ventured a riskier trip from France, where she had been living for years, away from her family for reasons I wouldn't learn until much later in life.

Albrecht was a restrained, lanky young man who wore a nightcap and a nightshirt to bed. I spied him on several occasions in that attire as he moved along the palace hallways, turning out the many lights that were normally left on throughout the night. His compulsive manner had me mystified, since I heard no sirens and no blackout was in force. He also looked unusually glum, which I understood better. His father had recently died, and I could imagine feeling the same.

Albrecht's mother impressed me much more vividly. The fact that she was seven years older than Father only partly explained the generation gap between my cousin and me. What really made the difference was that Albrecht had been born when my aunt was eighteen, while Father didn't start his family until twice that age. My aunt was exceptionally tall and wore a turban with a funny-looking ostrich feather, and pinned to the collar of her dress was a jade frog. Although expected to stay a week, she brought only a small valise that looked worn and was held together by a leather belt.

I took an instant liking to this lady because of the way she smothered me with hugs and kisses. For her own son she had only a dutiful peck on each cheek. Fleetingly I wondered why this was so. I was more puzzled the following day when I chanced across mother and son, standing silently at opposite ends of the drawing room. Was it because Rudolf the butler was there, dusting and straightening up? He had served the family faithfully for years, but thrived on whatever gossip he could pick up in the course of his work.

I was about to withdraw discreetly when my aunt pulled me toward her with a majestic sweep of the arm. Turning to Albrecht, who as the eldest son had just inherited the family estate in Austria, she said, "I need some money." It sounded neither like a request, nor a command, but an opportunity to comply.

Albrecht pretended not to have heard. He shifted his weight from foot to foot and began to stare at the large Gobelin on the wall, as if examining the design of its idealized pastoral scene.

Once more Albrecht's mother announced her need for cash, but again received no response. In a few energetic steps, she interposed herself between Albrecht and the country scene on the wall. Now there was rebuke in her voice. "For three years I don't see my son. Millions of innocents are about to be killed. Whole armies will go down in defeat. Great navies will be dispatched to the bottom of the seas. And I make over a thousand kilometers by train to see my son once more before these dreadful things happen – without wagon-lits, mind you – and he can't grant me a ridiculous little wish."

She paused to glance across the room at Rudolf. He was busy arranging some papers on a heavy Renaissance table in the corner. "Well, if you're so poor and cannot spare a few crowns for your own mother who wants only to buy a little something for your own cousin," she said, raising her voice, "I'll be compelled to get a little loan from Rudolf. I know he, at least, is a generous soul."

Albrecht's lanky form arched into a stoop, and a look of suffering contorted his face.

"Well?" his mother demanded with finality, "do I have to ask Rudolf?"

Albrecht's mother ended up with a few hundred crowns. "I want you to know," she informed her son haughtily, as she stuffed the modest sum into a faded alligator purse, "I consider this to be only a loan. I don't feel I should owe you any gratitude, don't you think? After all, I am your mother."

Without consulting anyone, my aunt whisked me out of the house. She shuttled me from store to store, buying whatever she thought caught my eye. A windup fire truck, a steam engine with a dynamo and a little bulb that lit up, and two live salamanders. My aunt had a regal bearing, and in her presence, clerks snapped to, treating her with a deference that bordered on fear. In the pet shop where she bought the salamanders, she had originally asked for a monkey. When the owner tried to explain that the international situation had disrupted monkey shipments from India, my aunt said a monkey from Africa would be fine. Ignoring the shop owner's helpless shrug, she began to search every corner of the premises for the monkey she was convinced he was hiding there. She even started to invade the exasperated man's adjoining apartment. That's when he confessed that irrespective of war or peace, his shop had never carried monkeys and never would. "Well, shame on you!" my aunt rebuked him. "If I had it my way, every young boy would have a monkey of his own. He could then study it and watch it like a reflection of himself. Not only for the bad things he must outgrow, but for the many good things he can learn."

By the time we returned home, it was evening and the long, mirrored vestibule was dark. Encumbered by my aunt's gifts, I started to grope for the switch. Just then Rudolf appeared from the side door of his adjoining quarters and turned on the lights.

"Is this any way to treat guests?" my aunt asked pointedly. "We could easily have tripped and dropped the salamanders in their glass jar. Imagine, *quel malheur* that would have been! The lights should always be left on in a proper foyer."

"I didn't realize, thousand pardons, Mrs. Countess," Rudolf muttered. "It was still daylight when your son left. On his way out, he turned out . . . "

My aunt interrupted. "Ah, yes, my son, of course." She nodded understandingly, then pursed her lips. "Did he say when he was coming back?"

Father's loyal butler stood there awkwardly. "His Grace packed everything, Mrs. Countess."

Rather than surprised or disappointed, my aunt seemed vindicated. She turned to me and laughed like a storybook witch, "Ho-ho-ho, what a coward that Albrecht! He knew we would return with not a penny left."

I thought I understood. If my gloomy cousin chose to depart so hurriedly, it probably was because he feared another request for funds. I had by then concluded that Albrecht was thrifty rather than stingy, which also explained his obsession with turning out lights. How could I have guessed he was formulating some strange theory about dead electrons? Or that his wonderfully unrestrained mother had once caused Albrecht a desolation that made the reunion too difficult for him to bear?

Perhaps most remarkable in retrospect — and to Albrecht's everlasting credit — was that despite his princely title and centuries of noble lineage on both sides, my cousin in no way betrayed what he must have been thinking when he saw his mother smothering this little mongrel with kisses.

3/

It was to be my last visit to the palace for several years. Realizing that war was inevitable now, Father bought a villa for Mother about a hundred kilometers north of Prague, where she and his children were more likely to be safe. On a gentle hill overlooking a small village, this stucco-covered modern structure had large terraces, windows that were two stories tall to light up the front hall, and a wood-and-brick fence enclosing acres and acres of orchards and woods.

Living in such a conspicuous way was not without perils of its own. Driving by one day, the wife of the district Nazi boss took a fancy to the house and right away wanted to requisition the upper floor. "So many rooms!" she kept exclaiming with proprietary interest, as she breezed from room to room. *"So viele Zimmer!"* Only her husband's sudden transfer to a distant town spared us untold grief.

As a first grader, I was confused by the war. I felt an unspoken conviction that my parents, teachers, and all the people in the village were against the occupying Nazis. Yet everybody seemed to be publicly rooting for a quick German victory. In school, we were taught how to sing *"Deutschland, Deutschland, Über Alles,"* and how high to raise the arm to give the *Heil Hitler!* salute impressively enough to please the Nazi inspector on his surprise visits.

I soon became adept at this game. If called upon, I could argue convincingly and in detail why a Nazi victory was inevitable. Spurred on by my rhetoric, I might even expound on the glories of the thousand-year *Reich*. In my best moments as an unwitting seven-year-old flack of German power, I might have made the Nazi propaganda chief, Goebbels, proud.

It didn't stop there. I somehow developed a secret yearning for one of the symbols of Nazi rule. What I wanted more than anything was the handy little dagger I saw all of the *Hitlerjugend* wear over their back pocket, strapped to a wide black belt around their waist. They were young boys, often no older than I, seemingly no different from troops of boy scouts dressed in black. How lucky they were to own such a knife! Its stainless-steel blade was sheathed in black, the black handle emblazoned with a small red swastika. This bit of red against all that black cast on me a hypnotic spell. It wasn't just another knife but a whole magical universe. To this day I wonder what I wouldn't have done for that knife. One thing I concluded already then. I wouldn't have joined the Hitlerjugend even if it had been possible. That would have meant leaving the comforts of home and always marching around in shorts, knees bare in the coldest months, in sleet and snow. But if that dagger had been dangled promisingly enough in front of me, I wasn't sure I wouldn't have revealed that Father listened to short-wave radio, which was strictly forbidden, or that I had overheard sentiments in our home with a decidedly anti-Nazi tone. Any thought of hurting the people I loved might have been temporarily blocked by the desire to please and be rewarded. No doubt, I would have been still more forthcoming if threatened with thumbscrews. I had always thought of myself as a potential hero. But not that kind; not if it involved pain.

At the time I entered the village school, I was free of any religious bias or creed. I didn't even know what denomination I was, when asked by the teacher on the first day in class. None of the choices she reeled off sounded familiar. But she thought I was a Roman Catholic and told me to check at home. I was surprised Mother knew what a Catholic was – and still more so, that I was one. How could I have been something with such a weird name without knowing it? But I was glad. Most of the other children in school were Catholics, and I didn't want to be different.

Religion was an integral part of the curriculum. The immediate objective was to prepare us for confession and communion – "the first stop on the only train to heaven," as the old village priest called it. He admonished us with great solemnity to let the thin, round communion wafer dissolve slowly in the mouth and never, never to bite into it. We shouldn't even unduly try to dislodge it with the tongue, if it happened to stick unpleasantly to the roof of the mouth. Otherwise, it might suddenly spurt blood, since it was the body of Christ. The old priest was sufficiently convincing to discourage any of us from yielding to the temptation of checking it out.

I soon came to understand the finer points underpinning the priest's words. The object of it all was the soul, which I clearly envisioned as being about eight inches long and having the consistency of the soft inside of a bamboo stick. It sort of floated or was suspended within the chest, a little off to the right from the heart. The purpose of going to confession was to cleanse the soul and make it sparkling white – the way it had been at birth after baptism, which supposedly took away some grievous sin with which we all came into the world. Not that I ever understood this very well. What could we have done that was so bad while being transported by storks, or carried in the tummies of our mums? The rest, however, made sense; that whenever we did something naughty, the soul would gradually lose its sheen and start to turn dark, from the bottom up, like mercury rising in a thermometer. The goal of life was to have your soul pure and white at the moment you died. Then you would go directly to heaven. This was a place wonderful beyond anything you could imagine; certainly beyond anything I had savored so far in life, whether jumping into my mother's bed for a few moments in the morning before getting up, or evoking that magic genie from my version of Aladdin's lamp. Heaven was the place where my grandparents, and eventually, my parents and all the people I loved would go. But if their souls had any dark areas, they would first have to be dispatched to purgatory for a thorough scrubbing. This wasn't a pleasant place, though like school, it would eventually come to an end. A soul that was totally black would be cast directly into hell, where it would stay forever. Yes, I was discomfited by the picture of hell, a place manned by furry devils with tails, gleefully prodding their victims with pitchforks into cauldrons of furiously boiling water. Yet the idea of *forever* discomfited me more. The mere attempt at trying to think how long that might be would leave me queasy. Whenever I seemed to reach a terminal point in time, I would ask, but what after that? And then, after that? And after that? Yet, I knew *forever* would be longer still and that my most far-ranging flights in time barely reached the point where *forever* began.

Of course, once first communion was over, I hardly bothered with such thoughts. Religion became a sporadic thing, usually a few seconds of silent prayer before going to bed. "Please, God, continue to keep me safe and sound, and protect my mother and grandparents whom I love, and my father, too." This formula seemed to have worked so far, and was a good insurance policy. As for Sunday church, I didn't always have to go. The only regulars were several toothless old women, their heads wrapped in black shawls even during the summer heat. They alone could remain spiritually vigilant for the nearly two hours it took the old priest to wade through Sunday mass.

Then a young assistant appeared on the scene; nobody was sure exactly from where, but he electrified the villagers. For the one weekly sermon his superiors assigned him to preach, the church was filled beyond the front portals. He would talk about the indomitable human spirit, soaring like a condor and providing a lofty perspective for our daily travails. Conviction infused his every word, power radiated from his every expression and move.

No wonder the old priest began to see more and more empty pews. The young people especially took to the newcomer's words, and I soon found myself volunteering to become an altar boy for that one mass the new assistant was allowed to say. I often accompanied him on the one-hour walk through the fields and woods to the next village, where he was assigned to hear confessions. The time always passed quickly. I was fully absorbed, listening and asking questions. He rarely talked about religion the way the old priest did but delved into what it meant to be a human being; who we were and what we could become. He always left me feeling excited about being alive.

Then about a week before I was to make my altar-boy debut, the assistant priest disappeared. The rumor had it that the hardy young woman who used to come from her parents' nearby farm to cook for him, clean his room, and launder his vestments was caught providing him with a more personal service. A petition was started among the villagers, asking the Church hierarchy to exercise Christian forgiveness and give this young man a second chance. But soon another rumor began to spread. The word had it that the assistant wasn't really a priest but an impostor, a dropout from a seminary; in fact, a barber who was now back at his old profession, clipping people's hair and shaving their beards in some undisclosed town.

Although I was to remain a sporadic churchgoer for several more years, I would never feel inspired the way I had been in the presence of this barber masquerading as a priest.

As a first-grader in that village school, I had no sense of being different. Like the rest of my classmates, I went barefoot from spring until autumn. I was proud that the soles of my feet became so hardened I could follow my friends over the stubble of freshly cut wheat fields. I had no idea that going shoeless for them wasn't a choice.

I did recognize a curious anomaly in my life: I had no idea what kind of work Father did. That he was a count, I knew. But what exactly did a count do? I normally wouldn't have cared, if only several of the boys in school weren't always hounding me about the nature of Father's employment, no doubt put up to it by their parents. Not that I blamed them. The fathers of all the other boys had some kind of a useful job. Most of them worked in a nearby stone quarry. Several were farmers. A few were store-keepers. There were also two blacksmiths, a tailor, a postman, a watch repairman and a chimney sweep. Some of my friends were already helping their fathers after school at their trades. It puzzled me to think what I would have to do if Father ever needed me to help him be a count. How could I have known that already in his early twenties – before inheriting the family properties following Sascha's death – Father had been a leading salesman of Czech lo-comotives to the Soviet Union?

But with the onset of the war and imposition of Nazi rule, Fa-ther considered it essential to keep a low profile. He continued to live in Prague and visit us once or twice a month. He seemed to have no set schedule, usually arriving in the middle of the week and staying for several days. His program consisted mainly of tak-ing my older brother and me on long walks in the woods, and at least once a day, going to the post office, where he placed count-less long distance calls on the only telephone in the village. The postmaster automatically assigned lightning priority to these calls, since he knew the surcharge was no object to Mr. Count and that Mr. Count didn't like to wait. At our villa, Father had a room of his own where he slept, although in the mornings, when I some-times went to spend those few precious minutes in Mother's bed, Father was already there. When the time came for Father to re-turn to Prague, he might at the last moment casually decide to stay a few more days. Whatever his line of work, I couldn't help but conclude a count could take his ease. I really wouldn't mind eventually being one myself.

It was at this time, still in the early stages of the war, that my privileged existence almost came to an end. The chain of events began with an invitation for Father to appear publicly with Konrad Henlein, who was the regional Nazi boss in the border area between Germany and Czechoslovakia, known then as the Sudetenland. That's where Father's family had for generations been one of the largest landholders, and the Turner-of-the-Wheel name was widely respected by the Czechs as well as the Germans living there. A disgruntled school teacher who muscled his way up the Nazi ranks, Henlein recognized that appearing with Father would give him the kind of status in his bailiwick he couldn't get by force.

Driving to the Sudetenland in a small four-cylinder Skoda (gasoline was difficult to find even at black market prices, and that eight-cylinder Tatra was on blocks), Father was poignantly aware of his position. An invitation from a Nazi was tantamount to a command, especially from a Nazi of Henlein's rank. To decline, no matter how tactfully, meant certain arrest, concentration camp, and most likely an unthinkable end. But to appear with this ruffian would be a betrayal of everything Father's family had symbolized for centuries. Photographers would surely be there to preserve for future generations this moment of shame.

Speeding along the narrow country road, Father was in a desperate trance. Glancing in the rear-view mirror, he made a nervous face, crinkling his cheeks in a way that narrowed his eyes into slits. Being a dead hero wasn't something he could readily accept. Life simply couldn't come to such an end! There was still so much to do, to enjoy, perhaps a destiny to fulfill. Why, one day, when the country was free, he might be president. And he had yet to marry the mother of his children and give them his name. God, if only there was a way he could disappear, become invisible for a while, take a temporary leave from this world . . .

Just then, a twelve-wheeled lumber truck roared down the on-coming lane. Father would always be unsure whether in his mental turmoil he had drifted unwittingly across the unmarked center-line – or deliberately tried to sideswipe the truck and be unavoidably delayed.

They hit practically head-on. The huge vehicle had a dented grille, while the tiny Skoda was a twisted wreck. The impact threw Father through the windshield into a ditch, and it was several hours before he regained consciousness in a hospital room. He was all bandaged up and in cumbersome casts, tended to by nuns. A wire ran through a hole drilled into the bone of his right knee, which was suspended from a pulley over his bed. There was no part of him that didn't hurt. For several days, he couldn't feed himself and was dependent on the ministrations of the nursing staff; yet Father felt an inner joy unlike any in his life. He had passed the test and was alive.

Unable to visit Father in that distant hospital, I couldn't comprehend the nature of his wounds. I worried about this man whom I admired and was beginning to love. Yet, what an opportunity this was to respond to those questions about Father from the curious villagers! They didn't even have to ask, as I rarely missed a chance to describe graphically how Father's arms and legs had been cut off, and he almost lost his head, which remained attached only by a thin flap of skin. When grown-ups looked at me askance, I hastened to assure them that the doctors had managed to sew everything back.

The accident gave Father fresh impetus to normalize his life, though the intent to marry Mother wasn't quite so simple to carry out. While recuperating at his residence in Prague, Father was exposed to a procession of aspiring brides who came to pamper him and give him a chance to prove how far he had recovered from his wounds. They sought to tantalize him with talk about what a sturdy family they could help him start. One young princess from Silesia shipped her trunks ahead to Prague and telegraphed that she was on her way. Being from a family of twelve, all in robust health, she was confident she could overcome Father's reservations about nobility as breeding stock.

For the second time within a few weeks, Father felt himself cornered. He had always been aware that a commitment to Mother was fraught with risks. Now, his intentions were weakening. Perhaps his eugenic experiment was bound to fail; the children wouldn't amount to much, and Mother's limited exposure to the world and lack of languages would hold him back in his political ambitions. *Maybe I should start all over again*, Father would catch himself thinking, and immediately feel his cheeks crinkle into that nervous face.

By the time the Silesian princess arrived in Prague, Father was nowhere to be found. After letting the princess wait in vain at the palace several days, Father instructed Rudolf to tactfully move her out. "I knew if I hadn't done what was right," Father would often say to me in future years, "I could have no more faced myself than if I had appeared with Henlein."

The marriage ceremony was held in Prague without fanfare, so as not to remind the Nazis that Father was alive. I found out about it only when my mother's maiden name on the official notebook I kept for each subject in the village school was carefully pasted over by my teacher with a little blue strip, identifying me as a Turner-of-the-Wheel. Otherwise, little had changed, except that Father on his subsequent visits had a pronounced limp, which was still detectable at the end of the war. The other notable reminder of the accident was a pink scar under his chin from a large shard of glass that had lodged against his jugular. If he happened to shave carelessly, the scar would ooze a few drops of blood. This must have been the wound that had prompted me to volunteer those reports about how Father had nearly lost his head.

4/

In the national euphoria of being freed from Nazi rule, little did I suspect I would be exposed to dangers more insidious than any during the war. Whatever emotions I felt at leaving my village friends quickly dissipated in the excitement of moving into Father's residence in Prague. Constructed hundreds of years ago in one of the city's quieter squares, the building was darkened with centuries-old layers of soot; inside, such modern conveniences as central heating rarely worked, and during the colder months, a full-time janitor was kept busy stoking the individual tile stoves in each room. Otherwise – if one were to overlook that ice cream store on the ground floor – the place was quite grand, even worthy of its official designation as a palace. An assortment of German Gothic and Italian Renaissance art was scattered over the walls of the high-ceilinged rooms. Here and there, huge Gobelins and other tapestries covered entire walls. Father suspected a number of these pieces were fake, most likely exchanged by some ancestor strapped for cash but unable to sell legally the hereditary originals.

Father was a hero now. The liberation government bestowed on him various medals for his wartime anti-Nazi stance, and articles on his resistance activities appeared in the national press. It turned out Father had provided financial help from secret funds to dependents of well-known concentration camp victims. And he had been involved in such risky forays as derailing German military trains and conveying strategic information to the Allies in London. No wonder I never managed to find out from my parents during the war about this aspect of a count's work!

I soon discovered we owned more than I could have imagined, properties recently returned after being confiscated by the Nazis during the war. In addition to the unkempt palace, there were two large office buildings in the heart of Prague, one of them called Chicago. While visiting the United States some years before the war, Father had been tempted to erect an office building in Chicago and call it Praha. His patriotic feelings, however, prompted him to make his investment in Prague and settle for calling the building Chicago. Beyond Prague, Father's properties comprised several farms, a large dilapidated castle, and extensive holdings in the forests of the former Sudetenland, including a modern sawmill and a plant to prefabricate affordable houses. A few hundred yards from the sawmill, on a gentle hill amid the majestic Bohemian woods, stood another much smaller but usable castle, overgrown with ivy and topped with a ceramic stag on its single cupola.

I became increasingly aware of what it meant to be a count. Wherever I went, people seemed to know who I was. In the nine-story Chicago, where I liked to ride the automatic elevators and push the buttons for people getting on and off, everybody I encountered appeared eager to listen to what I had to say. Already then I wondered: could my comments really be as interesting as all that?

I soon realized a count could behave unlike anyone else, as I witnessed while having lunch in the main dining hall of that Sudetenland ivy-covered castle. Among Father's dozen-or-so guests at the large round table was one of his junior officials, who inadvertently revealed he had turned in Father's pistol to the occupying U.S. troops. "What?" Father demanded with undisguised fury, "You gave them my pistol? I risked my life the entire war hiding it from the Nazis, and you make in your pants and hand it over to the first American who barks at you!" Without waiting for a response, Father lifted the empty soup plate in front of him and smashed it down on the remainder of his setting. The porcelain shards went flying, and a heavy silence ensued. While the young official didn't eat much during the rest of that meal, what surprised me was that within moments, Father was his genial self again.

Then there was the time I was with Father in his eight-cylinder Tatra in Prague, when he barreled out of a small street and sideswiped a car on one of the city's larger thoroughfares. Several witnesses immediately stepped forth, doffing their hats and offering to testify on behalf of Mr. Count. (Although titles had been abolished in 1918 with the founding of the republic, their use remained an entrenched tradition.) But Father stopped only long enough to shout instructions at the other driver for sending him the bill. Despite the heavy damage to his car, the driver didn't seem to mind. Father had a reputation of paying far better and faster than any insurance company.

Mother was far from happy now. She didn't like the pretense and hypocrisy she felt around her. She would often say to Father with a trace of bitterness, "I hope you never have to find out how loyal your employees would be if you didn't have money to throw at them." Sensitive and proud, Mother detected slights at every turn from Father's various friends. Her tormentors came not from the nobility, who seemed to act with impenetrable grace, but from the non-titled so-called *better people*. They were far more transparent in how they felt, especially some of the wives, who combined their contempt for Mother's origins and lack of higher education with jealousy over her looks. Then there were the little things, such as faithful old Rudolf failing to dust properly (or so it seemed to Mother) when Father was out of town, or the chauffeur getting stuck in traffic and being late if Mother was the one he was picking up. Whenever she complained, Father tried to calm her down. "People are all snobs," he would say, with an easy shrug. "Can you imagine what your father would have done to me if I had been a neighbor's son instead of Mr. Count? I doubt he would have stood by so patiently while we made all those children on the side!"

Father's commitment to married life, however, didn't transform him overnight. Satisfied with his flock of children, by now increased to five, he nevertheless continued the practice that had once served him so well: keeping his eyes open for potential mothers wherever he went. It had become a conditioned reflex, a spontaneous reaction as normal as the way he breathed or tied his shoes. He did it everywhere and all the time, no matter what the occasion or in whose company he happened to be. No wonder my older brother and I started to imitate him at an early age. It wasn't unusual for the three of us to rivet our eyes to the same woman on a busy street. And we didn't stop at that. While Father would limit himself to scanning those features most closely related to bearing and nourishing potential heirs, my brother and I tried to top off any encounter with a little bump and a nudge. This was easy when the enticing lady passed on our side. But if she happened to pass on Father's side, we had to employ the indirect technique of giving Father a nudge, usually against his leg. He became so used to our routine that if we failed to nudge him at the crucial moment, he still brushed against these women of extraordinary charm.

The most fun my brother and I had was when we started to play this game on our own. He was twelve and I almost eleven, and we had recently acquired a new set of clothes, fashioned by Father's tailors from materials they had been hoarding throughout the war. Each of us had a choice of a couple of gray flannel suits with short pants, a tweed herringbone jacket, and some soft, off-white silk shirts. We were nattily dressed as we walked along Prague's streets, bumping attractive ladies right and left. We would even cross the street if properly inspired. We were always careful to be polite, begging *Pardón!* of any woman who seemed to take note. But very few of our contacts showed any tendency to ire, since we obviously were only little boys. Some of our contacts even rewarded us with smiles.

It was exciting to contemplate the range of opportunities inherent in this approach. I had the whole city of a million from which to pick and choose, with no restraints or checks on who might be next. And who knows, I thought, now that the war was over, the whole world might become my turf on which to practice this special talent as I pleased. I saw it as a responsibility to the family line to miss no occasion for this training which surely would one day help me meet the ideal bride.

It was during these euphoric postwar days that I discovered what I was prepared to do to preserve my way of life; to keep my image shining bright and bask another day in my unique glow. Heaven forbid that people might think of me in anything less than a favorable light, especially in the school where I was enrolled in Prague. I was openly looked up to by my classmates from those *better* families of lawyers, doctors, and high government officials. Even the teachers seemed to treat me with a subtle deference.

Not Eugene, though, who sat directly behind me in class. A reputed troublemaker, he had already been sent twice to reform school for six-week stints. His widowed mother supplemented her state pension by taking in laundry, which she did by hand in a wooden tub at home. She had three younger children, who claimed much of her time. My school was supposedly in the best position to give Eugene the guidance he needed to straighten out.

In his frayed shorts and repeatedly mended shirt, Eugene was a marked boy in this class of well-dressed, well-behaved boys. He always seemed to be fidgeting behind me, and I had the feeling his eyes were boring into my back, watching my every move.

It happened during dictation. Through a clumsy swing of my arm, I made a big ink splotch in the official notebook every student kept. Right away, I could feel my face flush. Making an ink splotch was one of the worst things anyone could do. It was a mark of overall sloppiness, perhaps even a reflection of some corresponding stain on one's character.

Quickly, I tried to cover the evidence with my hand. But too late! I could already feel a commotion behind my back. I turned in time to see Eugene's arm shoot up and wave to be recognized.

"I'm going to tell!" he hissed.

I panicked. What would people think if I were to be exposed? It would be so uncharacteristic of my good behavior, neatness, and excellent marks. Maybe boys like Eugene could go around making splotches, but me?

In a flash, my brain went to work. If only I had a chance to take the notebook home! I could clean it up with an ink eradicator and the teacher would never know. I had to stop Eugene from giving me away.

Instinctively I reached into my pocket. I groped around and pulled out the first thing that came into my hand. It was a small, gold-colored pencil sharpener I had casually picked up the previous day at the Chicago building from the desk of Father's secretary. Now, like an offering, I placed it under Eugene's nose.

Eugene's arm dropped to half-mast. He took the shiny instrument with his free hand and appraised it carefully. Then he nodded and lowered his arm. I watched the pencil sharpener disappear into the pocket of his pants. I was safe. The teacher hadn't looked up.

The trouble began several days later. Father's secretary discovered the sharpener missing and wanted it back. She had bought it with her own money and regarded it as a good-luck charm.

Obviously, I didn't want her thinking I had stolen it and have her raise a fuss with Father. I promised I would bring it back the next time I dropped by.

The following day at school during the first break, I tried to explain the situation to Eugene.

"But you gave it to me," he protested coldly.

I shook my head. "Did you ever hear me say that? I only lent it to you . . . you know, for you to look at."

"Don't bullshit me!" He paused to give me a scornful look. "It's too late, anyway. I've sold it."

"Then you'd better buy it back."

"I wouldn't even if I could! You gave it to me."

For a while, we argued back and forth. I'm not sure whether we were overheard, or I asked the teacher to intervene. Either way, I lodged my complaint. I had lent Eugene a gold pencil sharpener, and he was refusing to give it back.

The teacher was appalled. "Hmm, what you really mean is that Eugene has stolen it!"

I wouldn't have put it in those words; no, that was a bit strong, I thought – and was considering how best to clarify my position. But the teacher was already lecturing Eugene, loud enough for the rest of the class to hear. What a shameful thing for his worst pupil to do to such a good pupil! The school should never have agreed to accept Eugene from the reformatory. Once a thief, always a thief. Maybe reform school was where Eugene still belonged. "How embarrassing," the teacher concluded, speaking more to the class than to me, "if your father, Mr. Count, should find out. What kind of a school would he think we run here?"

This was too serious a matter for the teacher to handle on his own. Although the bell for the next class had already rung, Eugene and I ended up in the principal's office. I stood silently by, increasingly discomfited as I heard more talk about Eugene's incorrigibility and his need for another reform school stint. What if Eugene had to go back to reform school on my account? As I listened to Eugene repeat the simple truth which no one would believe, I was feeling worse and worse.

More than once I volunteered to drop the case. I never intended to turn it into such an affair, I tactfully said. If Eugene sold the pencil sharpener, that was the end of that. I hinted it may have been a misunderstanding from the start.

The principal shared the teacher's main concern: what would Mr. Count say if he found out his son had been robbed at the school? No, the principal said, this was a grave matter, and he was sending for Eugene's mother right away.

I felt caught in a madness from which I couldn't escape. Where would it stop? I tried to tell myself it was all Eugene's fault. Why did he try to get me into trouble over a splotch that was no business of his? Fleetingly, I considered telling the truth. But that would permanently tarnish my image, besmirch the family name, and prove most embarrassing for both the teacher and principal. They were committed to my story, and I was stuck with an implicit lie.

When Eugene's mother came, I felt still more acutely what I had done. Wearing a shapeless soiled dress, she had a look of wizened suffering as if she knew that no misfortune would pass her by. I imagined she could have been one of the impoverished women in that hospital ward where Mother feared I had been exchanged at birth. Was Eugene really me, and I, in fact, her son?

I shifted my weight from foot to foot as she looked at me searchingly. I stood there, neat and scrubbed in my tailored clothes next to her son, who already had the stigma of irreversible poverty imprinted on his face. For a brief instant our eyes met, and I had to look away. How well she knew the truth!

Eugene's mother didn't try to dispute me, but dismissed me with her eyes as if to say, what else could be expected from one of my type? Her feelings were for her son, whom she was aching to help. Pleading his cause in a quietly desperate way, she never lost her dignity. When she finally managed to win for him one final reprieve, her face barely showed relief.

I couldn't hide my joy. At that moment I felt as if I were the one who was getting off. But it wasn't over yet. Eugene's mother, the principal said, would have to make good on the theft. He would personally escort us to a nearby stationary store where she was to buy me a sharpener similar to the stolen one.

In the street, I walked in a daze alongside the principal, with the poor widow and her son trailing close behind. We formed a bizarre little group. I tried not to think what I would say if by chance we met Father. I had recently come to know of his reputation as a crusader for the underprivileged; how he had taken the unprecedented step of building private homes with flush toilets for his rural employees, and at Christmas time, handed out two months' additional pay. How could I now explain these people with me in the street?

In the store, I felt like a thief as we went from shelf to shelf, looking for that accursed pencil sharpener. Anguished as I was by the thought of taking money from this scrubwoman who needed it for her children's bread, I was still unable to blurt out the truth.

When the clerk finally told us the store was out of sharpeners, the principal made Eugene's mother pick out several items he estimated to be of comparable worth. I didn't even want to nod or look whenever he pointed to something he thought I might want. I was hurting to get out of there, to wake up from that bad dream now.

We settled on a pink eraser and a large green blotting paper. At the cashier's, I watched Eugene's mother take out a few coins from somewhere deep within her dress. How much they must have meant to her, the way she held them as she slowly counted them out! Just then for a brief instant our eyes met again, and I knew that all the excuses I could find would never make right what I had just done.

5/

During that postwar summer of 1945, the foreign minister, Jan Masaryk, gave Father a choice. He could be appointed to the most important of all diplomatic posts, ambassador to Moscow. Or he could be sent to Ankara, Turkey.

Father gave a nod and wink to his friend Jan, and without hesitating said, "Ankara!"

To me, the job of ambassador made about as much sense as being a count; so I suspected it would be fun. But I was disappointed with Father's choice. Why Ankara? Although I knew nothing about politics, from what I had heard, Moscow surely was the center of the world, except of course, for Prague. Ankara I couldn't even locate on a map. Weren't the Soviets our friends? I still remembered overhearing Father during the war speak with admiration of Stalin's anti-Nazi drive. Hadn't the Soviets liberated our country at the cost of many lives? Granted, I had recently heard talk of Russian soldiers raping women and taking over homes where they cooked food over fires on parquet floors and relieved themselves wherever they pleased. But those were exceptions or only rumors. The newspapers and radio said the Soviets were more than ever our best friends. So why was Father going to Turkey and not the USSR?

Within days of arriving in Turkey, I was well along to my first addiction. Not to some nefarious drug that would addle my brain but a simple food sold on practically every street corner in Istanbul, where I was enrolled at an English boarding school. I would gorge on this food every chance I had. Just thinking about its aroma, texture and taste filled me with a yearning that could be satisfied in only one way: go out and get some more.

It was called a *simit* – a large, round pretzel, freshly baked and covered with sesame seeds. Young Turkish boys with dark hair cropped close enough to show old scars in their scalps usually sold simits from glass cases in the streets. The glass was supposed to keep the heat of the simit in and the street grime out. But some of the boys hawked their simits right off a stick, passed through the center of the circular rolls.

I preferred the simits off the stick. That way I could tell if they were still warm and freshly baked. I would often roam the streets until I found a boy who had a stick-full of simits capable of arousing these special desires of mine. The best way to test for oven freshness was to squeeze the simit first. If the boy wouldn't let you do that, it wasn't because he was worried about Constantinople's sanitation codes. The boys with warm simits were always eager for you to touch and squeeze their wares, though that soon wasn't necessary in my case. With a glance at the simit's golden crust, I could judge its crunchiness and the buoyancy of the dough within. What a treat to smell the baked freshness and scorched sesame seeds! Given an appropriately spaced succession of boys hawking warm simits off a stick, I might eat as many as a half dozen of these rolls.

My addiction to the modest simit inadvertently escalated to something incomparably more exotic. It happened at the old Park Hotel in Istanbul, at a café frequented by Americans, where I liked to stop for an occasional snack. On this unforgettable occasion, I ordered an iced coffee and a piece of chocolate cake with whipped cream. But what the waiter brought was unlike any iced coffee I had ever seen: a rich, chocolatey liquid in a tall, frosted glass, topped with a scoop of whipped cream. It looked so inviting that I wasn't about to protest the obvious mistake. And how glad I was from the first sip, whose delicate velvety taste absorbed my total concentration. It was as if I were inverting myself to follow this frosty liquid within my innermost self, luxuriating in the delicious trail it left behind.

Yes, those were the sensations aroused by my first chocolate milkshake, as I later discovered it was called. What I considered as marvelous as the taste was that by merely pointing to my empty glass, I could in a matter of moments have another, filled with the same exquisite drink. Was this what heaven would be like? Not only wonderful beyond anything on earth, but in unlimited quantities, too?

I had four that day, and came back to the Park Hotel as often as I could. On my way to these treats, I was now able to walk by what looked like the best of Istanbul's simits without slowing down. If I could have as great a pleasure as was awaiting me, why settle for less? When I eventually began to tire of the same old milk-shaky taste, I still didn't go back to yearning for simits. After all, if there was something that much better than a simit, wasn't there bound to be something that much better than a shake?

It was during this Turkish sojourn that I began to have an inkling of an elementary fact – that the sort of life I took for granted wasn't shared by everyone. Even in the sheltered environment of my English boarding school in Istanbul, I could see how fortunate I was. I needed to look no further than the school's janitor, *Effendi* or Mister, as the students respectfully called him. One of Effendi's tasks was to shine the several hundred pairs of special black slippers we all had to wear inside the school. Each student was entitled to one free shine a week, which was part of Effendi's salaried job. That work he usually did at night. During the day, he wanted to be unhindered to give individual shines for which he was allowed to charge. Although Effendi was always buffing and shining and took pride in his skill, he was hardly on his way to becoming rich. Day after day he wore the same pair of patched, baggy pants, and from his pail took out the same meager lunch.

Effendi never complained. He was grateful for whatever the god he called *Allah* sent his way. If Allah in his infinite wisdom had intended Effendi to be rich, he would have made him something other than a janitor. Effendi believed in Allah fully and unquestioningly. Several times each day, I saw Effendi take out his prayer rug and go through his routine. He entered a trancelike state in a corner of the school's lobby where he worked, oblivious to the throngs of students shouting and milling around. Praying wasn't something mechanical that Effendi did by rote as an obligation to be fulfilled. I could discern from his face that these were the most intense moments of his day. About halfway through, he would lean back, resting his buttocks against the tops of his heels. He cupped his hands around his ears and glanced apprehensively around to make sure no evil spirits were lurking near. Effendi then went into the final supplication phase, low on the ground, slithering snakelike in a way that kept him within the perimeter of his rug. Only when he was finished would he be the same old Effendi again, a smile of satisfaction on his lips — not unlike when he finished applying an especially lustrous shine, and he could almost see himself reflected in the shoe.

Effendi wasn't unusual in his faith. There was the old gardener at our embassy in Ankara. During Ramadan, the Moslem version of Lent, he wouldn't eat or drink from dawn to dusk while doing heavy labor in the scorching sun. As a truly devout man, he might even try to avoid swallowing his spittle or keep it from trickling accidentally down his parched throat. Once, when I watched him struggle with a wheelbarrow filled with sod, I wondered how well I could have done, if only for a day. And to do it day after day, for four weeks merely to get to heaven!

The thought made me feel momentarily depressed, but then I brightened up. The requirements for heaven were obviously different, depending on where you happened to be born, as was the promise of what the place would be like. The heaven where the old gardener and Effendi were going would have an abundance of those things they lacked on earth, most of which I already had.

But who was I to try to fathom God's or Allah's reasoning in creating these inequities? Perhaps Allah in his mercy made these people in such a way that they didn't fully feel their misery. What brought this to mind were the legless boys about my age, hobbling around Istanbul's better streets on the palms of their hands, a begging cup around the neck. A Turkish official from the protocol office told me with undisguised contempt that most of the injuries had been intentionally inflicted — usually with the parents' help — to create an ideal opportunity to beg, to give these children a certain advantage in life. For an instant, this seemed to penetrate and strike something responsive deep within. Advantage in life? What kind of a life must it be that they were willing to throw themselves beneath the wheels of a tram, or have their parents dismember them with an ax? I remembered when I was little, I would have been willing to end it all beneath the wheels of a Prague tram if my grandparents were to die. But that had been just a thought, a way of letting myself know how much I cared. How horrible the pain must be when you closed your eyes and made the fatal plunge that would leave you crippled for life! Sparks flying in your eyes, the searing explosion in your brain, the grinding in your ears, then the shock of blood spurting out and almost half of you no longer there . . . These little boys hobbling around so energetically on their hands had faced that reckoning. They had been there and known what it was like. Now, they were acting as if it was nothing at all, just a normal part of life.

I welcomed Father's decision at the end of my first year in Turkey to send my brother and me to school in England. This had nothing to do with any national preference but simply meant I would be able to see Mother on a more regular basis than vacations. She hadn't accompanied us to Turkey because, as Father explained, she didn't know languages, and how many people at diplomatic receptions would speak Czech? It would be an impossible situation for him as well as for Mother, he said, and packed her off with my two sisters and younger brother to London, where they could start learning English. But as Father would admit in future years, the real reason he didn't take Mother to Ankara was that he feared she might imagine he was unduly resting his eyes on the attributes of some diplomat's wife and cause an international incident. Father's fears may have been justified, for this is precisely what would happen at an even more critical juncture in his life.

Father enrolled my brother and me at a boarding school called Dulwich, whose name derived from its location in a pleasant London suburb where Charles Dickens placed the residence of his fictitious Mr. Pickwick. We were assigned to Orchard House, along with about thirty contemporaries uniformly clad in blue blazers, gray flannel pants, and multi-colored beanie caps for outdoor wear. Detachable white stiff collars were de rigeur, and they were a struggle to put on. To my great relief, one of my classmates tipped me off how to get away with wearing semi-stiffs instead. Otherwise, what I remember best of our first year was that twice a week we took communal baths, with four of us boys fitted into each of the bathroom's four, square-shaped tubs. Since hot water was scarce, crowding all those bodies into each tub had the advantage of raising the water level to cover our outstretched thighs. Being a member of the lower of the two grades, I was usually assigned to what could be called a second sitting in the same water. In this and other activities, we were supervised by two matrons, Miss Law and Miss Day. In retrospect, the former looked a lot like Margaret Thatcher, while Miss Day bordered on being cute — which may be why some of the more mature thirteen-year-olds were hesitant about stripping in front of her.

In my second year at Dulwich, my older brother moved from Orchard House to a residence on the other side of the campus for third formers and up. Not only did I relish this independence; I was now considered sufficiently seasoned to be appointed as one of the four Orchard House monitors. Besides bestowing on each of us the unquestioned right to a first sitting in the same tub with our three anointed colleagues, this post surely was among the most powerful any twelve-year-old could hold. To enforce the rules of the house, I was deputized to dish out a punishment called *lines*. These were one-sentence renunciations of the offense committed, such as, "I must not mack around," or, "I must stop acting like a blooming idiot." The minimum was twenty-five lines, but persistent or repeated misbehavior could bring some incorrigible wretch many hundreds, even thousands, of lines. A goodly third of the students in Orchard House spent at least an hour each day doing lines. To keep these misdemeanants in their place, they could be additionally socked with the most frequently imposed line of all, "I must not be cheeky to a monitor." It was the only punishment I remember meting out, and only once in a twenty-five-line dose.

By far the most intriguing event that year was the wedding of Princess Elizabeth. It was well-nigh impossible for any of us boys not to fall at least a little in love with the future queen. There she was, gracing the cover of just about every magazine, so wholesomely lovely, perfectly coifed, bejeweled and otherwise resplendent in her togs. And there was Prince Philip, her future consort, so handsome and no less resplendent in his bemedaled naval uniform, richly embroidered with gold and embellished at the waist by a mighty sword. And there we were, a bunch of twelve-year-olds in our colorful beanie caps and fresh semi-stiffs. What was making us squirm in our collars was an imponderable we never tired of discussing: given that the purpose of the forthcoming union was to produce an heir, which we also knew required a certain vile act, how could the newlyweds in those ennobling garments go about carrying it out? How could they signal to each other or put the unspeakable into words? Not surprisingly, we placed ourselves more in Philip's shoes. How would he know it was the right moment to make his move so that his young bride wouldn't be appalled? Getting undressed in front of the future queen surely wasn't the same as stripping down for Miss Law or Miss Day. How unspeakably embarrassing if they got their signals mixed! The contemplation of this dilemma held us schoolboys transfixed as we kept repeating to one another, "How can they let each other know? How, how, how?" It was as if we were trying to answer some ultimate riddle of life, such as when I had tried to imagine as a child the concept of eternity. Yet, we knew that by the morning after their wedding day, Philip and Elizabeth would have faced that unthinkable moment and penetrated its mystery.

The other enigmatic event during that second year occurred when Father came to reunite with us over Christmas in London, where his good friend Jan Masaryk also happened to be spending a few days. As the son of the country's first president and his American-born wife, the Czech foreign minister was thoroughly oriented to the English-speaking world and kept a permanent flat in London. What Father urgently wanted to discuss with him was the worsening situation between East and West. The Soviets were making a grab in postwar Central Europe for as much territory as they could get, and vast numbers of people who abhorred the thought of living under their sway were becoming refugees. Could anything be done to save Czechoslovakia from being next?

My brother and I found ourselves waiting for Father in the embassy car that brought us to Masaryk's flat. It was a freezing day, but the memory of World War II gasoline shortages must have been too recent for the chauffeur to let the engine idle for warmth. The first hour passed, then the second, and still no Father. I was cold as well as thoroughly bored by the time a man who identified himself as Masaryk's valet finally opened the car door and asked us to follow him. Next thing I knew, we were being welcomed by the man I immediately recognized from newspapers and magazines – a jovial open visage with an endless domelike forehead dominating a rotund body draped in a colorful silk robe, even though it was already midafternoon. He joked self-deprecatingly about having left us in the cold, and then turned to reproach Father in a lighthearted way for not letting him know sooner that we were waiting outside. I could understand why the country's most famous man was the most popular as well. Before resuming his dialogue with Father, Jan Masaryk personally fixed my brother and me each a large cup of hot chocolate.

That's the way I would remember the man who made headlines around the world a few weeks later when his broken body was found early one morning on the stone pavement three stories beneath the foreign minister's official residence in Prague.

Whether this national hero had been pushed or jumped of his own free will would be discussed by his compatriots to this day as intensely as Americans discussed the circumstances surrounding President Kennedy's death. However, what intrigued me at the time was that Jan Masaryk was the first person I knew who died shortly after I had seen him so humanly alive. He had crossed the line between this life and what may ensue – and now understood it all.

Trying to penetrate that barrier in my mind was no less futile than the attempt to figure out a few months earlier how Prince Philip would resolve his wedding night dilemma. Years later, when I realized how simple the solution must have been for the royal consort, I wondered: would the answer to the mystery surrounding death prove just as simple the instant it was experienced? Would we marvel how it could have remained hidden from us throughout life, since it wasn't a mystery at all?

As I thought back on Father's discourse with Masaryk, the phrase that stuck with me following the foreign minister's death was something about "the situation turning from bad to worse," which might force Father to emigrate with the whole family to the United States. The clear inference was that this would be a difficult step, no matter how inviting the opportunities in our prospective haven might seem.

I wasn't entirely averse to the possibility of things going from bad to worse; for I cherished what must have been a unique dream among the millions hoping for sanctuary in the United States. This dream derived from having discovered in England an exciting new genre of literature, comic books from U.S.A. The one that especially caught my eye was *Captain Marvel*, and right away I knew it would change my life. No, not the exploits of this miraculous man, which were fun to read, but the full-page ads sponsored by two men whose feats I found no less miraculous, Charles Atlas and George Jowett. These real-life marvels could take your body, no matter how puny and weak, and turn it into an impressively muscled physique. What more dramatic proof than those pictures in the ads?

It was as if a light had suddenly switched on in my brain. I, too, was puny and weak. Even the ninety-eight-pound weakling in the ads, who was perennially losing his girlfriend on the beach and having sand kicked in his face, didn't look bad to me. Surely, Jowett and Atlas must have discovered some unique secret if they could do what they claimed. How wonderful to have a body bursting with energy and strength, or to catch a glimpse of a reflection in a mirror and discover it's you! Surely those muscles would once and for all put an end to my older brother being able to impose his will on me. No wonder America was a great land of opportunity, if it would give anyone a chance for the sort of transformation shown in those comic-book ads.

Well, almost anyone. The offer of free literature clearly said, "Not good outside continental U.S.A." Hence only a deteriorating political situation would make it possible for me to clip out the coupon and take that first indispensable step.

The decision to leave came early in 1948 when our homeland fell under Soviet sway, and a forbidding curtain separated Czechoslovakia from the Western World. Fortunately, we didn't have to evade armed guards and police dogs, crawl across land planted with mines, or cut through electrified barbed wire to make it to the other side. This was the eventuality Father had foreseen three years earlier, when he turned down with a wink and a smile the important post in the USSR in favor of a small pro-Western country.

As a final gesture to the past, we made the voyage from England in style – first class on the SS *America.* In New York we were greeted by an unruly array of reporters amid popping flashbulbs and repeated shouts, "One more with the family, Count!" I couldn't wait to see the front pages the following day, and I got up early in our New York hotel to sneak down to the lobby for an advance peek. Boy, how surprised everybody would be to recognize me in the flesh! People might even offer their condolences on the world-shaking events that had brought me here. What a disappointment, then, to find the story in only one of the papers – and several pages back at that! Maybe my former homeland wasn't really the center of the world.

Father came to America relatively well prepared. Indeed, all our property had been confiscated by the Communist regime, including that unkempt palace in Prague and the ivy-covered castle deep in the Bohemian woods. But during the previous couple of years, Father had managed to whisk out a few antiques, Persian rugs, paintings, jewels, and other family heirlooms, most notably, a mahogany chest containing an unusually massive silver setting for twenty-four, engraved with the family crest by Vienna's leading craftsman at the turn of the century. Father also had a sizable horde of gold coins, mainly U.S. Eagles. He wasn't sure exactly how many, since he'd never needed to count his money before, but there were enough to fill a small attaché case. In our New York hotel, Father often left the case half-open on his bed, some of the coins spilling out, while we went out to explore the city. The hotel staff must have thought the gold was a police plant. While a number of prized items inexplicably disappeared from our rooms, including a set of very long Zeiss hunting binoculars and a Rolleiflex camera, the gold miraculously remained untouched. Father was relying on it to pull him through the next two or three years. That's how long he figured it would take for the Communist regime to be overthrown, either through a popular uprising or a quick world war, after which he would no doubt be restored to his former life.

What also comforted Father was that this wasn't his first time in the United States. During a three-month visit in the 1920s, he had traveled from coast to coast and later wrote a book extolling America's free enterprise system. He had interviewed Henry Ford and Herbert Hoover and made numerous useful contacts, which included negotiating with the head of Westinghouse on behalf of Czechoslovakia's largest industrial complex. Father's only negative experience had occurred when he showed up on a Miami beach without a bathing suit top, and the sheriff gave him twenty-four hours to leave town.

Grateful and excited as Father was to be in the United States, he harbored a vague sense of unease. What if his calculations proved wrong and he could never go back to his former life? What if his money ran out, and he had to enter the American free-for-all? Despite his accomplishments in public and private life, hadn't they all been facilitated by the prestige of his noble rank? How much would his title count in the United States?

6/

Father's foresight wasn't limited to choosing the right diplomatic post. Prior to leaving Ankara, he had secured from a colleague at the U.S. Embassy a letter of reference to a place called Hotchkiss. Located in Connecticut on a wooded hill by a picturesque lake, it was one of the leading boarding schools – or so this colleague explained. It corresponded roughly to the last four years of a European *Gymnasium* and virtually guaranteed its graduates admission to Yale, Harvard, or Princeton.

"I don't want you worrying about tuition," the school's distinguished-looking, white-haired headmaster advised Father when we arrived there during our first week in the United States. "I'm instructing our bursar to consider as payment in full whatever you can afford. And I shall let you be the judge of that. If it turns out you can't afford anything right now . . . well, we have other boys on full scholarships. We consider it an investment in the future. Our scholarship boys repay us many times over through helping others and by what they give back to the school."

The headmaster's voice was matter-of-fact, as if he were merely doing what anyone in his position would. We needed help, and that was reason enough for him to act. "I was an admirer of your President Masaryk," he volunteered after a slight pause. "Who knows, maybe the day will come when you shall return to your homeland, and your sons will be able to put to use over there what we teach them here." He glanced at my brother and me. "I hope they keep up their Czech."

I was glad to hear this implicit confirmation that we would be able to return, probably within several years at the most. Yet that very day I gained a different perspective from a boy deputized to show me around the school. As his opening gambit, my escort revealed how his own parents had abandoned their home in Saint Petersburg after the Revolution of 1917 and emigrated to the United States. I wasn't particularly surprised by this coincidence of fate; no doubt that's why this boy had been assigned as my guide. But then as we continued our cross-campus trek, what emerged was that my escort was unalterably convinced that he and his family would one day be able to reclaim their home in former Saint Petersburg. Well, I wasn't about to say it, but I knew he was wrong. Who in his right mind would have thought in 1948 that the Soviet regime, entrenched for thirty years, would ever collapse? And I wondered: Since this boy was no less certain than I about his family's chances of going back, couldn't I be just as wrong?

But that was no more than a fleeting concern. As soon as I settled down in a pennant-festooned single room in an attractive red brick building housing our class, I took that long-awaited step I associated with coming to the United States. From the latest issue of *Captain Marvel*, I carefully clipped out those no-obligation coupons and sent them to the two body-building greats. It was one of the most exciting days of my life when, about two weeks later, I received a response from both men in the same mail.

At first, I was inclined to give Charles Atlas the nod. Judging by the many photos he and Jowett had sent, it looked as if Atlas was taller and possessed the kind of smooth, fluid physique that represented what I had in mind for myself. Jowett seemed a bit chunky. Maybe all those muscles had stunted his growth. As a thirteen-year-old barely five feet tall, I certainly didn't want that happening to me.

There was one problem with Atlas: He wanted forty dollars for his Dynamic Tension course, which was out of the question for me. After days of agonizing over my quandary, I detected what seemed to be a loophole. As part of the forty-dollar offer, I would be receiving a free, ten-volume illustrated encyclopedia of sex. It alone was said to be worth forty-five dollars. As intrigued as I was with the promise of revealing photos (absolutely nothing held back, the literature said), what I wanted most was that Dynamic

47

Tension course, which Mr. Atlas was clearly eager to send. Why else would I have already received a follow-up letter, wondering when he might hear?

Hoping to make up for the delay, I penned a proposal I thought eminently fair. If Mr. Atlas mailed me his forty-dollar Dynamic Tension course, I was willing to let him keep his forty-five-dollar encyclopedia of sex – revealing illustrations and all. As a token of good faith, I wouldn't quibble about the five dollars he would be saving on the deal. To further enlist his sympathies, I explained I was a recent refugee from Communism and could use his help. Judging by the ready understanding and sympathetic reaction of the school's headmaster, maybe this exemplary body builder would come through for me, too.

I never heard from Atlas again. As for George Jowett, my dealings with him also came to naught. His secret was a unique, fully adjustable, fifteen-pound fulcrum bar. At thirty-five dollars, it too was beyond my means. Just as well, I thought. I didn't want to become chunky like Jowett.

But I didn't give up. I had discovered at the local newsstands two magazines, *Your Physique* and *Muscle Power*, which I started to read with religious zeal; indeed, with incomparably more zeal than anything religious I'd ever read. This for me was the Holy Writ, and what it made amply clear was that I could never reach my physical ideal without a real set of weights.

I came to the conclusion that the minimum I needed was an adjustable 118-pound combination dumbbell and barbell set, with a chrome-plated, revolving knurled sleeve. The cheapest set cost twenty-one dollars, and without the knurled sleeve, four dollars less – still far more than I could contemplate. I also knew I could never be satisfied with the cheaper set. How my eye immediately went for those sparkles reflected from the chrome on the revolving sleeve! It was the set I always saw myself using in my dreams.

A fortuitous event helped me out of this financial plight. Taking a shortcut one day across the roughs surrounding the school's nine-hole golf course, I found several golf balls just lying there. I was surprised to learn these balls were mine to keep – and then delighted to discover that depending on their condition, they could be sold to other students for better than a quarter apiece.

I spent the following weekends scavenging the roughs. As I crawled through brambles toward some inaccessible spot for a ball, being scratched and otherwise discomfited, I envisioned those weights with a chrome-plated sleeve that would enable me to mold the kind of mighty body displayed in the muscle magazines. Just conjuring up this image made my muscles feel vibrant and alive, as if anticipating their forthcoming evolution and growth.

Father had to contend with a challenge of incomparably greater consequence. He had by now learned that doing business as an émigré in New York wasn't the same as doing business as a count in Prague. There were no special considerations here; no magnanimity of spirit, no subtle winks. People seemed interested only in how much money he had and how quickly they could acquire a share of it – including some of his transplanted countrymen. A lawyer he had known in Prague, who had immigrated to the United States a decade before us, invited Father for a sociable lunch at a downtown restaurant. Ordering lavishly and insisting on picking up the tab, he thereafter sent Father a bill for his time and the cost of the meal. "In a way he earned it," Father would reminisce in future years about his presumed host, who would have been grateful in Prague for the mere honor of dining with Mr. Count. "He's the one who pointed out that few émigrés ever get ahead in the United States until they lose everything and have their backs against the wall."

What enabled Father to cling to his optimistic scenario was the worsening international situation. Surely, the Communist regime in his homeland wouldn't survive a clash of the superpowers; the United States would quickly win and his financial resources might last till then. This assessment didn't change when the Soviets detonated their first nuclear bomb. By that time Father was dabbling in New York real estate and had his eye on a large apartment house in Queens that he could buy for a down payment he could afford. The rental units promised to be a veritable money tree and provide us with a comfortable place to live, stemming the biggest drain on Father's funds. But at the last moment, Father rejected the deal. He was afraid the building was too close to the heart of Manhattan and would be obliterated in the first nuclear exchange.

Father had by now also learned that the free enterprise system he once extolled had little interest in hiring this fifty-year-old jobless man. There simply weren't any middle management slots designed for former Czech ambassador-counts. Any potential employer would have to wonder how this European gentleman could ever adapt to company ways. For starters, how should he be addressed? Although Father was indeed remembered at Westinghouse — and the new president invited him to lunch — it was only to make the inevitable turndown more cordial. The lone response Father received from his repeated *Position Wanted* ads in the *Wall Street Journal* was from a personnel consulting firm that wanted him to hire them.

"Ah, what a hard country America can be!" Father would sigh, crinkling his cheeks in that nervous way which narrowed his eyes into slits. On top of his employment woes, the New York State traffic bureau had lifted his driver's license for repeated speeding and recklessness at the wheel. In our cramped Riverdale apartment, where we moved to save on hotels, Father tossed and turned during the night on the living room couch and groaned in his sleep about ending up in Harlem or some other slum in his downward slide to God only knew where – a prospect surely no less grim than the *Schuldturm* of his grandfather's day.

Despite the weight of his immediate concerns, Father took a keen interest in émigré politics. Though powerless to do much to liberate his country from the Soviet yoke, he could at least keep his ambitions alive in case he ever managed to return. That's what prompted him to turn toward Washington, where émigré activities were centered. With no bona fide job remotely in the offing in New York, Father made a ten-thousand-dollar down payment on a four-hundred-acre dairy farm in a tiny Virginia village thirty miles from the nation's capital. The operation promised to be a profitable one, with a hundred milking cows and enough acreage to provide most of the feed. Since a substantial portion of Father's former estates had been agricultural land, this was an undertaking for which he felt qualified.

The final papers were to be signed in mid-August, at which time Father would make another ten-thousand-dollar payment and take possession of the farm. The balance would be paid off over the next thirty years.

Father had one reservation: shouldn't Mother see the place before the papers were signed? He felt a need for her support in this decision that would so critically affect the family's future. His ordeal in the United States over the past two years had undermined his self-confidence, and he no longer was the secure, decisive person he had once been. How ironic for him to have thought Mother might hold him back, Father would reflect, and again crinkle his cheeks nervously.

I was home for summer vacation and joined my parents on the trip. We made the 250-mile journey from New York in our second-hand car, which in those days of no superhighways took eight hours. After another hour of wandering along country roads, we found the village: a general store and about a dozen other buildings in all. The farm was three miles down the road; we couldn't miss it, we were told by a profusely sweating black farmhand taking a cigarette break. It was the only complex of buildings between here and the next village.

It had indeed been a sweltering day. Although the sun was about to set, the heat and the humidity hadn't diminished. Surrounded by an endless expanse of cornfields, the farm's whitewashed barns beneath the reddening sun created a shimmering silhouette like a desert mirage.

The farmer greeted us at the door. A wiry man with reddish hair, he gave us a brief tour of the simple two-story house and then offered us glazed doughnuts with milk. Sitting at the brown Formica-topped kitchen table, nobody had much to say. During one particularly long lull, a haggard middle-aged woman appeared in the entryway. Her gray hair was unkempt, a cigarette dangled in her mouth, and there were prominent sweat rings under both arms of her sleeveless cotton dress. She stood there, looking like an escapee from a mental institution, her gaze affixed to Mother, a smoldering cigarette dangling from between her lips. After a few moments of uneasy silence, the farmer walked over to the woman and peremptorily took her by the arm. With a few hushed words and a little pushing and pulling, he managed to turn her around and lead her out of the room. When he returned, he excused himself. "You see, my wife is ill," he explained. "That's why I have to sell the farm."

Shortly thereafter we left. For the next hour, Father drove around the country roads, trying to find the main highway. It was now completely dark, but the heat hadn't abated and it felt sticky in the car. There was no one in the sleeping villages to provide even wrong directions out of this rural labyrinth.

It was nearly midnight when Father came to a spot where he could pull safely off the road. I assumed he had stopped so we could all take a nap. But both he and Mother just sat there in the front seats, staring off into the night. I could feel a tension between them in the muggy air. Mother so far had said virtually nothing, and Father seemed hesitant to ask. Now, without turning to her, he finally uttered the words, "So, what do you think?"

"The wilderness, the heat . . ." Mother sighed. "No wonder that woman went crazy. It would be a disaster for our girls."

"Remember, I already paid down ten thousand."

For a moment, Mother didn't respond. Permeating the car through the rolled-down windows was the ceaseless whirring of cicadas from the surrounding fields. The enveloping sound came in gentle waves and somehow made Mother's silence all the more pronounced. Finally, with an undercurrent of distress, Mother said, "You just can't let such a huge sum lapse."

Father turned to me, stretched out on the back seat. "And you, how did you like it?"

I hesitated only an instant. "I didn't."

As mid-August came and went, Mother sporadically voiced her fears and Father had yet to make up his mind. The wiry farmer gave Father an extension till the end of the month, and with the papers still unsigned, he sold the farm to somebody else. Although Father tried to sue to get back his down payment, all it brought him was the additional expense of a lawyer's retainer fee.

In subsequent years, I often felt I was the one who had cast the decisive vote. As my parents agonized over how best to assure the family's existence, I weighed only two factors in rendering my response. On the plus side, the size of the farmhouse seemed to guarantee I would no longer have to share a room with my older brother. The far weightier negative was that living in Virginia would make it impossible to continue seeing the girl I had just met in our suburban New York neighborhood.

How ironic that several months later, she and I had parted.

The headmaster who had so generously taken in my brother and me would play a role in my life I could have hardly foreseen. Referred to as the Duke by students and faculty alike, this aristocratic-looking man occupied a special niche beyond that of running the school. It was rumored that he had been a confidant of President Roosevelt, and that President Truman occasionally called him now. The Duke was also reputedly among the few mortals who not only understood Einstein's theories but could make them comprehensible to an average fourteen-year-old. Yet the Duke was no less known for entangling boys in debates about whether Mickey Mouse ought to have a driver's license or the school's Lake Wononscopomuc should be stocked with freshwater sharks.

This was my second full year at the school. I was growing fast and the muscle training was bringing visible results. The custom-tailored flannel pants and blue blazer from my English schoolboy uniform were conspicuously inadequate. With the cuffs let down, my pants barely reached my ankles, and when I wore a hole through the seat, Mother fixed it with a large, square patch that was much darker than the rest of the pants. This, at a time when most of my classmates tried to look casually stylish in their Brooks Brothers pink button-down shirts and charcoal suits on Sundays, and plaid or check tweed jackets with wash khakis during the rest of the week. Although I considered everyone a friend, and said "Hi!" to anyone whose eyes I met, some of the big wheels I passed in the school's corridors pretended I wasn't there.

Not so the Duke. In the bustle between periods, his was often the friendliest face in the crowded corridor. Yet he was the headmaster, which made him far more important than the biggest of the wheels. In various ways, he let me know he regarded my nondescript wardrobe as something honorable, an asset that made me better than the rest. And whenever he probed my mind, it was on topics he thought to be my special expertise. I often felt his grip on my elbow, as he came up from behind, the way it was his habit, and ask questions like, "Do you think the Austro-Hungarian Empire should be restored, with Archduke Otto on the throne?" I had little idea who Archduke Otto was, and I would have been mortified to admit this to the Duke. But he was already trying to help me along, asking whether I thought I myself would make a good emperor. Now there was a subject for which I needed no facts and could expound on endlessly! The Duke listened to every word as if my opinion was as important as his.

I, of course, never failed to listen to the Duke. Not just in the corridors, or at the headmaster's tea, or whenever I sat at his table in the dining hall, but even in Sunday chapel, where I rarely listened to anyone. The Duke took to the pulpit about once a month. On those occasions, he wore the black robes of a minister but never assumed the typically somber ministerial pose. During one Sunday service, the Duke's golden retriever wandered down the chapel aisle, and everybody started to snicker, curious what the Duke would do. It was a serious disruption of a solemn occasion that the biggest pranksters in the school couldn't have planned. But the Duke never missed a beat. Stepping down from the podium and scratching his retriever behind one ear, he delivered an impassioned lecture on the virtue of dogs. "There's a great deal we can learn from them," he summed up. "How many people do you know you can trust as much as your dog? Do you have a best friend you can trust that much?" He paused to look over the rows of boyish faces and implicitly pose the question to each of us. "I often hear dogs can't get to heaven. I suppose the people who say it have all sorts of degrees in theology and know what they're talking about. The one thing I can say with certainty is that I want no part of any heaven where dogs are not allowed." The Duke glowered, visibly angered by the thought of a dogless heaven. Then, giving his retriever an affectionate pat and telling him to run along, he resumed his sermon as if no interruption had taken place.

Among the Duke's self-assigned duties was the woods squad, a punitive detail consisting of students who had been officially "sequestered" – that is, barred from athletic and social activities for breaking such rules as leaving the school grounds without permission at night. Working alongside the headmaster for two hours each day in the school's extensive forests was considered the most arduous part of the six-week punishment. Looking fit in his wash khakis and a checkered wool shirt, the sixty-year-old headmaster was the hardest worker on the squad and an exhausting conversationalist. "Wouldn't it be better to make golf a ten-hole or a twenty-hole game?" the Duke might suggest to a boy held captive on the other end of a lumberman's two-handed saw, half-way through a heavy log. "Why nine or eighteen? Those are pretty strange numbers, don't you think? If I were on the golf team, I certainly would want to keep score in round numbers. Maybe we should consult the mathematics department and find out what Dr. Renny and Mr. Hale have to say."

And so it would continue. There was no way a student could win debating the Duke. No matter which side the boy happened to choose, the Duke automatically took the opposite tack. Sometimes the Duke pretended he was agreeing only to demolish his own arguments. No wonder that by the end of the day, most of the boys on the woods squad felt done in.

Yet every now and then, a boy would see the light. Almost overnight, the woods squad would become for him no longer something to be dreaded, a painful bore, the worst part of being sequestered, but something he was inexplicably looking forward to. It might even turn into the brightest point of the day, infusing everything with new meaning and clarity. Some of the boys preferred to keep such newfound enthusiasm to themselves; a bit embarrassed, not unlike by an unexpected conversion to a faith they had previously scorned. But eventually, when their punishment was over and they were free to return to the normal life of the school, they would quietly request to remain permanently with the woods squad and the Duke.

Father was still reeling from his loss in Virginia when he made a similar down payment on another farm in Massachusetts. To do this, he literally had to sell the last of the family jewels, a sparkling diamond tiara, proverbially fit for a queen. Van Cleef & Arpels in New York, however, claimed the central five-carat diamond was flawed. "Sorry, there's a chunk of coal in it," the hunched-over man with an eyepiece said with a touch of disdain, and offered Father barely enough to meet the down payment terms.

There was no backing out, and this time Father presented the deal to the family as a fait accompli. The balance of seventy-five thousand dollars was to be paid off over the next thirty years in quarterly installments of about a thousand dollars each, including interest. "If you miss just one of those," the gruff old Yankee selling the farm warned Father on signing the contract, "I hope you realize you could lose it all."

Located in the western part of the state, the farm had several hundred acres of pastures and fields, about a hundred head of Guernsey cows, and a small milk-processing plant. Most of the people in the area worked at the state epileptic hospital, or at the Church Company, a toilet seat factory topped by a large neon sign, *Church Seat: The Best Seat in the House.* The area's largest daily ran a front-page story about a count taking over. "Only a mere handful of customers on his four milk routes are aware of his identity," the paper tantalizingly revealed, alongside of an elegant photo of Father in his English tweeds. "He prefers it that way, for to him, it is an indication that democracy in the United States is a real thing and that his success as a dairy farmer is due to his ability and not to his title. 'Here they call me Henry,' he explains. 'Count? That's nothing.'"

Beyond the ominous caution from the former owner, Father learned his lesson here even faster than in New York. His experience as a benevolent landlord in Central Europe with scores of loyal employees had little in common with trying to farm a few hundred acres in Massachusetts with several hired hands. Each day, well before dawn, Father quaked in his custom-made, manure-splattered wing-tip shoes until all of his employees showed up. The smokers would be clearing their throats in the chill of the early morning air, coughing out the phlegm between their barrage of four-letter words, sometimes holding up Father for a few extra dollars or other benefits before starting to work. The implicit threat was always there. What if the cows remained unmilked, the previous day's milk undelivered, and the following day's unprocessed? I remember helping Father fill in for one such absentee at the dairy plant. Father had on the same blue pinstriped pants from one of his Savile Row suits I had seen him wearing years ago at diplomatic receptions in Ankara. While I operated a carousel device rinsing 40-quart cans with live steam, Father tried to work a huge, clanking bottle-washing machine a couple of steps away. He inevitably failed to keep up with the relentless mechanism disgorging the clean bottles four at a time. They burst in a great hail of glass, while the hot water that was supposed to rinse the following batch squirted in his face. That's when I would leap over to press the red *Stop* button, and after cleaning up the mess, restart the machine for Father until the next bottleneck.

More frequently, Father had to fill in for one of the drivers who delivered our milk directly to homes of customers. On each route, this meant making approximately a hundred stops, scattered through several of the area's communities, and distributing some five hundred quarts of pasteurized, homogenized, or raw milk in glass bottles (as well as such smaller items as heavy cream, cottage cheese, and butter). The delivery trucks weren't refrigerated, and crushed ice had to be spread on top of the cases of dairy products during the summer. The regular drivers started loading around 5 A.M. and were usually back by early afternoon. Father, who started a little later – having supervised the loading by the other drivers – didn't finish until well after dark. Although he had previously accompanied each of the drivers at least once, that was hardly sufficient to become familiar with their routes. Guided by a loose-leaf notebook listing the customers' names, addresses, and what they took, Father had to search out almost half of them. Moreover, he had to contend with the housewives who had heard about him being a count and wanted to chitchat or invite him in for coffee. As he gingerly brought several of the one-quart glass bottles to someone's door, wearing an open-necked white silk shirt from his former days, this tall mustachioed man who spoke with a foreign accent was liable to arouse the curiosity even of those who had no idea who he was. The combined result was that by midaft-ernoon, we started receiving frantic calls at our house from other housewives, wondering what had happened to their milk. The calls often continued until late into the night. Although Father would have returned by then (his truck strewn with shards of glass from several broken bottles, and the case or two of unsold milk now tep-id because the ice had melted long ago), it was inevitable that he had missed a few stops. Tired and resting with a newspaper on the living room couch, he would rouse himself and drive off with the requested items in his car. The last thing Father wanted to risk was having a customer defect to one of the dozen or so other dair-ies peddling milk in the area.

7/

The Duke was pleased with my progress during the years under his tutelage. At least that's what he consistently wrote in his periodic reports home. No doubt, by my senior year, I earned a unique status of my own, especially now that my brother had graduated. I still didn't own any suits or shirts from those vaunted Brooks Brothers, but I seemed to have a flair for wearing my more modest wardrobe purchased on sale here and there. When my prize essay on the advantage of owning only one tie was read in class, some of the big wheels took note. What worried them was that my one-tie gambit could become a popular fad, like wearing heavily scuffed white buckskin shoes, without any of the big wheels being able to take credit for starting it.

I had by then developed quite a physique and was eager to show it off. Whenever it wasn't blatantly obvious, I walked around the dorms without a shirt, the muscles at least a little flexed to display them in the most impressive way, especially those under the arms. Just a subtle tension spread them out almost like wings, giving the upper torso more of that V-shaped look. The trick was to retain the appearance of being relaxed and loose; how mortifying if my effort to look better were to be exposed! But even without flexing, I was considered one of the best-built members of our class.

Indeed, I myself was becoming a wheel of sorts. One of my classmates invited me to drive down to Florida to spend the spring vacation at his mother's winter home in Hobe Sound. (Father said he could spare me from the farm, and Mother sent me fifty dollars for the trip.) This semitropical enclave of great wealth was teeming with Hotchkiss boys, and I soon realized I could count many more of them as my friends than my reclusive host. It also turned out my host had a sister, a freshman at Vassar who wasn't reclusive at all. She had been one of the most popular debutantes in New York the previous year, and while she normally didn't date anyone unless he was at least a sophomore at Yale, she accepted my invitation to the school's graduation dance.

The Duke was particularly impressed by this transformation from the small boy he'd taken in four years earlier to the young man I had become. He assumed my physical evolution to be a sign of a corresponding spiritual growth, since there was no evidence to suggest this wasn't so. His wisdom and experience told him I was becoming the sort of well-rounded person who would one day make him and the school proud.

Then, just a few days before graduation, disaster struck.

It started innocently enough. I was sitting at the headmaster's table, as usual next to the Duke at the head of the long table for thirteen. Most of the students were reluctant to sit near the Duke. They were afraid he would prod them into debating some of his favorite topics and they couldn't eat in peace. They crowded around the dining room entrance until the last moment before the doors officially closed, hoping that a few of the more obliging types had filled those undesirable seats.

I, of course, considered it an honor to sit next to the Duke. I enjoyed his incessant banter and inexhaustible ability to carry on about whatever subject anyone might raise. Moreover, the Duke's glowing recommendation was the reason I had been granted a nearly full scholarship at Yale.

This particular meal was a breakfast. It started off with a discussion of *How hot is hell?* "Don't tell me you don't know," the Duke chided the half-dozen students sitting on either side of him, when his query evoked a round of exasperated groans. "At one time or another, I've heard just about every one of you complain that it was *hot as hell*. Surely you know what you meant! Or are you in the habit of saying things you don't mean, or worse, don't even know what you mean?" The Duke took a sip of orange juice, then pretended to share the students' exasperation. "I can't understand why all of you refuse to tell me how hot hell is. It's terribly frustrating not to know. I'm asking simply because I'm curious. It's your expression, not mine. I can't use it because I don't know how hot hell is. And not one of you is prepared to tell me! That's not very generous, is it? I don't even know if they use centigrade or Fahrenheit in hell. Now, what do you think? Dan? Robert? Bill? Richard?"

Without getting a satisfactory answer from any of the students sleepily sipping their juice, the Duke launched into a simpler question: *How far is a stone's throw*? This time, he managed to evoke a couple of weak retorts, and after making his point, lapsed into a momentary silence to concentrate on ladling out the hot cereal and passing it down the table on either side of him.

Normally, the silence would have lasted only a few seconds before the Duke introduced another of his typical subjects. But, for some reason, I thought this was an ideal opportunity to interject a topic of my own that I knew to be of considerable interest. It involved two of the school's senior math teachers, Dr. Renny and Mr. Hale, who often thrust subtle barbs at each other in front of their respective students in class. The rumor had it that this enmity wasn't merely professional jealousy, but dated back to the time Dr. Renny flunked Mr. Hale's son on a final exam in math.

"Is it true what they say," I now asked the boy sitting next to the Duke across the table from me, "that Dr. Renny flunked Mr. Hale's son in math?"

I wasn't really expecting an answer from the boy. How would he know? This supposedly happened years ago. But the Duke knew, and he would authoritatively settle the question once and for all.

I was still looking across the table at that boy when I had the strange feeling that something had gone terribly wrong. I heard the Duke pause, arresting the motion to fill the next cereal bowl. I had the sense of him putting the bowl down deliberately. Then I heard him utter, with the incredulity of someone who had just been slapped by a trusted friend, "What a malicious thing to say!"

I turned in time to see a tense, quizzical smile dissolve into a scowl of great severity. The Duke's forehead became tinged with pink, and the little shock of white on top of his head began to quiver dangerously. His eyes, reflecting the dark clouds gathering within, transfixed me with a look of outrage. "That's the sort of poisonous rumor-mongering we can do without," he continued in a blunt, excoriating tone.

I was in shock, as if lightning and hail had struck both at once. No wonder some of the Duke's detractors compared his anger to the wrath of God!

"I was only trying to find out if it's true," I said defensively. "Everybody says it's so."

"Everybody?" Again, that tense, quizzical smile. The fact that the Duke hadn't resumed ladling out the cereal was adding to the gravity of his words. "What kind of talk is that? Who is everybody? There are three hundred and eighty-seven students in the school. Do they all say it? There are another fifty-four faculty and staff. How about them?" There was no trace of humor in the Duke's voice. He glowered at me, defying me to name my source.

Under the circumstances, of course, I couldn't think of anyone, except perhaps Dr. Renny himself, who had often implied as much in class. But my better judgment told me that this would be exactly the wrong thing to say.

"Well, there's simply no excuse for this sort of thing," the Duke said, as he resumed ladling. "All it does is create ill-will and undermine the spirit of the school. In the long run, it's the same sort of thing that causes wars. I would have thought *you* understood that especially well." The Duke paused to give me a prolonged, sorrowful look. I felt at that instant as if he was making me personally responsible for starting some future world war, as if my indiscreet remark about Dr. Renny and Mr. Hale would somehow interact and escalate to bring about a calamity on a global scale.

And he wasn't done yet. For the rest of the meal, the Duke carried on in a similar vein while I ate my hot cereal, then the soft-boiled egg and toast, and finally gulped down my milk. Fortunately, I was no longer the direct target of his words. I sensed the Duke didn't want to embarrass me in front of my classmates. He was lecturing the whole table on character flaws, how we must be on guard against them because we were all susceptible. This was a welcome respite for the other boys from the Duke's normal routine. They weren't expected to respond and could eat in relative peace.

I was the first to finish breakfast. As soon as I wiped my mouth, I asked the Duke, "May I be excused, sir?" This was a mere formality, which every student engaged in with the teacher at the head of his table.

"No, you may not be excused!" the Duke replied firmly.

It was the first time in four years I had been denied permission to leave. I noticed several other students glancing at me, as if to say they were glad they didn't happen to be in my shoes but serves me right for always trying to suck up to the Duke.

I sat there like a player in a penalty box, wondering how long before I would be released. The Duke waited, now uncharacteristically silent, until everyone at the table had left. The rest of the huge dining hall had also emptied, except for the few scholarship students assigned to sweeping the floors and washing the tables in preparation for the next meal.

"I am frightfully disappointed," the Duke said gently, a touch of sorrow in his voice. "You've always had such exemplary school spirit. I was so pleased to see how you developed since we first took you in. Now, after four years, to find this strange streak within you . . . it really is disturbing."

The Duke reached into his pocket to take out a pipe. He didn't light it but just held it in his hand. Determined though he seemed in this inquisition, there was no vengeance in his voice, no righteous desire for retribution. At times, he seemed embarrassed and pained.

"What does go on in that head of yours? I was always sure I knew pretty well. Not the details. But whatever it was, I had no doubt it was honorable and good. But now? Maybe you can tell me."

I sat there with a feverish glaze in my eyes, the sound of my heart in my head. I wanted to tell the Duke I was still the same person he had always known. Maybe in my enthusiasm, I did talk a little too much about people and their traits when they weren't around. The Duke was right about that. And if that amounted to a fault, I would watch myself. But otherwise, I was a pretty good guy.

"These little things are like icebergs," the Duke continued in an even, instructive tone. "Only the tip usually shows. What you don't see can be deadly. It can bring a lot of ships down, including your own. How can I be sure it isn't going to happen to you? How can I be sure there aren't all sorts of other things submerged within you, waiting to breech the surface?" The Duke looked at me intently, and I averted my eyes. "You're the last person from whom I would have expected something like this. It's a bad attitude to take with you no matter where you go."

I wanted to slither under the table and disappear. God, this was as bad as that incident with Eugene and the pencil sharpener, and yet it was so undeserved. I had only repeated what I heard dozens of times from others. The Duke knew about the rumor concerning Dr. Renny and Mr. Hale, just as he knew how hot *hot as hell* really was. Right now, I could have told him, if I thought he still cared. I was feeling the heat. But why pick on me? Every student had surely done something far worse during his four years at the school, me included. Maybe my classmates who didn't want to sit next to the Duke were right. At the other end of the table, I would have never been overheard. Why this, after I had gotten along with the Duke so well, and he had thought so much of me? And just days before graduation!

Meekly, I followed the Duke out of the deserted dining hall. I was hoping I would be able to bolt on the other side of the double doors. But when the Duke reached the threshold, he paused to wait for me, as if he had read my mind. Gently, he took me by the arm, as was his habit with students to whom he had something of vital importance to impart, and started to walk me down the corridor.

"To be a person of character . . . that is the most important thing we can teach you," the Duke resumed. His voice was gentle and fatherly. "To be popular, to be a *good guy*, that's easy. The world is full of good guys, but a good man is much more difficult to find. If we don't help you develop the proper character, your education is of little value. Knowledge can be dangerous if you use it for improper or selfish ends. I wish all this had happened two years ago. Or better still, when you first came to us. We would have had a chance to really work with you, to help you. Now, I'm afraid you'll have to do it on your own. I think you'll find that for the rest of your life you're going to be pretty much on your own."

We were nearing the Duke's office. Other students were passing us in the busy corridors, getting ready for classes or rushing off to the infirmary to have their noses sprayed and throats swabbed and get excused from morning chapel. I was desperately hoping the Duke would finally let me go.

He opened the door to his office, and once more put his hand on my arm. "I don't want you pushing this out of your head," he said somberly, and then was gone.

I walked down the busy corridor in an unhappy trance. That I should fall so unjustly in the Duke's estimation!

Suddenly I was gripped by a terrible thought: What if the Duke wouldn't let me graduate? Was that the meaning of his parting remark? Maybe he would give me only a certificate instead of a diploma. That's what happened to students who didn't pass all their courses. Obviously, I had failed in the Duke's estimation, which was far more serious than failing any course. Nor was it something like being caught in town after lights out, for which you could get censured or sequestered. My only censure had been for dropping a wrench out of my dormitory window and almost beaning Butch Stearns, the toughest teacher at the school. The Duke publicly made light of the incident, much to Mr. Stearns' dismay. But this was hardly a joking matter for the Duke.

I was beginning to succumb to my fears; indeed, the Duke would *not* let me graduate. I soon had evidence that made me more anxious still. In my mailbox the following day was a note in the Duke's careful script. He went on at length about character; how we must always be on guard that we do and say only those things that are truly worthy of us, regardless of whether anybody finds out or we get caught, which I saw as a pointed reference to my eleventh-hour gaffe. "We owe it to others," the Duke concluded, "to do what is right. In the end, we owe it to ourselves; for only then can we live with ourselves in peace."

I was already trying to reconcile myself to my fate. If the Duke didn't let me graduate, would I lose my scholarship at Yale and have to find another place to go? It would hardly be the same, and I would have to lower my expectations as to what life might hold in store. Still, if only the Duke stopped hounding me! He was like a crab that had locked onto me and wouldn't let go. He seemed at the point of obsession, almost irrational about the whole thing. As if he had nothing more important to do in these last days of school!

Twice more before graduation, the Duke called me into his office to give me similar talks. And twice more I was to find in my mailbox those detailed, handwritten notes in the precise, well-rounded script I had only so recently come to dread.

Finally, it was time to graduate. My parents had made the two-hour drive from the farm for the ceremonies, along with my two brothers and two sisters. They were sitting in the school chapel with all the other parents and friends, having no idea how I was sweating it out in my pew. My anxiety continued to mount as other students went to the podium to receive their diplomas, and the moment for calling my name approached.

Then I heard it, in the Duke's resonant voice. I couldn't believe it and thought it must be a mistake. I was not only getting my diploma, but the Fidelity Prize, awarded to that scholarship boy who had done the most for the school community as exemplified by his spirit and growth.

I had goose bumps running up and down my back. My knees felt weak as I heard the clapping and walked down the aisle amid the sea of faces on either side. And there, down at the other end, stood the Duke, like some fortress of strength, waiting to catch me if I stumbled or fell.

"Congratulations," the Duke whispered, as he shook my hand. I felt him draw me closer, until nobody else was there, just he and I. "I have done all I can. This prize is as much for what you've done for the school as for what I expect from you. Now, it's up to you . . ."

8/

Except for taking three days off to attend a debutante party for a sister of one of my classmates, I was busy seven days a week with tasks on the farm during that summer before going to Yale. I always found a way to make the most of my work and didn't really consider it a chore. In raking the fields on a sunny day, I tried to sit on the tractor at an angle that caught the most direct rays of the sun. When hefting those 40-quart cans of milk up a flight of rickety steps from the barn to the cooling room, I liked to watch the way the shoulder muscles beneath my T-shirt strained and became delineated in a powerful symmetry.

Now that I was old enough to drive legally, my additional task was delivering milk door to door. I was the substitute driver for the regulars taking their annual vacations. After two or three times on each route, I started to identify my customers by the number of quarts they took and where those should be put. *Three homogenized, two pasteurized, half-a-pint of heavy cream in the shade on the back porch.* Or: *Two raw milks in the refrigerator. Don't forget to move the old milk up front, put fresh milk in rear.*

One of my customers was an old New Englander, Mr. Heck. A feisty, red-faced little man, he had parched skin stretched taut like a mummy. Mr. Heck operated a tiny fast-food stand at a small lakeside resort. He took a case of half-pints, a half-case of chocolate, two heavy creams and a large cottage cheese. I often stopped there around noon, and Mr. Heck fixed me his special, a couple of hot dogs filled with melted cheese on toasted rolls. As he puttered between the hot plate and the little refrigerator within his tiny space, he talked incessantly about the women who had already been by that day. "I'll take my old lady any day," the dried-out little old man usually concluded. "Been married for forty years. Don't run around no more. You want to know why?" he once asked me, impetuously making a lengthwise slit in a hot dog to reveal the pinkish meat inside. He grasped one end of the hot dog in each hand, leaving about two inches of the slit exposed in between. Then he turned it into a vertical position so that the opening ran up-and-down. "Yup, that's what it looks like, from up close, when you get your face right against it. If I was to warm it up a bit, put a little of this here oil on it, and close my eyes, it wouldn't feel none too different from the real thing." Old Mr. Heck ran his gnarled finger along the pinkish, two-inch slit. "Yet, for *this*, men have been willing to lie, to cheat, to steal, to kill, to go to war – even make doggoned fools of themselves." He took a wedge of cheese, stuck it in the slit, and slapped the whole thing on his red-hot grill. "Take it from an old man who knows," Mr. Heck said, fixing me with his watery eye, "'tain't worth it. I can't say I wouldn't be the same dang fool all over again if I had the chance. But 'tain't worth it, 'tain't worth it."

That was easy for dried-out old Mr. Heck to say! He had his *old lady* who did whatever it took to keep him content at his age. But I was seventeen, supposedly at my biological peak, and feeling it, too. How well I had come to understand Effendi and the old gardener laboring so mightily for a heaven abundant in the things they lacked on earth! While I continued to evoke the pleasurable genie on my own, his magic no longer seemed complete, and he had been leaving tell-tale signs for the past several years that he needed the participation of a member of the opposite sex.

My various milk routes may well have offered countless opportunities for satisfying that persistent need. But Alfred Kinsey had yet to reveal the potential for such behavior in a surprising number of inconspicuous housewives. I never did consider as anything but kindness the invitations for coffee from several of the women who already had their curlers out and looked conspicuously well-put-together by the time I brought their milk. As for the younger unmarried prospects on my route, some of them thought I was *cute,* which enabled me to have things my way up to a point. I wasn't exempted from that early 1950s rule as to what a *nice* girl would and wouldn't do. Despite persistent efforts, I never managed to convince even one of them how much more I would respect her if she would just once, *please,* be less than nice. Their repartee, implicitly or explicitly, was always the same: "You mean you would marry me?" How tirelessly adept they were during drive-in dates in turning their chests and crossing their legs to thwart my moves! They seemed altogether content to keep this up throughout a double feature without seeing either film. I, on the other hand, would be so disoriented at the end of the show that I once drove off without removing the speaker hooked onto a partly rolled-down car window. The glass shattered, and it was a long

time before I regained the use the family car. Yet never for a moment did I consider, *'tain't worth it!* I remained confident that before long, I would prove dried-out old Mr. Heck totally wrong.

The cost of repairing that broken window was symbolic of our
family's financial plight. Having recently acquired the habit of
counting his money as if our future depended on it, Father realized
he hadn't factored in all his expenses prior to buying the farm.
How could he have known that the clutch on one of the milk
trucks would burn out, the boiler in the dairy would need a new
heating element, and the rocks in the fields would chew up a
half-dozen cutting blades, all within a week? How could he have
anticipated the loss he incurred when he tried to expand his dairy
line by manufacturing ice cream? The amounts Father paid out in
various bonuses and the accounting shortfalls he had because of
improper controls at loading time were by comparison trifling.
The real problem was that the seventy or so milking cows and the
small milk-processing plant couldn't support the fixed expenses
Father had. His biggest financial drain came from paying for our
schools, despite the various scholarships we had. My older brother
was in his third year at Princeton, my two sisters were at a Catholic boarding school, and my younger brother was a day student at
the local academy.

   With his finances continuing to deteriorate, Father tried to
supplement his income by selling life insurance. After a full day of
busying himself on the farm, Father drove off in the evening to
check out the leads provided by the home office. It seemed that
every family he called on had some relative, friend, or a friend of a
friend, who was in the insurance field. Father eventually focused
on nearby Westover Air Force base, where the transient personnel
made such ties less likely. The difference in his rate of success,
however, wasn't great. After a third visit to some sergeant and a
two-hour discussion about a policy that might eventually net a

few hundred dollars in commissions, the former count came home more exhausted than from any work in the fields. He took off his jacket and tie and stretched out on the living room couch, where he had recently taken to sleeping. He switched off the light and then tossed and turned and groaned. It was hard to tell when he fell asleep, if at all.

The situation for Mother was in some ways more difficult. When she first arrived in the United States, Mother was in her early forties and radiated an eye-catching blend of robust health, ethereal beauty, and simple elegance. A shipboard picture of my parents standing arm-in- arm on the promenade deck against a backdrop of the Manhattan skyline made them look more like a couple visiting on a honeymoon than immigrants.

Mother's determination to protect this lingering romance, combined with her heritage of a common Central European bias (which had never affected Father) soon led to the sort of incident Father had feared if Mother accompanied him to Turkey.

Among Father's romantic interests when he had visited the United States as a young man was a shapely young woman named Marjorie, whose family controlled one of the major brokerage houses of Wall Street. She had since become a widow, and Father was counting on her for introductions to people who could help him for the duration of his stay.

When Father first apprised Mother of this gilt-edged opportunity shortly after arriving in New York, she compressed her lips but otherwise didn't respond. Several weeks later, when Father told her that Marjorie had invited both of them to dinner, Mother again didn't say anything. Only after Father's repeated entreaties, pointing out what this relationship could mean to the family's future, did Mother finally respond.

"I suppose that means you've already seen her," she said quietly.

"We've only talked on the phone," Father said, raising his arm defensively. "Can't you get it through your head, this is purely a social relationship. That's why Marjorie insisted you come, and if you don't, I'm not going either." He paused, then seeing Mother's skeptical look, added, "Really I haven't seen her, I swear I haven't."

The dinner was elegantly served with butlers and maids in Marjorie's Park Avenue duplex. The conversation was almost entirely two-way, since Mother's command of English at this point was slight. Mother sulked and remained taciturn even when Marjorie addressed questions to her that Father translated. Things nevertheless moved along at a cordial pace until the interval between the main course and dessert. That's when Marjorie fetched a photograph of her daughter, which she proudly showed to Father and then handed to Mother. After studying the picture for a moment, Mother looked up and in her halting English observed, "But doesn't she look a little Jewish?"

The ensuing atmosphere prompted Father to leave with Mother immediately after dessert. When Father bitterly rebuked Mother on the way home, she again chose not to respond. As I would learn decades later, what had incensed Mother to act in such an appalling way was that before ringing Marjorie's doorbell, Father had fessed up that he had already seen her several times.

While Mother welcomed the move from our cramped New York apartment to the Massachusetts countryside, the sojourn in the United States seemed to her to be lasting particularly long. She lacked the cosmopolitan outlook that had been a part of Father's upbringing, and she felt forlorn to be separated from her parents and the small world she knew. What was imprinting the first visible wrinkles on Mother's forehead, however, was her sense of helplessness to affect the family's situation. No matter how hard she worked at her household chores, whether repapering the sprawling old farmhouse or mending our clothes and making sure we were neatly dressed, she felt it was all for naught. She saw Father's employees take advantage of him at every turn and play him for a fool at a cost she couldn't ever offset by what she scrimped and saved. "Now you see how loyal people are when there's no money," Mother would point out to Father more and more often. Mother's added woe was the mess the drivers and farmhands constantly tracked in and deposited on the Persian rugs in the living room. That's where Father had chosen to officiate at a long Italian Renaissance table from his palace in Prague – one of the few pieces he'd managed to whisk out in time – which now became cluttered with route books, milking ledgers, breeding records, canceled checks, and more and more unpaid bills.

Father's standard response to Mother's plaints was a good-natured shrug, not too different from the tack he took when he had been a count in Prague. But as the family's financial situation worsened, Father became less likely to react with a smile than with that nervous crinkling of his cheeks. He was liable to point out with an edge to his voice that if Mother hadn't so crudely ruined his contact with Marjorie and spoiled it for him with the farm in Virginia, we wouldn't be in our present fix. Those four hundred acres of agricultural land only thirty miles from downtown Washington had been sold recently for several million dollars as a real estate subdivision.

As in other families experiencing economic hardship, the tension between Mother and Father became increasingly evident. The situation reached a climax in the kitchen of our Massachusetts home. Several months in arrears on his mortgage payments for the farm, Father was so desperate for cash that he had lugged the mahogany chest with the massive sterling setting for twenty-four to a Boston pawn shop to secure a fifty-dollar loan. Mother was under additional stress from the news that her father had passed away in Prague and her mother was seriously ill. The dialogue escalated in volume until Father grasped from the kitchen counter one of the plates Mother had just washed and smashed it to smithereens. "I can do that, too!" Mother retorted, as she grabbed the three remaining plates in quick succession and dispatched them in a similar way. She then opened the nearest cupboard, and taking out plate after plate, smashed it to the floor. Father stood there aghast, watching the shards accumulate around his feet, until he said a bit uncertainly, "All right, that's enough!"

Having witnessed the scene, I became aware for the first time of Mother's underlying strength. While she implicitly portrayed herself as being subservient to Mr. Count, in a subtle way she was often the one in control. Whether holding off Father for five years in Prague before agreeing to bear his children or, as I had come to realize, dissuading Father from buying the Virginia farm, Mother knew how to get her way. Even in trivial matters, such as canvassing Father about his preference for Sunday lunch, Mother presented the options in such a way as to yield the desired result. And if that failed, she would still prepare what she had intended all along.

Mother had her own agenda and thoughts, and she didn't want anyone to penetrate the mystery of her ways. Though fiercely protective of her children and of her husband's image – she wouldn't allow any criticism of Father in her presence – the only member of the family with whom she had a close bond was my ten-year-old brother, Tom. Mother undoubtedly considered her emotional isolation essential to the survival of the butcher's daughter in the family of Mr. Count. That's why it was such crushing news when she received word from Prague that her last confidante, my grandmother, had died. Even so, Mother quickly wiped away the tears as if grief was an emotion she couldn't afford.

9/

The excitement I felt on entering Yale that fall was tempered by an unavoidable adjunct to being a scholarship student. As the recipient of university largesse, I was obligated to put in fourteen hours each week at some campus task. For freshmen, this usually meant duty in the commons, an oak-paneled Gothic-style dining hall of arena proportions, where more than a thousand students were served three cafeteria-style meals daily. The specific tasks were assigned by the dietitian, Miss Jones, whose sensitively lovely face and trim waist offered an enticing distraction from her ample legs.

I started out in the scullery on the glass-washing machine, but was soon transferred to a serving line, specifically on butter. Standing at the end of one of the four serving lines in a white waiter's jacket, I made sure that students passing by with their heaping trays took no more than two pats each. I considered it a compliment that Miss Jones seemed to favor observing the traffic flow by standing next to me at the end of my line. She looked refreshingly pretty in her lightly starched dietitian's uniform, and whenever she made some remark and leaned toward me to make herself heard over the din, our shoulders touched long enough for me to feel her warmth.

I didn't mind the work per se, even though it cut into my study time and curtailed my social life. While at Hotchkiss, I had looked forward to taking my two-week turn as a waiter – along with every other student at the school – because it assured priority on second helpings. What was different now was that only scholarship students were doing this work at Yale. Although the white waiter's coat supposedly served as a badge of distinction for having gained entry to this bastion of privilege purely on brains, it also marked the student as more or less a charity case.

What aggravated the situation for me were my pretensions to belonging to the privileged segment of my class. I took care always to be well dressed, especially after I had discovered Morris Widder's second-hand store, where Brooks Brothers togs were sold at a small fraction of their original cost. Yet my most frequent encounters with fellow students were to be while wearing a white waiter's coat.

This feeling of implicit inferiority assumed a more troubling dimension during my third week on the job. It was the day of the season's first football game, and many of my classmates had invited dates from Vassar, Smith, and other nearby women's colleges.

Walking across the Old Campus to take up my position in the commons, I had already encountered a couple of girls I knew from the occasional mixers at Hotchkiss. Now, as I cautiously leaned forward over the counter to see who might be coming my way, I felt my heart vault into my throat. Waiting to be served with her escort at the other end of the line was a girl with whom I had repeatedly danced at the one debutante party I had attended that summer. She had seen me in a white dinner jacket, playing the role of the suave continental to the hilt. God, what to do now?

"Are you all right?" I heard Miss Jones's solicitous voice as if through a fog.

My mind was racing in overdrive. "Just checking if there's going to be a break in the line," I said. "I think it's time to get more butter."

I disappeared in a trice but obviously didn't hurry back. By the time I retrieved several trays of the chilled pats from the walk-in refrigerator in the kitchen and resumed my place, the danger had passed.

The following Saturday, I had no warning. I spotted her only as she was picking up dessert; butter would be her next stop. She was one of the girls I had been trying to impress as a worldly count the previous spring in Hobe Sound. She had been skeptical then, and in a nice way told me she liked me for spinning tall tales. She was the last person I wanted to see me this way.

Reacting more by instinct than design, I turned abruptly from the counter and doubled over while holding both hands to my head.

I felt the gentle touch of Miss Jones's fingertips on my arm.

"It's just a muscle cramp," I explained. "I was trying out for the swimming team earlier today . . ."

By the middle of the following week, I had made up my mind. The problem wasn't limited to these embarrassing chance encounters. I had by now discovered that weekends offered an ideal opportunity for what was known as bird-dogging; that is, making a play for somebody else's date. In my case, it wasn't a matter of trying to recruit for a future weekend, which I couldn't have afforded anyway, but merely of peripherally participating. My debonair European act, combined with strategic upper body display and topped off by some provocative remark I had picked up in class about the human condition, was proving effective. Beyond evoking admiring glances, I was the occasional recipient of a sensuous embrace on the sly. It would hardly do if one of these conquests later encountered me on butter.

"I have a favor to ask," I ventured with unrehearsed intensity as I was taking leave of Miss Jones at the end of work that midweek day. "Do you think I could fit in all of my hours during weekdays? It looks as if I'm going to have to go home and be the relief milkman on weekends."

Miss Jones gave me a sympathetic look. "Aren't you trying to take on too much?"

"I can handle it."

"When do you have to begin?"

"They're counting on me this weekend."

"It's a bit sudden . . . but I'll see what I can do."

By the time I reported for work the following day, Miss Jones had revised the entire schedule for the fifty or so scholarship boys, which was posted on the kitchen bulletin board. The concentrated working hours would undoubtedly encroach more drastically on my study time, but I could make it up. As for myself going through the food line on weekends, I knew Miss Jones was off-duty at least one of those days. Since there were four separate serving lines, I could surely evade her if she happened to show up.

I felt a sense of self-justification in having to go home the first weekend to peddle milk. The next two weekends, however, I spent on campus practicing my bird-dogging technique. And it turned out my key assumption had been right. Miss Jones was nowhere to be seen on any of those days even though I had surreptitiously peeked at each of the serving lines. Maybe now that the term was underway and the kitchen functioning smoothly, Miss Jones felt she was no longer needed on weekends.

The following Saturday, I had a date for the football game. I was among those who had signed up for a subsidized, low-cost get-together with girls from Smith. Three busloads of them were disgorged in front of the Yale Bowl, where a like number of Yale freshmen awaited them. The matching had been done by lottery. I had little idea then that human worth could be measured by criteria other than movie-star looks, and I wasn't enthralled with my draw. Still, I wasn't about to step out of my gentlemanly role, especially since the encounter wouldn't last long. After the football game, dinner, and an informal dance, the buses would be taking the girls back.

I went through the serving line that evening in a lethargic mood, being polite to my date while not fully acknowledging her presence or my role as her escort. When we came to butter, I happened to look up perfunctorily from my tray — and that's when my heart stopped. Next to the person manning my post stood Miss Jones, looking especially pretty behind the waist-high steam table. I felt myself flush as she gave me a penetrating look and then walked away toward the kitchen before I could nod or say hello.

The next meal I worked was Monday lunch. I felt an emptiness within whenever Miss Jones walked by as if I weren't there. At no time throughout the meal did she take her customary position next to mine at the end of the line. Only as I was ready to leave did she confront me directly.

"I'm sorry . . . I really believed in you," she said, squeezing out the words, her voice quivering. "I had real sympathy for what I thought you were trying to do." She paused and then turned matter-of-fact. "I've asked the bursary office to transfer you to the Hall of Graduate Studies. I think it's best for all concerned."

I felt as if I had again grossly compromised myself. This realization stayed with me even after learning that the dining hall to which I had been reassigned not only would keep me out of view of my classmates but was the only one on campus closed on weekends.

10/

When I came home for Christmas during my sophomore year, our family affairs suddenly took an unexpected turn. To this day Father refers to the portly man with a stutter, who had been officially banned from the milk business in Connecticut and wanted to regain his reputation by going into the same business in Massachusetts, as Santa Claus. In his eagerness to buy the dairy, the trucks, and our customers, this benefactor agreed to pay the full price Father had asked but by no means expected to get. Although most of the money went toward the mortgage, enough was left to pay some of the more pressing bills piled on the Renaissance table. The other windfall came shortly after, when another buyer acquired the livestock and farm implements and rented from us the fields and the barns. Most of the proceeds again went toward the mortgage, but a few thousand dollars remained, providing Father with a thin cushion to try to begin anew.

The advantage Father now had over when he first started out in the United States was a roof over his head and six years of experience. On the other hand, he had virtually no money to invest and little time in which to secure a substantial source of income.

What kept Father from feeling backed against the wall was a discreet approach from the Central Intelligence Agency. Father had no idea how the CIA came to know of him. He had long since relinquished any ties to Czech émigré groups in Washington, which could have served as a conduit. Be that as it may, the CIA deemed Father suited for the job of controlling strategic goods that were being shipped, legally and otherwise, behind the Iron Curtain. He was to run the operation from Vienna and report directly to Washington.

This sounded good to me. It certainly seemed more suitable for Father than shoveling manure or peddling milk door to door. He would be paid enough to keep us in the United States, and we would occasionally visit him in Europe. I was already considering what new jackets to buy when Father left for a final briefing in Washington. His meeting with the director of the CIA, General Walter Bedell Smith, went as expected, with such details as salary and operational methods once more reviewed. It was only as Father was leaving that the general casually inquired, "By the way, do you have any suggestions for the name under which you'd like to operate?"

Father was puzzled. "You mean the code for my reports?"

"I mean your new identity. You obviously can't go to Vienna and do this kind of work without a cover. That's our policy. That's how we operate."

Father made it clear he also couldn't go to Vienna – where he and the family were known almost as well as in Prague – under an assumed name. "What if I meet somebody in the street who recognizes me?" Father asked sharply, as he shook hands with General Smith. "I don't think it would work if I were to tell him he was mistaken and that I was Mr. Jones . . . or Mr. Smith."

Having lost valuable time and further depleted his dwindling funds, Father resumed his search at a frenzied pace. He long ago gave up on the idea that some company might offer him a salaried job. He was approaching the sixty mark, when many of his contemporaries with company careers were retiring. Who would want to hire him at his age? His best bet, Father figured, was to go into business for himself as an independent distributor. If he could find the right item, maybe the commissions would enable him to keep up with his most pressing bills. He had recently read Arthur Miller's *Death of a Salesman* and was haunted by Willy Loman's fate.

To the existing clutter on the dining room table were added various magazines, newsletters, and pamphlets describing an array of "unique, once-in-a-lifetime" opportunities. Culling out those that seemed most promising, Father talked to dozens of companies on the phone, made dozens of inquiries by mail, and even made several abortive forays to check out several manufacturers whose products looked promising.

I was by then a junior at Yale, and Father was still desperately searching for a viable means of support. He had managed to stave off disaster over the previous two years only because of the kind heart of the gruff old Yankee who held the mortgage on our farm. Despite having threatened Father with the possibility of foreclosure at the time of the sale, he not only overlooked a pattern of late payments but allowed Father to sell off chunks of the farmland as building lots and pocket the cash.

As much as I empathized with Father's financial woes, I didn't allow it to cloud my outlook. I saw our family situation as a temporary aberration caused by political events. It certainly wouldn't carry over into my life in any decisive way. Once I completed my education and entered the job market, I could look forward to the same bright future as my college friends.

This optimism was unexpectedly challenged in one of my most interesting classes at Yale. "We take it for granted that our experience here on earth is supposed to be enjoyable, that it is our birthright to derive pleasure from daily life," Professor Franklin Le Van Baumer lectured our intellectual history class in neo Gothic Harkness Hall. "Gentlemen, this assumption blithely ignores the evidence." Professor Baumer was a tall, distinguished-looking scholar who liked to gesticulate vehemently when his back wasn't hurting him. With his lumbago acting up, he was careful to make no untoward moves. "There is no guarantee," he continued stiffly, "that our unexpected freak of history, when enjoyment of life is considered the norm, is assured any kind of a future. Virtually all of history, as well as the abject conditions in which most of humanity still lives today, point strongly against it."

Professor Baumer's prognosis resonated through the cavernous lecture hall but didn't strike a responsive chord. Though I would toe the line in any future test so as not to risk an inadequate grade, my outlook wasn't about to be affected by a few dire words. Most of my friends were sanguine about the future, too, and not just because they were at Yale. Why, even in the blighted parts of the world people were leading better lives, despite the likes of Effendi. Was Professor Baumer so isolated in his intellectual lair that he failed to understand the world in which he lived? Or was the professor's aching back more likely to blame? A permanent cure would surely improve his views! And I wondered, why was it that so many of the great thinkers in history had some physical problem or mental quirk affecting the ideas with which they tried to saddle the world? Saint Augustine went around for years moaning, "God, make me chaste ... but not yet!" – and then did his utmost to inflict the dubious blessings of his celibacy on everyone else. Was that because his personal ardor for intimate pleasures had waned? Having myself just turned twenty, this was a problem I could hardly understand. And I had an exciting thought. What if the world were to come under the sway of a philosophy formulated by someone with a healthy appetite for life? I was the 175 pound boxing champion, yet I had good grades. As a Scholar of the Second Rank, which was much better than it sounds, I was in the top ten percent of my class. Why couldn't I figure out a valid philosophical system for our times that would one day be taught in Professor Baumer's class – or at least be included on the optional reading list? It was a thought with which I occasionally liked to entertain myself, especially after a few beers at the Old Heidelberg bar. Under my socio ethical synthesis, those vague desires and dreams I used to have while nudging attractive women as a prepubescent on the streets of Prague could be gloriously fulfilled.

11/

Father's latest prospect for pulling him back from disaster was a Texan named Elmer Wheeler, who claimed to be America's greatest salesman, and many magazine and newspaper articles hailed him as such. "Sell the sizzle not the steak," was Elmer Wheeler's copyrighted motto. This meant you really didn't need to have much of a product if you knew how to sell.

Father was sufficiently inspired to fly to San Antonio, where Elmer Wheeler was apportioning chunks of the United States to individuals astute enough to recognize a once-in-a-lifetime opportunity. The item he was offering was a little miracle in itself. At a time when tape recorders were the size of a suitcase, his Minifone had been reduced to the proportions of an average book and could be inconspicuously worn in a white harness under a jacket or a coat. Elmer Wheeler's intent was to apply this technological breakthrough to a field more lucrative than undercover police work. Potential franchisees would be able to offer companies a new, dramatic way of improving the performance of sales employees by secretly monitoring their interactions with customers. From these recordings, Elmer Wheeler's diagnostic experts at the home office would then identify each employee's strong and weak points.

What this super-salesman was now offering were the Minifones at $500 each, along with exclusive rights to territories for marketing his revolutionary sales improvement technique. The cost of the franchises ranged from $1,000 to $50,000, depending on location and size, and included a proportional number of hours of free diagnostic time.

At the conclusion of the meeting in the packed Texas hall, Elmer Wheeler received a rousing hand. As Father watched more than a hundred aspiring Minifone moguls start lining up at several booths staffed by Elmer Wheeler's assistants, his lingering doubts began to dissolve. Hoping to put his mind at rest, Father asked for a tête-à-tête with Elmer Wheeler himself.

The super-salesman instinctively sized up what it would take to close a deal. For $1,000 Father acquired a complete Minifone package with harness and instructions, as well as an exclusive to the territory within fifty miles of our Massachusetts farm.

By the time he came home, Father's original doubts had returned. He had an uneasy suspicion that maybe he had succumbed to the sizzle and there wasn't much steak. Could this little machine and attaché case of materials really secure the family's future?

Father had no choice but to forge ahead. For his first prospect, he selected a nearby six story department store, whose owner agreed to see him because of their acquaintance from meetings of the local chapter of the Foreign Policy Association. As spelled out in Elmer Wheeler's instructions, the approach to a prospective client was predicated on surprise. The idea was to walk in, and after chit chatting briefly about this or that, reveal that everything said had been recorded – and then play it back. The coup de grâce would come at the recording's end, when Father was to ask the startled prospect, "Now, what would it mean to you and your company if you could eavesdrop this way on each of your sales-people?"

As I tried to help Father prepare in the living room of our farm, his remaining confidence began to evaporate. Awkwardly, he slipped on the heavy white harness over his shirt and tucked the book sized Minifone into a pouch under his arm. A complex machine, it used filament-thin wire instead of tape to record the sound. The first time I turned it on, the wire became hopelessly tangled and I had to snip off several yards. An array of buttons had to be activated in the right sequence by feel in the hidden hol-ster. Considering that Father's impatience with delicate mechanics often caused him trouble tuning a radio, I didn't allow myself to think what would happen when the critical moment came. I ad-justed the hidden microphone under Father's tie, helped him put on his jacket, and then spent some time instructing him how to hold himself so that neither the microphone nor the bulge made by the Minifone would show.

Mother drove us to the department store. During the twenty minutes en route, Father couldn't make himself comfortable. He kept wriggling in the bulky harness as if he were in somebody else's suit that didn't fit. But he didn't complain and seemed re-signed to his fate. As I watched him from the back seat sitting in silence next to Mother, he repeatedly crinkled his cheeks into that unsettlingly grimace.

Mother managed to park about twenty yards from the person-nel entrance to the store. I jumped out of the car to open Father's door and help him get out. He reached for the attaché case on the floor and then gingerly straightened up.

"All set?" I asked.

"Good luck," Mother whispered.

"Let's go," Father muttered to himself, and with a visible effort began to stride uncertainly to the personnel entrance of the department store.

I watched Father for a moment or two, then turned to Mother. She was watching him too, and I saw tears flooding her eyes. "How fate can twist your life!" she moaned, and broke down in quiet, stifled sobs.

In retrospect, I recognize that as Father was taking those labored steps, I was seeing someone who had his back against the wall. According to that New York émigré lawyer who sent him a bill after a purely social lunch, Father could expect his fortunes to change. And that's what seemed to be happening now. Within days of Father's humbling Minifone experience (he never did manage to get the contraption to work at the department store, whereupon the owner gently told him he wouldn't consider spying on his employees anyway, nor would the unions allow it), Father fished out another opportunity from the ever-mounting jumble on the Renaissance table. Shortly thereafter Father sold his first Exercycle and started on a new career.

"It was easy," he would explain in future years, "because I fell in love with the machine."

Surely, Father's association with the Exercycle represented a unique chapter in the already bizarre employment annals of dispossessed nobility. One of the most expensive of all exercise machines – it cost about $500 in 1955 – the Exercycle was an electric-powered device with pedals that went around in a range of 30 to 90 rpm, a large chromed seat that moved up and down, and three way adjustable handlebars that swung back and forth. What attracted Father to the Exercycle was that it looked like a machine he himself could use. Now that he no longer worked on the farm, he needed something to keep himself in shape. Father had always made exercise a part of his life. As a younger man, he had worked out with a set of rubber chest expanders and taken long treks amid the mighty firs of his Bohemian woods – though his main muscle toning activity in Prague derived from the hands of a masseur.

Having installed an Exercycle at home, Father conveyed to prospective customers his own enthusiasm about the machine. By the end of the first week, he had closed three sales, which was what the home office in Hartford had projected for his first month. And by the time I returned home for Christmas vacation, Father had already chalked up twenty that month, approaching the performance of the company's most successful distributors.

12/

In the fall term of my senior year at Yale, I finally made it *all the way* with someone I was completely smitten by. This was still no easy matter in those days, when attitudes were not too different from what we had believed as schoolboys at the Orchard House. There was a strong presumption that sweethearts worthy of that designation were infinitely too nice – along with mothers and sisters and virtually all the girls who went to Vassar or Smith – to engage in something so base; and, heaven forbid, enjoy it. The most promising prospects for such dishonorable behavior were local girls of the sort one would hesitate to introduce to family and friends. The first time I did succeed was with a lanky girl from town who seemed to meet those criteria. The only feeling I had toward her was a vague sense of gratitude for the chance she was giving me to practice this skill and gain experience in such a vital area of life. Our sporadic affair ended abruptly when I naively revealed to her how I felt. I thought she had known all along and didn't in the least bit mind.

It was in the Green Room of the drama school that Avis and I were fated to meet. I occasionally dropped by this traditional actors' lounge on the pretext of thespian interests, but in reality to ogle some of the budding ingenues, which was far cheaper than trying to make it to one of the closer women's colleges. The drama school girls seemed to be also more yielding, as if they had basic needs similar to mine. Was it because they were actresses? Or were those proper, uptight college girls the ones who were putting on the act?

I first glimpsed Avis as she sat quietly in a corner chair, studying a script. She had dark, shoulder-length hair and infused that corner space with a tangible grace. I liked what I could make of her aesthetic proportions beneath the yielding yellow cashmere sweater and the greenish plaid skirt she wore so stylishly. While her refined profile suggested someone not likely to go beyond holding hands, there was an intensity in her face, as if all of life was happening at that instant and she wanted to respond with everything she had.

I approached with a hesitant, "Excuse me, but . . ."

She looked up and gave me a luxurious smile, as if she had been expecting me and now was glad I was there. "Well, hello," she said, and then cued me through the introductions in a way that banished whatever nervousness I felt.

I couldn't believe how easy she was making everything seem, as if I was an experienced man-of-the world with an irresistible technique. In no time, we were walking down York Street for a cup of coffee at George & Harry's. Sitting across from me in the dimly lit booth, she listened to everything I said in a way that made me feel I was the most special person on earth. With just the right smile and a few well-chosen words, she could make my most banal observations sound witty and fresh. Especially the way she exclaimed with bedazzled amazement," I don't believe it!"

There was a misty rain when we started back, a copy of the *New Haven Register* over our heads. I felt an exciting intimacy in the way we were so effortlessly keeping pace. While crossing the street at the intersection of College and York, I suddenly found myself holding her hand. The sun had momentarily brightened the overcast sky, and Avis gave me an exuberant smile. "I feel so delicious," she said, licking the misty droplets off her lips. "I never, ever want to stop feeling this way as long as I live."

We had dinner that evening, and again the next. Everything was happening of its own accord, as in a dream. I felt spontaneous and free, relieved of any need to maneuver or scheme. She didn't even engage me in debate when I followed her up the two flights to the little apartment near the drama school where she lived.

What I experienced next revealed to me a new world. I needed no seismic instruments to recognize that what was happening was the same as when the earth had moved in Hemingway's *For Whom the Bell Tolls* back in freshmen English; especially those sensuous sounds Avis made, as if possessed by some buoyant spirit over which she had no control – an unforgettable but rare event according to Hemingway, and he certainly ought to have known. I had also read, in the few discreet manuals available on this subject at the time, that even a vastly milder response shouldn't be expected among newlyweds until after weeks of diligent efforts in the conjugal bed. Surely, Avis was less experienced in this field than I, I said to myself, though I did wonder where was the sort of evidence that used to be publicly displayed in old Russian villages after the wedding night to confirm the honor of the bride? Nevertheless, I came to an unshakable conclusion: It must be something special I had done, or some special attribute I possessed, which brought about this miraculous response.

But what?

For a while, I was at a loss as I went down the list. Obviously, it had little to do with size, which I recognized to be modest and no standout in the communal showers of the Yale University gym. Just as obviously, it wasn't my clothes. Although I owned my first suit and several pink button-downs acquired at Brooks Brothers on York Street, that didn't begin to compare with what most of my contemporaries had. Was it perhaps because I was a count? Mother warned me that young females might go for me solely because of that. But I knew she was liable to be projecting, and I hadn't even told Avis yet.

Then suddenly, it was so clear. Why, Avis herself intimated as much in repeatedly marveling how *special* I was. Maybe that crazy idea which occasionally flashed through my brain about my consciousness being the only one in the universe wasn't so crazy at all. Maybe everyone else was merely playing a role for my benefit, irrevocably pledged never to let me know. Any moment I could expect someone to falter and give away the game, though I was hoping not just then; not when I was having such a great time.

Of course, that was fine as a theory. What I really suspected in the back of my mind, despite everything I have said, was that I must have been quite a stud, which is what pleased me the most.

We were a radiant pair, Avis and I, walking across campus arm in arm or holding hands. People would turn and look, often wistfully, as if reminded what they were missing in life. How many Yalies came close to having it that good? Not the captain of the football team, or the chairman of the *Daily News*, or the president of Skull and Bones, the most exclusive secret society on campus. I had no doubt they would gladly have given up their vaunted positions to be in my place.

"Promise me one thing," Avis said after one of these cross-campus walks, with her characteristic intensity but unusual concern. "Promise you will never, never talk about us to anybody. What we have . . . well, I don't want to sound corny, but it's sacred. It's *ours*. Nobody must ever know."

"Whom would I tell?"

"I want you to promise."

"Oh, all right, cross my heart," I said lightly, and raised two fingers. "Scout's honor."

"I mean it!" Avis sounded anxious. "I know it's difficult for you to understand. For a young man, this sort of thing is just another feather in his cap. For a young woman . . . well, the world is hardly so kind."

I could see her point. That leering query, "You getting any?" was so frequent on campus it was almost like saying, "Hi!" I had in fact been tempted to boast a little to a few select friends, just to see their reaction. They would never believe it, not with Avis!

"Really, I haven't breathed a word to anyone," I assured her.

Sitting close to me on the daybed of her apartment, Avis looked relieved. "It's only because I love you so much," she sighed, and gave me a tender kiss. "We should be careful about people seeing us together too often. There are so many busybodies around. It could ruin everything."

I thought she was overreacting; yet I recognized I was too simplistic a soul to figure out someone as mysterious as Avis. Why question my incredible luck? If only old Mr. Heck could see me now. '*Tain't worth it?* Hah!

The relationship soon settled into the pattern of student life. While my studies unexpectedly improved despite a lessening of effort on my part, Avis continued to be immersed in her drama school work. Her parents, both of whom were doctors on the West Coast, didn't consider the theater an appropriate career. This was the only year for which they had agreed to pay, and Avis wanted to get as much out of it as she could. Homework and rehearsals were taking up most of her time.

"Oh darling," she whispered one night, as she emerged from an especially profound litany of those passionate sounds, her features becoming reanimated by her more familiar self, "how I wish we could be together . . . always. You're a shining thread of something nice interwoven in my life. If you only knew how wonderful you make me feel."

A shining thread of something nice! Gee, nobody had ever called me that before. I didn't mind that two evenings a week were the most she could take off from her work. At this rate, I wouldn't overspend my limited funds, earned during the summer operating a jackhammer drill on the future Mass Pike. The three or four intervening days would also whet my appetite to a deliciously acute stage. More so than ever in my life, I felt I held the upper hand.

It was in this smug mood that I received a near-perfect grade, with little effort on my part, in Samuel Flagg Bemis's demanding *Diplomatic History of the United States.* This kind of good news couldn't wait. Determined to share it with my love, I immediately tried to give Avis a call. But her line was busy – and remained busy on several subsequent tries.

This wasn't anything unusual. I knew Avis preferred to study with the phone off the hook and, I reflected with a contented smile, also make love. Hm . . . why not go over right now? Surely, she would welcome this respite from her work!

On the way across campus, I was already getting excited, thinking of what would happen next. The images, sounds, and tastes were becoming so vivid I quickened my pace.

There was no answer when I rang her downstairs bell. It was an old apartment house, and the bell often didn't work. But as usual, the front door was unlocked.

Quickly I bounded up the two flights of stairs. Then just as I was negotiating the final steps, I heard a sound that stopped me in my tracks. I recognized the special intensity which had always been so welcome to my ears. Now it had an ominous effect. I felt as if I should retreat before it was too late. Still, I couldn't resist pressing on and placing an ear against the door.

How quiet everything was! Maybe it had been my imagination playing not-so-funny tricks.

Cautiously, I raised my hand and was about to knock. But just then another of those familiar sounds came forth; more intense, more passionately marked. I recoiled, as if struck below the belt. And now more sounds came cascading from behind that door. Their familiar tempo and crescendo left no doubt that the buoyant spirit was in charge — and my darling had not evoked it on her own. Gasping for air, I fled down the stairs.

It wasn't until the following morning after a sleepless night that I reached Avis on the phone. Trying to remain calm and be as tactful as I could, I alluded to my suspicions.

"How could you suggest such a thing," she retorted, with overwhelming sorrow. "Oh, I'm so disappointed . . . you, of all people. But I'm glad you called." she continued in a calmer tone. "It serves me right. It just goes to show I've been neglecting my studies. I shouldn't have been seeing you in the first place. I really can't see anybody until I catch up. When I do, I'll call . . . I promise."

"But Avis . . ."

"Don't sound so grim," she said, as if trying to cheer me up. "I'll see you bye and bye."

She neither called nor saw me during the rest of my year at Yale. But I did glimpse her at least a half-dozen times walking across campus, always with an escort at her side or holding hands. Each time, I managed to take a divergent path before it was too late. Under no circumstances did I want to approach close enough to discern what was going on. I hurt enough as it was.

13/

A few months after I graduated from Yale, the Hungarian uprising against Soviet might in the fall of 1956 brought the Cold War
dangerously close to heating up. For the first time in years, I
dared entertain an impossible thought: Would there one day be a
similar but successful revolt in Prague, and we would be going
back? My more immediate and practical concern was the effect of
such flare-ups on the draft. Now that I was no longer a student,
my deferment was over, too. This meant I could summarily end up
as a foot soldier subsisting on K rations in some highly uncomfortable place. Surely I could discharge my obligation in a more appropriate way. The previous year I had become an American citizen – the Duke had been one of my sponsors, and the judge shook
my hand and said, "Congratulations, Count!" – which meant I
could become an officer. From the war movies I had occasionally
seen, it appeared that officers in the Navy enjoyed the greatest
prestige and led the most gentlemanly life. Always clean linen on
their beds, stewards serving them wardroom meals, and except for
carrier pilots, they were about as safe as civilians on the street.

Or so I thought when I decided to apply.

In no way do I lay blame at the Navy's door; they did all they
could to warn me in time. Already at the Officer Candidate School
in Newport, R. I., they tried to explain, through the compulsory
moral guidance program of the chaplain's office, why it was wrong
to succumb to the tempting offers from willing ladies we would
encounter in the side streets and bars of the hungrier parts of the
world. We were supposed to memorize the four reasons why we
shouldn't give in, just the way we had to memorize in damage control the six ways to save a listing ship. I quickly learned from
practice sessions in a simulator that I could never save a sinking
ship. Soon, I would find out I was equally inept at putting into
effect the moral points that would spare me grief ashore.

It happened in the Taiwanese port-town of Kaohsiung. That's where the fleet tanker to which I was assigned returned after refueling a division of destroyers on continuous patrol in the Formosan Straits. COMTAIPATPAC was the bureaucratic designation for that command. Its operations were in line with the brink-of-war policies of the secretary of state, John Foster Dulles, to keep up the pressure on the Communist Chinese. They, in turn, were sporadically shelling the tiny islands of Quemoy and Matsu, a few miles off the Communist mainland, still held by the Nationalist troops of Generalissimo Chiang Kai-shek.

Our Kaohsiung contact was Henry Wu. He was a local businessman who brought scores of laborers to touch up our ship, clean out the scuppers, and take on various jobs that the sailors appreciated being spared. As payment, Henry Wu was allowed to draw off some of the sludge from the bottom of our fuel tanks, which was normally pumped over the side at sea. In anticipation of drawing off a few hundred barrels more than we had agreed, Henry Wu treated several of us officers to a traditional twenty-course Chinese feast, with lots of drinks and all the trimmings afterwards. By the time I came face-to-face with the lithe young woman who was to serve as a trimming for me, I was feeling pleasantly woozy and uncontrollably bold. What I liked best was the way her body was devoid of the teeniest hair, providing the first unobstructed view of the mysteries within. That kind of a peek Avis would have never allowed. Even if so advanced in other ways, she preferred to be possessed by that buoyant spirit in the dark, a light left on in the bathroom and the door slightly ajar. And there hadn't been anyone since, which was over a year!

Though it was way too late to reflect on the chaplain's words, I did remember the urgent tone of Chief Hospital Corpsman Andrews advising us at the Newport OCS at least to play it safe. Yet somehow, all caution went to the wind. It was as if I didn't have a mind of my own and was being propelled by an inexplicable force.

It was a force that chose to ignore where I was – in a brothel in the middle of Taiwan, where locals and military from all over the world bought time shares of one hour or less. Obviously, not even my genial Chinese host could guarantee anything beyond the external quality of the goods. By the time the effects of any internal flaws might be felt, he would have long since cashed in on his hundreds of barrels of sludge, and I would be far out at sea.

That's exactly how the scenario played out. It started out as a funny feeling in the groin, though not the kind likely to make you laugh; an itchy, burning sensation at the tiny opening at the end, which looked reddish and puffed up as if it had been in a fight. And, when squeezed like an empty tube of toothpaste from the bottom up, several drops of fluid, abnormal in color and density, would slowly drip out.

God, this wasn't supposed to happen to an officer, especially not to a count! Weren't such inherently dirty afflictions the lot of an altogether different segment of the human race? If only I had been impressed rather than entertained by the chaplain's moral spiel! For the first time I had an inkling what Mr. Heck may have meant, '*Tain't worth it.*

The ship's hospital corpsman prescribed the standard antibiotics, but a check-up by a bona fide doctor had to wait until our ship docked in Hawaii. There, I found myself in a bizarre situation. At the Pearl Harbor Naval Hospital, during a high-level readiness inspection conducted by several admirals, I was literally caught with my pants down. Bent over, my ailment was being probed from behind by a doctor's rubber-gloved finger inserted in my rear. I couldn't see the inspecting party, nor they my face. But my officer's hat and coat, lying on a nearby chair, was enough for one of the admirals. "This is something I don't care for at all," I heard in a shockingly familiar voice, as the party hastily started to withdraw. "What a shame, even officers these days not being able to keep their noses clean!" It was a voice I instantly recognized;

not because as a lieutenant junior grade I had much official truck with admirals, but because this happened to be the voice of COM-SERVPAC – Commander Service Force U.S. Pacific Fleet – whose lovely daughter Pam I frequently escorted around town during my ship's stopovers in Hawaii. That very evening I was to dine with Pam and her parents at their sumptuous Makalappa Drive quarters, high above the naval base. Pam's father was the ultimate superior of our ship and eighty other ships under his command; hence his title, COMSERVPAC.

Thank God he hadn't seen my face!

I had originally requested assignment to a ship on the East Coast. This would have meant routinely joining up with the Sixth Fleet and visiting Mediterranean ports. How interesting it would have been to see if the old shoeshine man, Effendi, was alive. Or were his prayers answered and he was now in paradise, at last enjoying those things he had so sorely lacked in life?

Yet I wasn't disappointed to find myself in the Pacific on a Navy tanker. Home-based in Long Beach, California, our ship steamed to Hawaii every six months, then continued to the Far East to join the Seventh Fleet and visit ports such as Manila, Tokyo, and Hong Kong – in addition, alas, to Kaohsiung.

Undoubtedly the biggest break of my Navy career came from having at one time been a Czech national. Due to the militant suspicions between the superpowers – and because I still had several relatives from Mother's side living in Prague – the Navy withheld from me the highest security clearance known as *crypto*. The reasoning was that I could be blackmailed with the lives of Mother's relatives to hand over top secret codes and theoretically compromise the communications system of the Free World.

When I first reported on board, the captain was furious. "God damn those idiots in Washington!" he railed. His intent had been for me to replace the ship's communications officer, who was being reassigned to shore duty. Far from sharing the captain's distress, I felt as if I had been saved from a premature scuttling of my Navy career. My aptitude for maintaining an orderly system of communications records and files was about the same as Father's, and it would surely have been merely a matter of time before some top secret *registered* publication couldn't be accounted for. Any such discrepancies the Navy didn't regard lightly.

Lest my feelings be hurt by Washington's lack of trust, the captain appointed me to be the ship's security officer for the upcoming Operation Hardtack. My main task was to prepare the crew to remain mum about what they were about to see. Operation Hardtack was to be the next to the last open-air test series of nuclear weaponry before President Kennedy and Chairman Khrushchev would agree to end all above ground explosions.

During our six months in the Bikini-Eniwetok proving grounds, I witnessed from the bridge of our ship through high-density goggles more than a dozen of the so-called devices going off. These goggles were so dark they practically blocked out the brightest sun. Even so, we were directed to turn away from the biggest explosion of the lot, a multi-megaton H-Bomb about thirty miles away. There was no immediate sound, which made the spectacle all the more eerie. No combination of words could convey the searing force of the blinding fireball suddenly bursting outward on this oceanic expanse to consume the horizon. It was like a thousand midday suns in an instant engulfing the sea and the sky; an awesome display of unbounded power, worthy of contemplation of humanity's potential to create and to destroy. Yet how unthinkable if transposed over a familiar skyline where people lived! No wonder many of the top Bikini brass didn't care to concern themselves with implications of this sort. If not getting pleasantly soused at the little makeshift officers' club at Camp Blandy, they were busy trying to add to their collections of spotted cowries and giant clamshells before heading home to wife and kids. The biggest flap of the operation came when somebody stole an admiral's entire horde that had been buried in the sandy ground at the Enyu Island base to rot out the flesh.

I certainly imbibed my share at the Camp Blandy Club, where happy hour prices of ten cents a drink seemed permanently in force. "Don't sweat it!" was the popular Navy refrain, and I tried to take it to heart. In the Pacific, this was still a time of relative peace, two years before the first advisers would be sent to an obscure country called Vietnam. Knowing whom to salute and keeping your hair appropriately trimmed could be more relevant than having the courage to insert your body as caulking into some gaping torpedo hole.

Being a naval officer was not unlike being a count. As head of gunnery and the ship's first lieutenant, I was a liege-lord to ninety men, with the cargo deck for my fief. I realized I could never penetrate the mystery of the refueling rigs in my charge, with their intricate maze of pulleys, wires, and lines. But I knew on whom to call. Several times each day, I made it a point to stroll around the ship, exchanging words with each of the men, praising their work, approving their liberty chits, and bestowing whatever other largesse I had it within my power to dispense. I didn't mind the reputation for listening to every hard-luck story and perhaps being taken in. After all, the sailors bunked forty to a small compartment below decks without air conditioning or ports, their worldly possessions crammed into a footlocker no larger than those rented out at bus stations for a quarter a day. I had my own stateroom with two portholes, a shower and a toilet. Every morning, a Filipino steward awakened me with a gentle knock and a fresh cup of coffee, and later made my bed.

"The men think you're a great guy," one of my career petty officers told me, when I solicited him after several beers for a frank opinion, "but they also think you're here on a pleasure cruise. They'd like to see you . . . well, sir . . . carry your load."

I felt the sting of his words, though only momentarily. What counted was that the captain considered me to be a highly effective officer, or so he had written in his quarterly fitness reports to Washington. My gunnery department earned the top rating in the fleet after I discovered a creative way of conducting firing exercises of our manually operated World War II vintage guns that produced scores worthy of the latest in automated weaponry. What pleased the captain no less was that I had rewritten the ship's history in a way that made it seem as if his command was the culmination of all of the ship's previous activities since its commissioning in 1943. And he did not remain unaffected by what COMSERVPAC finally revealed to him during the ship's most recent stopover in Hawaii." What a coincidence," the admiral casually remarked at his Pearl Harbor headquarters, during the captain's official ten-minute call. "One of your officers has been squiring our daughter Pam around town. We had him at the house for dinner last night." The admiral reminisced briefly in front of my startled commanding officer, then raised his bushy eyebrows. "I leave it to you to convince this fine young man to make the Navy his career."

God, what if the admiral had seen my face!

14/

Until practically my last day on board, the captain tried to get me to stay. Why, Washington would most likely honor any request I made. I could be assigned as a flag lieutenant, perhaps even as an aide to COMSERVPAC. That would be quite a plum and look good on my record at promotion time.

The Navy had been exciting at times, but I was ready to move on. I no longer wanted to have to prop open my eyes on interminable mid-watches, or take the risk of being assigned in the course of a lengthy career to some martinet for a superior with absolute say-so over my fate. I had seen several of those in my time, and didn't want to press my luck.

I was twenty-five when I mustered out of the Navy at the Treasure Island Naval Station in San Francisco during President Eisenhower's final year as commander in chief. I had saved a few thousand dollars of my pay and saw this as a chance to break out of the lockstep of life. Having so strictly forged ahead through prep school, college, and the military, I wanted a respite before going on to a career.

Fortunately, my parents were doing fine. The thought that I might have to help out and grab the first job I could get had occasionally clouded my horizon, but that wouldn't be necessary now. Father's continued success with the Exercycle was restoring his confidence, which further increased his sales. His inherent expectation of having his way, combined with his Old World mystique, made it harder and harder for prospects to say no. With five Exercycles loaded into the back of his Chevrolet station wagon, Father made frequent forays from his Boston office into the half-dozen states of his New England territory, calling on prospects who sent in inquiries in response to ads. His record for one day was more than five hundred miles traveled and all five machines sold. He repeatedly received the dealer-of-the-month award. At the annual sales force convention, other dealers from all over the United States would approach him and ask, with a touch of awe, "Henry, how do you do it?"

Indeed, Father's income was now sufficient to keep up with his mortgage as well as pay the full tuition for my younger brother Tom at Hotchkiss. When three Exercycles were stolen from his station wagon (while he was sunning himself between appointments on Revere Beach), Father was able to shrug it off. "Think how much worse it could have been," he observed with a laugh, "if I'd had five instead of three machines in the car!"

When I phoned Father from San Francisco, he was supportive of my plans. "This is the time to do it, if you want to fool around," he said. "I hope you find a place you enjoy, but that shouldn't be difficult in California. You really have a golden life. I don't envy you, but in a way I do." He paused, then added in an amused aside, "Who would have believed when I was born that I would end up this way – Mr. Exercycle!"

As soon as I hung up, I headed for Laguna Beach, a prosperous, artistically oriented community clustered on several gently sloping hills at the edge of the Pacific, about halfway between Los Angeles and San Diego. I had often retreated there from my ship on a weekend pass, returning with the freshness of someone who had been swimming in chilled champagne. Now, for $125 a month, I rented a small house on a rocky bluff directly over the beach. From the window I could watch the activity on the crescent strip of sand below, especially those high school girls exposing their exquisite shapes to the rays of the sun. What a repository of potential brides! On my very first evening, one of these lovelies whom I had been ogling earlier while sitting on the beach knocked unexpectedly on my door. Things progressed at a seemingly unstoppable pace. Only when it was almost too late did she caution me, still in a seductive voice, about her age, and proudly showed me her junior high school I. D. card. The reason she had been trying to set me up, I eventually found out, was to blackmail me into doing her English composition homework. Under other circumstances, I would have been delighted to help her out.

Toward the end of the second week, I had an unsettling surprise. The caption beneath the photo on the society page of the *San Diego Union* identified her as "Mrs. Dewey King III, of LaJolla." She was organizing some charity ball, and although the picture and newsprint were partly smudged, I would have known her anywhere — my first carnal love, now bearing the name of a former classmate from Yale.

LaJolla was an even more prosperous community than Laguna Beach, about an hour's drive down the Pacific Coast. We met for a drink that same afternoon at the Marine Room of the Beach and Tennis Club, not far from her home. Wearing a chic gabardine suit, her hair perfectly coifed in a lustrous bun, Avis seemed no less sensuously predisposed than at Yale. Yet where years ago I had sensed a barely contained bursting forth of joy, I now perceived a barely subdued misery.

She shook my hand gravely. "You certainly look as if you've found your groove," she said, with a not altogether happy smile as she slipped into the seat across the table from me, in front of the panoramic window of the Marine Room.

Avis ordered a margarita, and we started to chat politely. There was a tacit recognition between us that her life had drastically changed; it was as if she had suffered a grievous wound that she wasn't ready to discuss and I would be cruel to point out.

"You wouldn't want to hear about it, anyway," she finally said, with no attempt to smile. "My life is hardly fun. Dewey . . . that is, my husband . . ." She paused. "I don't think you knew him at Yale, did you?"

"There were a thousand of us in my class. I knew of him."

Indeed I did; not because of his Nordic good looks and powerful physique, which might have qualified him for the romantic lead as a Viking hero in some Hollywood film. Dewey King's renown at Yale — perhaps notoriety is more accurate — derived from his vociferous leadership of the most conservative causes on campus, be it organizing rallies in support of Senator Joseph McCarthy's Communist witch-hunt or raising alarm about government plans to fluoridate the nation's water supply. Moreover, at a time when most of the students were partial to casual attire, he dressed as a traditional gentleman in elegant double-breasted suits.

"I guess I knew of Dewey mainly because of his political views," I elaborated.

Avis nodded and her lips parted in a bittersweet smile. "Would you believe I once subscribed to that crazy political stuff? Oh, I loved him so! I would cry if he'd walk out of the room for even a moment." Avis paused to take a sip of her margarita, then licked the salt remaining on her lips from the rim of the glass. "We lived in an enchanting dream until some of his friends started to spread awful rumors about me . . . and Dewey believed them." Avis sighed. "Afterwards, he was terribly remorseful, but it was too late. In place of all that love, I felt only a painful void. If it weren't for the twin girls, I might have already done away with myself. They aren't even three. They need me so . . ."

Avis looked out the window at the ocean's edge. She watched the surf lapping gently at the sand, leaving behind streaks of whitish foam. She turned to me, and though verging on tears, made an attempt to smile. "If you ask me," she said, as if exposing some astounding conspiracy, "life is nothing but a dirty trick."

Seeing Avis so fragile and sad, I couldn't help but recall her exuberant moments at Yale. How did she ever get so messed up? In my benevolent view of the universe, life wouldn't have meted out such a fate without her active complicity.

"I'm sorry," she apologized. "I didn't mean to ruin your afternoon." She took a few quick sips of her drink, then brightened up. "Enough said?"

"It's a deal."

"You always did understand," she sighed, then smiled at me with a nostalgic intensity as if all along I had been the only one. "That's what makes you so special."

I would see Avis again, but not that close to home. We would occasionally meet for dinner at some quiet ocean-side restaurant about halfway between where she and I lived. Although we did little more than talk, I felt uneasy about these trysts. I often wondered, what was her husband doing alone at home? Even if Dewey and Avis no longer shared a marital bed, they lived under the same roof paid for by Dewey from his salary as a corporate lawyer with a conservative San Diego firm. Despite the divergence between his views and mine, I felt a curious kinship for Dewey, as if we had both not only taken part in the same war but sustained wounds from fragments of the same shell. Were those "awful rumors" Dewey's friends had supposedly spread related to Avis's previous affairs at Yale, perhaps mine included? Besides, how did Avis manage to free herself for these late evenings out? Or did she go out on other evening dates? Of course, I realized this was a topic I couldn't broach. She never thought it fit to volunteer what had ended our relationship beyond dismissing that whole year as terribly confused.

"You really were a legend at Yale," I said to her one evening, trying to cheer her up and get her to talk about those days. "At least, to me you were."

She looked distraught. "A legend?" she moaned, as if I had deliberately wounded her. "How could you say something so awful! You seem to forget, Mister Smartypants, I'm a mother now. I can hardly afford to be a legend. If only for the twins' sake."

"Gee, I'm sorry," I stammered.

Avis reached out and touched my arm. "It isn't your fault," she said, now again composed. "You're young and carefree. One day you'll understand what responsibility means. Believe me, I've suffered for that crazy, mixed-up year in more ways than you can imagine."

Even in her depressed state, Avis was scintillating company. Though sad and wan, her dark eyes projected an untamed intensity for life, a passion waiting to be released. She retained the ability to constantly elevate life, to imbue every incident and word with the drama of a Greek play. She saw herself as a tragic character but never lacked a certain humor over her fate. "Maybe this was all meant to be," she once remarked deadpan, "because I only swing my left arm when I walk. I bet it's one of those human peculiarities the Olympian gods especially abhor."

Then one evening after a seafood dinner at Dana Point, instead of driving to our respective homes, we parked on a high cliff overlooking the Pacific. Avis got into my car, sliding just a little toward me on the front seat. There was a near-full moon, reflected in a shimmering line of yellow that ran thirty-five miles over the gently rippling waters to the darkish silhouette of the mountains on Catalina Island. Avis tilted her face invitingly close, and I could practically taste the warm moistness of her breath. She made no effort to restrain me when I leaned over and lightly kissed her lips. While she didn't respond the way she had at Yale, I felt an excitement in how she remained so pliant, as if to let me know I was free to do whatever I wished.

I realized it was only a matter of time. Fortunately, I was feeling cured from that after-dinner trimming provided for me in Kaohsiung by Henry Wu. That's all Avis would have needed to cheer up her life! Moreover, Avis and Dewey were now sort of separated, or so Avis claimed. What that exactly meant I wasn't sure, and at times wondered whether Dewey did. But this wasn't something I racked my brains over. Perhaps not unlike Adam when offered the apple by Eve, I figured it had to be all right to partake of what Avis was offering.

Avis declined to come to my little Laguna Beach house. It would be too deliberate, too premeditated, she said. But she didn't resist in any other way. Our candlelight dinners soon acquired the momentum to merge into more actively romantic moments on a blanket under the cover of a warm summer night, not far from the ocean's edge, or on the red leather upholstery of the seven-year-old Cadillac convertible I had bought the day the Navy and I parted ways.

But it was all no good, this new thing between Avis and me. That same buoyant spirit was indeed there, perhaps more exciting than before, as Avis now struggled in vain to stifle those sensuous sounds and try to check the way she would so vehemently twist and turn. It was her helplessness to control these throbbing moves and the intensity of her half-suppressed moans that seemed to raise her passion to the limits of physical tolerance. And afterwards she felt so guilty that I was afraid she might soon have me believing we were committing some sort of a heavy sin.

This feeling of guilt is what tipped me off. Maybe Avis wasn't so complex after all. Maybe she simply had a touch of that peculiar disorder that so many of my contemporaries hoped to encounter in the flesh. Was it nymphomania she was trying to disguise? I could clearly perceive how she mobilized her ingenuity to cater to that insatiable spirit while trying to camouflage this behavior from herself and the world. In a way, she was like a kleptomaniac and equally ashamed.

Avis continued to bemoan the fact that her life was over now; that at twenty-six she had nothing to look forward to, no feeling of hope. "You should find yourself a beautiful young girl," she repeatedly told me, "one who is footloose and fancy-free." Then, with a touch of sarcasm, she would add, "Like you." She went through this spiel so often, on the telephone and on those occasions when we met, that she soon convinced me she was right. Especially after we met for the first time in the morning, and I saw her looking blanched out and at least ten years older than I, with little of her mystery left.

We parted as friends, though not without a last dramatic flourish. I had finally become involved with precisely the sort of person Avis had been urging on me for weeks, and I assumed Avis would be delighted to hear the news. I felt only a little sheepish when I told her the next time we met.

"That certainly is all right by me," she assured me with a bittersweet smile on the open patio of the LaJolla Beach and Tennis Club. "You're a lucky man, judging by the lovely pictures you so thoughtfully brought. Frankly, I expected all along that one day I'd end up as just another feather in your cap."

"It's not that way at all," I protested.

"I really don't mind."

"That relationship isn't like ours," I tried to explain. "It's only temporary."

Again, a bittersweet smile: "What in life isn't?"

"It's the truth. My friend has to return to Chicago to start her freshman year. I've got to get back to New York to look for a job. When I leave here, I still want to have a little money in reserve."

"Very wise," Avis nodded, "and it also makes it easier for me." She paused, then made a startling disclosure of her own. Yes, she too had met somebody. "A serious man who will make a wonderful father for the twins, and I expect to marry soon. And when I do, I don't think I should let you have my new name." She sighed warily and gave me a tender look. "You know the strength of what's between us. It will always be there, at least for me . . . no matter what. So this has to be good-bye. Think of me kindly . . . and don't ever forget me."

A curious postscript to the Avis saga would herald the revolutionary social changes of the 1960s.

I was already back in New York for several months, sharing two floors of a ramshackle brownstone on the Upper East Side with several friends, when the city's dailies gave prominent coverage to a bizarre incident. It involved Avis ex-husband, my former classmate Dewey King, and caused considerable discussion with two of my roommates who had also known Dewey at Yale. What reportedly happened was that during the divorce-and-custody proceedings initiated by Avis in a San Diego court, Dewey made a disruptive appearance, dressed only in jeans and a T-shirt, with his three-year-old twin girls in tow.

"Do these children belong to you?" the incredulous judge snapped.

Dewey planted himself in front of the bench in his bare feet. "No, your honor," he replied calmly, "I belong to them." He then pulled out a marijuana cigarette, lit it, and blew smoke in the judge's face.

Sensational though the story was, it seemed incomplete in one respect. None of the newspapers mentioned the name of the man Avis intended to wed. Since I also failed to find it in any of the weeklies recycling the story, Avis would indeed have to remain just a memory.

II. The Perfect Universe

Let me reintroduce my much older cousin, Albrecht, whom I had encountered briefly on the eve of World War II at our unkempt Renaissance palace in Prague. A courtly, silver-haired gentleman, he is fervently working to save the universe. He labors endless hours, filling lined yellow sheets with penciled numbers, sheet after sheet after sheet. Though still of sound body and apparently sound mind, Albrecht claims to have been assigned this task by God.

There isn't much time, according to Albrecht's calculations. Humanity's wasteful, self-indulgent ways are threatening the firmament — its myriad of stars and planets and moons clustered in uncounted galaxies. Albrecht believes he is about to prove what he has suspected since his youth: that the world's excessive consumption of electricity for frivolous goals is creating too many used-up, dead electrons. Accumulating in unseen vast piles, these dead electrons have already slowed the spin of the earth in measurable ways, or so his figures indicate, and eventually could disrupt the harmonious paths of even the most distant celestial spheres. It is this irreversible universal chaos which my fatherly cousin is striving to prevent.

Albrecht is not out to save the human race. He gave up on that years ago and regards the prosperous masses of the industrialized world with a strained tolerance. Especially those overfed tourists from neighboring Bavaria who park their ostentatious cars just outside the open gates of his *Schloss* and have no qualms about wandering in. Traipsing around Albrecht's castle as if it were a public monument, they point their emblem-festooned walking sticks at architectural details here and there, even at the windows beyond which my cousin is grappling with his sacred task. How plainly these people exemplify the corruption by Lucifer of God's greatest handiwork, Albrecht thinks; how obviously hell-bent on destroying themselves they are by perpetuating in an infinite variety of ways the sin of Adam and Eve and wantonly devising still more pleasurable ways! Albrecht isn't about to make an effort to redeem them from their fate, even if he could, because they have only themselves to blame. As for himself, he isn't worried. In any terminal disaster on earth there would be pockets of survivors, made up of those deserving God's grace for having led dutiful lives. Surely Albrecht would gravitate to such a pocket and manage to slip into it, and then slip out when it was safe again. Failing that – and in the absence of more practical alternatives – he would settle for the option of heaven.

In the little Tyrolean village where he lives, no one considers Albrecht weird. On the contrary, he is highly respected by almost everyone. Frau Kunst, who has been his housekeeper for twenty years, addresses Albrecht as "His Grace." So do many of the villagers. Whether the affection in their tone comes from the heart is hard to tell; such is the effect my cousin's title of *Fürst* still exerts on their tradition-bound emotions. To this day, a matronly woman who lives near the Schloss displays in a special glass cabinet all of the cups, saucers, and other utensils this nobleman of princely rank once touched on a visit to her house.

Albrecht doesn't often socialize, not even among his peers. Whatever time he can spare from his celestial task he devotes to running his estate of thousands of hectares of timberland. Though his profits rarely reach a hundred thousand dollars a year, Albrecht once refused to acknowledge an offer of fifteen million for the land alone from a German industrialist who wanted to develop a luxury resort. What gall, Albrecht thinks. Doesn't this man understand Albrecht's duty is to care for his forested land, even if the financial returns aren't what he might hope? Albrecht personally knows thousands of his trees, especially the larger ones. For decades, he has watched them mature to their impressive girth. He marks with a cross whichever of these mighty firs are to be cut down for his lumber mill, giving primacy to sound ecology over human needs. Attired in a well-worn green loden coat and lederhosen that have over the years mingled human smells with those absorbed from the woods and the fields, Albrecht is indistinguishable from the nature around him. He could pass for a stately fir, when standing straight to his full height. When stooped over at the end of a long, wet day, with drops of rain turning the green felt of his old hunting hat a darker shade that matches the permanently sweat-soaked headband, he looks like a moss-covered giant mushroom. If there indeed were in nature a human instrumentality of God, it could hardly be embodied in a more appropriate form.

Albrecht's other duty is to assist nature in controlling the deer running wild in his forests and fields. Long before dawn, he sets out with his *Forstmeister* to track these animals and, from time to time, shoot the right stag or doe. None is overlooked, none escape. He has observed them since birth, as they grew, thrived, and reproduced. Now he is the instrument for selecting the fittest. Those he has blessed with abundant years and knows particularly well, he likes to warn in advance when their time has come. Albrecht claims he has merely to think it, and they'll get the word. Still, they can't evade him, not even his most majestic stags. Albrecht can stalk any one of them all day long, and know exactly where to find him at the first light of the following dawn.

Bam! One shot is usually all it takes.

Albrecht's Tyrolean Schloss isn't much as castles go. Headquarters for a monastic order until the early seventeenth century, the whitewashed mansion stands three stories high with a massive front portal eight feet tall of rotting wood, reinforced diagonally by rusting iron strips. The castle's thirty or so high-ceilinged rooms are in various stages of repair. There is a small, unpainted room beneath the rafters filled with old steamer trunks, and another room next to it, where scores of good-sized chunks of home-smoked bacon hang all year around. On the second floor is the most luxurious suite, occasionally occupied by Albrecht's daughter, Stephanie, and tastefully decorated by her in a blend of the old and the new. Gilded stars twinkle on a pale-blue ceiling and soft carpeting to match stretches from wall to wall. Her suite is the only one throughout the Schloss equipped with an odorless flush toilet instead of the traditional type that inverts directly into a hole.

Albrecht often acts as a gracious host to as many as a dozen relatives and friends, some of whom stay for weeks, even months. There are no liveried servants; only the cook, old Frau Kunst, indefatigably scurrying around in her immaculate dirndl, her silvery braids coiled like cinnamon rolls above each ear. Less skilled hands are recruited as need be from several of the nearby farms, which also supply the Schloss with eggs, milk, and other agricultural goods. The cuisine is on the simple side but extremely tasty, due to Frau Kunst's culinary skills. She favors venison from Albrecht's woods and trout from his lakes and streams, which she prepares with lots of butter and tops off with a creamy sauce. Wine, both red and white, is served with every meal, poured from carafes filled with the cheapest bulk brands from the local grocery store. Anything of better quality Albrecht would consider extravagant or an outright waste, an unnecessary pampering of human taste, though he thoroughly enjoys, if without comment, the vintage bottles occasionally brought by guests.

When nobody has to be entertained, Albrecht takes his meals in his private quarters directly off the entrance to the Schloss. His cramped, two-room suite looks as if it would make a more suitable wine cellar than a prince's private lair. The rooms have low vaulted ceilings and small recessed windows hollowed out of six-foot-thick walls that seem to bulge under the weight of the floors above. Several engravings of hunting scenes enliven the white-washed walls, the upper portions of which are lined with mounted antlers of deer, mountain goats, and two twenty-four-point stags whose horns are still attached to their bleached-out skulls. Carefully inscribed on each mounting is the date and place of the kill, dominated by Albrecht's initials. The furniture in both rooms is simple and sparse. Except for one delicately inlaid chest, dated 1763 in an elegantly flowing hand, the simple wooden tables, bed, and other pieces look more like those one would find in a peasant's hut. And there is no radio, no television, not even a telephone, though Albrecht did have one eventually installed in Frau Kunst's quarters directly across the hall. Whenever she rushes in to report a call, Albrecht calmly follows her back and obligingly answers the phone. He prides himself on being what he describes as a passive user. This means he will accept calls but would initiate one only in an emergency. For business matters relating to his estate, Albrecht prefers to depend on the mail.

While working on his theories, Albrecht sits in the dim light of one of the battlement-like windows and delays turning on the small overhead lamp until he can barely see. Sometimes he prefers to remain in the dark, contemplating the mysteries of the firmament and reflecting on humanity's role. He is proud to have publicly shown he can do without the comforts for which others yearn. During the war, the Nazis evicted him from his Schloss and placed him on punitive restriction. For two years he pedaled an old bicycle fifteen kilometers each day to a stone quarry for twelve hours of compulsory work. Albrecht never complains about this difficult interlude and seems to regard his suffering as just deserts for his human lot. Should he encounter similar duress through whatever untoward twists of fate, he is prepared to submit with comparable grace.

Submitting to God's will is what Albrecht's life is about; especially, submitting for a worthy cause. And what could be worthier than trying to save the universe? Albrecht is ready to suffer all manner of frustration to complete the task for which he believes he alone was called. His classical education by private tutors more than half a century ago hardly prepared him for this specialized work. His mathematics went no further than addition, multiplication and similar elementary skills. But over the years, Albrecht has painstakingly acquired on his own a working knowledge of algebra, spherical geometry, and integral calculus, though for a long time he didn't think he needed them, just as he long disdained the use of calculators. Now he has a basic pocket model with a floating decimal point that he still uses sparingly. Rather than assuming the universe to be more complex than anyone can conceive, Albrecht believes the universe to be far simpler than anyone has previously guessed. After all, what is more simple yet as perfect as a sphere? Or more useful than the wheel? Simplicity is to Albrecht a sign of divinity, while complexity is a reflection of human conceit.

Sitting there in his vaulted quarters in the dark, Albrecht often turns sentimental. He has been a widower for fifteen years, and in a leather frame on his desk is a small photograph of his departed wife. How vibrant and vigorous she had been! Then shortly after the birth of Stephanie, their only child, she began to feel inexplicably weak. For three difficult years Albrecht watched helplessly as the woman he adored became an emaciated invalid. He cared for her the best he could, carrying her from room to room and helping her to the toilet. When she finally left this world, Albrecht's grief over what he saw as God's will was made bearable by what he recognized as God's infinite love. How providential that little Stephanie had been brought into his life! At least he had her to devote himself to with equal care, shielding her from the corrupt influences of the world and teaching her what was right. And in what seemed to him like an eye blink, his Stephanie was transformed from a golden-tressed child into a dazzling eighteen-year-old princess being joined in holy matrimony to her storybook prince in a feast celebrated by throngs of the Tyrolean village folk.

Albrecht's invitation to Stephanie's wedding had been sent to our family in Massachusetts, and Mother routinely enclosed it in her next letter to me in New York. She must have assumed I was the only one in the family remotely in a position to attend. But I hadn't seen Albrecht in more than twenty years, and he probably barely knew I existed. I had never met his daughter, the bride-to-be, and I couldn't be sure the invitation addressed to Father even extended to me. Besides, a closer reading revealed the event had already taken place months ago. I felt that sending the newlyweds an impersonal card with an imprinted salutation was about the right response.

Not that I could have gone anyway. The financial cushion from my Navy days was looking less and less comfortable with each week I remained unemployed, even though I wasn't yet seriously pressed. The two top floors I shared with several contemporaries in the ramshackle East Side brownstone provided relatively inexpensive rent, and I didn't need to spend much on clothes. I owned a closetful of suits, patterned after one of my Brooks Brothers off-the-rack numbers by a Hong Kong tailor during an R & R visit of my ship. His copies could be readily distinguished by the four handcrafted buttonholes on each sleeve that actually worked.

It was partly because of the way I dressed that I became involved with the New York Republican State Committee. I happened to stop by to see a friend at the committee's Roosevelt Hotel headquarters in the aftermath of Nixon's defeat; by the time I left, I had been appointed field coordinator on the premise that I would make a favorable impression on the politicians upstate. Nobody bothered to ask whether I was a Republican, and I wasn't about to bring it up. Frankly, I hadn't given it much thought. Unlike in the politics of Central Europe, belonging to one party or the other could hardly land you in prison and certainly not cost you your life.

Because JFK's inroads into traditional Republican strongholds had given him the votes to carry the state, my task was to help the party recoup in the next midterm elections. Two or three times a week, I boarded Mohawk Airlines for such destinations as Binghamton, Ogdensburg-Messina, and Buffalo to meet with the respective county chairmen. After a convivial dinner accompanied by a fine Riesling from vineyards surrounding the Finger Lakes, I would address the county committee. I always tried to offer some nugget from Cecil Driver's unforgettable political science course at Yale. "It has often been said that politics is the art of compromise," I liked to quote, mimicking Cecil Driver's British twang. "Ladies and gentlemen, I prefer to think of politics as the compounding of interests." Ultimately, it didn't seem to make much difference what I said, as long as I said it with verve. And those Hong Kong suits certainly helped.

What I particularly welcomed about this part-time work was that it left me free to investigate a variety of other careers. In the job interviews set up by the Yale placement office, I tried to be no less credible whether talking to Morgan Guaranty about becoming a financier or to J. Walter Thompson about writing copy for some hot automobile account. I even managed to put on what I thought was a spirited performance across the river in New Jersey at

Lightolier, Inc., trying to convince them of my eagerness to represent their lampshades and similar wares in retail outlets.

The fact was that I still had little idea of what I wanted to do. Without any viable role model besides that of a count, I had only my naval experience on which to draw. I felt unabashedly confident, however, that I could succeed in practically any nontechnical field, be it in industry or government. Wasn't that what a Yale liberal arts graduate was supposed to be able to do – with no less ease and grace than the proverbial Renaissance man? I did, moreover, have a specific aim or goal, which for obvious reasons I was careful not to disclose in job interviews: to have fun, to enjoy myself as I had done in Laguna Beach, to make the most of my one and only time around on earth. Not that I was unmindful of the expectations of my old prep school headmaster, the Duke, whose largesse provided me with my privileged education. But I had plenty of time to focus on helping others after I became established myself. Right now, the world I saw beckoning was a veritable Garden of Eden; better still, since there would be no forbidden trees. This was the early sixties, and I sensed a new freedom in the air, as if the world was at last coming under the sway of the kind of healthy philosophy I personally hoped to formulate back in Professor Baumer's class.

I was still working for the Republicans when Albrecht's daughter, Stephanie, unexpectedly rang the downstairs bell of the Upper East Side brownstone, where I lived. From the first breath-stopping glimpse, I recognized about her a familiar air. This was the second year of the New Frontier, and Stephanie had the same chic aura of some of the young women on the White House staff featured in the media. She also reminded me of illustrations of enchanting princesses in the fairy tale books from my childhood, though purely in looks and physical attributes, Stephanie could have doubled for a young Marilyn Monroe.

"How did you ever find me?" I asked, as soon as we became slightly acquainted.

"Your tacky card to the newlyweds fortunately had a return address."

"Well . . . I knew I had a little niece . . . but this sort of niece?"

"And I knew I had an *Onkel* . . ." Stephanie's voice momentarily trailed off, as her lips sparkled with a smile. "Actually, I checked you out. I shouldn't tell you this, but I waited across the street for a good half-hour . . . until I saw you come down for the mail. I knew immediately it was you, even though the front door was only half-open."

"Didn't want to take a chance, eh?"

"Take it as a compliment. I am here."

"Where's the rest of the family?" I asked, remembering Albrecht's letter to Father about Stephanie having had her first child.

"We decided little Diana wasn't ready for the trip," Stephanie explained.

"And the lucky groom?"

"Oh, him!" Stephanie said dismissively. "He'll be around soon enough."

Stephanie liked the casual, disordered atmosphere of the brownstone, and she quickly felt comfortable there. As she became unguarded and thoroughly relaxed, I realized that the real reason for her familiar air was the heritage we shared. I was able to detect, within her overall glamour, some of the less-than-flattering characteristics that neither of us had been spared: a sensuous dimple on the tip of her nose, which in my case was almost a cleft; a forehead that sloped back a touch more than it should, but nowhere nearly as much as mine; and a head that was just a bit too flat in the back, but hardly with the prominence that had earned me the nickname of *Platehead* at Hotchkiss. Yet, when together, Stephanie and I seemed to radiate a special something that would blind others to these flaws and often make people turn their heads. Even Hansi, Stephanie's titled husband from a distinguished German family, appeared to be a little jealous the day she finally brought him the few blocks from their suite at the Regency Hotel. Fifteen years Stephanie's senior, Hansi was a handsome, well-dressed man of mountainous proportions who, on shaking hands, undermined his Old World dignity by bestowing on the other person an overpowering wink.

"So you're the famous Onkel," he said, giving me the first of those monumental winks, as if trying to enfold me into some co-conspiratorial endeavor.

I ignored the gesture as if it were an involuntary twitch. "Stephanie and I are actually second cousins once removed," I explained.

"That still makes you an Onkel in Germany," he said with authority, then laughed nervously.

"I like the idea of your being an Onkel," Stephanie chimed in, in her British-accented diction acquired at a boarding school in England. "Second cousins once removed is such a mouthful."

Hansi was visibly relieved that the blood ties between his wife and her New York Onkel appeared to rule out what he otherwise might have feared. Still, he was reluctant to let Stephanie stay at the brownstone while he flew to Detroit and Saint Louis for a few days of meetings with potential clients for his modest import-export business. Having come by on a Saturday morning, he encountered the assorted roommates and transients lounging around in various states of undress, unshaven and sipping beer directly from cans. What, allow his wife into the midst of this? The only reason he finally relented was that Stephanie assured him she would have a room she could lock.

"Can I see the key again, *Liebchen*," Hansi said stiffly. "I want to check if it works."

"How demeaning!" Stephanie exclaimed, feigning outrage. "Isn't my virtue beyond suspicion?"

"It's not you, Liebchen," Hansi said, in a conciliatory tone. "It's the others. After all, you're the one who'll have the key."

"The others!" Hansi's little darling continued with her huffy act. "I don't think I like that at all. How do you suppose that makes my generous Onkel feel?"

"I meant the *others*!" Hansi said testily. He managed a smiled in my direction, then surprised me with another enormous wink. "I'm sure your Onkel will take excellent care of you. Don't you see, Liebchen, that's why I'm letting you stay."

"Yeah," Stephanie grumbled, "under lock and key, and only because you want to save on the hotel."

"Well, Hansi," I interjected cheerfully, "I hope you have a good trip. You're going to be visiting our Midwest at the right time . . . when it's no longer cold and before it gets too hot."

Two days later Stephanie was back at the Regency, due to Hansi's sooner-than-expected return. But she continued to come to the brownstone whenever she could, if only for an hour or so. We had a unique understanding in the way we thought and viewed the world, and in that respect seemed to be more like twins than merely second cousins once removed. I could often tell what she was thinking before she began the thought.

"Your motives are altogether transparent," I teased her during one such visit when no one else was around, "and they aren't consistently noble."

"That's because I'm more open than you," she protested. "You've got all these little tricks that leave you smelling like a rose. Soon you'll have Hansi liking you."

"It's called public relations. In the Navy, I was our ship's PIO."

"God, whatever that means."

"Public Information Officer. It was a collateral duty. My main job was gunnery and deck."

"That's still no excuse for not taking my side when Hansi and I have an argument."

"The whole point of public relations is to smooth things over, to prevent unpleasantness; especially with someone who's a prince and wears a size fifty jacket."

"So, if Hansi made enough of a row over that key, you might have PR'd me into a chastity belt!"

"And why not?"

"Hypocrite! You're almost as bad as Pappi . . . speaking of which, you really ought to come for a visit. You've become so very American. It's time you went back to your roots for a while. I know you'll love the Schloss. Hansi has to stay in Munich and tend to business, but I'll be there practically all summer."

I shook my head. "I don't want to lose my job with the Republicans."

"It's summer! Isn't everybody on vacation?"

"I'm afraid it doesn't quite work that way here."

"But it isn't going to cost you anything at the Schloss."

"That's not the point," I said, then added half-heartedly, "I've got a career to . . . "

"Oh, come on, Onkel dear," Stephanie interrupted again, "don't be such a drag. Why don't you at least try."

As it turned out, my employers at the Republican headquarters weren't averse to my taking the summer off, since political activity for the midterm elections wouldn't begin in earnest until Labor Day. No less decisive was that one of the transient roommates agreed to assume my share of the rent for the summer months.

With Stephanie's guidance I wrote her father, more or less inviting myself for an extended stay to coincide with hers.

Albrecht's response was prompt but cool. He didn't feel he really knew me after all these years, he wrote (using a worn-out typewriter ribbon that made the letter barely legible), and he hoped I wouldn't take his reservations personally. Albrecht doubted whether anyone brought up in the United States could adjust to castle life. "Living in a castle is like living in a glass house, and I expect you to keep that in mind if you still intend to come. A scandal is the last thing I need," he concluded cryptically. "Also do not expect to have your wash done or your bed made. My housekeeper is old and new people are impossible."

"What Pappi is really worried about," Stephanie explained, when I showed her the letter during her final visit before flying back to Munich with Hansi, "is the irresponsible family blood on his mother's side. As a first cousin, you're automatically suspected of having the potential for mischief. But don't mind Pappi. He's an old fuddy-duddy. Just think what fun we'll have . . . my favorite Onkel, your favorite niece!"

2/

I went as cheaply as I could. From New York's Idlewild Airport, I flew Icelandic via Reykjavik to Luxembourg, then took the train the rest of the way. That meant almost a full day on the turboprop and another night on the express to Innsbruck. To resurrect myself before arriving, I tried splashing cold water on my face in the toilet of the jerking local taking me the final few stops.

Stephanie was waiting at the village station with her red Fiat convertible. It was a bright afternoon in early June, and the surrounding Tyrolean peaks were still covered with glittering caps of snow. How great to see Stephanie again, then sit at her side as we raced along the greenish meadows, tinged with the yellow of dandelions in bloom! The air felt brisk and clean. When I put on a pair of sunglasses to shield my tired eyes, I felt almost human again.

Albrecht was standing outside the open portal of the Schloss, on a small balcony of crenellated stone, sipping his post-luncheon demitasse in the warming sun. I would have known him anywhere. He had the same serious demeanor of the lanky young man I still remembered from our prewar meeting in Prague. The silvery streaks in his wavy hair and the deep lines in his ruddy, weather-beaten face imbued him with a dignity that had been denied him in his youth. Even the unaccustomed sight of someone his age in well-worn, overly short lederhosen held up by suspenders with little antler buttons across the chest failed to undermine his imposing presence.

Albrecht shook my hand, then took a long puff on his tiny cigar butt. He squinted slightly in the sun and gave me a discreet once-over. "So this is what they're wearing in America these days," he said with a critical chuckle.

I had no idea what he meant. I certainly considered my Brooks Brothers tweed jacket and gray flannel pants more apropos than his outfit. If the camera around my neck looked too touristy, surely he would appreciate the photos I intended to give him when I left. For the moment, however, I thought it best not to respond.

Albrecht took a prolonged puff on the stubby butt that must have been burning his fingertips. "I have to go in the woods for the afternoon," he said, grinding out the cigar carefully on the heavy stone of the small balcony, then stowing the remnants with equal care in his lederhosen pocket. "The Forstmeister is waiting. Stephanie will show you to your room. Tea is at four-thirty, for which I'm always back. If you're hungry, Frau Kunst will fix you something. So, welcome . . . and till then, *Servus!*"

I watched the tall, stooped Fürst select a long walking stick from among several rudimentary poles stacked in a corner by the entrance to the Schloss. He grasped it about a foot from the top, and using it like a staff, made his way energetically down the balcony steps. As he passed Stephanie's sporty car, he made a slightly wider arc with his arm, and seemingly by accident, hit the bright red door with the metal tip of his stick. But he continued toward the woods without disrupting his step.

"Isn't Pappi something?" Stephanie said with a mixture of affection and disdain. She watched Albrecht merge into the darkness beneath the tall pines, then shook her head. "He does that every time. He thinks a car should be the simplest possible box, just to get around in. At least the Fiat, thank God, seems to have taken his mind off the plumbing I had installed last year. That corner of the second floor is mine, so what does he care? I thought he'd disown me over that! And the Fiat, too, even though he actually bought it for me. That made him all the more sullen. He felt I had beguiled him into compromising his principles."

"Do you think he ever would?"

"Disown me?" Stephanie made a distressed face. "He's always threatening." Then she laughed. "Fortunately, I'm the only child."

Stephanie was still looking in the direction of her car, parked below the balcony, when I took her lightly by the hand and pulled her around until she was facing me. "Tell me Stephanie, do I look okay?"

She smiled. "I'm hardly an unbiased observer."

"I'm not interested in PR."

"Well, you do seem a bit tired. But a little rest will fix that."

"I mean, what I'm wearing. "

"What about it?"

"Was Albrecht expecting me to show up in lederhosen or something? Or is it perhaps the camera?"

"Oh, that!" she laughed. "It's your sunglasses. Pappi hates sunglasses. It's a sign of a *Hochstapler*. Literally a high-stepper, a shady character."

"But it's bright as hell," I protested. "Especially if you've been up two nights straight."

"You'd get no sympathy from Pappi. He refuses to wear goggles even when he skis the Corvatch in the sun. That's up over three thousand meters. At the end of the day, he's blind as a bat."

"That's crazy."

"That's Pappi for you. Another thing, if you want to stay on his good side," Stephanie warned in her lighthearted way, "don't ever mention Kurt Jurgens."

"The German actor? *The Enemy Below* with Robert Mitchum?"

"I've only seen his German films. Anyway, a total degenerate, Pappi says. Absolutely hates Jurgens."

"I didn't know they traveled in the same circles."

"God forbid! It's because of the stories Pappi can't avoid seeing in the press. You know, those torrid romances old Kurt supposedly has all over the world."

"What does your father care?"

"Because Kurt does it in the light for the whole world to see. *Stern* and *Paris Match* are always there, as if on cue."

"Does Albrecht expect everyone to live in a glass house?"

"Pappi believes in moral example."

"Come to think of it, your father looks a lot like Jurgens. An austere, somber twin."

"That's just the point," Stephanie said, then seemed to reflect a bit. "Except I'm sure old Kurt is no fuddy duddy. I wouldn't mind at all meeting him, if you know what I mean, Onkel dear. Now let me show you to your room. Poor boy, I'm sure you could use a little rest."

Within two weeks of arriving at the Schloss, I came to understand the rudiments of Albrecht's ways; how he viewed humanity in those pessimistic, apocalyptic terms; the sacred responsibility he felt in caring for his forests and deer; and above all, Albrecht's obsession to solve single-handedly the riddle of the universe before it was too late. He retreated to his dimly lit quarters after the late afternoon *Jause,* or tea, to struggle against this insuperable challenge with whatever God-given talents he had. He emerged three hours later at dinnertime, with the weary countenance of someone who had been juggling the planets and stars in a Newtonian universe and knew the incalculable consequences of dropping a single one. Sitting at the head of the long table in the stately second-floor dining room, he silently ladled out the soup from a simple porcelain tureen. Next to his plate was a lined yellow sheaf of the jottings he had just made. He would sporadically glance at them throughout the meal, adding a few figures and notations and perhaps scratching others out, the latter accompanied by a painful, "Ach, ach!" Everyone at the table knew well enough to ignore the Fürst in his mealtime travails. This was obviously a subject only he was privileged to understand.

One mystery I soon managed to unravel was the fate of those finger-burning cigar stubs Albrecht stowed in the pockets of his lederhosen. He would take them out at the next appropriate occasion, lite them again, and start puffing away as long as his fingers could bear the pain. He would then insert the remnants in a holder and smoke them to the very end, with a look of satisfaction for not having wasted a puff. This habit confirmed my impression years ago in Prague that he was thrifty rather than stingy.

Of the various guests and relatives he entertained, Albrecht's unabashed favorite was Stephanie's little Diana. Already adept at wandering around the Schloss, Diana never tired of her favorite ploy: to remain hidden as she slowly opened her grandfather's door, then abruptly reveal her face and shout, "Guess who!" Hunched over his sacred task, Albrecht would pretend to be startled. This always evoked from Diana an exuberant squeal as she rushed into his arms. She called him *Opapa,* and he dubbed her *Angelina,* his little angel – a name that would gradually supplant her real one. He talked to her about how wonderful heaven was and how much God loved little girls like her.

My relationship with Albrecht remained unchanged. He continued to treat me as if I were just another guest rather than someone with whom he shared a set of grandparents. Considering what I had come to know of my cousin's outmoded views, this was fine by me. I might have found it embarrassing if other guests were to think he and I came from too similar a mold. Yet I didn't in any way want to antagonize my host. I put away the sunglasses for the duration of my stay, and I refrained from commenting in any way on Albrecht's uncanny resemblance to the rugged movie idol, Kurt Jurgens.

There was one subtle tension I was determined to resolve. Although Albrecht never failed to invite me, along with the other guests, to join him on his afternoon outings in the woods, he seemed to regret it for the rest of the day. While he didn't say so directly (I had by then learned Albrecht avoided personal confrontation if he could), I suspected it still had something to do with what I wore — a long-sleeved, red-and-white checked shirt, a pair of wash khaki pants, and matching chukka boots.

This time Stephanie wasn't much help. "Pappi can be mighty strange," she said, when I stopped by her quarters after lunch. "I think you look fine."

"The only thing I don't like are the shoes," I said. "Clambering up those steep hills, the crepe rubber slips on the pine needles."

That afternoon, Albrecht and I walked alone along the mossy trails of his mountainous woods. The other guests had departed earlier in the day, and the Forstmeister had to do some paperwork at the *Forstamt*, Albrecht's Schloss-like administrative building in the village.

On the narrow paths, I kept several paces behind my cousin in his lederhosen outfit. He occasionally stopped and wordlessly marked a cluster of trees with his telltale cross.

131

We came to a large clearing. In the distance on the other side, at the edge of the woods, we spotted a pair of young roebuck. They were grazing placidly, but by the time Albrecht planted his pole firmly in the ground (which he used to steady his binoculars), the deer had bolted into the woods.

"Ach!" Albrecht glanced at me as if I was to blame and slightly shook his head.

I was determined not to let the opportunity pass. "If it will help," I said, ready to make the concession I suspected Albrecht had been expecting from the moment I arrived, "I'll get a pair of lederhosen."

"Aber wo!" Albrecht said vehemently. He yanked the pole out of the ground. "That wouldn't be at all appropriate." He turned away as if to resume our silent trek.

I didn't budge. "So what do you recommend?"

Albrecht swung around to face me. "Ach, don't you see, you dress the wrong colors. They're too bright. That's why the deer run away."

"I thought they could only smell."

"Ja, of course, that's true," Albrecht interrupted, "but they also see very well." He shook his pole toward where the deer had been, then stuck it again in the ground. "Those deer were upwind. They always look around when they pasture. You must wear something green. Or something much, much darker than now." Albrecht grasped his lederhosen suspenders at the level of the antler buttons halfway up his chest, as if to support himself, and glowered at me. "But it doesn't have to be exactly the same as I."

So that was it! Albrecht didn't want me wearing lederhosen any more than I wanted to be wearing them. Lederhosen were his official attire, his cassock, his priestly robes. They were as much a part of him as his divinely inspired views. He had been trying to send me a signal over the past several days about dressing differently, yet he feared I might misinterpret it precisely as I did. If I had bought an outfit, I would have been no less of an impostor in my lederhosen than if Albrecht somehow turned up in my naval officer's uniform.

I had to laugh inwardly at the dilemma we had shared. "So you don't think lederhosen are necessary," I said casually. "I have a dark green sweater and a pair of charcoal pants."

Albrecht's grasp on his suspenders relaxed, and his hands dropped to his sides. He nodded, and there was a trace of a smile. "Lederhosen wouldn't suit you, I don't think."

Albrecht retrieved his pole, and we started toward the woods on the other side of the clearing. Walking side by side through the moist grass, it was my cousin who uncharacteristically broke the silence. "I have at home some pairs of mountain shoes. There's no reason you should spend money on something you'll never use in the United States. The color doesn't matter, but your shoes have not the right soles. I also noticed they're sometimes still wet the next day. Not very comfortable. I think we wear about the same size." The way Albrecht said it made me feel for the first time he wasn't just playing the polite host.

Later, when we returned to the Schloss, I found in my mail a large envelope with finished photos from the rolls of film I had sent to a processing lab. One of the pictures was of Albrecht and his little granddaughter. It showed my cousin standing in the sun on the crenellated balcony against the darkness of the open portal at his back. His beloved Angelina was perched on his shoulder, a tiny hand clutching onto his silvery hair. Too bad they were both squinting! Then I noticed an amazing congruence in their gaze. They were looking past me, as if at some infinite object beyond this world, an identical expression animating each face.

Albrecht accepted the picture without comment, as if it were one of the vintage bottles of wine occasionally brought by guests. But that evening, when Stephanie and I came down to his private quarters for dinner, I saw the photo propped up on the desk next to that of his departed wife.

At the end of my first three weeks at the Schloss, Stephanie unexpectedly decided to return to her Munich home. Hansi wanted her to resume her duties as hostess to his business friends. He was in a position to expand his import-export company with a foreign exclusive for a fast-growing, Munich-based manufacturer of specialty paints — automobile undercoating, to be precise. Hansi's stopover in Detroit that spring had been to investigate opportunities on the U.S. end. The only reason Stephanie agreed to interrupt her summer at the Schloss was in anticipation of more such trips. "I promise you'll have fun in Munich," she assured me. "No boring dinners. Those business types are already taken by the idea of being represented by a prince. All I need to do is get them invited to a few parties. And don't worry, silly old Hansi won't mind having you around the house. Why should he? You are the Onkel."

They lived in a luxurious duplex (in which Hansi had invested his relatively modest inheritance) on the Widenmayerstrasse overlooking the Isar River. From the sunny breakfast room on the third floor, there was a clear view of the Englischer Garten park on the other bank, punctuated by the Maximilianeum, the seat of the Bavarian parliament — a huge, yellowish structure that looked as imposing as its name.

"More coffee, Onkel dear?" Stephanie asked, as we were finishing a late breakfast. We had arrived in the middle of the night, and Hansi was already out of the house. "This will perk you up."

"I shouldn't," I said, but nevertheless passed Stephanie my cup. As she poured, I placed a hand just above my stomach. "In about two hours, I'm going to feel it right here. Little hot flames leaping up toward my throat."

Stephanie seemed delighted. "*Sodbrennen*," she explained in a conspiratorial tone. She had filled the cup and now was topping off hers. "Two hours. That's exactly how long it takes me, too."

"Another damn weakness to share!"

"I think it's sort of fun."

I looked at her skeptically. "Sodbrennen?"

She laughed. "I mean this sharing of weaknesses. Why do you think we understand each other so well?"

It quickly became obvious that Stephanie was the light of Munich's social life. Despite the normal summer slowdown, practically every night there was some party, reception, or ball where handsome young men were vying for a dance with the glamorous young princess, or pined to exchange a few whispered words. And Stephanie's phone seemed never to stop ringing throughout my stay. Hansi's old housekeeper, grim Frau Trepper, usually took the calls, then silently scurried in to report. "It's the Count von Bismarck. Mr. Count wanted to speak to His Serene Highness. I told him that His Serene Highness at the moment wasn't here, but Her Serene Highness was. Mr. Count said he would call later."

Stephanie nodded, but seeing Frau Trepper start dusting nearby, added firmly, "Thank you, Frau Trepper. That will be all."

"Yes, thank you, Princess," Frau Trepper said, and withdrew with an irrepressible scowl.

"Yes, thank you, Princess," I mimicked with a laugh. "*His* Serene Highness isn't here, but *Her* Serene Highness is. It seems this folderol isn't only good for Hansi's business but does wonders for your ego, too."

Stephanie put a finger to her lips, then spoke in a whisper. "I think Frau Trepper is a spy. She isn't even supposed to be dusting. It's beneath her station. She was Hansi's *Erzieherin*. He was only a few days old when his family took her on. She wiped his fanny and brought him up. Deep inside, she feels Hansi is her little boy. She's terribly protective of him."

Hansi and I got along surprisingly well. He sensed I had a way of smoothing over the subtle but ever-present friction between him and his wife. By the end of the second week, he was so used to my presence that he appeared at breakfast with his hairnet still on, a bobby pin beneath the webbing holding his forelock in place. No wonder he always seemed so perfectly groomed.

Stephanie and I still hadn't finished eating when Hansi, now without hairnet, was ready to leave for the office. "Well, Lieb-chen," he said, giving his wife a kiss on the cheek, and bestowing on me an especially grand wink, "I'll see you both at lunch."

As Stephanie poured more coffee, I said, "Gee, I think Hansi's okay."

She smiled sarcastically. "That's easy for you to say."

"Why did you ever marry him?"

"You know perfectly well, I was only eighteen. Everybody kept telling me Hansi was the best catch in Munich." She took a sip of her coffee. "Some catch, eh Onkel! And he's so stingy. I have to fight for practically every Pfennig. I guess I can say that at my tender age, I didn't know any better."

"Weren't you supposed to be the best catch in Innsbruck? Or was it Salzburg?"

"God, what do you take me for?" Stephanie laughed. "In Vien-na. And I was, too!"

"Maybe you deserve each other after all."

"He's no angel, I assure you. He's got a twelve-year-old son, whom he has barely acknowledged. But that's his business. Where I had to put my foot down was when he tried to slap his Liebchen around. We were married hardly a week. It was on account of some stupid dinner I wasn't too keen on going to."

"Considering his size, I'm surprised you survived."

"That's not the point. You see, it was an *Ohrfeige* . . . the palm of the hand across one cheek, then the back of the hand across the other." Stephanie flicked her hand back and forth to demonstrate. "An Ohrfeige is so demeaning, as if I were some juvenile. I told Hansi he does that once more, I'm walking out for good."

"You seem to have scared the hell out of him."

"I'm not fooling myself. He wants the Schloss. As the youngest son, he didn't inherit much. He thinks that being in business isn't quite up to his dignity."

"You have to admit, he is being nice to me."

"That's only because I'm right now being extra nice to him, if you know what I mean, Onkel dear. And that, let me assure you, isn't easy."

"Poor Stephanie," I laughed. "Always ready to sacrifice. Just like your Pappi."

She glanced around the breakfast room, then reached across the table to touch my hand. "Only for a worthy cause."

I was still in Munich in August when Stephanie's little girl turned two. No big celebration; as usual, we took the precocious child for a midmorning stroll in her baby carriage to the Englischer Garten park, where she would get out and walk.

"It sometimes scares me," Stephanie said, as we crossed the Isar River via the Maximilianstrasse Bridge, "she's so much like me. Thank God she doesn't have Hansi's winking eye."

"Thank God she has his nose."

"Well, he should be good for something," Stephanie laughed. "Most of all, she has my attitude. Do you think that's good? Look at her, she's already flirting with you.

"An-gel-leeh-nah!" I called to Diana in her carriage, mimicking Albrecht. "I don't think she's going to turn out exactly an angel."

"Was sagt er, Mammi, was sagt er?"

"See? Always wanting to know everything, just like me, eh Onkel dear? My grandmother is that way, too. Always putting her nose where it doesn't belong. That's how she got her name, *Issten* — by always asking, *'Was ist denn? Was ist denn?'* Pappi says I'm going to end up just like my grandmother. An old witch dragging her nose through mud. Silly Hansi now says it too, whenever I do something he doesn't like. As if the poor woman had committed some atrocious crime!" Stephanie paused to straighten Diana's polka dot cap, then resumed pushing the pram. "Does that mean she'll also end up like poor old Issten?"

I shrugged. "The one time I saw your grandmother was when I was four years old. She wangled some money out of your father only to spend it on me."

"That's typical. I've seen Issten circle Pappi like a prey for days, waiting for the right moment to strike. I must say, Pappi has developed some ingenious evasive tactics. What's so peculiar is that my grandmother hardly ever spends anything on herself."

We reached the other side of the Isar. Stephanie stopped to lift Diana out of the carriage, and the three of us continued toward the riverbank, down a narrow winding path beneath tall willow trees.

"What I find peculiar," I resumed, "is that during the entire time at the Schloss, I sensed it would have been safer to bring up Kurt Jurgens' name than anything about your grandmother."

"It's a terribly sore point with Pappi. Despite all that's happened, he's devoted to her. He feels it's a family affair and nobody else's business."

"I thought I was family."

"It isn't something I often discuss with Pappi either. I don't know much more than you."

Stephanie again went through the basic facts, which no longer had the startling effect as when I first wormed them out of my father a few years back. The scandal occurred in the 1920's and involved one of the most famous black singers of the time, Roland Hayes. "He was a favorite of King George V and Queen Mary," Stephanie now elaborated in the park. "At one time, Roland was clearing over ten thousand dollars a week. Not bad for a black concert soloist in those days, eh? I wish Hansi was making half that today!" The liaison produced an extramarital child to "blend the races" – Maya, a half-sister to Albrecht. She, by now, had several children of her own, and they all lived with my aunt in her crumbling château at the foot of the Pyrenees in France. "This isn't exactly what Issten had in mind," Stephanie concluded, "when she embarked on her affair with Mr. Hayes."

"Meaning?"

"I'd rather you found out for yourself."

"Another family secret?"

We came to a little kiosk where Stephanie bought a package of birdseed for Diana. The little girl immediately began to throw tiny handfuls toward the pigeons beginning to congregate around us.

"You really should visit Issten before returning to New York," Stephanie said. She sat down on one of the public green metal chairs. She kept an eye on her daughter, while I sat across from her. "It's not a bad trip. You can go by train through Zurich and Geneva to Toulouse via Lyon. First class, it can be quite pleasant. When my grandmother visited Pappi last year, she came second class, all the way. Not even a couchette. And she's seventy-five." Stephanie paused, then leaned forward on the small rounded seat. "I take it back, that's not entirely correct. She did finally shame Pappi into buying her a first-class berth. But just before the train left, she cashed it in for second-class coach. You should have seen poor Pappi's face! Anyway, I know you and Issten will get along famously. She's the only person who really understands me. That is, besides you, Onkel dear."

Though it was only a few days before I was to return to the United States, I could feel the effect of Stephanie's words. The memories of my aunt in Prague were as vivid as anything from my past. How she had tried with such determination to buy me a monkey, as if it were the most important thing in the world! Whether confronting the shop owner or her own son, she had the sort of unrestrained, commanding presence I aspired to having one day myself.

Sitting at the river's edge, I was for the first time giving thought to Albrecht's mistrust for the heritage we shared. I could readily discern a parallel between my aunt's affair with the black singer and what Father had done in recruiting Mother on the tram to test his genetic theories. Both had been experiments of sorts, though my aunt's was incomparably more radical – and one that nobody on either side of the Atlantic had been prepared to support. It was a subject that even my father, so open about everything else, didn't care to discuss. "What my sister did is nothing to trumpet to the world," he had said tartly, when I tried to get him to elaborate before I left the United States. "Regardless of whether the father is black or white, a lady cannot behave that way. But I wish her well," he continued in a gentler tone. "As long as she's alive, she's my longevity insurance, since she's seven years older. I'm in much better shape than she and should make at least a few additional years. I hear she has become quite a bent-over old witch."

3/

I left the next day on the first express. Stephanie drove me to the *Hauptbahnhof*, and Hansi came to the station directly from his office. I offered only a perfunctory protest when he insisted on taking my hefty suitcase and carrying it along the length of *Gleis* 5 to my reserved seat. Amid the tumult of international arrivals and departures, several passers-by recognized the dapper prince, bowing to him and doffing their hats. Despite my bulky bag, Hansi managed to acknowledge each greeting with a smile and that enormous wink. As I walked arm-in-arm with Stephanie alongside her spouse, I was savoring the scene.

I took Stephanie's advice and made the entire trip by train, which was as pleasant as she claimed. Due to a schedule mix-up, however, I arrived in Toulouse two hours later than I had wired my aunt. It was past midnight, and I was wondering whether the woman Stephanie called "Issten" would still be waiting at this dimly lit station of multiple tracks and platforms. And if so, would she recognize me? Or would it be the sort of embarrassing meeting of the only two people left standing there?

I spotted her as soon as I walked several coach lengths to the end of the platform. She was within a small cluster of people just beyond the ticket collector, waiting to welcome their relatives and friends. And she, too, already recognized me among the dozen or so passengers lining up to go through the gate.

It was a reenactment of our meeting in Prague. Before I had a chance to put down my bag, she smothered me with hugs and kisses. "Blood is thicker than water," she said emphatically, as if to confirm a lifelong belief. "It is absolutely remarkable. You're exactly as I imagined you would be."

I felt it was only yesterday I had last seen my aunt. Pinned to the collar of her dress I recognized the same jade frog she had worn then. The only noticeable change was that she no longer looked so tall. This was probably as much due to the fact that I had grown in the intervening years as that she had shrunk and become stooped. Although there were dark hollows beneath her eyes where the skin hung loose, Issten appeared spry at this fatiguing hour and ready to bid lesser mortals carry out her commands.

"You look younger than I expected," I said.

She smiled, then flicked her hand in a gesture of confident dismissal. "Bah! I'm sure the picture my relatives paint of me is of a bent-over old hag dragging her nose through mud."

"I really appreciate that you waited."

"Of course I waited! There was never any question in my mind, since there was no train two hours ago as you told me. But I had absolute faith you would come on this one."

"When I changed trains in Lyon, I found out that the one I was supposed to take won't start running until the autumn schedule."

"Ah, yes, the autumn schedule . . ." Issten's voice trailed off, then she resumed with great immediacy. "We had not a penny, Yura and I. He's outside with the car to drive us to the château. I had to telephone a family I know here in Toulouse. The husband came and brought us a thousand francs, old francs, so we could eat something. We hadn't eaten anything all day. We had each a sandwich. I had mine with cheese. I don't know what Yura had. Then we just sat here, and sat and sat . . ."

"I'm sorry," I began to apologize.

Issten gave me a quick hug. "You poor dear! I didn't mean it that way. You must be tired after your journey."

The station was deserted except for a man waiting in the shadows at a respectful distance. My aunt nodded to him, and he came rushing to take my bag.

"This is Yura," Issten said. She assumed I knew who he was. From what Stephanie had told me, I figured Yura must be the husband of Maya, my aunt's daughter with Roland Hayes. About forty years old, Yura wasn't a big man but appeared strong. His muscles bunched up by his neck, and he handled my suitcase with no more difficulty than Hansi. Yura's corduroy jacket was patched and looked as if it had never been to the cleaners. His hair was unkempt, and his leathery face had the sleepy appearance of someone dunked in cold water after being roused in the middle of the night. But it was a gentle, shy face.

Issten and I followed Yura to the only car in front of the station, an old Volkswagen Beetle. In the light of the street lamp, its paint job seemed to have faded to an indistinguishable gray. The body had countless dents, and one of the rear fenders was missing.

Yura put my bag on the front seat, then tilted the backrest forward to enable my aunt to get in the rear. To fit beneath the low roof, Issten had to hunch over from her normal crouch and then draw up her knees at an angle to squeeze them into the narrow space between the seats. Yet, she didn't seem in the least bit discomfited. It was as if she had merely folded herself into some special contour seat of her royal coach.

Yura tried to start the engine. After several attempts, it began to cough, rocking the car and reverberating explosively through the stillness of the night. Although we were all squashed in and Yura was sitting practically in our laps, he tilted his head back in my aunt's direction, as if opening an imaginary glass partition, and said, *"Oui madame?"* Then, having received his pro forma instructions, he sped off.

The château was on top of a steep hill. Using the lowest gear, Yura coaxed the Volkswagen up the long, narrow winding road. It was a clear night, and a full moon delineated the irregular hefty blocks of yellowish stone from which the château had been built. The massive square structure looked like a medieval fort. Over the entrance was a high, pointed arch of delicate but eroded masonry that could have graced an early Gothic church.

We went into the kitchen, dimly lit by a single bulb dangling on a wire from a high, vaulted ceiling. Although it was almost 2 A.M., Maya had waited up and now greeted me with a warm embrace. She had prepared some tea and started to grill a chicken over the smoldering logs in a huge, stone fireplace. She was a hearty middle-aged woman with a brownish moonlike face that had an unmistakable family resemblance, though with a trace of sadness somewhere deep within. There was a distinct aloneness in how she stood over the fire, flanked by an old mutt and a Great Dane puppy trying to keep warm. The chilly late-August air from the Pyrenees was rolling in through several broken windowpanes.

Issten poured herself some tea. She was sitting across from me at one end of a long, rudimentary wooden table. Yura sat at the other end, quietly smoking a cigarette. The five grandchildren, I was told, were asleep.

"The twins wanted to wait for you," Issten said. "I had to phone twice from the railway station . . . PCV, because we had not yet borrowed the thousand francs."

"PCV?"

"Yes, it means the other party pays. I told the twins they must go to bed. They have to get up early to go to school. They're almost thirteen. You'll see a great family resemblance when you meet them. Very unusual and gifted boys."

A large rat distracted my attention as it scurried along an exposed water pipe on the kitchen wall. Overcoming the initial shock, I wondered if I shouldn't discreetly alert my aunt. But as I glanced at other pipes along the soot-darkened walls, I discerned at least half dozen similar shapes. I was beginning to understand why Stephanie might have felt she couldn't adequately depict Issten's situation and urged me to see for myself.

"I look forward to meeting the twins," I said, picking up the conversation. "Stephanie also feels the family tie. She says you're the only one who understands her. She really identifies with you."

"Ah yes, Stephanie, of course," Issten said absently, and took another sip of her tea. Then she abruptly put down the cup. "But not at all! We are not at all the same, Stephanie and I. We are close, yes. But we are not the same. I always had a purpose, a mission. What mission does Stephanie have? To buy a new dress? To go to a party? To have a good time?"

Issten started to discourse on the imperative of having a purpose beyond any personal pleasure or material gain. Suddenly she surprised me by bringing up in this context *that so terrible thing I did* – her faintly sarcastic appellation for the affair with Roland Hayes.

"It wasn't something rash that a silly young girl might do," she explained in a quiet, forthright tone. "I was almost forty. Albrecht's father and I hadn't been living as man and wife for some time, though he still loved me very much. I married him because I didn't want his great family line to die out. I was certain he wouldn't have another chance with somebody else. He was twenty-five years older than I and a head shorter. But now our sons were grown up. I was ready for something else than having teas with old ladies and playing bridge . . . yes, a new mission, a new sacrifice." Issten paused as if recollecting her thoughts. "It was destiny. It really started when I was quite small, when I read *Uncle Tom's Cabin*. It made such an impression on me. I thought, how is this possible?"

"But Roland Hayes?" I asked, trying to be tactful. "How could someone in your position in those days . . . I mean, you were so well known."

What I was trying to say was this: Not only had she been a member of two historic, wealthy families and married a man who, until the final days of the Hapsburgs, had been a noted confidant at the imperial court, my aunt had also been a personality in her own right. Over six feet tall, she had a way of making herself strikingly visible wherever she went, as I still remembered so well. With all eyes on her, how could such a grande dame in the 1920s start any extramarital affair, much the less one so unorthodox and conspicuous?

"Well, the whole thing of how we first met was the following," Issten answered eagerly and without hesitation, as if the memory was indelibly etched onto her soul. "It was in nineteen-twenty-three, when we still had the *palais* in Prague. An old friend visited me from Vienna who was always involved in arranging opera and theater and so on. And she said, 'I made the acquaintance of a perfectly delightful Negro who was singing in Vienna. You must know him, you must make his acquaintance. He's coming to Prague. Do write him a line and tell him from me that he should see you. And speak with him because he's a really charming fellow.'"

I turned to glance at Maya, tending the chicken by the fireplace. I had to remind myself it was *her* father that my aunt was about to meet. Yet Maya was no less my first cousin than Albrecht. As she quietly petted the dogs, I could detect still more of the family traits – though she was also vaguely reminiscent of the motherly woman who came from Harlem once a week to tidy up our East Side brownstone in New York.

Issten continued without a pause, "So I thought, well why not? I'm going to do it. It already was too late to write. But when he came to Prague, I went to the hotel where he was staying and asked the porters if I could see Roland Hayes. The concert was to be that evening. And the porter said, 'Yes, go upstairs to his drawing room suite on the *premier étage.'"

I could picture my aunt fearlessly making her way from the hotel's main lobby up the grand stairway, and as soon as she was out of sight, the incredulous porter rushing to inform his confreres at the front desk, "Jesus Maria, Mrs. Countess is going to the room of the American black!"

"So I went upstairs. Roland came out of his bathroom and said, 'Oh, excuse me, I haven't quite finished dressing.' He was just knotting his bow tie. I thought that was so charming, so nice. I noticed he had a delicate figure, perfectly formed in black. We sat down and talked as if we had known each other always. And he said, 'I'm so glad you came. I hope you will like my concert to-night. After all, Prague is quite a new round for me. I don't know how the people will like my singing and my message.' You see, he didn't only sing, but he brought a message. The message that everyone should understand that he did it with all his heart, that he did it to help his race, and he did it to show he was capable of doing it."

I was feeling the predawn chill, despite being closer to the fire-place than Issten. I also spotted what looked like a bat that had flown in through a missing window pane. Still, I didn't want to interrupt, now that I was learning the details both Albrecht and my father had sought to keep under wraps.

"I took Fräulein Gartner," Issten went on, impervious to the cold and ignoring the dark, filmy creature fluttering overhead in widening circles around the glowing bulb. "Do you know who Fräulein Gartner was? That was an old lady who gave me lute and singing lessons and loved Albrecht very much when he was little. We sat there together in the fourth row and waited."

An unexpected drama occurred that evening in the concert hall in Prague. There was to be a program change, and Roland Hayes stepped forward on the podium to make the announcement in his limited German. Immediately, there were shouts from the audience that he didn't understand.

"The poor fellow, he thought they were attacking him," Issten continued in anguished tones. "I was so ashamed, so ashamed. I wanted to tell him, 'No, they want you to say it in Czech or have somebody interpret it.' You see, this was the time of the new re-public. German had been the official language of the old empire and wasn't at all popular. But how could Roland have known that? He just stood there on the stage, a slight dignified figure in his *smoking* . . . a tuxedo I think you call it, no? He looked calm, but how he was trembling underneath! Then he said, this time in English, 'If you don't want to listen to my songs, go out!' Great

147

courage, no? For an audience he never knew! By now, others in the audience realized the terrible misunderstanding. They were so apologetic. 'They beg you to say the title in Czech,' somebody explained. And he said, 'But I don't know any Czech. I can say it in English.' Then the man who started the shouting went up to him to ask his pardon. Roland kneeled down on the platform to give him a little pat on the shoulder and muttered, 'All right, all right. I can begin my concert now.'

"And that gave it such an intimate atmosphere, a feeling that everything was going to be perfect. Really, things then went wonderfully. Roland always had wonderful programs. Classics, then at the end, spirituals that I had never heard before. When they came, I had the feeling that all of my life had been rolled back to the beginning of time, and there he stood and I stood and we belonged together. I can't explain it otherwise."

Issten seemed to be in a different world, in that concert hall in Prague, reliving her meeting with Roland Hayes. For a moment she remained silent, then glanced at me in a most aware way. "People will snicker and say it was sex," she continued, in a tone that was a blend of detached dignity and immediacy of feeling. "Yes, it was there, of course. How could it not have been? Roland had such fragile, beautiful hands. I often watched him when he slept, all curled up, those delicate hands covering his face . . . though that didn't happen until years later, after we had exchanged hundreds of letters."

Issten paused to take a sip of her tea, then silently nodded several times.

"It sounds romantic," I volunteered, eager for her to continue.

Issten sighed. "Ah, but Roland also had this tremendous jealousy, a tremendous jealousy of everything I did, of everybody I spoke to, against every newspaper I read. When I wanted to go buy something in a shop, he trembled I might deceive him with some hairdresser or a porter or anyone. But never, never! I was the last person who would deceive him. It was such an awful struggle never to know whether he believed, sitting there for hours, not speaking a word, only ruminating in this awful, awful jealousy. Remind me to show you the photos I had taken in Copenhagen where he gave me a terrible swollen eye. Yet what was I to do? I knew I was only paying the price for what our race had done to the blacks. No, no, sex was not the purpose at all. I could have hidden in a haystack for sex and not traveled openly with him for three years, humiliated even in the advanced countries . . . looked upon like a pair of curious beasts."

The scandal was more subtle than the exposés in today's gossip magazines on supermarket checkout racks. My aunt's affair had been considered too bizarre for the predominantly conservative press. The only articles on both sides of the Atlantic were brief denials from "knowledgeable sources" concerning the countess and Roland Hayes. Not that anyone had been left in the dark in the exclusive Central European society of the day. The nobility was no less prone to gossiping than the kitchen help, and often, with more malicious intent.

Sitting there in the primitive, drafty kitchen of the château, Issten momentarily closed then opened her eyes. "Yes, one must be prepared to suffer and suffer if the world is to be advanced. What is life if not to do what one absolutely must?"

She paused to look at me in a penetrating way. Hunched over, she reminded me at that moment of Albrecht; not only in her physical bearing but in that readiness to sacrifice. Even in mentioning the bruised eye, she had done it with the pride of atoning for humanity's sins.

"The purpose was," she continued in great, rounded pontifical tones, as if proclaiming a higher truth to the world, "to bring a new light to humanity. I couldn't stand the idea that this gifted man might not think he was good enough. The blacks, you know, have quite a different human contribution to make than we. And far, far more important! Well, what have we done that is extraordinary? In ethics we haven't done anything really extraordinary. We have done great things in . . . in engineering, in inventing things and all that. Yes, marvelous. But the things that really matter have always lacked."

God, she sounded so much like her son – the same indifference to technology as Albrecht, the same contempt for Western man's lack of moral worth.

By now, Maya had served the chicken and stepped back toward the open fireplace. Issten's forty-year-old daughter was standing close enough to hear what was being said, as she petted the puppy while the old mutt was sporadically trying to lick an open sore near its tail.

Issten declined to eat anything and continued to sip her tea. "I only wanted to bring that child into the world to prove one can have perfection just as well in black as any other way," she said impersonally, as if her daughter weren't there. "Of course, it ought to have been a boy, not a girl. I wanted to give it to Gandhi to be properly . . . how do you say it in English, *élevé?*"

"Raised," Maya interjected. Though she had never been in the United States, she spoke without an accent.

"Ah yes, of course, raised," my aunt repeated. "I wanted to give it to Gandhi to be properly raised so he could make his mark on the world. But a girl? Impossible! Not in those days. Unfortunately, my daughter also has no feelings whatsoever for the blacks. Only for Indians." Issten sighed. "For that, I suppose I'm to blame, too. When she was little, I read her the stories of Karl May about your Wild West. Her hero to this day is Winnetou, the romantic young Indian chief in May's books."

"I also love horses and dogs," Maya said. She laughed with a trace of that lingering sadness, then added softly, "My children, of course, I love the most."

It was only because I excused myself at this point to go to bed that I drew an erroneous conclusion. Considering the privileged life my aunt had forfeited and the poverty and social disgrace that was her lot, hadn't her experiment failed? That's what Stephanie must have meant by her observation that things hadn't worked out as Issten had hoped. I recognized an especially ironic parallel between my aunt and her son. In their individual ways, each was intent on saving the world. Issten's final remarks about her misbegotten daughter were no less rueful than Albrecht's pained, "Ach, ach!" when he detected some basic error or flaw in his calculations. Yet, for him it was merely a matter of crossing out a few penciled figures and starting anew – hardly a possibility open to Issten.

I found out the following afternoon how infinitely beyond her son Issten considered herself in her quest. The grandchildren were back from school by then, and I met them in the dank kitchen. In the glinting shafts of light streaming in through a small recessed window high up on the wall, the place looked even more primitive. Besides the scurrying denizens of the previous night, I was able to discern large spiders spinning their webs in musty dark corners, en guard in their individual gossamer worlds.

"You see, all is not lost," Issten said cheerfully, as she glanced around the table at the grandchildren, complexioned in various shades from delicate brown to creamy white and each buoyant with life. "Not at all, not at all." Her eyes came to rest on two identical boys, clearly the eldest in the group. Sitting close together and a little apart from the others crowding a proudly contented Maya, the boys were in their teens and looked like the exotic sons of some multiracial prince. "One day, the twins will do great things," Issten said, with total admiration and a matter-of-fact confidence. "I know it, even if I'm no longer alive to see it . . . though I certainly hope to be. I see no reason why one can't live to be a hundred or even a hundred and twenty, if one still feels well, no? I have a lot of work left, and I do feel well. The twins need me.

I must do all I can. But I also must do something about my feet. They're terribly swollen. Otherwise I would pay no attention. I ought to have done it already last year. I wanted to go to Bad Gastein. They have a very good cure, especially for swollen feet. But Albrecht wouldn't give me the money, the miser! He has millions, you know. What does he think?" She paused, and came out with her rapid *ho-ho-ho* laugh. " . . . That he can take it with him?"

By the time I was ready to leave the following day, I felt no less a part of the château than I had at Stephanie's Widenmayerstrasse home and at Albrecht's Schloss, despite the various predators sharing my quarters here and the shortness of my stay. I was comfortable calling my aunt "Issten" with the same intonation as did her grandchildren. My aunt probed and inquired about everything, and though she spoke English at the château when not speaking French, I could almost hear her saying in German, which was her first language, *Was ist denn? Was ees-ten?* What is it? What is it? I also felt a close kinship for my cousin with the brownish face. Especially after Maya and I walked down to the lively village bistro at the bottom of the hill for a farewell Pernod. "I'm sorry to have been a disappointment to Mamma," she said somberly, amid bantering with the ruddy-faced regulars in the local Basque dialect. "Life for me hasn't been what I would have preferred either. Luckily, we have the children, and I suspect Mamma and I are much closer than either of us think." Maya glanced at the lottery stubs she had bought earlier from the squat, black-bereted proprietor and spread out on the table around her drink. "Do you know *Tiercé?* It lets you dream. Everybody in France plays it. It's with horses and numbers. Maybe one day I'll get lucky." She looked up earnestly. Her eyes again seemed sad, but she laughed. "My dream has always been to ride off into the sunset with Winnetou."

I was sorry I couldn't extend my stay when Maya implored me to do so over a second Pernod. I had to catch a train to Luxembourg for my long-standing reservation back to the United States on Icelandic. It was less than a week before Labor Day, when I was expected to resume my job.

4/

When I showed up at the New York Republican headquarters, it gradually dawned on me that I wasn't about to be re-employed. The staff had been reshuffled and many familiar faces were no longer there, including my chief benefactor, who had been forced to resign. After trudging from office to office most of the day, I was in effect told, "Don't call us, we'll call you."

This was a rude awakening from my fairy tale existence of the past three months. What now? Would I have to start the not-so-merry-go-round of trying to sell myself to potential employers? From the dozen or so companies where I had interviewed during my previous job-hunting whirl, I had no pending offers I could readily tap. Was it because they had all concluded I wasn't entirely sincere and lacked the requisite enthusiasm for any of those jobs? Yet I needed to find something fast. Not only did I have to resume paying rent; the financial aid people at Yale were insisting I start making good on my promissory notes. If I had suspected things would turn out this way, I might have never yielded to Stephanie's entreaties.

As I was putting away a second six-pack that evening at our East Side brownstone, one of the roommates from the revolving roster volunteered he might be able to help. He was employed in the advertising department of Scholastic, Inc., a leading publisher of school periodicals and books. He offered to arrange an appointment with the editorial department, which was constantly losing young writers to more prestigious publications such as *The New York Times, Collier's,* or *Look.*

Whether because this intermediary happened to be the son of one of Scholastic's major stockholders – or because of the trial piece I wrote on Saudi Arabia – I got the job: general assignment writer for the company's two high school publications, *Senior Scholastic* and *World Week.*

One of the first stories I covered for Scholastic resulted from pressure on my employers by the American Legion to send a reporter to Washington for their annual Boys Nation convention. The weeklong activities culminated in the reception of the Boys Nation delegates by President Kennedy in the White House Rose Garden. While the conservative Legionnaire supervisors were concerned about being photographed shaking hands with the liberal president, the youthful leaders gushed the usual clichés: "Shake the hand that shook the hand . . . I'm not going to wash this hand for a week . . ." But following his moment with JFK, however, a tall eighteen-year-old with light, wavy hair stepped quietly aside. Encircled by his friends, he stared into the palm of his hand as if electrified by the touch of Michelangelo's God, then muttered seemingly to himself, "I'm going to do it . . . yes, I'm going to do it!" Now his friends were the ones who became electrified. Turning outward toward the rest of the Rose Garden group, they relayed the news with the excitement of informing the world of a historic event, "He's going to do it . . . yes, he's going to do it!"

The youth was William Jefferson Clinton, and that was the instant he had decided to run for president. The only reason for my presence at this footnote to history was that the American Legion reimbursed Scholastic for my expenses. Otherwise, it was my employer's policy that writers research their articles from the array of newspapers and magazines kept on the premises. This wasn't exactly a momentous endeavor, and the salary was about what a good secretary earned in those days. But the magazines didn't publish during the summer months, which meant I would be free for future visits with Stephanie.

The job held more immediate advantages, too. Because of the reliability of my work and the sympathetic attitude of my editor, I soon joined the privileged ranks of employees allowed to set their own working times. This meant I was free to spend the sunniest part of each day on the rooftop of our East Side brownstone, or take a whole day off to go to Jones Beach. Prior to deciding on the one-hour drive (plus a half hour by subway to the Bronx, where I parked my old Cadillac), I would check the tides to ensure having a hard surface on which to run. This was a full decade before jogging became a fad. I had discovered already at Yale how effectively such exercise could clear the brain and restore the body's energy. I had done my laps there on the quarter-mile indoor track on top of the huge neo-Gothic edifice known as the Payne-Whitney Gym, most often after overindulging in New Haven's incomparable brick-oven pizza and countless bottles of Haffenraffer beer. I had by no means moderated my appetites since then (although I did continue to evolve my tastes) and found this form of exercise especially therapeutic in New York. I once set out to do thirty-five miles on Jones Beach to see what it would be like. It turned into a test of stamina and will; a self-imposed challenge in a world where daily survival was hardly the physical struggle it had been for so much of human history. Toward the end of that run the tide was coming in, forcing me to plod the last miles through soft, grasping sand. I felt dehydrated by the five hours in the blazing sun. My legs bounced back and forth like disembodied leaden weights, and my chest was raw from swinging my arms. Yet when I finished, I felt resurrected, filled with a triumphant peace and an unbounded love of life. Was that how our ancestors felt after subduing some savage beast they had taken on with bare hands? As I was cooling off at the water's edge, I spotted an injured horseshoe crab dragging its broken tail through the liquid sand. I helped it back into

the safety of the surf, if only to give the creature a few more precious moments before the inevitable end.

Considering the unexceptional nature of my Scholastic job, the
basic challenge I faced in New York was how to differentiate myself from so many contemporaries who were also trying to make
their mark. In practical terms, how to get invited to the parties I
had occasionally gone to with classmates at Hotchkiss and Yale,
the best of which weren't too different from those I had enjoyed
throughout the summer at some spectacular palace or Schloss as
Stephanie's guest.

Even if I did have an unusual background, making something
of it was another matter. I couldn't exactly go around introducing
myself as a count. A little hint here and there was fine, especially
when dropped by somebody else. While I felt no special urge to
publicize the butcher side of the family – or Father's growing reputation throughout New England as Mr. Exercycle – I wasn't
averse to proffering some choicer episodes of our family history to
launch a social career.

Fortunately, I had a launching platform of sorts. One of my
New York roommates happened to be in *The New York Social
Register* (aka *The Book*), and I was soon accompanying him to all
kinds of affairs. The invitations I particularly coveted were to the
summer debutante balls held in striped circus-sized tents on mani-
cured lawns of posh country clubs or private estates. The best ones
had Lester Lanin personally conducting his society band till dawn
and vintage French champagne that never ran out. Standing a bit
off to the side and sipping glass after glass, I liked to keep an eye
on the debutantes being whirled around, as well as on some of the
younger-looking mothers. I was at an age when it was easy to
straddle the generation gap, even if I did gravitate toward the
more youthful side. Anyone I happened to be particularly smitten
by I would later look up in my roommate's copy of the Book – on

the sly, of course, since I didn't want people getting the idea that I really cared about this sort of thing. I might have been taken for an outright opportunist, which wouldn't have been entirely fair, since I had to like them, too. For how could I fulfill my primary goal of having fun with somebody I didn't like? When I had first approached COMSERVPAC'S daughter years ago, it was because she happened to be the prettiest girl around the officers' club swimming pool and the lifeguard at that. When she gave me Quarters D as the address where I was to pick her up for dinner that evening, I thought it sounded like multifamily housing for chief petty officers.

Still, I could be shameless in what I was prepared to do. At one coming out party in upstate New York by a beautiful lake, the rumor had it that Janet Auchincloss, who was making her debut that year, was there. This was the peak of New Frontier days, and the fact that Janet happened to be Jackie Kennedy's half-sister was something most people could only pretend not to be curious about. Roaming the tented dance floor on that enchanted evening, I was alert to cut in on anyone with a semblance of the Jackie look — and then tried not to betray my disappointment on finding out she was not who I thought. When I finally did cut in on a lively debutante who in response to my self-introduction said she indeed was Janet Auchincloss, I tried to keep my cool. "Auchincloss, Auchincloss," I repeated, as if trying to place the name. "Any relationship to the writer Louis Auchincloss?"

With little effort on my part, Janet and I became friends. She had a bubbly sense of humor, and I soon came to think of her more as someone who was good company than a conduit to a White House job. There was no question of our relationship taking a romantic turn, since Janet was already in love with the man she intended to wed. Even so, I looked forward to driving occasionally to Sarah Lawrence College, where she was in her first year, and taking her out for drinks and bantering about all sorts of things.

Or Janet would come to Scholastic, where I had recently been given an office. I would close the door, open the bottom drawer of my desk, and offer her a light snack of Gruyère cheese, macadamia nuts, and a goblet of a fine Bordeaux red, all of which I invariably kept on hand, while she rambled about the details of her life, sometimes seeking advice as one might from a person with an edge in years and down-to-earth experience.

I took it as a social milestone when Janet unexpectedly invited me to escort her to a mental health benefit sponsored by the Kennedy family: a black-tie premiere of *It's a Mad, Mad, Mad, Mad World*. Jackie had given Janet her tickets, since she was planning to be with the president on a trip he was taking to sample the public mood in several Texas cities and towns. Janet and I found ourselves sitting in the midst of New Frontier luminaries who unexpectedly had to settle for sitting next to us.

More than usual, Janet was brimming with good cheer. Just before the lights began to dim, she volunteered that somehow John seemed to have suddenly, miraculously fallen in love with her sister again. It all sounded so mundane I had to remind myself who it was that Janet meant.

"Isn't it wonderful?" she exclaimed. "I can't believe how perfect everything is. Absolutely perfect!"

I watched Janet's eyes sparkle, as in studio photographs after they had been touched up with little white dots. Yet, the perfection of it all was what suddenly made me think. Over the past several years, I had evolved a theory that seemed to have an uncanny application to what Janet just said. Though merely a restatement of what had been observed since the days of Ancient Greece by people far wiser than I, my version was rooted in what I had personally learned about the perils of overstepping the limits of our human lot. I had come to accept without grumbling whenever something was just a little bit askew or had gone a little bit awry, such as having a conspicuous pimple break out on my nose on a day I otherwise felt on top of the world. It was this blemish that protected a human being from anything worse in a universe that for some reason couldn't tolerate total happiness on earth. Yet if Janet was right, there was now no such blemish between the presidential pair.

"Perfect," I heard Janet repeat, as the lights began to dim. "I'm so happy for them."

I glanced at Janet at my side, in her exultant mood. I didn't want to spoil her special moment of joy, yet neither could I let the matter rest. "Let's hope, Janet," I heard myself say in a level voice, "there is some little imperfection here and there."

She glanced at me, vaguely perplexed. "What do you mean?"

"You see, Janet, I've had this theory for years. *When you're ready to two-step with the gods, they'll strike you down every time.*"

I paused. Seeing the sudden apprehension superimposed over Janet's joy, I smiled and reached out to touch her arm. "Janet, you know me and my crazy theories."

That was only five days before America's Camelot came to its shattering end on a sunny November day in the midst of an exuberant smile and a wave to a Dallas crowd.

5/

I invariably managed to take advantage of the publishing pause at Scholastic to spend the time at Albrecht's Schloss. It was at the beginning of my third summer there that Stephanie chose to cause precisely the kind of scandal her father feared. She had recently become the mother of a baby boy, predictably named Hansi.

I was what could be called the first witness on the scene. It was barely dawn when I vaguely heard Stephanie walk into my room, on the other side of her odorless bathroom on the second floor, and quietly close the door.

"Hey, Onkel dear, are you awake?"

"What if I say no?" I opened an eye and saw her standing by the bed in her pink bathrobe, looking strangely excited as if something momentous had taken place.

"Guess what, Onkel dear . . . I just told Hansi that little Hansi isn't his."

"I think I want to go back to sleep," I mumbled, and pulled the pillow over my head.

I had known of Stephanie's predicament since day one, and of her determination to marry Jonathan, the English musician who prided himself on being the father of the boy. They met during a two-day stopover in London, shortly after Hansi had signed his specialty paint contract. While Hansi was talking undercoating at British Motors, his wife was surveying the Portobello Road flea market. Outside one of the stalls, she became enraptured by a slim youth strumming a guitar. A year younger than Stephanie, Jonathan unwittingly made himself even more attractive when he confided that he had never made love. With Stephanie's diligent assistance, he managed to remedy this condition before she departed the following day, and later discovered he was a prospective father as well. For an initiate, Jonathan considered it quite a feat. He was already planning to give little Hansi a more appropriate name as soon as Stephanie was free. And that was certainly fine by me, since the relationship I had with Stephanie over the past couple of years precluded jealousy. Yet I consistently urged her not to disrupt the status quo. She was in a position to continue her affair indefinitely on the sly. (She had recently convinced Hansi to allow her to fly to London for a week's visit with "former classmates.") So why look for trouble? Jonathan was only sporadically employed with a nightclub group as a singer-guitarist, waiting for a break that would vault him to greater fame. His father, a somber British diplomat, wasn't about to help in any way; at least, not as long as Jonathan refused to consider more appropriate work.

Worst of all in my view was that the divorce would devastate Albrecht and might lead to consequences that couldn't be foreseen. I had been careful to give Albrecht no cause to regret his original decision to invite me to the Schloss. After our uncertain beginning the first summer, we had been getting along increasingly well. I found it easy to be sensitive to his views, and I wasn't about to do anything that would alienate him as my host. A scandal, especially, was something I knew how to avoid. I had a reputation among my New York friends for dispensing advice that would help them look good no matter what personal or professional straits they were in. It was a question of managing the truth in an appropriate way. "You could make the devil look good," my friends used to jest, meaning it as a compliment.

"Come on, Onkel dear," Stephanie said, pulling the pillow off my face. "I said I *told* Hansi."

"That wasn't very smart, was it," I said testily, then sat up in bed.

"He's been suspicious. Stupid Frau Trepper has been telling him little Hansi looks just like the princess but not in the least bit the way the prince looked when he was a baby."

"It seems old Frau Trepper isn't at all stupid."

"I just couldn't lie to Hansi anymore," Stephanie sighed, as if resigned to her fate. "Not about something like this. You should have seen him. I was barely awake, and there he was, sitting up in bed, staring at me. He looked so idiotic in that hairnet. He had a pathetic scowl on his face and asked me point-blank. I guess I'm just too honest for my own good."

"Yeah, for your own good."

"What's that supposed to mean?"

"I think you'd lie to Hansi forever if it served your purpose."

Stephanie was sitting at the edge of my bed, a vapid blankness in her doelike eyes. For a moment I thought she might get angry.

But then her eyes abruptly became alive, as if she realized the truth and felt relieved for no longer having to pretend.

"I guess you're right, Onkel dear," she said, and started to nod in unison with me. "I really do have to get a divorce. One way or another. If you only knew, Hansi's such a bore. And how he snores so terribly, and has such morning mouth."

"I don't think you're being fair."

"You just don't get close enough."

"I don't need to remind you that the undercoating business has been good."

"I don't care if he makes millions."

"I guess I have a soft spot for any prince who lugs my suitcase the length of the Munich Hauptbahnhof."

"You would, wouldn't you!"

"Besides, I thought his fame reached far and wide as a lover."

"Hah, that's what he'd like you to believe!" Stephanie burst out. "It's all his own PR, to use your phrase." She paused as her face reflected an array of unpleasant emotions. She seemed about to explode again, but then checked herself and sighed, "Let's just say that he has his shortcomings."

Stephanie broke the news to her father immediately after breakfast, while Hansi remained secluded in their suite. As she enumerated her grounds for divorce in the privacy of Albrecht's lair, he became more and more appalled. *What did marriage have to do with snoring, bad breath, or a pathetic hairnet? Marriage was forever, for better or for worse, a solemn contract sealed in heaven. Be serious,* Albrecht told Stephanie, and assumed the problem had been solved.

She then told him about the child.

Albrecht looked stunned. Now he knew the situation was irretrievable, like death or the loss of a limb. It was a horrendous sin, an outright sacrilege, an insult to God. How could his Stephanie, whom he had brought up with such care, do this to him? First it was his mother who dishonored the family name and offended God. Now his only daughter! Was there a curse on the women of the house? Surely there would be a terrible price to pay – and a scandal, too! How could he, the prince on the pedestal, face the knowing looks of the villagers in the streets when they bowed and doffed their hats?

That was the gist of Albrecht's reaction, at least as reported to me by Stephanie. She had to endure an hour of her father's jeremiads before managing to break away. His long pauses of wordless reproach were the most trying part of the ordeal.

Giving Frau Kunst barely time to fill his rucksack with sandwiches and a thermos of tea, Albrecht retreated into the woods. A little later, I saw Hansi peel out in his Volvo from its parking space in front of the Schloss, his face frozen in a grimace of pain.

Albrecht didn't return until dusk. I watched him preside over dinner in the stately dining hall, wordlessly ladling out the soup to the half-dozen guests. Everybody knew what had occurred, and it was a somber group. Sitting next to me at the far end, Stephanie whispered, "Thank God, you're here, Onkel dear. I didn't think it would be this bad." At the head of the table, Albrecht seemed to be engulfed by impenetrable gloom. His eyes glistened sporadically, and when a tear began to worm its way down his weather-beaten cheek, he made no move to wipe off this symbol of his grief. Not once throughout the meal did he glance at the sheaf of lined yellow sheets on the table next to his plate.

Over the next several days, I realized my presence wasn't much help. Whatever cheer I tried to provide evoked only a fleeting smile. Albrecht seemed mortified that it should have been Stephanie who brought this scandal about, rather than I, who had in his veins so much more blood from the side of the family known for mischief of this sort. My cousin, no doubt, remembered the warning he had once sent me that living in a castle was like living in a glass house.

Now this from his daughter!

Stephanie's scandal surfaced in curious ways. Unlike in her grandmother's day, the respected media – not to mention the tabloids – now clamored for stories of this sort. Yet it was Hansi who transformed the case into a cause célèbre. He was determined to prove in court that Stephanie was fabricating the story to get a divorce, and that he, in fact, was the father of the child. Hansi's willingness to risk public humiliation wasn't motivated entirely by fatherly pride. (If Stephanie hadn't told me about his pre-marital child, I certainly wouldn't have found out about it from Hansi.) But if this little boy turned out to be his, Hansi could still wind up as the master of the Schloss. Such a position he could hardly attain merely through selling more undercoating paint.

Although the blood tests failed to prove who the father was, they demonstrated to the satisfaction of the court that Hansi was not. In being granted the divorce and exclusive custody of little Hansi, Stephanie lost Diana. Living in England as Jonathan's wife, Stephanie wouldn't see her daughter as often as she might like. The only one in heartfelt accord with the verdict was Frau Trepper. An unmarried twenty-two-year-old when she had taken on the assignment of raising Hansi, she was overjoyed to become *Erzieherin* for the "little angel" as an unmarried sixty-year-old – and once again have a clear purpose in life.

The scandal resurfaced after the final decree when Hansi tried to get the marriage annulled by the Church. This was an essential step for any Catholic who hoped to remarry but one that Stephanie chose to skip. For Hansi, this meant having to seek out less-than-pleasant testimony, mainly from Stephanie's Munich friends, to demonstrate a special form of incompatibility between husband and wife. Because of Hansi's title, social position, and involvement in lay Catholic works, the Vatican appointed a special legate to hear the case; a thin, austere monsignor with two front teeth of

gold. The salient details of the testimony were soon being discussed all over town; not only the hairnet and morning mouth, but
an array of other intimate complaints most likely provided by
some of Hansi's other disgruntled lovers from his past. Whatever
the source, this wasn't the kind of talk one of Munich's most eligible bachelors might like to have going around.

"I don't know why Stephanie was always complaining about
me," Hansi remarked, when I returned to Europe the following
summer at the height of the proceedings. "I was on business in
Brazil a couple of weeks ago, and the girls there had no complaints." Hansi smiled confidentially, and then for emphasis gave
me a monumental wink.

When I arrived a few days later at Albrecht's Schloss, I tried not
to appear shocked by how much my cousin had changed. In less
than a year, his silver-speckled hair had turned a dull gray, and
the heavy lines on his face appeared more deeply etched. He had
always tended to stoop, but now he rarely straightened to his full
height.

Yet there was one light in Albrecht's life: his five-year-old
granddaughter, who also happened to be visiting on this occasion.
It clearly wasn't the first time since the divorce that Frau Trepper
brought her not-so-little ward to stay with her Opapa. For his precious Angelina, Albrecht was ready to suspend his labors on the
universe; whether to pretend being startled by her exuberant invasion of his quarters, or to watch her ride her pony in the fields,
or to sit at the edge of her bed reading fairy tales before tucking
her in, and waiting like a shy suitor for her tender good-night hug
that would mist his eyes.

This wasn't exactly the Angelina who accompanied me during
the same visit to a nearby pond, which was the domain of several
semi-wild geese. At her urging we edged closer and closer until one
of the large birds made a hissing lunge in our direction, evoking a

scream from the little princess as she scurried to safety behind my knees.

With the attacker swimming off placidly, Angelina composed herself and looked at me with lively eyes. "I fooled you," she boasted. "You really thought I was scared."

"All right," I said, grasping her by the hand, "let's go see that goose again."

"No, no, no!" she started shrieking, pulling me back. "I'm not fooling this time. Please, please!"

I relented. "See?"

"Fooled you again," she exclaimed triumphantly, while keeping a wary eye on that goose. "And if you try it again, I'll fool you again."

"Until you're old enough and you don't need to fool me anymore?"

She seemed to think that over, then looked at me in a coquettish way. "*Vielleicht ja . . . viellicht nein*. Why should I tell?"

Watching Albrecht with Angelina day after day, I recognized the distant look I had captured in the photo of him and the little girl gazing at the same infinite point. Was it the future Albrecht was trying to discern? I knew he didn't want to think of his Angelina as ever growing up. *How young and pure she was, yet already how much like Stephanie!* "Oh God, please spare Angelina from being corrupted by this evil world," Albrecht said with a sigh during one of our solitary walks in the woods, and then confided that he included this request in his prayers every night.

When Angelina left at the end of the week, Albrecht again withdrew into his impenetrable world, and a somber mood once more permeated the Schloss. I didn't especially mind that I had to leave a couple of days later to start fulfilling a professional commitment in France.

6/

I had accepted a daring offer from a friend: to act as principal for a group of U.S. high school girls enrolled during their summer vacation in a four-week study program at the University of Grenoble. I still shudder on remembering the thankless task of assigning rooms late into the night at the university's Résidence Hector Berlioz to three busloads of disoriented teenage girls and their disgruntled teacher-chaperones, who had traveled for two days without sleep. Yet, when I read their evaluations at the end of their stay, it made it all worthwhile. Indeed, I had done my best to ensure my young charges got their money's worth. Take, for example, the frequent dances I organized. I personally recruited the stag line while walking across the *Cité universitaire* and along Grenoble's public boulevards, inviting the local Romeos I thought my girls would like, as well as some young men I thought they should meet; especially those classy students from Africa, dreaming of becoming heads of state, or at least ministers, with chauffeured Mercedes limousines and all the perks. "If only Daddy could see me now," I heard a belle from Charleston gloat, while cheek-to-cheek with one such type. My girls felt secure, knowing I was there to save them from any less-than- gallant moves, though only if they gave me the sign. Otherwise, they were free to do as they wished, provided they continued speaking French. How much more of a cross-cultural experience could my charges have had? I also managed to reform the university's traditional academic fare by prevailing on some of the French pedagogues to teach my girls how to ask *"Où est la toilette?"* and read a menu in French, instead of confusing them with the pluperfect tense.

The program in Grenoble was one of a half-dozen organized throughout Europe by the American Institute for Foreign Study. When I returned to the United States, the same friend who had hired me for the summer now offered me a full-time job in public relations.

I welcomed the chance to leave Scholastic. I had been promoted to world affairs editor, but my articles were still limited to library research. The trick was to make the reader believe the writer was always on the scene, as I evidently succeeded in doing in the trial piece on Saudi Arabia. Only on such unique occasions as JFK's funeral did management splurge to send a reporter on location – and then merely from New York to Washington.

As director of information for the Institute, my mandate was to make its name synonymous with student travel abroad. I would be starting at about the same modest salary I had at Scholastic. Only now I would be able to travel for free and have an expense account. Moreover, my employer-friend, who was one of the Institute's three owners, assured me that the real payoff would come when the company was acquired by some large conglomerate. In the meantime, it was necessary to keep salaries low and show steadily improving balance sheets.

In trying to obtain free publicity for the Institute, an indispensable part of my task was developing strong links with magazine writers and editors in New York. No less important, however, was gathering the raw materials from the Institute's enrollees during their summers abroad. Overwhelmed and euphoric to be in Europe for the first time, students were willing to give credit to the Institute for almost everything short of building the Eiffel Tower or writing the Magna Carta. The programs were mainly well administered and worth the price, despite the inevitable snafus and inconveniences of group travel. I categorically avoided publicizing any such problems that could discourage potential participants from signing up. But I did make a point of including some criticism in each press release or article. For instance, "Exclaimed seventeen-year-old Don Lick, of Aurora, Illinois, with a trace of exasperation as he crossed the thirteenth century moat, 'I've seen so many castles in the last two weeks, I've got castles coming out of my ears!'" The Institute's publicity thus gave the impression of being objective, while making countless students in the United States yearn for the problems of Don Lick.

The most formidable challenge I faced in connection with this work was one I truly relished. With the bulk of the programs located in countries known for their wines and culinary expertise, I had to figure out a sustainable response. Specifically – let's say I am in France – how should I handle daily a full lunch, including a heavy paté, half a bottle of red, and a double serving of goat cheese with countless pieces of that addictive crunchy French bread without getting fat? How to be ready for an even more sumptuous meal at dinnertime? Here, planning was of the essence. If I finished lunch at two-thirty, I would have about six hours before having to sit down again. The time-tested formula I developed for this between-meals interlude was to keep moving, to do as many interviews as I could, tracking down the Institute's students and chaperones all over Paris. On days when no tour groups were passing through, the pace was less hectic. I usually walked leisurely along boulevard Saint Germain until midafternoon, pausing to survey the clientele at Aux Deux Maggots and then watch a different crowd trooping into Le Drugstore across the street. Just minutes away were les jardins de Luxembourg, where I could stretch out in the sun for a little nap on a couple of green metal chairs, and eventually jog a few laps on the gravel paths beneath the chestnut trees. I would get back to my hotel room for some energetic push-ups and deep-knee bends before relaxing in a long shower or a bath. With a clean shirt and a fresh pair of socks, I would then be ready to step out and do justice to any meal. Besides the patés and cheeses and breads, among my favorites were the *carré d'agneau* topped with a crust of garlicky butter-soaked crumbs. Although the salads and other green vegetables were of world-renowned quality in France, I favored potatoes, especially the thinly sliced *pommes de terre Lyonnaise* baked in a thick cheesy sauce. And of course, I didn't skimp on the desserts or the wine, starting out with a bottle of the house Beaujolais, and if need be, ordering another half-bottle to accompany the *crème brûlée* or *tarte aux pommes*. This would put me in just the right mood on a warm summer night to amble up the Champs Elysées, watching the Arc de triomphe all lit up, a huge *tricolore* unfurled from the highest point within the arch, fluttering in the breeze and filling the entire opening with waves of red, white, and blue – all gently blurred before my eyes.

Crisscrossing Europe throughout the summer in connection with my PR work (the Institute's programs were in more than a dozen countries), I found it easy to stop by Albrecht's Schloss. Though I rarely stayed longer than a week, I was now able to return several times during the summer months. Stephanie, on the other hand, no longer visited as often as before. This was partly because she lived in London and had to draw on her modest trust fund to pay for the trips, and partly because Jonathan didn't feel sufficiently welcome at the Schloss. Albrecht couldn't forget that his daughter's second husband was the cause of the scandal that had practically collapsed his life. When Jonathan openly protested during a recent visit that Albrecht's icy silence was no way to treat a guest, his reluctant father-in-law felt compelled to respond, "Ach, but what makes you think you're a guest? You're merely tolerated."

Even without Stephanie there, I sensed I was welcome at the Schloss, free to come and go as I wished. Everyone made me feel at home, including Frau Kunst; she, especially after I started tipping her in advance on a weekly basis, regardless of the length of my stay. I wanted to spare her the insecurity of wondering to the end whether the tip would be commensurate to her efforts on my behalf. She, in turn, insisted on making my bed, doing my laundry (despite what Albrecht had once written me), and filling my rucksack with sandwiches for a day in the woods, even if there were a dozen other guests and she had to call on a neighboring farmer's wife and daughter for help. When I stopped in the kitchen to let Frau Kunst know her efforts hadn't gone unnoticed, she sometimes used the occasion to emphasize the family ties. With open admiration she would remark how much little Hansi, on his latest visit to the Schloss, was looking more and more like *der Onkel,* me.

Frau Kunst's cordiality was in part a reflection of how Albrecht felt. My cousin and I had become understanding friends, despite the generation gap. I took my meals regularly in Albrecht's quarters when no other guests were at the Schloss. To be invited to eat here rather than in the stately dining hall on the second floor was an honor reserved for family and close friends. Albrecht seemed to recognize I had a special insight into his travails; not only those with Stephanie but the no less painful memory of what his mother had wrought. Within certain bounds, I felt free to bring up the Roland Hayes affair and the situation at the château, though never at meals. That's when I knew Albrecht wanted his peace. I would then try to draw him out on his theories about the universe, nodding as if all of his points made eminent sense. This would continue until the next course was served. When something was on our plates, we were equally afflicted by the family indisposition of concentrating on our food to the exclusion of any cerebral concerns.

But between courses, especially before dessert, Albrecht could be coaxed into sharing some of his latest insights and conclusions. Did I know that flying saucers moved around by mastering the secret of standing absolutely still in a universe rushing headlong in countless directions? That the saucers had to keep spinning because their mass was so great that if they stopped, they would expand and blow up? Yet these were merely sidelights to his more fundamental discoveries. Albrecht was convinced he had succeeded in working out to the last millisecond the life span of the universe, accounting even for the final grunt of its ultimate compression. According to my cousin's formula, this added up to some thirty billion years. His one proviso was that humanity didn't interfere in God's grand scheme – which, alas, was already happening because of our excessive use of electricity.

Dead electrons were Albrecht's bugaboo. He was alarmed that they were accumulating at a dangerous rate and ultimately represented a more serious threat than nuclear waste. "You're a logical person," Albrecht remarked, as I finished a large venison steak and was awaiting Frau Kunst's chocolate soufflé, whose aroma was already permeating the entire lower part of the Schloss. "You know that every form of energy has its residue. Nuclear fuel . . . radioactive waste. Gasoline and fuel oil . . . noxious fumes. Even the wood in this fire," Albrecht said, nodding toward the green-tiled *Kachelofen* wedged in one corner of the small room and radiating pleasant warmth against the outside chill from a persistent mountain drizzle, "even here you have a residue of ash. Why should electricity be any different? As a logical person, haven't you wondered what becomes of those trillions and trillions of electrons once they're used up? Think of that the next time you switch on a light or turn on a radio. Those are dead electrons! I suspected it already as a young man. Now I have proof."

I barely managed to stifle a smile. Was that the reason Albrecht had been so earnestly turning off those lights at our residence in Prague when I was four years old? But I wasn't about to make some irreverent remark. I knew Albrecht was a sensitive soul, especially when it concerned the mysteries of the universe, which he considered to be his private domain. Besides, I had already been surprised more than once when some seemingly absurd assertion of his eventually turned out to be closer to the truth than what bona fide scientists had previously theorized. Such as Albrecht's conviction, years earlier, that somewhere near the sun was an extra, yet-to-be-discovered planet – a possibility respected astronomers were beginning to concede.

"Yes, dead electrons," Albrecht interrupted my thoughts. He nodded gravely. "The world is littered with dead electrons. They're slowing the spin of the earth and shortening the life of the universe." He tilted his head to put us squarely face to face, then looked at me with a hard intensity. I could see a fresh crispness in his tired eyes, as if the gray within each pupil were turning to steel. There was an implicit accusation in his stare: I felt he was making me personally responsible for America's wastrel ways, for America's monstrous pile of dead electrons, as if I alone, single-handedly, had piled them up. It was the same look my old headmaster, the Duke, had given me in making me feel responsible for some future world war because of that indiscreet remark at breakfast concerning Dr. Renny and Mr. Hale.

Albrecht finally averted his eyes and sighed. "Unfortunately, the spin of the earth has slowed. It's been proven over and over again."

"But is that any cause for panic?" I asked cautiously. "I thought you said the universe had a thirty-billion-year life span."

Albrecht was not to be easily stumped. "Ja . . . yes, thirty billion, more or less. You have to use my formula, C square plus two seconds plus one over *hoch zwei*, if you want to be accurate. C is the speed of light in kilometers per second. The two seconds is how long it takes for the original explosion to reach its most extreme dimension, and for the final implosion to shrink the universe back into an infinitesimal speck. One second for each. It's the only exception to Einstein's theory when light travels almost infinitely faster than three hundred thousand kilometers per second."

"That may well be," I interjected impatiently, "but what I want to know is how much have these dead electrons . . . especially the countless zillions in America . . . how much have they shortened the life of the universe?"

"Ach, ja, that!" Albrecht nodded, again with utmost gravity and visibly agitated. "Ach, ja," he repeated, nervously rubbing the right side of his face. "I should say already at least a few seconds. Perhaps as much as a minute. And that's only in the last fifty years."

"Well, what's a few seconds, even a minute, in thirty billion years? I don't see . . ."

My sentence remained unfinished. A pained expression contorted Albrecht's deeply lined face. He hunched over in evident despair, cradling his furrowed forehead in his hands. No doubt I had pursued the question too far. I wanted to say something to calm him down, but Albrecht already resumed, as if prodded by an implacable force.

"Ja, of course, what you say is perfectly true. But don't you see, you don't understand!" He was shaking his head and the longer wisps of his silvery curls trembled. "You see, even a few seconds . . . a few seconds here, a few seconds there . . . what it means is that *we are going in the wrong direction!*" Albrecht made an agonized grimace but was too wound up to stop. "We should be extending the life of the universe! Our ultimate aim, the purpose of life, is for us to become immortal partners to God. God waits for us . . . even right now he waits. We can become immortal. You see, there's a way to lengthen the life of the universe into eternity. I haven't worked it out yet, but I know it *is* possible. The trick is to rotate the axis of the universe. And then you've got it . . . ja, somehow rotate the axis."

Just then Frau Kunst entered briskly with her soufflé. All thought of rotating the universal axis momentarily forgotten, Albrecht and I reverted to a silence interrupted only by an occasional clinking of spoons from the overeager scooping against the sides of our plates.

7/

The Institute offered programs at a half dozen study sites within two or three hours' drive of Issten's château, and I was prepared to brave the rats, bats, and spiders to spend several days with this unusual aunt. Brought up to reflect the glitter of European society, she had chosen a drastically different life to become a luminary for the children her hapless daughter produced. There were now six instead of five. "Those twenty minutes after giving birth are an indescribably wonderful time," Maya told me, a sad smile stretching her generous lips. "Six children makes two hours. Little less, really, because the twins came practically together. A little less than two hours of pure joy. Not much to show for a lifetime, eh?" She paused, then laughed a bit raucously. "I might as well have been born in your Harlem ghetto!"

In addition to Maya and her brood, Issten's château had a varied accumulation of occupants. Like the meandering clouds trying to cross the mountains between Spain and France, most of these people got caught in the inclement peaks. Having banged on the massive wooden portal to seek shelter from the elements or lodging for the night, some of them ended up spending the rest of their lives. That was the story of Yura, the husband of Maya. He had come as a young Russian boy, having served as an orderly to a certain General Murayev, who turned against the Soviets and sought refuge in Spain. Issten took in Yura, as she would have anyone who had no place to go and was endowed with a kindred spirit she especially liked. "He was only sixteen," Issten said, recounting how Yura became involved with her daughter. "They both liked horses very much, and they were almost exactly the same age. When I noticed Maya was every day becoming bigger and bigger, I went to the barn, and right away, I gave Yura two sharp slaps . . . an old-fashioned *Ohrfeige*, which he certainly deserved. The poor boy seemed too stunned to say a word, but we both understood. It was a kind of wedding ceremony, and they also had an official one later, though one must not conclude they lived happily ever after. Two of the children are not from Yura because Maya for a time went away with a canalization worker. He was an extraordinarily handsome man but had absolutely nothing in his head. I went after him once into the sewer to try to question him. Quite different from Yura, with whom she again had a child after she came back. Yura loves her very much, poor thing, and suffered terribly."

Despite Issten's obvious penury and the lack of interest among her more permanent guests in seeking gainful work, she refused to send any of them away. "When someone has been with you for twenty years," she explained, shocked that anyone could entertain such a thought, "you don't suddenly tell him that he cannot eat soup with you!"

During my latest visit at the château, an old Rumanian diviner happened to be there. After eating Issten's soup for several days, he disclosed that a golden Madonna was buried somewhere on the grounds. The signals from his divining rod (which he kept stored in a Havana cigar box) were vague, he said, but there definitely was something there.

That was more than enough to rejuvenate the eighty-year-old Issten and inspire her to throw herself body and soul into an all-out search. Instead of tending to her three hectares of Bordeaux grapes, a dozen chickens, and a decrepit draw horse, she mobilized her establishment to help uncover this providential horde. She marked the ground where each hole was to be dug and spurred her diggers on when their persistence began to flag in the afternoon sun and they wanted to take a glass of wine and nap in the shade of an apple tree. "Yes, yes, I can see the Madonna now," Issten excitedly mumbled to herself, loud enough for the various digging crews to hear, as she puttered energetically among them from hole to hole. "It definitely is fourteenth century. I would say thirteen-fifty-eight to be exact. It measures just a few centimeters short of a meter and weighs precisely sixty kilos." She turned to give me a triumphant look. "Can you imagine what we'll be able to do with sixty kilos of gold?" Then, peering down at one of her crews digging furiously several feet in the ground, she cautioned, "Now be careful, be careful! If you hit anything hard, it's probably the Madonna. I don't want you to scratch it."

After several days of frenetic activity, the property was pockmarked with six-foot-deep holes. Absorbed in their momentous task, no one thought of taking the time to fill them in again. The result was that my aunt's old draw horse fell into one of the holes, broke his hind legs and had to be destroyed.

Taking it as an omen, Issten called a temporary halt to further work. "It must mean the time has not yet come for us to find the Madonna," my aunt explained to her dispirited stalwarts, gathered around the dead horse – though she herself remained undaunted. "We must have come extremely close. Otherwise we wouldn't have had the omen, and we would still have a perfectly good horse."

Issten certainly could have used the gold. Throughout my stay, there seldom was any move to prepare the evening meal until I offered to take Maya shopping in my rental car. (Her old Volkswagen had been replaced by an even more decrepit Morris Mini.) After endless protestations enroute, Maya would accept an advance to cover the groceries for the château's sizable retinue. There simply was no other money around, and the procedure repeated itself from day to day. I wondered how Issten paid for the twice-weekly flying lessons for the twins. She went up with them in a little rented plane, and they swooped low over the château and did Dutch rolls for my benefit. "I want to show them I have confidence in everything they do," Issten told me after they landed. "It is more important than anything I can put on their plates."

Issten was uninhibited in her efforts on behalf of the twins. I was at the château when she read in the regional *La Depêche du*

Midi that Sammy Davis Jr. was visiting Paris. By the end of the day, Issten had spent over a hundred dollars on the phone, trying to track him down and contact him personally at his hotel. "I love his book, *Yes, I Can!* Wonderful title, no?" She smiled at me, again undaunted by failure. "Just think how much the twins could have learned from meeting Sammy Davis!"

My aunt's paramount concern was to imbue the twins with pride in their heritage. "They can't get it from their mother, who has no feeling whatsoever for the blacks," Issten said, explaining why she took over the upbringing of the seventeen-year-olds from Maya. "She spends too much time in the bistro and brings the younger children with her. We've had dreadful arguments, simply dreadful. She had a wonderful governess, you know, Miss Muirhead, and even though Maya wasn't a boy, I gave her the best. She knows the classics perfectly. She speaks four languages fluently. She could have an enormous influence because the children love her very much. Unfortunately, the influence is in the wrong direction. One of the twins now reproaches me for going with Roland Hayes. 'If you hadn't gone with him, we would be like everybody else,' he says. Of course, I tell him they wouldn't be here in that case at all! The children must realize they have a great advantage in not being the same as everybody else. One day I hope they'll understand not the faults but the perfection that Roland had. Especially the twins. They must never forget who they are. They must carry the message as long as there is a need for it in the world. That was the whole purpose of that so terrible thing I did with Roland Hayes. It is my greatest legacy to them."

I heard more on this theme from Maya, when she and I went for our daily shopping tour, and, as usual, stopped at the village bistro for a drink. "Mamma says I inherited the impossible qualities of my father but none of his great ones," Maya said, sitting across from me in a cramped booth near the bar. I watched Issten's daughter take another sip of her Pastisse, her buoyant hair streaked with gray and deep worry lines clouding her moonlike face. "The truth is, I inherited the incompatibilities of both. That's why I can't live with Mamma, though I can't live without her either." Maya laughed sadly. "When I was very little, I thought she was my fairy godmother. She told me she found me in a shoebox, and I wasn't allowed to call her 'Mamma' until I was ten. She says she was afraid for my own good." Maya paused and sighed. "What I really want is peace. . . ." She glanced at the blackboard propped up on the bar listing the line-up of horses for next Sunday's *Tiercé*. "I want you to pick the numbers this time. Maybe you'll have better luck."

Maya drained the last of her Pastisse. She put down the glass and smiled in a way that momentarily dissolved those worry clouds. "I know Winnetou is somewhere waiting for his squaw," she said, her eyes reflecting an ethereal sheen. "All I need is the right horse."

Maya allowed me to pick up the tab for the drinks, but she again insisted on herself paying for those chances to paradise. It was all loose change that she must have been saving up throughout the week.

I could understand why my aunt was going deeper and deeper into debt. Over the past forty years, she had sold off the valuable antiques and paintings that had once graced the interior of the château. Next to go were the sixty hectares of adjoining land. Whatever remained was mortgaged to the last centime.

"When did you first start getting into this money mess?" I asked on the final morning of my weeklong stay at the château. Issten and I were having breakfast outside, at a small stone table adjoining the yellowish ramparts of her medieval domicile. The rays of the early sun were bringing out the delicate pinks and blues of the wild flowers in the unkempt formal garden in front of us. Even though the fresh tablecloth looked tattered and the Limoges porcelain was chipped and cracked, Issten's regal presence gave the setting a feeling of opulence and style.

My question was posed in a perfunctory way, more as a commentary on my aunt's state of affairs than in anticipation of any meaningful response. I didn't think she'd even heard me. She was absorbed in filing open a vial of apiserum, an extract of queen bees from China, with which she liked to start the day.

I resumed scooping out my soft-boiled egg resting in an old silver egg cup deformed by multiple little dents, when I heard Issten's rapid *ho-ho-ho* laugh.

"Oh, that's easy," she said, looking out over the untended lawn strewn with chunks of broken statuary. "I can tell you exactly when my financial troubles began. It was when I found out that if you get a loan, you have to pay it back!" She came forth with another of her disarming chuckles, then drained the small brown vial, tilting her head back to get the last drop. "Before that, I thought one could just go around getting loans, and that's all there was to it. It was a wonderful system, no?" She placed the empty vial next to her teacup, then concluded defiantly, "Of course, the loans with Albrecht I still feel I don't have to pay!"

Before I left later that day (I was driving across the border to Spain for a two-day visit to the Institute's program at the University of Salamanca), Issten charged me to use whatever influence I had with Albrecht on her behalf. She was on the verge of irretrievably losing the château and also needed funds to send the twins to the Sorbonne, where they had been accepted. She glanced with immense pride at the two of them sitting beneath a nearby chestnut tree on a green bench, improvising on their electronic guitars. "They'll do great things, don't you think? They have excellent minds, and they are two instead of one, yet they are one. In this case one plus one makes far, far more than two. That ought to give them a great advantage, don't you think? But in the meantime, they have to eat."

"I'll do my best."

"Not that I think it will do any good, mind you. But I hope you try. Albrecht's father would have acted differently. He was a great gentleman and always continued to love me. Even after all that happened, he still bought me the château. But my son will not want to listen, no matter what you say. Albrecht has a closed mind, especially about the château. His ideas about the stars, they're excellent. In every other way, I'm sorry to say, he's old. That's why I could never bear to live at the Schloss. Old age is contagious. The week I spend with him each year already is an ordeal."

Standing in front of her feudal edifice, Issten looked spry, with youthful anticipation of what life might still hold in store. Hunched over though she was, she had a splendid, regal presence. It wasn't until after I left that I realized how shabbily dressed she had been; her sweater pinched in places where the holes were sewn together, the heavy rough material of her skirt faded and frayed, multiple runs in her stockings, and on her swollen feet, a pair of cheap, durable shoes. And she still had that green jade frog affixed to the collar of her blouse. It occurred to me that Stephanie was right in what she had once observed. With all the money Issten had wangled and spent over the years, she never really bought anything for herself. Except for her occasional complaints about those problem feet and her partiality for a daily vial of Chinese apiserum, Issten was indifferent to any personal comforts and wants – more so than Albrecht, who made his self-imposed privations seem like such noble suffering.

"Well, bye, my dear," she said, giving me repeated hugs. "Blood is thicker than water. I feel a special connection exists between us, between you and me. It will always be there. How could it possibly not be there? And should I draw my final breath before we meet again, you'll be the one to whom I shall send my ultimate message from this world. You can tell Albrecht that, the old miser!"

Two weeks later, I was at the Schloss – this time, only for a day. I made the special trip after finishing a series of student interviews at the Institute's program in the Swiss mountain resort of Leysin, once a retreat for rich tuberculosis patients. Thomas Mann used it as a setting for *The Magic Mountain*, or so several of the local hôteliers told me.

I knew Albrecht would welcome any news I might bring of his mother from the château. It was touching to see this courtly gentleman, well into his sixties, so imbued with filial concern. He called her *Mammi* and loved her as if he were a little boy. Yet I also knew that when it came to discussing Mammi's inexhaustible need for loans, Albrecht would abruptly change. If I merely thought of bringing up the subject, an invisible barrier would drop between us with an implicit warning for me to back off.

I understood why. How vividly I remembered that painful scene in Prague of my aunt extracting a loan from her hapless son "to buy a little something for your own cousin." I felt as an accomplice and was at least glad we couldn't find that monkey in any of the stores. Over the years, I had heard similar stories of financial strife between mother and son. Such as the time Albrecht wired her, after agonized soul searching, five thousand Swiss francs, in response to her insistent appeals for twice that sum. "Where's the other five?" she immediately wired back. "What do you think? That I would ask for ten when I needed only five?" Or the time Albrecht tried to settle all of his mother's debts and lent her fifty thousand Swiss francs. But before she paid off a single franc, a medium in nearby Toulouse prophesied a unique opportunity to make a fortune by placing pinball machines into cafés and bars. That the medium also prophesied where the machines should be bought failed to deter my aunt.

"Mammi always had a weakness for this sort of thing," Albrecht remarked sadly, as if anticipating the plea I was contemplating on her behalf. He had eyed me warily throughout the day, wondering why I would make a special trip for such a brief visit. Now, we were finishing dinner in my cousin's cellar-like quarters. This was the one chance I would have to make my pitch, since I had reserved a berth on the ten o'clock sleeper for Italy, where the Institute had a thriving program at Perugia's Universita per Stranieri.

"Of course, Mammi lost everything," Albrecht continued, seated across from me at the small, rough-hewn wooden table near the window. As was his habit, he had yet to turn on the light. "To this day, she sends appeals to whichever of our family friends she can think of. Naturally, they come to check with me. It's all very embarrassing."

"What do you tell them?"

"I must tell them to ignore her." Albrecht rubbed his eyes. "It's not an enviable position to be in . . . but I'm faithfully following my father's wishes."

This was precisely the issue I would have to dispute. Over the years, Albrecht had indeed followed his father's practice of sending Issten monthly checks, sufficient for any genteel woman with a child to live on comfortably, even in luxury. What my cousin refused to acknowledge was that the situation since his father's time had drastically changed. As far as Albrecht was concerned, his half-sister Maya didn't exist, nor did that array of dusky nieces and nephews. It would be the height of immorality, or so Albrecht claimed, if he were to support offspring from the illicit union that had hastened his father's death. As for those hangers-on at the château, unwilling to do honest work, what sin it would be to support such indolence!

"Mammi knows she's welcome to live here," Albrecht said. "She would have everything taken care of; everything, including doctors and so forth. It means she would have no expenses what-soever. I would continue her stipend, and she could dispose of it as she wished. Throw it down a bottomless rat hole, for all I care. That's what she's been doing all these years, anyway."

Albrecht paused, as if he wanted to elaborate, but held back. I was familiar with this subtle bribe my cousin proposed to his mother from time to time. It would have little effect on staving off the foreclosure Issten faced, even if she were willing to abandon her life at the château.

"Mammi forgets she's no longer young," Albrecht sighed. "She must think of retiring and being here, with me, where I can take care of her in her old age."

I watched Albrecht turn and fixedly stare beyond the darken-ing window. In the dim valley below, village lights were beginning to flicker against the massive blackness of the Tyrolean Alps. A long, glowing strip delineated the railway station, where a tiny electric engine moved back and forth, connecting up loaded freight cars from Albrecht's adjoining lumberyard. Gazing at the shut-tling silhouette of the toy-like train and listening to its distant, high-pitched whine, my cousin stroked his chin with the back of his hand, his eyes sadder than moments ago. It occurred to me that for the past forty years, this aging son had been waiting for Mammi to come back, to come back to him for good.

"She's about to lose the château," I ventured quietly.

Albrecht became agitated. "Ach, ja, yes!" He turned from the window and again faced me across the narrow table. The dark in the room deepened the lines in his face, reflecting the conflict within. "But there's nothing I can do! Even if I wanted to, there's nothing I can do. You know that, too."

I nodded. I understood by now how deeply my cousin felt about deflecting funds from the property. It wasn't so much a matter of being parsimonious. As far as Albrecht was concerned, he was merely the steward of the land. This meant he didn't really own the Schloss and the land, but held it in trust from God. It was his moral duty to preserve and improve the estate, regardless of what personal pain this might cause him.

Remembering my promise to Issten, I nevertheless pressed on. "All it would take to meet your mother's debts," I ventured, in a low-key way, almost as an aside, "is less than one percent of the value of your estate."

I immediately felt the impact of my words. That invisible barrier abruptly dropped into place, surrounded by electrified barbed wire and mines. *"Ausser Frage!"* Albrecht exclaimed with threatening certitude. He flashed me a look that for an instant lit up the room as if I had set off one of those protective mines. He repeated, "Out of the question!"

I had been feeling him out and wasn't surprised. I realized I would have no choice but to employ a strategy I had carefully prepared over the past several days. "Let's talk about the ultimate issue," I began, in a friendly and relaxed way. "We've been through a lot, you and I. I think we understand each other as well as any two people. I hope I don't sound out of line, but I've got to tell you this, as I see it, and almost . . . well, almost as if God was prodding me, the way you say he often does. The ultimate issue isn't the Schloss or the land, but something you understand far better than I. How can you, or I, or anyone attain the eternal life that you yourself say is our one overwhelming purpose on earth?"

I paused to gauge Albrecht's response. I didn't feel hypocritical for resorting to this ploy. I was merely taking advantage of a tactic integral to my PR work, deploying words to evoke a desired effect. And I had in this case an especially worthy cause. I was trying to save an old lady from financial ruin, and help my cousin, who was getting on in years, from dying with guilt on his mind. Perhaps by the time I reached Albrecht's age, I might become genuinely interested in salvation myself.

Peering through the dimness of the room, I detected the first results of my approach. Albrecht seemed transfixed, as if I had succeeded in getting past a watchtower he had neglected to man.

I leaned forward in my chair to be still closer to where Albrecht was sitting in the dark. "I know how painful the situation at the château is for you," I resumed, intent on not losing momentum. "The question you have to decide is this: What will serve your ultimate purpose best? Keeping the property intact or pursuing commandment number six? Or is it commandment seven? I'm not too up on the numbers, but the one about honoring your parents, which I know you have always tried to obey. I could also refer to other Christian principles, like loving your half-sister and those nephews, and helping them, as if you were helping Christ himself. But that's compounding the issue. I guess it's really a toss-up between that commandment and the estate. I'm sure you understand . . . I mean about eternal life and so forth . . . far better than I. I feel presumptuous just bringing it up."

I discerned a further transformation in Albrecht's barely visible face. It was as if he no longer wished to resist my words. I seemed to be articulating what had been on his mind all along, perhaps for years.

"Right now, you're in an enviable position," I pressed on. "You have a choice. You can decide. It's up to you. But you won't always have that choice. Who knows how long your mother will live? And once she's no longer here, you'll no longer have that choice to help your mother out, to give her that loan. Can you imagine what it would mean to wish forever to undo what no longer can be undone? Never mind eternity; just having to live with that every day here on earth would be difficult enough."

My eyes never left Albrecht's, which glistened in the dark. "I remember your mother telling me how one must always be prepared to suffer, to suffer, and to suffer," I continued, trying to infuse each word with Issten's grandly eloquent tones. "What is life if not to do what one absolutely must?"

As we sat silently in the dark, I suddenly realized there was nothing separating us, not even the lack of light. I was within those sacrosanct walls Albrecht had been so zealously guarding.

He was nodding slowly, as if agreeing with everything I had just said. "Yes, ja, ja, you're right. My God, you're right. I remember on his deathbed, my father told me, 'Take care of Mammi because she'll never do it on her own.' Those were his last words." Albrecht paused to reflect on that final scene, momentarily helpless to blink back the tears as his mind spanned everything that had happened in the many years since. "I've tried, I've tried. God only knows how I've tried."

I was beginning to feel guilty for trespassing too long on Albrecht's most private domain. I knew it would take time if he were to change his mind, and there was nothing I could do but withdraw with grace. This I did after an appropriate pause by switching the conversation to Albrecht's favorite theme, especially at moments such as these, when he could look out from his darkened room and see stars filling the heavens above the black outline of the Tyrolean peaks: How to reorient the axis of the universe?

Both of us seemed relieved by the change.

8/

"Reorient the universe? I think Albrecht must be going gaga," Father said, when I phoned him from New York shortly after returning to the United States. "If Albrecht had to make a living, he wouldn't have time for such stupidities."

Father had reached the seventy mark. He still lived on the Massachusetts farm and sold Exercycles throughout New England. He earned enough to be comfortable and was the company's senior distributor in length of tenure as well as age. His most effective sales technique was to heft the unwieldy 135-pound machine up a flight of stairs into the master bedroom of a prospect's home without being winded. Straightening up from the familial stoop, he would then casually reveal his age. Father enjoyed his life, including the old habit of ogling every attractive woman in his path. His one disappointment was that I hadn't yet produced a child, preferably a son, especially after all he had done to endow me with the proper genes. "I don't understand why you're wasting your time fooling around with Stephanie. Whatever you have with her, it's not leading to anything. Before you know it, you'll be too old to even ee-yaculate," Father observed tartly during another of our weekly conversations on the phone. "I'll have to concentrate on your younger brother now. At twenty-six, Tom should be ready soon."

Mother, for her part, felt sufficiently represented for posterity by the eleven offspring produced by my older brother and two younger sisters. Drained of the robust beauty that forty years ago had captivated Father on the tram, Mother was marked with deep worry lines and had a deformed arthritic thumb. From time to time she cautioned me about remaining alone into old age.

I had by no means given up on having a family, and above all, finding the woman of my dreams. One reason I had remained unencumbered was to save myself for such a magical occasion. I had a vivid picture of what it would be like; how she and I would merge into an inseparable unity and live in a special dimension of our own. It would be the most passionate encounter of all, somehow extended into perpetuity.

I had been involved in a number of these dreamlike affairs, some lasting a matter of hours, others stretching to weeks and months. But I always managed to wake up before binding myself in some inextricable way, though I wasn't always the one to wake up first. Take the case of the exquisite, intelligent shoe heiress from Saint Louis, who had an affinity for Pucci prints and Louis Vuitton purses and could spend hours shopping at Bergdorf Goodman with unflagging zest. The instant we became serious, she succumbed to an irrational, all-consuming fear; that as my wife, she would immediately have to go to work behind the soda counter at Woolworth's. She could already see herself fixing malted milks and BLTs on toast, wiping crumbs and spills off the Formica countertops and scooping up nickels and dimes left as tips. There was no way to allay her fears; no way to convince her that she had more than enough money of her own, and that no matter what the situation, she could certainly keep her present job as a travel writer for Condé Nast.

But I knew what she meant. Even if I appeared affluent, I was far from rich. My starting salary at the Institute had hardly nudged despite the results of my public relations policies. I had obtained extensive coverage in most of the major newspapers and national magazines, including spreads in *Seventeen, Family Circle,* and *Parade.* The full-page article in *Parade* alone was worth over $50,000 in advertising space. The editor, Jess Gorkin, appended the Institute's address, which brought in more than 3,000 leads. This level of exposure in the media had the additional effect of spurring interest among several powerful conglomerates in acquiring the company.

"Don't forget, it's *our* company," my friend the owner reminded me over an after-dinner brandy in the library of his twenty-room suburban estate, where he had recently moved from a more modest house. "When the deal is sealed, we'll all be rich. In the meantime, it's to our advantage to show low salaries."

I didn't mind postponing my plans. When the right time came, I had ample reason to believe I would find that woman of my dreams, turndowns such as that by the shoe heiress notwithstanding. I liked to comfort myself with the thought of how many prospective brides, or ideal partners for affairs, could be found in New

York merely in the seven choice blocks on Fifth Avenue between Tiffany's and Saks. My early training on the streets of Prague had not been in vain. Though no longer resorting to a bump or a nudge, I still couldn't pass by an attractive woman without a glance, if not actually turning my head or even changing direction. Thanks to my keen vision, a willingness to risk being rebuffed and a spontaneous approach, my habit continued to yield sufficient rewards (in that pre-AIDS era) to become ever more deeply in-grained.

For street encounters of this sort, it was essential to exude a special confidence. A suntan from some tropical isle in the middle of winter undoubtedly helped. No less important was wearing a custom-made suit from Morty Sills. Morty cut his suits to empha-size the best contours of a customer's shape, with double vents pinching the waist and peak lapels flaring the chest. What a dif-ference from that boxy Brooks Brothers style, whose main re-deeming grace was to drape amorphous or paunchy bodies with the traditional Ivy League look. Morty gave you four buttons on each sleeve (just like that labor-intensive tailor in Hong Kong), with handcrafted buttonholes that actually worked. These were more of a secret status symbol than the Rolex Oyster Perpetual watch I had recently picked up in the tax-free shop of the Zurich airport. At chic parties, I would see people with such buttonholes, if not speaking to each other, at least eyeing each other with re-spect. And in the pockets of my suit, while striding along New York City streets, I made a point of always having several dollar bills to hand out to beggars, whose show of gratitude would make me feel like a king.

Radiating that confident glow and sporting a Morty Sills suit, let's say I am on my favorite turf, those few choice blocks on Fifth Avenue. Along comes a raven-haired beauty, elegantly slim, carry-ing what looks like a shoebox in a Charles Jourdan shopping bag. The variable-speed approach will determine whether or not to initiate an interview. This means positioning myself sufficiently close as I walk down the street, and slowing down and speeding up so that I can inconspicuously gain the necessary input to form an all-around image. A frontal once-over is best performed at a pedestrian light by turning sideways as if to check for oncoming cars. Good peripheral vision is a must. All this time, the intricate maneuvering has provided ample opportunity to devise a spontaneous approach. Anything short of an original ploy could result in a frigid stare or even an official call for help. Fortunately, in the case of this prospect with the Charles Jourdan box, I have noticed a unique opening. She seems to be uncomfortable as she walks; obviously, she's wearing the shoes she has just bought, with her old ones in that box. As I again edge myself impersonally alongside her in the crush of the afternoon rush hour crowd, I suddenly turn to her and catch her off-guard. "Excuse me, I couldn't help but notice," I say with concern, "your left shoe is killing your foot." I pause, while she glances at me as if I have uncovered an embarrassing secret. She doesn't know whether to be angry or to laugh. So I give her time, at least a few steps more, before saying, "I really wouldn't have brought it up, except I think I can help. It's in the heel, isn't it?" Reluctantly she nods and gives me a skeptical look. We're now rounding the corner at Tiffany's, and I step out of the mainstream of the sidewalk crowd. "Over here!" I say firmly, and motion her to join me in the little alcove by the service door. She hesitates an instant, but then impulsively makes the move and ends up standing next to me. I quickly bend down and gently grab her heel. "Hurts right there, doesn't it?" Then I straighten up. "What you have to do is to raise your heel inside the shoe. Last week, I had the same thing happen to me with a new pair of Church's English shoes. Hmm, do you happen to have a Kleenex?" When she shakes her head, I pull a handkerchief out of the pants pocket of my Sills suit with a diplomatic stripe that is three quarters of an inch from line to line. "Now," I say, bending down once more and folding the handkerchief into a little square, "I have to take off your shoe. Here, hold onto my arm . . . "

One point I should clarify: by no means did I think of myself as a lover endowed with exceptional attributes or irresistible technique. Ever since my affair with Avis, I had learned not to take as absolute truth the accolades from any woman under the spell of passion or love. Moreover, I had the dubious talent of being able to rise or fall to whatever level the situation seemed to demand. While some of my relationships had evolved with the spontaneous excitement of a dream, I have to confess there were times when I acted like an out-of-control teenager attempting to secure a strategic position. I might on such occasions lunge or otherwise try to get close, despite an intuitive feeling from the start that my date wasn't favorably predisposed. This usually happened with prospects I didn't truly like, making me reproach myself afterwards for having even tried, in the parlance of day, *to put the make* on this date.

Incidents of this sort, though incomparably rare, would temporarily disrupt the image I had of myself and tried to project to my friends, which wasn't entirely accurate in other ways, too. While I never was one for collecting feathers in my cap, as Avis claimed, I didn't actively discourage others from thinking I was more of a Lothario than was the case. Yet I probably averaged no more than two or three liaisons per year, including the briefest encounters, and some of those I would just as soon have skipped. Not only that Kaohsiung mercenary, who was merely trying to survive and could hardly have been expected to look out for the long-term interests of a partly irrational customer. Indeed, I had been exposed to post-debutantes listed in the Social Register who harbored germs no less hardy than hers. Take that stunning young woman I met in the street, carrying the Charles Jourdan box. She turned out to be in the Chicago version of the Book, and her father was a high-ranking White House adviser to President Lyndon

Johnson. Even before I had a chance to do anything more than take her to a two-hour lunch, this young beauty had to be rushed for emergency surgery to relieve a fulminating pelvic infection. The doctors excised both of her ovaries, and she was happy to be alive when I visited her in a flower-bedecked private room at New York University Hospital. As I eventually found out, her malady was due to a long-neglected multiplication of those microscopic assailants that cause VD.

Unlike in the foregoing case, I didn't always emerge unscathed. Suffice it to say I had occasion to become acquainted with "Big Stick" Beneventi, a top New York urologist who carried his nickname with pride. It derived from his treatment of choice, which he administered with a long metal probe as thick as a fountain pen and shaped like a J. He would plunge it deep into the tiny opening at the tip of the affected part, then give it a quick twist and a turn. The idea was to rouse out any of those noxious invaders lurking in the soft nooks and crannies along the path of this searing probe. They would then start pouring out in veritable armies, looking like thick ribbons of yellow, especially the following morning after getting into formation all night.

Despite the omnipresent worry about picking up or passing along some insidious bug, I wasn't about to abandon my romantic quest. And despite the disclaimer of my amorous potential, I did pride myself on having a certain talent or feel, perhaps akin to the way I could intuitively concoct a salad dressing from random ingredients, adding and mixing and tasting until I knew I had brought them to their potential peak.

I had an ideal venue for putting this sensitivity to use. For starters, I was now a member of Le Club. The dim lights and continental ambiance of this superb place to dine — where adventurous women in chic gowns were romanced to slow music on a small dance floor by mysterious men in custom-made suits with four buttons and real buttonholes on each sleeve — made seduction almost inevitable on the first date. Moreover, I had moved out of the communal brownstone to an apartment of my own, an expansive studio on the twentieth floor in a new building right off Park Avenue and on the same block as Bloomingdale's. It was painted burgundy red and had a queen-sized brass bed, soft velvety furniture, a couple of Bokhara rugs on loan from home, and enough potted palms strewn around to tempt any new interviewee to stay awhile and demonstrate what she could do as a bride.

It was in my new apartment that I most liked to entertain. Le Club was fine for a one-time initial splurge. If that failed to advance a relationship, probably nothing would – not to mention that I couldn't have sustained a lengthy campaign at Le Club until my bonus from the Institute's prospective sale came through. But money wasn't the only consideration. In my burgundy red studio, I could at the most propitious time discreetly display my physique, which I had worked hard to keep in shape since buying that barbell set with the knurled, chrome-plated revolving sleeve. By far the greatest advantage of being at home was that I could engage without restraint in both of my favorite activities at once, sometimes intensified by a few drags on a powerful joint. This would make everything super-sensuous, especially the two-pound Maine lobsters with hot garlic butter and the 1935 bottles of Saint Estèphe I could buy as a special for eight dollars a bottle at Surrey Liquors just a few blocks away. I realized even then, somewhere in the back of my mind while sipping this wine, that it would one day be selling for five hundred dollars a bottle or more. Thank heavens not enough people had this awareness yet! To think that the grapes had been picked in France the same year I was born by some squat, rosy-cheeked farmer with garlic breath who may have long since died! Yet, that wine had continued his work, changing from within, maturing on its own. Life in its highest form would rarely mellow that evenly for so many years – and was much more likely to end up spoiled.

What often did me in was a dessert I invented: a quart of rum-raisin ice cream from a new, then little-known company called Haagendazs, whipped up in a blender with a bottle of vintage Sauternes. I could easily gobble down the entire batch without help from my date. This invariably resulted in waking up before dawn, head groggy and stomach so full of acid I was afraid to turn on my side and risk having the corrosive liquid slosh around. That's when I forced myself to go for a run in Central Park, usually several miles, still in the dark. By the time I returned, I would be feeling light- footed and pleasantly relaxed, purged of those painful devils within. I would buy an early edition of *The New York Times*, then go back to bed for a couple of hours of contented sleep, knowing what I could look forward to: breakfast, the *Times*, and my enthusiastic friend, in whatever order that might turn out to be. On the grand scale of human existence – in terms of the billions of people who had ever lived or were now living on earth – I felt I was enjoying at least a thousand times the pleasures allotted to a normal life. I considered that an accomplishment and a distinction of which I had every reason to be proud.

9/

Despite my frequent visits to Albrecht's Schloss and the special relationship I enjoyed with the host, I was in no way exempt from a strict rule that applied to every guest: no overt discussion of sex. It was a taboo subject in any explicit form and could precipitously lead to a fall from grace, especially if such a discussion happened to pertain to His Grace, the Fürst.

Not that I remained ignorant of my long-widowed cousin's intimate habits. The most revealing details came from Albrecht's brother, Ferdinand, whose visits to the Schloss sometimes coincid-

ed with mine. Though almost as old as Albrecht and equally conservative in many of his views, Ferdinand had an open, cherubic
face and freely admitted to the family tendency for indulging the
flesh. Years ago in Vienna, before we'd ever met, I had pointed
him out to Stephanie on a busy street – a face in the sidewalk
crowds that looked strikingly familiar. "It ought to be," Stephanie
exclaimed, "it's Uncle Ferdinand!" He had inherited no vast estates, since everything of that sort went to the eldest son. But
Ferdinand lived in a comfortable apartment in Hietzing, a pleasant suburb of Vienna, where his brother visited him once or twice
a year. It was during these visits that Albrecht occasionally succumbed to one-night trysts with various professionals beckoning
from the dimly lit alleys off the city's luxurious Kärntnerstrasse.
"My brother always tried to pick up the cheapest merchandise on
the street, though he'd certainly want to get his money's worth,"
Ferdinand told me, with the typical relish of one member of the
family revealing the silly secrets of another behind his back. "I
remember the girls once took us to a fleabag hotel with very thin
walls. I could hear my brother in the adjoining room sounding like
a grand old stag. I must say he seemed to go at it with quite some
gusto most of the night. But when we met the next day at the Mo-
zart Café for breakfast, he was terribly silent, almost in a daze.
Finally he said to me in a funereal voice, 'Can you imagine, I gave
that whore two hundred schillings. Ach, two hundred schillings!'"
Ferdinand shook his head. "Typical of my brother to have his fun
ruined over a few dollars."

Although I laughed, I wasn't surprised. I could appreciate Albrecht's distress over this unauthorized expenditure from the estate entrusted to him by God. In this respect, I understood my
cousin better than did his brother.

Such mercenaries of the streets had not been Albrecht's sole relief. From what Stephanie had told me in the past, her father preferred to satisfy his needs with a woman who had once been a

friend of his departed wife and now lived in Canada. That she was on the unattractive side helped Albrecht justify the affair over the years. How could anyone think he would have picked her if pleasure was his goal? This woman had helped care for his wife in her most difficult days – surely a lifetime debt! Moreover, there was no visible exchange of funds, no quid pro quo, although the amounts Albrecht spent for her occasional visits to the Schloss would have kept several of the more expensive streetwalkers in Vienna comfortably fixed.

Then Albrecht met Elizabeth, while taking a cure in the hot springs of Bad Gastein for an arthritic joint. Albrecht indulged in such pampering (yet continued to ignore his mother's appeals to take care of her swollen feet) because the pain had affected his shooting arm, which was an indispensable adjunct for enforcing God's will among his deer. Still, my cousin thought it only right to stay at one of the cheaper hotels at the luxurious spa. That's where the vigorous and attractive fifty-year-old Elizabeth happened to be staying with her spouse, a graying professor of medieval history residing in a pleasant Munich suburb.

They started out as partners in chess; soon, as I could see for myself, Elizabeth's husband of more than twenty years considered it an honor to deliver his wife to the Schloss, himself spend the weekend there, then leave Elizabeth behind for an indeterminate time. The pretext continued to be the interest she shared with her host in chess, which they played after dinner in the main drawing room on the second floor in the presence of other guests. Although Elizabeth also accompanied Albrecht on his mountain treks – and they often went alone – she consistently slept on the third floor rather than in one of the more convenient guestrooms on the floors below. That would have placed her incriminatingly close to Albrecht's quarters on the lowest floor. My cousin in no way exempted himself from the rule that living in a castle was like living in a glass house. His objective was the opposite of Kurt Jurgens, his movie-star look-alike: everything for Albrecht had to be kept hidden in the dark.

Thus it remained, even though other guests were unexpectedly awakened in the middle of the night by the purposeful stride of the Fürst's slippered feet, making his way up the main staircase with the same gait as when mounting a steep hill in quest of a stag. The loudest commotion occurred on Elizabeth's top floor on opening and closing the stairwell door. Fashioned by hand centuries ago of wood and glass, the door would clatter resoundingly at the merest touch. About an hour later, another reverberation marked the end of Albrecht's tryst. Then it was back down the three flights of stone steps, deftly avoiding the protruding antlers and horns from trophies covering the darkened stairwell walls. In his nightshirt and nightcap, which he still wore, Albrecht played the noisy ghost once or twice a week. This charade, as far as I could figure out, wasn't for Frau Kunst's benefit, whom no one could fool; nor out of deference to the absent husband, whose tacit blessing the affair obviously had; nor was it solely an attempt to deceive other guests. This went on even when I happened to be the only one there, and Albrecht wouldn't have bothered to be so discreet just for me. It really was for Albrecht's own peace of mind. Such a limited encounter was what my cousin could best justify, not unlike his passive use of the telephone. He considered himself no more compromised than when he walked across the hall to Frau Kunst's quarters to accept a call.

"Pappi's such a hypocrite!" Stephanie laughed. "He believes as long as you do it in the dark, it doesn't count. He also likes to make a big thing about not marrying again. Supposedly it's on my behalf because any entanglement could break up the estate."

"Another sacrifice?" I suggested.

"He doesn't fool me. I think he's too cheap to get married, though in this case I'm not about to urge him."

The location of the Institute's overseas headquarters in London made it easy to visit Stephanie. It was more than three years since she left Munich, and I knew her second marriage wasn't going well. She and Jonathan were drifting apart, if only by default. Slim and pallid, the young man was still waiting for his musical talents to be recognized. His nightclub engagements as a singer-guitarist were fewer and further apart. He whiled away his nights with friends, smoking hash in the avant-garde places around town. During the day he slept.

"Don't ever marry, Onkel dear," Stephanie warned me in her cramped Chelsea flat, paid for from the small trust fund she had. "The first biggest mistake I made was marrying husband number one. He was a consummate bore. The second biggest mistake was marriage number two. Jonathan turned out to be no better than Hansi and has no money on top of that. Thank God he isn't around much," she said, pouring me afternoon tea from an elegant sterling silver service I recognized from her Widenmayerstrasse days. "Husbands, alas, have an uncanny way of turning into a pain, like a toothache that won't go away. I'm sure, so do wives. Let's face it, Onkel dear, marriage isn't for people like you and me."

"How about little Hansi? You never did change his name."

"Why get the child confused? He was already too old to be suddenly called something else."

"I guess it's a confusing situation," I said, taking a sip of tea. "Frau Kunst keeps telling me how much little Hansi resembles *der Onkel*. She always gives me this mysterious wink. I'm never sure what to think. Does she mean I'm endowed with an abundance of the same family genes as the mother? Or does old Frau Kunst suspect that my share of the family genes was somehow combined with the mother's to produce this remarkable resemblance?"

"Good old Frau Kunst," Stephanie said lightly. "Her darkest secret is that she had a child at fifteen and had to give it up. I don't know what Pappi would do without her."

"About little Hansi . . ." I persisted.

Stephanie put down her cup. "I wish I could tell you he's yours. You certainly understand me better than anyone. But little Hansi has a weird blood type, not at all like you and me."

I knew Stephanie wasn't eager to pursue the matter. She didn't mind the reputation of being impetuous and romantic, which she gained from that contested fatherhood. But a three-way dispute could lead people to an altogether different – and erroneous – conclusion. I was almost certain Stephanie had made love to no more than half-dozen men in her life, including the two she married and one premarital crush. This may have been shocking a few years back, but it was hardly a cause for raised eyebrows in the late 1960s. Our own affair started within minutes of when we first met in New York with a light brush of the lips, which had a startlingly intoxicating effect beyond anything relatives were supposed to feel. The affair reached its peak that summer at Stephanie's Widenmayerstrasse home: two hours of blissful energy exchange on weekdays after lunch while baby Diana was taking her nap, Hansi was back at his office, and Frau Trepper had gone out to buy groceries, though only after frustrating delays and volleys of darting, suspicious glances as if Stephanie and I were about to commit some heinous crime. (Fortunately, Stephanie was right, and Frau Trepper never abbreviated her daily rounds of a half-dozen specialty stores.) The affair gradually tapered off into a sort of pleasurable occasion, not unlike a fine meal or a massage at a gym, limited to the summer months I spent in Europe and the week Stephanie was in New York in connection with Hansi's semi-annual undercoating trip. The confusion concerning little Hansi required no special malice or excessive license on Stephanie's part. It happened when she met her future husband for the first time during her two-day stopover in London, and then continued with Hansi to New York, where she didn't want to frustrate my expectations. Stephanie wasn't the type to leave her Onkel hungry just because she had unexpectedly feasted the previous day. It turned out to be one of the last times before that aspect of our relationship was phased out for good. But who would believe this relatively tame account if any questions about little Hansi's paternity were to be raised now?

I didn't, in fact, mind Stephanie's indifference to pursuing further genetic tests. During those divorce proceedings, I worried that someone might suggest drawing a sample of my blood. Then as now, I feared the implications of finding out. To think I was to blame for the scandal Albrecht had taken so heavily to heart! I might also have had to assume some fatherhood role and offer child support rather than watch others pay the bills — a secret fear that shamed me even then. Yet, I did take a quiet satisfaction in recognizing in the six-year-old the same passive, cheerful personality as I had shown at that age. When I first arrived at Stephanie's flat, the boy had given me an unusually curious look; then, with his little index finger, he distinctly traced the bump and cleft on my nose, and with a self-satisfied smile, did likewise to his own.

"Don't forget," Stephanie now said, "my nose is unfortunately a little that way, too. All it proves is we're related."

"I guess only Frau Kunst knows for sure," I joked.

"I certainly hope she doesn't go blabbing her suspicions," Stephanie said with a touch of concern. "Pappi would have a fit. Once is enough."

"Afraid he might disinherit you after all?"

Stephanie shrugged. "Who knows what Pappi might do? He'd never leave the Schloss to little Hansi, but he might to Angelina. That wouldn't be too bad having my daughter inherit, except that her father would always be showing up at the wrong time." Stephanie compressed her lips in mock disappointment, the corners of her mouth momentarily curving downwards. Then she laughed contemptuously. "But I'm not worried. I don't think deep inside Pappi likes silly old Hansi, either."

"Poor Hansi," I sighed. "He's always such a good host when I'm in Munich."

"Poor Hansi!" Stephanie mimicked. "That's all I hear. I hear it even from Angelina, 'Poor Daddy!' She's living with him, so I can understand that. What worries me more is how Pappi is always filling her head with all that stuff about *good* girls and heaven and God. Maybe that's because he suspects that my little angel is getting to be a little bit of a devil. I'd hate to see her become all screwed up." Stephanie paused then brightened up. "I think I've finally figured out what Pappi means by God's punishment. You know that child Hansi had before he married me? Well, I think I was God's punishment on Hansi for not accepting the boy. Doesn't it make sense?"

I couldn't resist. "And Jonathan has been God's punishment on you?"

Stephanie looked puzzled for a moment, but then nodded and laughed. "Sometimes it certainly feels that way. Now, more tea, Onkel dear?"

From what I would later reconstruct, at virtually the same time as Stephanie and I were speculating lightheartedly in her Chelsea flat about God's wrath, Albrecht was making the most difficult decision of his life. From the outset of his deliberations, Albrecht had firmly established that he would *not* leave the property to Stephanie and, as she had correctly surmised, not to little Hansi either. Yet after additional months of agony, he resolved to rule out Angelina as well. All three would be provided for in his will. The Schloss and the surrounding forests, however, would go to somebody who could be trusted to do the job; who wouldn't cause scandals or pursue selfish ends. Angelina was indeed innocent and pure, and she still hugged Opapa goodnight with the unalloyed affection of a child. Yet at seven, she was already acquiring some of the beguiling characteristics of her mother. Who could guarantee that this angel wouldn't follow in Stephanie's steps, and in not too many years cause a monumental scandal of her own?

That's how Albrecht came to adopt Andreas, his brother's only son. It should have been done in the first place, Albrecht reasoned, in line with the old imperial law – and still-honored tradition – of restricting inheritance to males, no matter how distantly related. Never again would he allow his emotions to sway him in an irresponsible way!

At nineteen, Andreas was a shy and awkward youth who had a tendency to turn beet red whenever speaking or spoken to. The previous year at a big dinner in the formal dining room at the Schloss, little Angelina had taken note of this fact. Sitting on Albrecht's left, she glanced at Andreas at the other end from his uncle, then asked, "Why do you always become so red when you speak?" Instant silence ensued as the dozen guests turned toward Andreas, at which point Angelina exclaimed, "Now, you've become even redder!"

Albrecht liked to recall that he too had been bashful in his youth, and he considered it to be an advantage in life. (Andreas, in fact, looked more like his uncle Albrecht than his own father with the cherubic face.) But what Albrecht especially valued were his nephew's parsimonious ways. Andreas would surely never beguile him into expenditures that would unnecessarily burden the estate. No more frivolous remodeling of the Schloss, especially the pale blue ceiling full of gilded stars that so brazenly trivialized God's firmament, and the odorless plumbing that so wastefully replaced toilets not even fifty years old. Andreas seemed content with a three-year- old Deux Chevaux, the least expensive of cars. And he had already proved himself worthy of Albrecht's trust in terminating a relationship with a young woman whose parents harbored leftist views. The young man had instead directed his attentions to Elizabeth's fifteen-year-old Tasha from the very first time her mother brought her to the Schloss. Albrecht's feelings for Elizabeth promised to eliminate the risk of having to endure some hypothetical in-laws he might not like; perhaps even some socialists, who were becoming so tastelessly vocal in the country's affairs. *What a providential match*, Albrecht thought. *Maybe Andreas would at last break the curse on the women in the family.*

"Anyway, I think he's quite courageous to say openly he intends to do so," Albrecht concluded, when he shared with me the rationale for his decision. "I mean, to break that curse."

It was the end of August. I was spending a couple of weeks at the Schloss after a hectic summer of nonstop traveling since seeing Stephanie in London. In addition to my regular PR work, I had been directing a promotion film about the Institute's programs throughout Europe. I could use the rest before returning to New York for the editing phase.

"You will, of course, always be welcome at the Schloss," Albrecht said as an afterthought. I was sitting next to him in his five-year-old yellow Taunus, and we were driving along a narrow dirt road winding around a steep mountain on his property. Carved out by my cousin's construction crews, the road was used to transport timber out of the harvested area. Albrecht was on his way to check how his new bulldozer was progressing farther up on the hill. About a hundred yards behind us in the dust, following in the Deux Cheveaux, was Andreas with Tasha, the demurely luscious teenager destined one day to become his wife.

It was a peculiar ride. Considering the condition of the road and the lethal drop into the majestic valley below, Albrecht was moving at a fair clip through the sharp curves. He had an unconscious way of driving, due to his reluctance to acknowledge modern technology, and it was hard to tell whether he was fully in control. But I was accustomed to that. What surprised me was how he deliberately slowed down on the straightaways to glance repeatedly in the rearview mirror. Only when the Deux Chevaux reappeared behind us from around the curve did he speed up again.

"Afraid of losing the future heir over the side?" I joked.

Albrecht's intense demeanor didn't change nor did he respond, and we continued down the straightaway in silence.

"Well, do you think it will work?" I finally asked.

"Ach, the bulldozers up ahead?"

"I mean this thing between Tasha and Andreas."

"Why shouldn't it?" Albrecht retorted. His voice had the same edge as when he suspected I was challenging his theories about the universe. "I have absolute confidence it will work. How could it possibly not work?"

"Things aren't always what they seem," I said, keeping my response deliberately vague. Albrecht was about to whip into another unprotected curve, and I didn't want to disturb his concentration. If I were to share with the Fürst my concern about his chosen heir, we might be the ones to roll down that mountainside. I knew Andreas well enough to recognize he was afflicted by many of the same characteristics as Stephanie and I. Why, he even had the same susceptibility to Sodbrennen! Wasn't Albrecht mistaking his nephew's lack of opportunity for self-restraint? As a student whose father wasn't rich, how extravagant could Andreas be? Moreover, I was privy to some startling insights concerning his intended-for-life. During the past several days at the Schloss, this remarkably mature *Gymnasium* student had found opportune moments to slip into the privacy of my room and display her intimate charms. Not that there was anything too entangling. We had only a few minutes before her absence might be ascribed to something other than heeding nature's call and prompt Andreas to embark on a Schloss-wide search. Flushed crimson, he often barged into my room just moments after Tasha had disappeared behind the connecting door to Stephanie's odorless toilet. Dashing through Stephanie's empty suite, Tasha made it back to the drawing room in time to await Andreas and resume their game of chess. What I learned from those brief visits was that the future mistress of the Schloss didn't lack a normal, calculating mind. She would hardly have given Andreas a second look had he been just another promising Forstmeister. For my benefit, Tasha contorted her face into a playful grimace to illustrate how she felt about the prospect of having to fulfill her marriage vows someday. But she knew how Andreas felt. Her satisfaction would come from being able to sway him to do whatever she wished; above all, to fill her life with precisely the sort of luxury and excitement her future father-in-law abhorred. She had already told me she couldn't understand why somebody in Andreas's position drove such a pathetic car; and more than once, she expressed admiration for Stephanie's suite as being exactly the way she would one day refurbish the entire Schloss.

"I have a responsibility," Albrecht interrupted my thoughts. He was starting to slow down after negotiating yet another curve. When the Deux Chevaux with the young couple reappeared in the rearview mirror, he speeded up. "Young people can never be completely trusted," Albrecht continued calmly, "but Andreas is sensible. He has proven it."

"Because he dropped that girl you didn't like? Her parents were socialists or something?"

"Communists, practically. That couldn't have worked. Not here at the Schloss. Andreas made the break before he had any inkling he would one day inherit. With his new responsibilities, I know I can expect from him even more."

"I understand she wasn't too attractive."

"Ach, that girl? Not at all! Not even superficially."

"Tasha certainly is."

Albrecht's response sounded curt. "That has nothing to do with it."

Since he was about to negotiate another curve, this wasn't the moment to point out the obvious: that until meeting Tasha, Andreas had refused to budge under the entreaties of both Albrecht and Ferdinand. Yet how deftly Andreas had dropped his controversial friend the instant Tasha came on the scene!

Albrecht was well out of the curve and again slowing down. The Deux Chevaux this time seemed to be taking especially long to appear. Seated next to me in his lederhosen shorts, Albrecht looked more and more anxious as he continued to peer into the rearview mirror. Finally, he stopped the car.

"Ach, I told Andreas he absolutely must not fall back more than one hundred meters!" Albrecht was staring in the mirror with the same zealous gleam as if stalking a stag. "Andreas must realize anything serious has to wait. Tasha still has two years in the Gymnasium and he needs two years to complete his *Matura* and earn his forestry degree. I'm not blind. I know sometimes he gets too eager with Tasha, and I intend to keep an eye on him. You can be sure of that."

The Deux Chevaux finally reappeared. The delay had hardly been caused by some wild romantic attempt. Having a respect for the technology his uncle disdained, Andreas had been more careful in the curves. It took the smaller car longer to accelerate, and no doubt Andreas also wanted to keep out of his benefactor's dust.

As Albrecht abruptly put his car in gear and let out the clutch, I stuck my head out the window and turned back to wave. Looking red-faced over the frustrating incident, Andreas continued to concentrate on the road. But Tasha put her hand out and waved.

Albrecht noticed the exchange and nodded. "Tasha is such a good girl. That's the reason I haven't really intervened. I know she wouldn't do anything that isn't right. Have you noticed her with Andreas, how reserved she is?"

I didn't say anything, since we were approaching another curve with a precipitous drop.

"For a young girl in love, that isn't easy," Albrecht continued with admiration, then sighed, "If only Stephanie could have been more like her. Think of what she would have spared me and herself too . . . especially God's wrath!"

All I could think of was how earlier that day in my room, the future mistress of the Schloss had so deftly disencumbered herself of her blouse.

10/

My public relations work in Europe was no longer restricted to the summer months. I took another lengthy trip in February to gather stories on students enrolled in the Institute's full-year programs based at various European universities and schools. This turned out to be arduous work. Some of the programs were new, with many problems yet to be resolved. The bleak midwinter atmosphere of big-city life, moreover, wasn't conducive to inspiring the kind of comments I needed for promoting the Institute. The students were more likely to gripe than to say anything positive. Even with the most receptive ones, I had to plead and cajole just to get them to write an article for a fee.

This hassling left me ready for a treat: a skiing vacation in Switzerland. I had just completed the final batch of those thankless interviews in Salzburg, where the Institute recently launched a home-stay program. I was drained by the double dose of complaints from students and host families. It was late in the evening, and I wanted to get out of there. I had a rental car and could safely manage the hundred-or-so kilometers to spend the night at the Schloss. It would then be easy to make the rest of the drive to Switzerland the following day.

After a quick telephone call, I was on my way. Although Albrecht was asleep when I arrived, I got up the next morning in time to join him for breakfast. Considering the brevity of my visit, I was glad to find him alone. This meant my cousin and I could have a relaxed chat.

I was enjoying my fifth slice of Frau Kunst's raisin-and-almond-studded *Stollen* when I noticed Albrecht glancing at me furtively. Sitting in his quarters at the table across from me in a frayed blue terry cloth robe, Albrecht smiled bashfully. "As a young man, I knew your dear uncle Sascha. He weighed more than a hundred kilos. You seem to have inherited his appetite."

"I take any such comparison as a compliment."

"Aren't you worried . . ." Albrecht didn't finish, reluctant to get physical. As with the lederhosen misunderstanding years ago, he shied away from being direct.

I helped him out. "That I'll get fat?"

"Well, one never knows, does one?" Albrecht observed, now deliberately impersonal. He let his eyes travel around his vaulted quarters, brightly lit by the early morning sun reflected from the snow- covered countryside. He poured himself another cup of coffee and methodically began to heap sugar into it.

I waited until he finished and began to stir. "You aren't exactly a practitioner of temperance," I pointed out. "That was six spoonfuls."

Albrecht shrugged. "Oh, really? I didn't notice."

"Well, I did. That's how many you always take. I rarely take more than two."

"Don't forget," Albrecht said smugly, "I'm climbing the mountains already for three hours before breakfast. Then I do another three hours in the afternoon. The deer and the forests take all my calories. I can imagine what kind of a life you lead in the United States."

"I work out at a gym for an hour four times a week and run a total of ten miles in Central Park."

"I cover at least ten miles each day."

"It's the intensity that counts."

"In America it's always the intensity. Everything all the time has to be stronger, more concentrated, newer, better."

"That's what makes the economy go."

"Ach, ja, yes, the economy. I'm afraid it's already happening here, too. Always tempting people into more sin."

"Do you want to go back to the cave?"

"Not at all!" Albrecht gulped down his coffee and started to refill his cup. "What I oppose is misleading people that a new fur coat, a new car, a new perfume can somehow change us for the better; even more ridiculous, that if we get enough of these things, they will somehow fulfill our ultimate yearning on earth." Albrecht sighed, then looked at me reproachfully. "I must tell you, you exercise for the wrong reason. You do it so you can have more pleasures. I do it so I can do the work of God. It isn't easy to care for the forests and deer. Especially the shooting arm must be healthy." Albrecht raised his right elbow and made a circular motion in the air. "This one, unfortunately, is becoming stiff."

"My purpose isn't entirely selfish," I pointed out. "I also like to bestow pleasure."

"Yes, ach ja, but that's worse. In our times there's already a great overindulgence. There's no virtue in giving an alcoholic a drink. That's the snake again tempting Eve."

"I like to think I'm a bit more versatile."

"It doesn't matter what the pleasure!" Albrecht exclaimed, momentarily agitated, but then continued in a more subdued, plaintive tone. "All pleasures are addictive, and in the long run, deadly. If not for the individual, then for society. The more people have, the less it means, so they want still more. Ach, what do you call it, a vicious circle? Your Puritans in America understood the dangers of pleasure. They weren't just a bunch of unreasonable fools."

I was tempted to remind Albrecht of his clandestine trysts with Elizabeth but settled for a safer retort. "I've personally seen pleasure dispel depression. Now doctors are discovering pleasure can cure even physical disease."

"Ach, ja, yes, that's true. Don't forget, pleasure once helped us survive . . . in primitive times, in great scarcity. But in our abundance, it only deceives us with benefits, though this deception is brief. In the long run, pleasure is deadly. It is almost exactly the same as low-level radiation. The individual doses seem harmless enough, but the damage accumulates. Eventually, a terrible selfishness results. The person becomes more and more like a heroin addict who is desperate to get a fix. That's when morality goes out the window." Albrecht shook his head. "Normally upstanding people are then ready to lie, to cheat, to steal. Ach, one hears of it more and more."

"In any case," I said, in a lighthearted way, "you don't see me getting fat."

"The point is not whether you get fat," Albrecht said somberly, "though there is a practical side to it also. This is that one day the world will go bankrupt. People, and now also governments, are borrowing and spending in a terribly irresponsible way. With all they have, they want still more. They forget they must inevitably pay it back."

"Yes," I nodded, then mimicked Issten, "if you get a loan, you have to pay it back!"

Albrecht glanced at me warily, and for an instant, our eyes met. He recognized the intonation and feared a thrust about his mother's financial plight. Quickly, he continued, "But the danger is still greater than moral and financial bankruptcy. The threat is to the *Universum.*"

Resisting the impulse to point out that my aunt's loans had at least been for selfless aims, I asked with appropriate gravity, "Oh, you mean because of all those dead electrons?"

Albrecht nodded. "Call it what you will," he said evenly, no doubt relieved to continue on this tack. "Your Robert Kennedy in America would like to become president. I could never vote for him, especially when he's in his sunglasses. Then he really looks like a Hochstapler. Terrible, terrible. But there's one thing true he says. *You can make a difference.* Yes, you can make a difference. I can make a difference. Each of us can make a difference. It isn't necessary to join the Peace Corps and go to Africa. The biggest difference will come if people deny themselves pleasures of their own free will. It's the same as when Stephanie bought herself the Fiat. I told her I was against it. I also told her I didn't want her to remodel the second floor. The pleasures have to be limited much, much sooner than when you get to marijuana and so on." Albrecht shrugged helplessly. "Yet what can you do when practically the whole *Wirtschaft*, the whole economy, is based on pleasure? Telling people there's a pleasure they can't have is again trying to tell Adam and Eve not to eat the apple."

"Don't expect Bobby Kennedy to tell them," I laughed. "If he runs, it'll be to get votes."

"Another thing he isn't telling people: Everybody already *is* making a difference." Albrecht paused to take a restrained sip of his coffee, then glanced at me significantly. "But it is a negative difference, and that is the real danger to the universe. People are making a negative difference by just being who they are . . . ach, always wanting more! That is original sin. In Paradise, Adam and Eve had everything, yet they wanted more! People today have forgotten that original sin exists."

Albrecht turned to gaze through the small recessed window directly at the alpine sun climbing over the snow-covered peaks. He didn't squint, nor did he blink, as he continued to sip his coffee.

"Yes, there will be a terrible price to pay," he resumed, as if in a trance. "It doesn't take much to unbalance everything. We're no different from Adam and Eve. They lost Paradise because they ate an apple from the forbidden tree. It was a willful act for which we're still paying the price, and all the time, we are repeating the act in still more irresponsible ways." Albrecht shook his head and turned to me, his unblinking eyes riveted onto mine. "Reorient the universe . . . that's our only hope!"

I didn't make it to Switzerland that day. A sudden March snowstorm closed the Reschenpass, as well as all other passes over the Alps, and I was forced to spend the night a few kilometers from the border. Fortunately, the local hotel had an unusually fine restaurant. After finishing a leisurely dinner with a *Nusstorte*, topped off with freshly whipped cream and washed down with what I had left of a liter bottle of a *Spätlese* Mosel, I felt I still had room for more. The nut cake had been excellent, moist and with a delicate flavor, and the wine had the bouquet of golden sun-ripened grapes. I was one of the last people in the restaurant, and the waitresses in their white paper tiaras were already spreading fresh linens for breakfast. When I asked if they had any more of that cake and was told yes, but it was a whole one and they didn't want to cut it up for one slice, I said I would take the entire cake. All eight slices. And another full bottle of that same nectar-like wine, *bitte*. Gradually, the dining room staff gathered at a respectful distance to see if I could manage it all. For a moment, I felt reincarnated in the guise of my legendary uncle Sascha, polishing off an entire goose half a century ago at some restaurant not too far from where I was sitting now. How sad he had died when he was only a little older than I, reduced to merely gazing at Marlene Dietrich's charms.

I smiled at the waitresses in their wilted tiaras as if to indicate an unwavering confidence. I knew that whatever Sodbrennen I might feel, whatever raging fires might engulf the cavity between my chest and waist, I would be able to recover on the slopes of Saint Moritz. That was the old exercise formulation I had by now learned to supplement with freshly squeezed juice of two oranges and a large grapefruit at breakfast. I would especially enjoy it because of the Italian blood oranges served in the Alpine hotels.

In Saint Moritz, I always stayed at the Palace, where the owner, Andrea Badrutt, would let me have one of his small *chambres sportives* with full board for what dinner alone at the Palace normally cost. Monsieur Badrutt had a half dozen such rooms and bestowed them on younger people who would add balance to the older clientele of Greek ship owners, New York socialites, and those relatives of the Shah who preferred the more ostentatious Palace to the privacy of the Suvretta House.

It would have been easy to succumb to the glamour and luxury of this resplendent hotel. While I did usually dally over a six-course meal till midnight, I resisted the temptation to walk down a flight of stairs to the King's Club disco, which would have taken up the rest of the night. My primary goal was to ski, and I felt compelled to be up in the morning for the first funicular to Corviglia at eight. Most of the people going at this hour were members of the ski patrol and employees of the mountaintop inns, carrying basketfuls of freshly baked baguettes and croissants, and cases of half-liter cartons of milk in the shape of inverted red-and-white cones. In the pinkish rays of the morning sun, I would wait with this assemblage for the ski lift doors to open, watching my breath condense and feeling the air bite my cheeks.

On reaching the upper slopes, I preferred to bypass the gondolas and chair lifts for the T-bars, so as to continue getting a workout even when being towed uphill. I would shift from hill to hill to be always facing the sun, and when not actually making a downhill run, I removed my sunglasses. I didn't want white circles forming around my eyes and giving me the look of a raccoon. I kept up this routine into the late afternoon, when the last warming rays disappeared beyond the silvery Alpine peaks as it suddenly turned crystal cold. I often rushed to make the last lift in the darkening bluish light, returning numb to the Palace at dusk.

Then came the biggest treat of the day. In the bathroom at the end of a wide corridor thickly carpeted in royal red (a chambre sportif had only a sink and a toilet) I immersed myself in the body-length bathtub filled to the top with steaming spring water. I liked to soak there until the heat was penetrating deep, banishing the cold stiffness and suffusing me with delicious warmth. After drying with one of the hotel's thick terry cloth robes, I shaved and splashed on Eau Sauvage, which would leave my face pleasantly tingly while bringing out the suntan from the rays absorbed during the day. I then slipped into a pair of strawberry-colored corduroy pants, a yellow cashmere turtleneck, and a soft blue blazer adorned with the same brass buttons that had once been on my naval officer's uniform. I invariably passed up the elevator, preferring to stroll down the two flights of the ornately balustered staircase, and then stopped at the concierge's desk to pick up the latest copy of the *International Herald Tribune*. I was now ready to make my entrance into the grand lobby for tea and for the delicious circle to start again.

If this was going in the wrong direction, as Albrecht claimed, I wouldn't have wanted to change it for anything in the world.

III. The Price to Pay

I felt on top of the world as I made my way among the early afternoon shoppers on Fifth Avenue. I had just left the protective
warmth of the intimate apparel department at Saks and was
headed toward Tiffany's and the luxurious 57th Street stores, surveying the scene as I moved along. It was an unusually bitter
end-of-March freeze, though the sun still shone brilliantly between
the tall buildings in the cloudless sky. Dazzling sparkles of light
reflected from the mounds of frozen snow piled along the edges of
the street. I felt so resilient that even without sunglasses I didn't
have to squint. I had by now discovered a practical rationale for
Albrecht's stance against unnatural shading of the eyes. Without
glasses, the chances of successfully initiating a spontaneous interview were considerably improved, since eye contact with the wary
prospect was essential for creating the necessary trust.

As I continued past Saint Patrick's Cathedral, several strangers in the street nodded and smiled as if to share in my well-being.
This catchy jauntiness didn't come solely from the midwinter tan
acquired in the Alpine sun. During the previous ten days in Saint
Moritz, my body had adjusted to the thin mountain air by manufacturing extra red blood cells. Now, at sea level on Manhattan's

streets, I was experiencing the euphoria of an oxygen high. I didn't even mind being approached for the second time by an inebriated derelict who spotted me as an easy touch.

The cold was more biting with each step. Especially between the blocks, the gusts of icy winds felt like stinging nettles whipped across my cheeks. Huddled in the warmth of a heavy cavalry overcoat I had picked up in London at Harrods's annual sale, I felt insulated against the cold; indeed, against human misfortune in any form.

I paused in front of Doubleday bookstore for a once-over of the best-sellers and new titles, then momentarily shifted focus from the elaborate display to my image in the glass of the store window. By glancing at this exuberant reflection as if it were somebody else – then reminding myself who it was – that oxygen high was reinforced.

Savoring this euphoric glow, I had barely resumed my recruiting jaunt when I stepped into a wrenching scene. Beyond a semicircle of stunned onlookers in the middle of the block, a frail elderly man was kneeling on a small curb jutting out from the base of the building, his inflamed nose only inches from the heavy stone façade. The pants of his tattered suit were rolled up so that his knees rested against the icy curb. He had on no overcoat, and the gusty frigid air was sending involuntary spasms through his emaciated frame.

Hovering over this wretch like a bird of prey was a chunky Korean. Dressed in a topcoat of heavy blue serge, a warm muffler around his neck, he was brandishing an open Bible and sporadically reading brief passages, which he then tried to get the derelict to repeat.

"Louder," the Korean urged him, "louder!"

The shivering penitent tottered in his upright kneeling position, then his rear collapsed against his heels. Right away his spiritual guide prodded him with his boot and pointed to a spot on the wall that was to serve as a marker for his nose. With a rough shove of his gloved hand, the Korean pushed the derelict's face until the tip of his bluish red nose was pressing against the icy stone.

I thought it almost indecent to look, as if I were peeking at a human's most private moments on earth. Surely this wretch wouldn't live out the day. His fingertips were white from being so tightly clasped in prayer. Racked with sobs, he was oblivious of the gawking crowd.

I pulled up the heavy collar of the cavalry coat over my ears. Feeling a slight shudder within, I figured it was time to move along. Get the blood circulating! I had been standing too long. I should be scanning the streets for the woman of my dreams.

Then I spotted something that made me pause. Vaguely discernible on each soiled sleeve of the penitent's threadbare jacket were four real, handcrafted buttonholes. My first thought was that the jacket was a hand-me-down provided by the Salvation Army. The way it hung from his skeletal frame, it could hardly have been custom-made. Yet I also realized that this crumpled coat may have once stylishly draped his unravaged frame. Was it possible that before his downward slide this derelict had been elegantly dressed in suits from Morty Sills?

I couldn't resist a step forward for a closer look. With his unkempt graying hair and patches of ulcerous skin, he appeared to be a generation older than I, though I suspected that no more than a few years separated us. Beneath his devastated exterior, I could detect vestiges of a life I understood. He might at one time have been a successful businessman, a lawyer, perhaps a clever executive in advertising or public relations. God, what despair had driven him up against this wall and made him submit to this bizarre contrition?

I was increasingly aware of the gathering crowd, kept at bay by the threatening glances of the Bible-wielding Korean. He had already warded off several sympathetic souls as they sought to ascertain from the penitent if they shouldn't call an ambulance. Most of the people around me were slowly and inconspicuously shoving, trying to move closer to take in the words and glean the macabre details. The way they were craning their necks reminded me of a scene at one of the farms near Albrecht's Schloss, where Frau Kunst obtained most of her eggs, milk, and other provisions. On this particular occasion, I had accompanied her to help bring back a suckling pig. We walked into the barn just as the farmer was grabbing the plumpest from a large litter. I saw him swiftly club the squealing unfortunate over the head, stunning it into unconscious silence, then hoist it up by its hind legs and slit its throat. Something about its life irreversibly spurting out seemed to trigger an emergency center in the piglet's brain. Though still unconscious, it began to squeal with a piercing cry. In response, the other piglets lined up in their stalls, their snouts curiously thrust in the air, yet somehow detached from what was happening to their littermate. It was as if they had an instinctive awareness on the periphery of their consciousness of the monumental import of what was taking place before their eyes. But feeling no pain, they couldn't make a meaningful connection with what would one day happen to them. This same puzzled fascination I now recognized on the faces of the crowd on New York's Fifth Avenue. They sensed they were witnessing something that could be of crucial personal import, yet they weren't capable of tying it in with their individual lives. The reason I knew how they felt was that I felt that way, too.

The scene toppled me from my oxygen high. Instead of continuing the delectable prowl toward Tiffany's, I went directly home. More than once on the way to my burgundy red apartment, I wondered, *Did that derelict's distress have something to do with the price Albrecht claimed we would all one day have to pay?*

2/

This wasn't the time to entertain maudlin thoughts. The American Institute for Foreign Study had just been sold, and I would finally be compensated for my role in the company's growth. The winning bid came from National Student Marketing — or NSM on the over-the -counter stock exchange — a fast-emerging conglomerate, whose projected earnings were based on satisfying the ever expanding array of student desires and needs. My employer-friend and his two partners walked away with three million dollars in cash, and some twenty-five million more in NSM stock.

My payoff amounted to a long-delayed three thousand-dollar annual raise, a yellow Camaro convertible for my exclusive use as a company car, and fifteen hundred stock options which I could exercise three years hence. While my friend didn't dispute that the publicity I had secured for the Institute markedly affected the amount he and his partners received, he rejected whatever reproaches I made about my paltry reward.

"I fought like the dickens to get you those options," he explained. "One day, they could be worth hundreds of thousands."

"I'll be glad to sell them to you for just a few thousand now."

"I don't want to deprive you . . . "

"I thought you said it was *our* company."

He shrugged. "I'm sorry you misunderstood. I gambled everything to start the Institute, including my house. What did you risk, by your own reckoning a mediocre job at Scholastic? Well, nothing ventured, nothing gained."

As disappointed as I was, especially since it was a friend who had let me down, my immediate concern was to safeguard the magazine articles already in the pipeline. In my ongoing communications with our benefactors in the media, I would have to be careful to give no hint that the Institute had been acquired by NSM. These writers and editors were willing to publicize the Institute because of its nonprofit designation. They might not feel the same about providing free space to a blatantly commercial conglomerate known for its glib young executives with private jets and yachts.

Fortunately, there was no need to resort to outright lies. The nonprofit Institute, at least technically, had not been sold. The three million dollars and all that stock had been paid for International Study Services, a little-known subsidiary into which the Institute had channeled its profits since day one. That's how the merger was reported in most of the financial press: "National Student Marketing Acquires International Study Services."

This little deception, alas, would not remain unexposed. The breach occurred when I stopped by to see Bob Fitzgibbon, editor in chief of *Family Weekly*, a Sunday newspaper supplement with the third-largest circulation in the United States after *Readers' Digest* and *Parade*. I phoned Bob's office earlier that day and learned that the proofs of his article on the Institute had just arrived.

"Looks great, Bob," I said, scanning the text and pictures. "I especially want to thank you for including the Institute's address."

"Glad I could be of help," Bob Fitzgibbon said with a gracious nod, as he sat coatless in his large, simply appointed office. An unassuming man with an open face, he reminded me of a Midwestern Grant Wood farmer-type who hadn't allowed big city life to add a single twist to his straightforward demeanor. "I consider providing the address as much a public service as the article. We want to let our readers know how they can participate."

"I'll keep you posted on the response."

Bob Fitzgibbon nodded. "I only wish there had been programs like this as I was growing up."

"When do you think I can see a final copy?"

"The presses are already rolling. It takes several days to complete the run. Our circulation is over eight million." Bob paused, then absently hiked up above each elbow the elastic bands that constrained the billowy sleeves of his white shirt. "Why don't you give me a call the day after tomorrow? I should have some first-bounds by then."

I approached Bob's long, rounded work desk to take my leave. As he stood up to shake hands, his forthright gaze touched something deep within that made me want to reciprocate. "By the way," I heard myself say casually, "it may interest you to know that the Institute has joined forces with National Student Marketing . . . with NSM."

Bob glanced at me suspiciously. "Joined forces?"

I had instinctively used the evasive terminology my owner-friend employed whenever he couldn't avoid disclosing the transaction. I realized I would now have to be more forthright. "As a matter of fact," I stammered, "we merged."

Bob blanched. "With NSM? Those youth marketing people . . . with over-the counter stock at forty times earnings?" Bob's voice shook, and he sank back into his leather chair. "I don't understand. I thought the Institute was non-profit."

I nodded. "NSM acquired the profit-making subsidiary."

"Profit? On students? NSM . . ." Bob's face was turning red. I could feel the tension in the room. It was as if on the pretext of soliciting for the Girl Scouts, I had extorted from him an open-ended commitment to a despicable cause.

Abruptly Bob reached over to a stack of papers on his desk. His hand shook as he picked up what I recognized to be a brown-line proof of the entire issue.

"Where there's a profit, there can be a loss," I heard myself say feebly, parroting more of the rationale of my employer-friend. "With NSM's financial resources, the Institute is in a stronger position to guarantee its programs."

Bob Fitzgibbon was ignoring me. He was rapidly paging through the magazine brownline, flipping back and forth, as if taking a mental measure of the various articles and ads.

I surmised Bob's intent. He was ready to stop those huge presses whirring away somewhere in the Middle West. If there was a simple one-step way to rearrange the layout, he would pull the offending article.

I stood there, heart thudding in my head and feeling as if my knees wouldn't support my weight. Obviously, I hadn't learned since my remark about Dr. Renny and Mr. Hale in front of the Duke. Bob was the one editor who had repeatedly declined my invitation to lunch at Le Pavilion, New York's trendiest restaurant. I should have known he would react this way.

Bob closed the magazine and put it back on his desk. He shook his head wearily, then slumped in his chair. "How long have you known about this . . . this joining of forces?" he asked quietly, without looking up.

"The negotiations dragged on . . ."

"That wasn't my question," Bob persisted woodenly.

"Little over two months," I said, in a barely audible voice.

"Thank you," Bob said, still not looking up. "I hope there was a good payday in it for somebody."

As I watched him sit there wishing he could eat the entire eight million run, I understood how he felt. In a way, Bob Fitzgibbon had trusted me as much as I had trusted my owner-friend.

It began shortly after the episode with Bob Fitzgibbon.

At first, I didn't know what was wrong. One of the most noticeable symptoms was waking up with an eyelid all puffed up, as if I had been attacked during the night by a squad of mosquitoes with infallible aim. Then I would get occasional blemishes or itchy patches on the skin. These were more embarrassing than any cause for concern. There was something icky about being beset by eruptions of this sort, which is why I preferred to pass them off as scrapes or poison ivy.

I now became concerned with symptoms I had previously dismissed as the body's normal reaction to excess, especially that bloated, burning sensation of flames leaping toward my throat from blazing stomach walls. This was increasingly accompanied by lower back pain, which would persist for days and sometimes made me cautious on standing up. My time-tested formula of vigorous exercise for whatever was ailing me no longer seemed to yield results.

The medical profession wasn't much help. The constellation of symptoms I described didn't correspond to any known disease, nor could the doctors discern any meaningful pattern in the slightly elevated blood pressure and minor abnormalities of laboratory tests. My main problem, though, was that the moment I disrobed, I forfeited all credibility. One glance in the examining room at my thirty-five-year-old physique, which looked as if it belonged to an athlete of college age, and I was categorized as a hypochondriac in need of psychiatric help. I didn't even have to broach the subject of the buzzing in my head for them to draw this conclusion.

Cautiously, I ventured into health food stores. These were still rare, catering to a hard-core clientele. What made me uneasy were the waxen people I saw there. Whether customers or employees, they looked ready for the grave, shuffling along with cotton stuffed in their ears and wearing extra sweaters and scarves no matter how balmy the day. I remember thinking, did these people come here for help because they looked so bad? Or did they look so bad because they had for years come here for help? I found out quickly enough when I ordered their special health concoction: a tall glass of freshly squeezed beet-carrot-celery juice, laced with lecithin and a square of baker's yeast. Before I put down the glass, I was feeling worse than when I had walked in

I didn't entirely dismiss what the doctors said. No doubt, the tensions resulting from the Institute's sale to NSM had affected me. Ironically, within less than a year the high-flying NSM stock had collapsed and the company's president was on his way to jail for stockholder fraud. My owner-friend emerged from the fiasco with a cease-and-desist order from the Securities and Exchange Commission but otherwise unscathed. He merely returned the near-worthless stock and regained full control of the Institute. The three million dollars in cash, he and his two partners kept.

Meanwhile, I was on the lookout for a new job. My opportunity came when one of those partners, who had remained uninvolved in the financial machinations, left the Institute to answer a call from Washington. He had been a roommate of President Nixon's new Peace Corps director at the University of California and now agreed to head up executive personnel for his old college friend. Embarrassed over my treatment in the Institute's merger with NSM, he had me appointed to a position with the salary and rank comparable to that of a two-star admiral, the same as COM-SERVPAC had been. My mandate was tacit but clear – to make the new director as famous as the Peace Corps's first director and JFK's brother-in-law, Sargent Shriver.

Too bad my client wasn't also married to a Kennedy! As it was, we jetted around the country, sometimes on VIP government planes or rented private Lears, eating good food, drinking fine wines, and impressing important people, and above all, impressing each other what swell and indispensable fellows we were. If only those unruly volunteers in the godforsaken parts of the world wouldn't cause trouble by demonstrating whenever Vice President Agnew showed up on their turf, promoting the government's Vietnam stance! The White House would never let us hear the end of that.

Yet the Peace Corps volunteers were the ones I would remember best. Upon completion of their two-year stints, they usually dropped in at our Washington headquarters for a debriefing if they intended to extend for an additional tour. Even the most ordinary-looking ones seemed to possess an extraordinary dimension, as if surrounded by some special aura or sheen. They appeared to be functioning on a higher plane, elevated above the normal Washington concerns, which suddenly looked absurd. Of course, if they tarried too long in this sanitized, air-conditioned capital, their sheen would begin to fade, which was perhaps why they were eager to return to their distant posts and resume their work. But try as I might to alert the media to this subtle phenomenon, it wasn't the kind of stuff that commanded headline news. *So what else is new?* the press inquired with an undisguised yawn – and continued to yawn even when the Peace Corps director courageously if obliquely castigated Attorney General John Mitchell for trying to repress youthful dissent.

One thing was clear: The sojourn in Washington was hardly helping to improve my health. None of the old symptoms diminished, and I had new ones, too. During the night, parts of my body would turn numb; my fingers, toes, arms, even parts of my face. To the touch, they felt as if they belonged to somebody else who had sneaked into my bed. My limbs flailed around like so much lifeless flesh, whenever I awoke every half-hour or so, and I would have to massage them back to life.

It was time to concentrate on getting well. Over the past decade, and especially over the past year, I had saved about twenty thousand dollars as a freedom buffer that would allow me to pick up and go. Why not try Europe, where I had spent so many memorable times and the doctors were held in such high esteem?

There was nothing to hold me back. The Washington apartment I would be giving up didn't have nearly the ambiance of my burgundy red studio in New York. As for the comfortable, well-paying conditions of my work, surely I would be able to do as well when I was healthy again. And in New York at that, where I retained my membership at Le Club. Besides generating all that hot air, my efforts in Washington hadn't amounted to much. Perhaps the only lasting effect of my work was that the Postal Service issued a special Peace Corps tenth anniversary commemorative stamp. But in my primary assignment, I had undoubtedly failed; for who today remembers the name of the Peace Corps director I was trying to make known, the Honorable Joseph P. Blatchford?

3/

"Ich gratuliere Ihnen," Dr. Angela Hommes said. She smiled as she handed me the latest lab report. "Your results are now completely normal. You're fortunate to have recovered so well. *Ja, ja,* I congratulate you."

I certainly didn't feel recovered. In fact, I felt no healthier than a dozen visits ago when I first started her intensive treatments with Vitamin B-12 shots, mild tranquilizers, and various other elixirs and pills. Now this attractive Munich internist, recommended by Hansi when I arrived to visit Angelina, had just proclaimed me as cured. She reminded me of those senators who at the very moment were suggesting in Washington that we resolve the Vietnam war by proclaiming a victory and withdraw.

Not that I was blaming Dr. Hommes. I had already scoured most of Europe for a cure, and she certainly was more pleasant and at least as competent as any of the doctors I had seen. In England, where I briefly visited Stephanie, I was told I had gout after suffering in a London taxi an excruciating attack of kidney stones, which felt as if a dull knife was being pushed into my back. "I say there," the driver inquired solicitously but with total aplomb, as I writhed on the rear seat of his cab, "everything perfectly all right, sir?"

The diagnosis in England was partly confirmed in Germany by Professor Schmiedt, who headed the *Urologische Abteilung* at the University of Munich. I had a kidney disorder, he said, and should be very careful about the overall intake of proteins. But he assured me it was a common affliction in the *Bundesrepublik,* and I should be able to manage just fine. Then in Paris, one of the most famous of all homeopaths, Professor Vannier, told me that the kidneys were not at all the cause. The liver was where the real problem lay. But you shouldn't worry too much, monsieur, he said. It was a national malady as French as the *tricolore* on Bastille Day. *Mais attention, pas trop de matière grasse!* Not too much fat, and only one glass of red wine a day.

That's pretty much the advice I also received from Issten, who was the main reason I had come to Paris. "You must not allow yourself to worry but try to be more spiritual about these things, although I must say it doesn't help with my swollen legs when I have to make four flights of stairs to my room." Not only had my aunt somehow managed, without Albrecht's help, to hold off the creditors seeking to evict her from her tottering château. She was subletting here a tiny walk-up over a bakery to be near the twins as they started their studies at the Sorbonne. My aunt looked a bit more bent over and shrunken than the last time we met, but she seemed just as undaunted by the vagaries of life. As we stopped on the dimly lit street in front of where she lived, Issten chuckled in her familiar witchlike way, "Ho-ho-ho, who would have thought when I was born in our Schloss with a hundred rooms that I would end up this way? In a little cubbyhole over a *boulangerie!*" She paused as if to smirk at her fate. "But I don't mind, not at all. I also don't mind that you will live much, much longer than I. You will get well, and as I promised, you're the one to whom I shall send my ultimate message from this world. When you see Albrecht, the old miser, you can again tell him that!"

Albrecht's Schloss became the headquarters for my medical pursuits. On arriving in Europe, I had picked up at the Ford factory in Cologne a new Capri, which served as my primary conveyance to wherever my search for a cure took me. And wherever I went, I was prescribed a fresh batch of powders, tablets, or pills of various potencies and intended therapeutic effects. At best, they had no effect; more frequently, they made me feel worse, especially at night. I often woke up with a start maybe fifty times before dawn, my heart racing like a motorcycle and making so much noise I could have recorded the beats by opening my mouth. I could feel my blood coursing within, winding its way through the arteries and veins like a pack of racing cars taking hairpin curves at a grand prix race. How long before there would be some sort of an internal crash?

I remained increasingly ensconced at the Schloss, alone with Albrecht except for Frau Kunst and occasional guests. On weekends, Elizabeth arrived from Munich with Tasha, who was in her next-to-last year at the Gymnasium. Following another secretive encounter with this older guest on a previous visit, Tasha must have had second thoughts, though she in no way appeared to be warming up to Andreas.

The relationship with my cousin during these months was placid. Because of my subdued mood, I didn't in any way challenge Albrecht about his theories or raise the issue of his mother's financial needs. He, in turn, was sympathetic to my health concerns, forgoing any *I told you so* jeremiads.

The one puzzling lapse in this humdrum truce came after a two-day visit by Stephanie. In a deliberate attempt to lift me out of my doldrums, she had invited me to her star-speckled pale blue quarters for a night of the sort of intimacy we used to indulge in with such gusto years ago. While there was no miraculous cure, my spirits did lift a bit. Whether this tipped the balance in my symbiotic status quo with her father, or he noticed something different in the way I bid Stephanie good-bye when she left the next day, I could only surmise.

That evening as soon as we finished dinner in Albrecht's vaulted quarters, my cousin suggested we move to the main drawing room on the second floor. Adjoining the stately dining hall on one end – and Stephanie's corner suite on the other – this expansive salon with high coffered ceilings was invariably used before and after meals when there were numerous guests. The decor had a simple formality, with several small Persian rugs spaced over parquet floors between three separate enclaves of comfortable furniture, each consisting of a couch and a few high-backed upholstered chairs around a small, square table. A half-dozen walnut-stained bookshelves were built into a portion of one wall, and over the double-door entrance was affixed the stuffed head of a twenty-two-point stag. When Andreas or Ferdinand were the only guests, they often accompanied Albrecht to the salon after dinner for a game of chess. Since I didn't play, my guess was that Albrecht for some reason wanted to give special significance to what he was about to say.

Albrecht chose the enclave in the center of the room. He seated himself in one of the high-backed chairs, and I occupied the corner of a green brocade couch directly across from him. On the wall immediately to my right was a large painting of Albrecht and Ferdinand as young men. They were portrayed in hunting outfits, and Albrecht looked exactly as I still remembered him from our first meeting in Prague. During my initial visit to the Schloss, when I offered to photograph him and Ferdinand in front of the painting in the same pose, Albrecht had not only produced the same gun but showed up wearing the same jacket. A black-and-white 18" x 24" enlargement highlighting every wrinkle and every line was now tucked into the lower corner of the frame, captioned by Albrecht, *The Price of 40 Years!*

Frau Kunst came in promptly with a platterful of her delicious *Kipferl*. At the end of her twelve-hour day, she looked no less fresh than when she served breakfast, her silvery braids still perfectly coiled above each ear. Now that I knew of her youthful misfortune, she occupied a far broader dimension in my mind. As I watched Frau Kunst set the porcelain platter on the small, delicately inlaid table between Albrecht and me, and then bid us a cheery good night, I wondered: what was she thinking as she observed the goings-on at the Schloss?

Albrecht finished the remnants of his afternoon cigar. He leaned back in his chair and with obvious relish lit up a fresh one. I didn't mind that this impeded the conversational flow. I enjoyed watching my cousin indulge in long pauses to puff away greedily and savor the smoke in its refined subtleties. It also kept him from competing for the Kipferl. I knew these butter-hazelnut cookies meant certain Sodbrennen; still, I didn't want to be deprived of my share.

"The Catholic Church comes closest to understanding the Perfect Universe," Albrecht remarked in an offhanded way, gazing at the wisps of smoke rising toward the ceiling. "Why? Because the Church understands the Holy Trinity. The Perfect Universe is like the Trinity. It loves us and is eternal."

Albrecht took another puff on his cigar, a long, slow inhale. As he gradually let out the smoke, his eyes shifted from the ceiling and past the billowing haze before him. He seemed to be looking off into a great distance, as if trying to focus on infinity. But then his gaze abruptly bolted from that indeterminate space and focused on me. Hunching over in his high-backed chair, he leaned slightly forward over the antique table, bringing his face closer to mine. "I hope you realize," he said with a zealous gleam, "that in the Perfect Universe, *there will be no focking.*"

I devoured several of the Kipferl in silence, trying to remain outwardly unfazed. I wasn't particularly surprised at this revelation as to what would or would not be allowed in Albrecht's heaven; nor at the slight mispronunciation of this most common of words. Old-time Europeans never did get it straight. (Father still thought it was *fick*, due to incorrectly overhearing his employees back in the days of delivering milk.) What left me speechless was to hear from this courtly cousin such a crude and modern expression, spoken with such aplomb.

"No focking in the Perfect Universe," Albrecht repeated, eager to reinforce his assertion and dispel whatever skepticism he discerned in my face. He shifted in his chair, the thick green material of his Austrian felt jacket pressing against the suede upholstering from the hides of his deer. He looked at me in the same steely, accusatory way as he did when he tried to blame me for the dead electrons imperiling the firmament. Again, it was my fault. It was as if I had personally invented the practice of *focking* and was alone responsible for its universal spread until it reached out to addict and corrupt his daughter Stephanie and threatened his own Angelina. Would she too be eventually on my conscience, this pubescent charmer who liked so much to roughhouse with me in her Widenmayerstrasse room, and have me teach her headstands against the wall and do somersaults on her bed, or wrestle with me while I held one arm behind my back? Not at all like the granduncle that I was, and the proper little princess she so often pretended to be. I couldn't help but wonder: What would Albrecht do if he found out about my affair with Stephanie? That I could have been the cause of her scandalous divorce just as easily as husband number two? What if he found out about my past sessions with Andreas's pure bride-to-be? I remembered Albrecht's vengeful gleam whenever he spotted yet another futile attempt of his nephew to hold Tasha's hand. Would he shoot me like one of his favorite stags to whom he had transmitted his intentions in advance? Nobody in the village would doubt the Fürst's word that it had been an accident. *God, was he thinking it now?*

"*Ganz ausser Frage,*" Albrecht's voice interrupted my contemplative pause. "Completely out of the question. You can't have immortality and focking too. You have to choose. It's impossible to have both."

"But why, Albrecht, why?" I shifted slightly in the corner of the couch and crossed my legs. "Is it because there would be too many people and eternity couldn't accommodate them all? Surely you don't need to worry, even if you personally believe birth control is a mortal sin."

"Venial," Albrecht corrected me promptly, as if eager to set the record straight on a point important to him.

"Whatever," I allowed. "By the time we've reached the Perfect Universe, focking probably won't be used for reproduction, and all venereal disease will have been eliminated. Sex will be there solely for our pleasure, to do with as we wish."

"I'm sorry I must correct you again." Albrecht said firmly. He took a quick puff on his cigar and set it down on the table, the lighted end resting against the edge of the cookie platter. (An ashtray would have been too open a recognition of his indulgent habit. This also meant he absently let the ashes drop to the floor for Frau Kunst to sweep up the following day. She knew exactly where the little piles were likely to be.) "God didn't make sex only for procreation," my elderly cousin continued. "He made it also for commitment, though it should not be used very often. On the contrary. Only when it remains special is it a cement. Too much . . . and it doesn't bind."

I leaned forward to reach for another cookie, then settled back once more against the green brocade of the couch. "What's wrong with sex purely for enjoyment?"

"Ach, after so many years . . . that you should ask such a question!" Albrecht shook his head vigorously. "I've told you many times pleasure is addictive per se, ipso facto, and you must always be careful. But sex is still more dangerous. Why? Because it is used as bait to sell other pleasures. Hochstapler cars and fashions, absurdly expensive watches . . ." Albrecht reached for his cigar, this time flicking the ash onto the half-empty porcelain platter. He looked at me steadily. "Not only by using suggestive young models; I understand in America they have hidden sex scenes in advertisements for cigarettes and whiskey."

"I'll have you know it works," I volunteered. "It's called subliminal advertising."

"Ach, of course it works." Albrecht again groaned. "But at what price! What do you think it does to us as human beings? Of all pleasures, focking brings us closest to the animal. Even the sound is the same. It means we're going in the wrong direction . . . backwards to being more and more like animals. Worse than animals! My stags, they at least have a purpose." Albrecht took a hurried puff, as if not to interrupt his thoughts. "Some of my stags perhaps think that with so many does around, they're in heaven right here; yes, in the Perfect Universe. That is until I come along, and *bam!* " He paused to give me a victorious grin. "That's what I mean, you cannot have focking and immortality, too."

I glanced toward the entrance at the lifelike head of the majestic stag mounted above the double doors, his glassy eyes impersonally presiding over the grand salon. "Albrecht, do you resent your stags?"

"But not at all! I admire them. A stag is the most graceful of animals. Everything about a stag is magnificent. I have even seen one fock, which is rare in nature. They're private animals and always withdraw to a secluded spot, away from other deer. But that still doesn't mean we should be like stags. They *are* animals."

"You mean they don't have a soul?"

Albrecht looked pained. "Ach, ja, the answer isn't so simple," he said, crinkling those weather-beaten cheeks. He was groping for a response that wouldn't contradict the Church's teaching that animals lacked souls. "Certainly, stags have not the same souls that God gave us. A stag can never become a part of the Perfect Universe. God made us so we could. That is the purpose of creation."

I figured it couldn't hurt to be conciliatory at this stage. "I have no quarrel with that."

"Hah!" Albrecht exclaimed, with evident triumph. "But there will be no focking there . . . in the Perfect Universe. How much plainer can I make it, my dear cousin? It isn't up to me to change eternal laws. I'm sorry . . . sorry to disappoint you."

Far from sorry, Albrecht was gloating. Leaning back in his chair, he looked at me from across the table as if I were the rich young man in the Bible who had just been told by Jesus that to get to heaven, he would have to give up everything he owned. *No focking in the Perfect Universe!* That would be the sacrifice I would have to make. For Albrecht, on the other hand, moving to a non-focking stage would be no problem at all, nothing to give up — or so he was making it seem.

Puffing away on his shortening cigar butt, Albrecht sat there smugly. "We will see, we will see."

I didn't mind participating in this discussion as if it were of immediate and practical concern. I had often done so in the past with topics no less removed from real life. But maybe this was the moment to turn things around. After all, Albrecht was my first cousin and the father of Stephanie, whose appetites I knew so well. He certainly had the same gusto for food as I; even how he intently sucked on that cigar was a giveaway.

As I glanced at my host in his strange, gloating mood, I decided to take a chance. "But Albrecht," I heard myself remonstrate gently, "you yourself like to fock."

There it was, I had come out with the unspeakable.

Albrecht couldn't hide his surprise. I had sneaked in a punch that didn't hurt but stunned and left him disoriented. He glanced around the drawing room, from the mounted stag's head to the bookshelves off to one side. His eyes scanned the irregular assortment of hardbacks and paperbacks in plain white, tan, and yellow covers, then shifted to the lowest two shelves and rested on a neat array of two dozen maroon volumes of the *Fürstliche Gotha,* the periodic official listing of his noble peers.

My cousin seemed to be deciding how best to react and deliberately looked serious about this severe breech. I thought he might shake his head and chastise me with silence until I left the room. But then almost involuntarily, Albrecht's deeply lined features began to open up, and a mischievous smile parted his compressed lips.

"I never really did *do* anything until after forty," Albrecht said, looking complacent as if making a boast. "I didn't even know what it was until I married. Then my poor wife got sick and that was the end of that . . . until she died three years later. It's only since . . ." Albrecht abruptly broke off, as if thinking things over, and then resumed in a different vein. "If I had it my way, people wouldn't be allowed to start before forty."

"Because you didn't?"

Albrecht's features again dissolved into the smile of a naughty boy, but this time he made no response. I wondered, was his rationale for celibacy the same as I had detected between the lines in Saint Augustine back in Professor Baumer's class – if you didn't or wouldn't or couldn't, no one else should be doing it either?

"Is that why you're watching Andreas like a hawk?" I persisted, wishing to make the most of Albrecht's frank talk. "Afraid he might begin too soon?"

Albrecht put down his cigar on the platter again. "You must remember Tasha is only seventeen. She has no idea about these things. Her mother . . . Elizabeth tells me Tasha gets easily upset. Frankly, I find it refreshing."

Ah, Elizabeth, a wonderful lady, though I wasn't surprised she was acting as tactical adviser to Tasha. What mother wouldn't want the best for her child?

"And you still think Andreas can break the curse on the women in the family?" I asked.

Albrecht looked grave. "Ach, ja, the curse is certainly there. Not only the curse on my mother and Stephanie. I felt the curse when my wife died. Also don't forget, Andreas's mother ran away from his father, from Ferdinand. Yes, it's in the family, definitely. My hope is that Angelina will be the one to break it first. She seems so much like Stephanie but has also a completely different side. Andreas, he has an excellent chance, too. Tasha is a very good girl."

"I admire his taste. Deep inside, I think Andreas is not unlike me."

"*Quatsch!*" Albrecht said haughtily. "I beg to differ. He's almost exactly the same as I."

Seeing Albrecht rapidly withdrawing into his private domain, I decided to take a chance. "Oh, but I agree," I said, nodding for emphasis. "Like both of us, he likes to fock . . . or at least, would like to."

For an instant it looked as if Albrecht might again respond with that smile. But then he abruptly picked up his cigar and stuck it in his mouth. I could see I had gone too far. His face became rigid, and his lips conformed tightly to the proper shape for drawing in the smoke. It was a long puff which Albrecht let out with studied concentration in a seemingly endless series of concentric rings. He watched them recede, one beyond the other, his eyes following them into the distance until he again stared into infinity.

Albrecht stood up. He ground out the half-smoked cigar on the cookie platter and carefully stowed the remnants in the breast pocket of his Austrian jacket. He looked around for an instant, then scooped up the remaining Kipferl.

"Ach, ach," Albrecht sighed, as he began to walk out over the Persian rugs and parquet floors. At the double doors, he paused and turned toward me on the couch. "Please, whatever you do," he said, in a plaintive tone, "don't forget to turn out the lights. It would be a *Katastrophe.*" Then he disappeared beneath the stag's impersonal gaze.

I was still at the Schloss when my cousin suffered a particularly painful setback in his work. It so happened that Elizabeth's father had been a physicist who at one time worked with Werner von Heisenberg. Acting on his daughter's word, Elizabeth's father endeavored to arrange a meeting between the recognized giant of modern physics and the Austrian Fürst, who supposedly had some original insights to share. When it began to look as if a meeting might indeed take place, Albrecht decided to provide the decisive nudge. In a lengthy letter to Heisenberg outlining the scope of his work, Albrecht included a three-page explanation that the American *billion* used in his calculations was the same as a European *milliard*. The result, alas, was that the originator of quantum physics let it be known that his health precluded any possibility of meeting with the Fürst – now, or in the future.

4/

During my final weeks at the Schloss, I had a further decline in health. On certain days my brain felt as if large chunks had been replaced by Brillo pads. My mind seemed too fuddled to pursue even routine mealtime conversation with my host. At night I had to get up countless times to relieve myself of seemingly endless, copious streams. This meant having to walk to the toilet through an adjoining bedroom and startle another guest, be it some night-capped old count or a prince I had just met. After two or three such interruptions between midnight and 4 A.M., I would opt for the window in my room and hope that the cascading stream didn't awaken Frau Kunst in her quarters below.

I returned to the United States via Antwerp, the most convenient port for shipping my car. My experience with doctors on both sides of the Atlantic left me skeptical. Not only did I question the medical profession, which sought to project such certainty in its field; I was beginning to wonder about everything we as humans allegedly knew. Our grasp of reality still seemed no better than that of the proverbial two blind men confronting an elephant for the first time from opposite ends.

When I returned to our Massachusetts farm, Father made it clear he didn't think I suffered from anything that wouldn't be cured if I settled down and had a family to worry about. He offered to take me into his exercise business, which would help me focus on something besides myself and put money in my pocket, too. He had just emerged from a yearlong crisis occasioned by the sale of the Exercycle Corporation to a consortium of financiers. The new owners lacked any understanding of the fitness trade beyond the balance sheet. With their first decree they practically put Father out of business by cutting his commission on each machine by two thirds. When Father rushed to the company's Hartford headquarters to protest, he didn't help his cause. "The best thing you can do is to start exercising on the machine yourself," Father advised the company's new president, and then poked the excitable, grossly overweight middle-aged man in his stomach. "In your condition, you could drop dead in six months." Fortunately for Father, his prediction turned out to be correct. The Exercycle Corporation was again sold, and the new owner immediately reverted to doing business the old way. With prospective customers now increasingly coming to Father's Boston office instead of just making appointments at their homes, he needed to have somebody there throughout the day – and that could be me. As it was, Father found it more practical to stay in Boston during the week rather than make the 160-mile round-trip drive from the farm each day. This meant that except for weekends, Mother was at home alone. She slept with a baseball bat by her bed to ward off potential intruders, and under her bed kept a rope ladder in case of fire. "If you were here, " Father concluded his invitation, "it would certainly be more cheerful for Mother."

The offer made sense, but with almost half of my savings intact, I wasn't about to relinquish my dream. I had, in fact, decided already in Europe on Laguna Beach. Maybe I could recapture some of the vigor I had invariably felt there during my Navy days.

I could hardly wait to pick up my Capri on a Jersey City dock, load a few essentials, and head out West.

In Laguna Beach, I found almost right away what I had in mind: a comfortably furnished condominium with a spare bedroom and a large, open verandah with potted palms and exotic plants, perched more than fifty feet over the Pacific surf. It was available for the next three months. In that time I would either get well or go out in style.

Here is where Dr. Bieler came into my life. I first encountered his name in New York during my initial foray into health food stores. Semiretired after fifty years as an M.D., he was the author of a big-seller, *Food Is Your Best Medicine*. Now, I came across his book again while browsing at Whipple's Healthy Foods in my ongoing search for a miracle cure. When I realized from the dust jacket that Dr. Bieler was still alive and resided only a few miles away in San Juan Capistrano, I felt a ray of hope.

I phoned him the instant I returned home, only to be hurled back into my gloom. No, he wouldn't see me, Dr. Bieler said curtly. Not next week, not next month, not next year. He wasn't taking any new patients because of his age. Good-bye . . . and click!

In desperation, I composed what was perhaps the most earnest letter of my PR career. Having noticed in his book that he liked to drop names, I detailed how some of the greatest specialists in the world had been stumped by my case. "From reading your book," I concluded, "I'm convinced you're the one person who can help."

The appointment was two days later.

He turned out to be a spry little old man whose alert eyes and kindly smile showed an undiminished interest in people and in life. He worked out of a large office attached to his ranch-style house high over the Pacific. He had no nurse and penciled little notes on index cards. Unlike Professor Schmiedt in Germany, who always seemed to be crowding me to the door, Dr. Bieler listened to the story of my life as if he were a minister or a priest. He went through the normal steps of a physical, taking my blood pressure, counting my pulse, and putting a stethoscope to my chest and back. He also held a pocket watch suspended on a chain over my liver and heart, observing carefully which way the watch would swing. Whatever mumbo-jumbo this was I didn't care, as long as he could diagnose my case.

"Well?" I asked, trying not to sound impatient, as I pulled up my pants and started tucking in my shirttails. "Does my case make sense?"

Dr. Bieler looked smug, then smiled in a way that seemed to validate his life. "I knew what was wrong with you the minute you walked in."

I felt intense relief. At last, someone who didn't take me for a hypochondriac or a nut!

"What you've got," Dr. Bieler continued in that same self-satisfied tone, "is starch toxemia."

"Starch toxemia?" I repeated, as I slipped on my shoes. Not having any idea what that was, I didn't know whether I should feel relieved.

Dr. Bieler nodded happily. "It means your body is rotten with starches and you've depleted your alkali reserve. Your cells can't do their work properly. They become sluggish . . . like you."

"Is it serious?"

Dr. Bieler again nodded. "In your case, the cells have also been weakened by all of those medications you've been taking. But nowadays, practically everybody has some form of this condition. Maybe not as bad as you, though some people have it a lot worse. In one respect, you're lucky. Your cells haven't gone haywire yet. That's what happens to people with cancer. Their cells go haywire."

Dr. Bieler believed starch toxemia to be the principal disease in the United States, just as Dr. Schmiedt in Germany maintained it was kidney disease in his country, and Professor Vannier, liver disease in France. Far too many acid-producing foods were being consumed, Dr. Bieler claimed, especially in fast-food chains. A snack of French fries, a hamburger, and a milkshake was one of the most lethal combinations that could be devised, while colas and other soft drinks were poisons in a category of their own. Moreover, fast-food chains served virtually no green, watery vegetables to supply the essential alkali antidote (this was in the days before salad bars). Result? A bonanza for companies promoting antacids to mask the early stages of a serious underlying condition. "Even worse are the tranquilizers doctors nowadays prescribe. The purpose of most of that junk is to keep the body from shouting for help . . . often, until it's too late. But in your case, you'll get well," Dr. Bieler assured me, then added in a conditional way, "if you're careful."

I soon found out what Dr. Bieler meant: a devoted adherence to the diet he wrote out on a little white slip. Starch in its multiplicity of forms was his main culprit, I now learned, the way various proteins had been for Dr. Schmiedt in Germany and fats for that homeopath in France. Lucky I wasn't going to all three doctors at once!

As it was, I ended up with no choice at all, committed to the weirdest diet in the world. Zucchini and yellow wax beans were to be the miracle foods that would neutralize the acids suffusing my cells and build up my alkali reserve. I was to eat literally pounds of them each day. On first getting up in the morning, a glass of warm water with a dissolved square of baker's yeast would gently get my system prepared. A half hour later, I was to start the day with an oversized bowl of steamed zucchini mixed in with two raw egg yolks. (Unlike the rest of the medical profession, Dr. Bieler believed the harmful portion of the egg was the fried or hard-boiled white, not the raw yolk.) At lunch, I was to have more steamed zucchini, and also wax beans, along with a piece of broiled lean meat. For supper, it was to be the same, with a piece of fish or fowl instead of meat. No condiments or sauces at any time except a single, small pat of butter twice a day on the zucchini and beans — unsalted, of course. And everything preferably steamed in a pressure cooker, including the meat. I also was to have a large salad twice a day, which would further help replenish that alkali reserve: lettuce, cucumber, and celery, again completely bare. The only remotely sweet item on this draconian regimen was a box of unsweetened blueberries for an afternoon snack, with a pint of tepid raw milk. The blueberries, Dr. Bieler explained, would neutralize the acids in the milk. "Don't ever drink milk from a glass," Dr. Bieler warned. "It's a protein. Always eat it with a spoon."

I couldn't believe my ears. What, no wine, no cheese, no cakes? No coffee to wake me up? No sauces, potatoes, or even bread? How could life exist without them?

I tried to get the kindly old doctor to relent. "Can't I vary the diet a bit?" I asked cautiously.

"What's wrong with it the way it is?" Dr. Bieler countered, with undisguised hurt in his voice.

"I merely thought if I could add or substitute something every now and then . . ."

"Not if you want to get well, you can't," Dr. Bieler snapped. "I've been on this diet for thirty-five years myself." He paused to take my measure in the Morty Sills off-white, double-breasted linen suit I had selected to give extra substance to my case. "What do you want, French gourmet cooking?" he asked, as if it were the greatest absurdity in the world.

"I'm afraid I may be allergic to the yeast," I said, trying a different tack. "I took it once and it didn't agree with me."

"Then don't take it," Dr. Bieler retorted, with a dismissing wave of the hand, "but drink that warm water all the same."

One more thing, Dr. Bieler said. I should make sure I had at least one bowel movement a day, even if that meant taking a warm water enema. When I skewed my face into a distasteful look, he reached into his desk and handed me a little booklet as if dispensing final authority for his words. It was *The Essene Gospel of Peace*, a translation of a third-century Aramaic manuscript supposedly containing the teachings of Christ that had never made it into the New Testament. From a copy of his own, Dr. Bieler read aloud: "Find a large trailing gourd, having a stalk the length of a man; take out its inwards and fill it with water from the river which the sun has warmed. Hang it upon the branch from a tree, and kneel upon the ground before the angel of water, and suffer the end of the stalk of the trailing gourd to enter your hinder parts, that the water may flow through all your bowels."

Dr. Bieler looked up, satisfied he had made his point.

Despite the way I felt, I couldn't resist a touch of levity. "What would the neighbors say? I mean the tree, the gourd, the hinder parts . . . "

Dr. Bieler didn't disguise his annoyance. Obviously, one didn't make light of such matters any more than one would have joked with a Soviet commissar about the withering away of the state, or about the Holy Trinity with Albrecht. "Just do as I say," he blurted out. "You're a very sick man. You'll get well, yes . . . but only if you're careful."

Almost right away I started feeling worse, if in a different way, on Dr. Bieler's fare. I was now constantly famished, with a gnawing emptiness that seemed to transform the area where my stomach had previously been into a vacuum chamber. I also felt strangely headachy and unwell, which had not been a part of my original symptoms at all. It was almost as if I were withdrawing from some potent addiction or a drug.

"That's good," Dr. Bieler chortled on a subsequent visit, not at all surprised when I told him how I felt. "That's called surgery without knives. Your body is throwing off poisons. It's pulling them out of your organs and tissues and joints where they've been stored for years. They're in your bloodstream now, on their way out of your body for good. That's why you're feeling so rotten. I'd be worried if you weren't feeling this way."

It sounded like exorcism, with the devils angrily protesting their eviction from a favorite lair. But I was too timid to tamper with a formula that was at least partly working. I was no longer feeling any of that burning sensation between my stomach and throat, which I had accepted as normal for so many years, and I was able to stand up from a chair without an audible groan.

Dr. Bieler wouldn't tell me how long I would have to put up with his regimen. "How can you expect to abuse your health all your life and make up for it in a few days? No sir, there's always a price to pay," he continued with the gentle righteousness of one who has already paid up in advance with decades of steamed zucchini and raw egg yolks under his belt. Then he added his standard creed. "But you'll get well, if you're careful."

It occurred to me that Dr. Bieler's formula was not unlike a religion, demanding that a harsh road be traveled in return for the promise of an ultimate salvation or a cure. When I felt especially headachy, famished, and weak, I would think of the old Moslem janitor, Effendi, burying his nose in a prayer rug several times a day; or the old gardener at our embassy in Ankara, laboring in the scorching sun without a drop to drink to fulfill the requirements of his faith. I remembered thinking back then how lucky I was not to be a follower of Mohammed, considering the sacrifices exacted merely to be saved in some hypothetical afterlife. Why had I now been stuck with such arduous demands, when others in seemingly worse state of health could manage on far more relaxed regimens?

There were days I was sorely tempted to give it all up and resume my old ways. But the memory of that awful brink from which I had so recently stepped a few paces back was still vivid in my mind. Moreover, Dr. Bieler continued to urge me on in our weekly appointments. "You'll get well," he would assure me, while giving my back a rubdown with his gnarled hand, "if you're careful!" I would thereafter resolve to stick it out until the following week. At this rate, maybe by the time I was ready to leave California in a month or so, I would be well enough to return to normal fare. My once-racing motorcycle heart was again running at near-normal speed, and I no longer felt those Brillo pads being stuffed into my brain. And if I awoke in the middle of the night, my limbs would do so too, rather than waiting until I massaged them back to life.

I was gradually beginning to appreciate the beauties of Laguna Beach again – the balmy air, the brisk ocean surf, the spectacular sun, the flowers blooming throughout the year. In this frame of mind, it wasn't long before I started to entertain the thought of how I would celebrate my cure when I returned to New York; perhaps a beef Wellington or a rare rack of lamb covered with a heavy crust of fried, butter-soaked garlicked crumbs; or a big dish of thick, creamy fettuccini Alfredo, the way they made it at Gino's on Lexington Avenue. And, of course, a suitable bottle of wine; a vintage Vino Nobile de Montepulciano or a Paternina Rioja Gran Reserva. I couldn't wait and almost could feel myself salivate.

It wasn't until the last visit prior to returning East that Dr. Bieler told me the truth. No, he said, I could *never* go back to the old ways, not even after I fully recovered. That would only undermine my health the same way as in the past, and the cure next time might be far more difficult than now. Yes, the rigid diet he had prescribed was for the rest of my days. "You might as well get used to it," he chuckled in an elfish way. "For all you know, you might get to like it."

In one respect, Dr. Bieler proved to be wrong. I never came close to developing a yen for that unique menu of his. Yet for almost two years, I somehow managed to put up with its demands and constraints; lugging a pressure cooker wherever I went, avoiding restaurants as if they had a skull-and-crossbones symbol on the door, and always making sure I had a supply of zucchini on hand. Whenever I stayed with friends, my hosts would wonder about the peculiar smell of this freshly steamed vegetable in their kitchen at breakfast time. Rather than accepting my explanation, they preferred to see it as some avant-garde fad.

I continued to get better, though. After I left Laguna Beach, Dr. Bieler encouraged me to consult by phone, free of charge, from wherever I happened to be. By then, I knew his refrain by heart. Yet I was gradually finding out on my own, by cautious trial and error, that I didn't have to be quite that careful and *still* stay well.

By the time I saw Dr. Bieler's obituary in *The New York Times* a few months later (God, how lucky to have gotten to him in time!), I was pretty well liberated from his creed. I could at last indulge in that grease-soaked, garlicked rack of lamb, along with a good half-bottle of red, without a sense of sin. Not that I often did. I would still hold back, especially on those overly sweet pastries and heavy sauces, which I didn't yearn for as before.

My real debt to Dr. Bieler wasn't so much in what I had given up from my gourmet days as what I added from his regimen. With

every protein, starch or fat I would now consume a watery vegetable or fruit. And with every major meal, I would be sure to include extra-large servings of zucchini or string beans and an extra-
large quantity of lettuce. If traveling by air, I would often attract
curious stares at the boarding gate, munching away on a bunch of
romaine leaves or celery sticks by way of preparation for the
starchy, alkali-poor in-flight meal and the several little bottles of
wine I would inevitably have. And as a last resort, if I overin-
dulged for too many days in a row, I could rely on that unpalatable breakfast mix of steamed zucchini and eggs yolks for a miraculously rapid cure.

I could say without reservations that Dr. Bieler had saved my
life. My body again worked like a clock, without me hearing it
tick. I had lost twenty pounds of a weightlifter's bulk and now had
a much leaner swimmer's build. Yet I would often wonder: how
much of that original draconian regimen had been necessary to get
well? Could I have adhered from the beginning to what I eventually distilled and still recovered my health?

This posed a question of a fundamental sort. What was truly
necessary for our well-being on earth – and what just human presumption or chaff? I knew only too well the shopworn joke about
the attractive virgins in heaven, perpetually kicking themselves in
the rear now that they realized it made little difference whether or
not they had remained chaste. Was there a universal answer for us
all? Or was the answer as individual as our fingerprints, with each
of us mandated in this life to search out those patterns and
grooves that were our own?

The experience with Dr. Bieler led me to a concept I called
Survival Overcompensation Trauma or SOT. The most insidious
aspect of SOT lay in its apparent logic: If one of something helped
us to survive, twice as much, or more, should be correspondingly
beneficial. Thus, if fifteen hundred calories per day were essential
to sustain life, why not up it to five thousand? If two or three

children provided continuity for one's family line and security in old age, why not have a dozen? If two nuclear bombs ended the war with Japan, why not stockpile ten thousand?

Indeed, I saw myself as a victim of this Survival Overcompensation Trauma; for hadn't I been merely seeking out those elemental pleasures that helped humanity survive and evolve over millions of years? The problem stemmed from the body's lack of an overriding mechanism to command *Stop!* when the pleasure was no longer promoting survival but was, in fact, undermining it. Our ancestors needed no such physical overrides. The scarcity that prevailed throughout virtually all of human existence was the most inexorable control of all. And I wondered – was that perhaps what Albrecht meant about the moral urgency to control our desires and wants if our civilization was to survive?

5/

In the years immediately following Dr. Bieler's miraculous cure, I never acquired an apartment of my own, a permanent place I could call home. Not that I didn't care about getting back into the mainstream of things and again having a chic Manhattan address. I talked to just about every major public relations firm in New York, as well as the personnel agency that made the better placements in this line. But I simply didn't look like a midlevel office employee ready to do someone else's bidding in my Morty Sills suits, invariably suntanned as if I had just jetted in from an exotic resort. The fact that I had been without a job for so long sealed my fate.

Drawing on skills acquired in the course of my PR work, I gradually created my own niche as a writer and producer of promotional films. My first client in New York was an elderly multinational builder of paper mills, whose exotic young Chinese wife had befriended me some years before. Though I tried to tap more of my New York contacts, I was increasingly finding work in Florida, where my younger brother Tom was a cameraman-director. Between shooting commercials with exquisite models romping on the beach, he introduced me to most of my clients there. Tom owned a tiny house in North Miami, where I often stayed for weeks at a time, sleeping on the living room couch and going to Golden Beach every day between jobs. I enjoyed my work, and with a couple of months of effort in this semitropical retreat, I could earn enough to keep me comfortable for the year. While I would have preferred to stay busier, this was a field where others starved. Most of my friends thought I had it made.

I knew better. I didn't deceive myself about the importance of my work. Mine wasn't exactly an achievement for which the Duke would have declared an unexpected school holiday, as was his custom several times each year in recognition of highly successful alumni. The defining moment for me came at a chicken-and-peas banquet at a rustic lodge in northern Florida, where I was among those being honored for their promotional work. Amid congratulations from my local associates, I couldn't help but painfully consider, if with amused detachment, what others of my vintage had attained. There was Lewis Lapham, who had sat next to me both at Hotchkiss and in many of the same classes at Yale, due to the inexorable order of the alphabet. He was now editor of *Harper's Magazine*. Another classmate, Don O'Brien, was the chief counsel for the Rockefeller family. And Winston Lord, who had been a couple of classes behind me, was meeting secretly with Mao Tse-Tung as Henry Kissinger's top aide. Meanwhile, I had just won second prize for the best public service TV spot in northern Florida.

Long absences from New York also affected my personal life. I had allowed my membership at Le Club to lapse, where the continental ambiance and soft lights made seduction on the first date so pleasantly inevitable. I was now relegated to staying with friends, which under the best of circumstances could hardly provide the intimacy of the burgundy red apartment I once had. Any romantic quest during my brief visits to New York was thus incomparably more difficult to implement, though I could still count on the initial impression created by a Morty Sills suits.

That's how I became involved with Annette, a statuesque stockbroker I had spotted on the Lexington Avenue subway on my way to a downtown video editing facility. Though Annette and I got together at her apartment rather hastily, it took several weeks after I had moved in before she realized I would never evolve into the man suitable to father the children she was eager to bear, now that she was professionally established and had passed the thirty mark. Determined and outspoken, she tried as a last resort to convince me to go into counseling. When I merely shrugged, she issued her parting salvo: I was a fraud, impressing unsuspecting girls with my suits and charm and that responsible look. I really ought to carry a warning placard or a sandwich board, just like people advertising somebody's eatery, spelling out the truth: I didn't have a place to live, lacked a reliable job, and certainly harbored no intentions of settling down.

Was I indeed a fraud? The question continued to resonate in my mind and lead to a chain of distressing thoughts. Would I one day end up like that shivering homeless penitent kneeling on an icy curb on Fifth Avenue? Was that the price I would have to pay, as my cousin Albrecht claimed would one day be exacted from each of us?

Albrecht's notion of a retributive universe was unexpectedly confirmed in a way he would have given anything to forego. Though my interpretation would diverge from his, what happened was a *Katastrophe* I could hardly believe. It was all the more unreal because I found out about it from a letter Stephanie had sent several weeks after the fact. Yet in reflecting on that wrenching event, I realized I really shouldn't have been surprised. I had recognized something ethereal about Stephanie's child ever since taking that photo of her as a two-year-old holding onto a strand of Albrecht's silvery hair. There was a curtain beyond which I couldn't see her growing up and crossing the threshold to womanhood. On my last visit to Hansi's Widenmayerstrasse home, I had shared this mystification with Frau Trepper (who regarded me more kindly in recent years). I tried to keep it low-key, but still the old *Erzieherin* blanched, as if I was articulating her deepest fears. Albrecht's Angelina had, in fact, just turned fifteen and was becoming an accomplished *Reiterin* with an impressive collection of equestrian ribbons and cups when the freak accident occurred. While driving the young princess and a girlfriend to Poland to buy a promising horse, their riding coach fell asleep at the wheel and the car smashed into a tree. Neither the coach nor the friend was hurt, and Albrecht's granddaughter had only a reddish bruise on her brow, obscured by a loose curl of blond hair. But she never regained consciousness and two days later was taken off life-support.

Everybody at the funeral appeared stunned. Stephanie, now divorced and seeing a young London barrister, stood silently next to Hansi in the little chapel in Munich over the family crypt, sharing his grief in a way they had never shared anything as husband and wife. My aging aunt, who couldn't raise the funds in time to make the trip, sent an uncharacteristically brief telegram. "My great-granddaughter has been deprived of life," Issten cabled from France. "I have been deprived of the next generation." And Frau Trepper, who couldn't stop blaming herself for not accompanying her charge on the trip and perhaps changing fate, was at home under heavy sedation.

Only Albrecht was voluble. Mingling with other mourners after the internment, he seemed to be in a trance as he insisted on making it openly known what he thought. Wasn't it obvious to anyone who knew about divine ways? Since no one else was hurt, surely this was the punishment of God. It was the punishment he had so often predicted for Stephanie's transgressions, if not for those of his mother, visited on the next generation and perhaps on generations yet to come. *Such could be divine wrath!*

Albrecht's perspective made the tragedy no easier for him to bear. Angelina was dead; his little angel was no more. He made no effort to hide his tears, whether waiting in the crisp air of the early dawn, hidden in a pine tree perch, gun at the ready for the stag whose time had come; or sitting alone in the dim light of his cellar-like room, intently penciling figures on those lined yellow sheets and wordlessly finishing off Frau Kunst's best. Day after day, the tears would worm their way down his face in glistening rivulets, his grief made all the more poignant by his princely dignity.

Yet Albrecht eventually found comfort in God's divine ways, just as he did after his wife's death thirty years before. In what appeared as such stern justice for another's thoughtless acts, hadn't God also shown his infinite wisdom and love? Angelina was now where she belonged, in heaven, in the Perfect Universe, saved from the perils of this world and the incalculable risks of eternal hell, of eternal separation from Albrecht and from God. Wasn't that what Albrecht had prayed for all along? Perhaps God knew this was the only way. Although Albrecht never put it into words, he recognized that the intervention had been delayed until the last moment. His Angelina was already blossoming into a mature beauty whose sole imperfection was a roving eye. The reason Albrecht had encouraged her to go on that fateful journey to Poland to buy a horse was to keep her interests focused on something that was safe.

The tragedy impelled me to give new credibility to Albrecht's life-long views. I had just completed – between gainful employment on a variety of films – a manuscript titled *Future Pleasure*. Seeking to reaffirm my own lifelong quest, this work amounted to a self-help manual for maximizing pleasure while evading some of its more obvious side effects. Now, as I was beginning to question anew the premises on which *Future Pleasure* was based, an old friend in New York offered to give the manuscript to a literary agent noted for promoting new authors. "Whatever the case," he said, "you'll be in good hands with Kathryn."

In response to her non-committal note, I made an appointment with Kathryn at the mid-Manhattan agency where she was employed. The demure young woman who took off her reading glasses to greet me in her office had the looks of a Grace Kelly, her low-key, understated manner amplifying her allure. She somehow maneuvered me into holding forth for over an hour without herself venturing an opinion about my work, and then invited me to lunch. The mutual empathy during our two hours in the Plaza Hotel's Palm Court prompted me to reciprocate by offering to make dinner at the apartment where I was staying. The owner happened to be away, and when Kathryn finally rang the bell and we found ourselves alone with the door latched, I felt the anticipation of being in a situation without limits on my fantasies.

The very next day I moved my suitcase to Kathryn's small but comfortable apartment in a stylish Upper East Side building. I was amused to learn that two floors below resided my classmate, Lewis Lapham. Living out my romantic dream in this milieu, I was beginning to feel on top again for the first time in years. Kathryn combined a tenderness of character with a tumultuous physicality that continued to propel both of us into a special dimension of our own. It was as if we had been specifically designed to arouse and delectably satisfy the full range of each other's sensory appetites. I had no explanation for this carnal synergy, except perhaps that she had been born on exactly the same day as I, a decade after me.

Kathryn's one imperfection was a blemish just beyond the right corner of her mouth. It was a stress pimple, she explained on a day it happened to be more noticeable than usual. Quiet almost to the point of being taciturn, she rationalized her silence by saying she preferred to speak to me with her body. Unlike that statuesque stockbroker Annette, Kathryn seemed to understand my comings and goings, whether to spend a week with my parents in Massachusetts or three weeks on a film project in Miami. "I've finally figured out what you are," she quietly interjected one evening with a smile, as she folded her arms in mock resignation in the midst of listening to a discourse on my unsettled life. "You are a civilian of fortune!"

Although Kathryn had yet to express herself about *Future Pleasure* with a contract or even in words, our relationship revalidated the basic assumptions espoused in that work. The purpose of life indeed was to maximize our pleasures while evading the side effects! Yes, that had to be the ultimate plan, our human destiny. And if there was a God as Albrecht claimed, the most convincing proof of his love for us creatures here below would be reflected in how he continued to make everything on earth such absolute and perpetual delight.

Book Two
IN QUEST OF REDEMPTION
I. Exposed

EXPOSED

It was a little after seven when I awoke to a gray midwinter dawn, the lower panes of the half-open window covered with frost. The small radiator clattering under the sill was hardly sufficient to heat the frigid air rolling in in visible sheets of mist.

I took refuge deeper in the warmth of my bed; oh, to have just a moment more within this pleasurable retreat! Then I made the lunge to release the latch that let the window down.

I could feel the room start warming up. It was a small room, but it had remained mine all these years I had been coming back to stay at my parents' Massachusetts farm. On one wall hung a permanent display of some of the more illustrious ancestors from Father's side, clad in fine silk robes of confidants at royal courts, or in gilded military uniforms. On another wall were several framed photographs depicting cherished moments from my past, including one with Stephanie walking arm-in-arm on the beach in Lignano, Italy. The biggest photo of the lot had been taken more than a decade ago by the alluring shoe heiress from Saint Louis, who had balked at marrying me for fear of falling into immediate penury. The poster-sized rendition showed me standing on the pink sands of Bermuda's Elbow Beach, with every muscle deline-

261

ated almost as well as when I had been the light-heavy-weight boxing champion at Yale. I was slimmer now and the muscles were still there. It was a standard from which I was determined not to retreat for as long as I could.

This was usually my favorite time in bed, when I could roll over and nap, waiting for the room to become pleasantly warm. I was vaguely aware of Father downstairs going through his morning exercise routine. He was over eighty now and continued to do justice to his honorific title of Mr. Exercycle. He could still charm most women at will, especially if it meant selling one of his conditioning machines. I could hear him doing leg raises, banging his heels energetically on the floor.

I wasn't having much success falling back to sleep. As I moved around in bed, I was feeling strangely restless as if I wasn't completely myself, as if a part of me had been taken over by something that didn't belong. I had never felt this way before and wondered: was this what male menopause was all about? There were other tip-offs, too. I had been beset lately by dreams of missing trains, usually at one of the great European stations like the Hauptbahnhof in Munich or the Gare de L'Est in Paris. Dashing with my bags through the crowds along a seemingly endless boarding platform, I would sometimes get almost close enough to jump on the moving train; more often, the rear car would be disappearing beyond the maze of winding tracks, leaving me alone on the deserted platform.

I sat up abruptly with an unwelcome thought. Had I passed my prime, and somewhere along the line missed the waiting train? Indeed, I had recently scaled down my aspirations. Instead of further massaging the prose of *Future Pleasure* in the hope of having it published, I took on a series of film scripts for a producer in Miami on daycare centers in the Southeast. The money promised to be good, but the job would be tedious and extend over several months, which was far longer than I could expect to sleep on my brother's couch in his little house. This had led me to a drastic step. After nearly a decade of a peripatetic existence, I had signed a one-year lease for an apartment of my own. It was in an attractive modern building at the water's edge in Miami's vaunted Coconut Grove. Yet rather than being relieved over this constructive step, I felt as if I had fallen into a trap. My dream for years had been to settle in California, preferably Laguna Beach. That old stomping ground would surely have worked its magic once more and lifted me out of the latest doldrums! But alas, California would have to wait. While I hadn't moved into my Florida apartment yet, I had been driving there every few days from my brother's house to literally take on the fleas left behind by the previous tenant with a Siamese cat. I didn't want the management to use one of those sprays which would deposit a poisonous residue. My own method consisted of leaving a bear rug I owned in the middle of the empty living room. In the absence of a cat, the furry rug attracted the forsaken fleas. I would then take off my shoes and socks and walk back and forth on the rug, providing an opportunity for the fleas to jump at my warm ankles and calves. This they did in droves; I would then pick them off by hand and dispose of them down the toilet. During each visit, I repeated the rug-walking procedure several times, eventually tempting even the most recalcitrant to take the fatal leap. In the process, I met an airline stewardess who held a long-term lease on an apartment only two doors down from where I was going to live. Her smile seemed to be as beckoning as in that famous *Fly Me!* advertising campaign, and before long she invited me to dinner at her place. As we sipped glass after glass of champagne, I tried to caution her, remembering Annette's parting words, that I might not be a good prospect for a sustained affair. I even implied I was the immature superficial type partial to passionate sex. I suspected already from the way she kissed that she had never experienced passionate sex and perhaps never would. Where would that leave me for the duration of my lease? As soon as the champagne wore off, I found out. Coming to with a start at her side in bed, I felt distressed over what I had done and tried to sneak out without waking her up. But in the dark, I couldn't find my pants. I fell fitfully asleep again for an hour or so, and then tried to make a discreet exit once more under the cover of the night. This time, I found my pants but couldn't find my socks and shoes. Nevertheless, I tiptoed out barefoot to my car parked downstairs in the apartment lot, and with great relief fled the scene. I spent the rest of the night on my brother's couch, and called the stewardess the following morning with a plausible explanation for my vanishing act. But I had yet to return to pick up my shoes or launch any further missions against the fleas.

Contemplating this episode at my parents' home, I realized there was no way I could fall asleep now. How did I manage to get so messed up, I wondered half-aloud. I didn't blame the stewardess and still felt terrible about the way I had behaved. Her misfortune was to have been the first since my breakup with Kathryn, who had set a new standard in my continuing quest for the ideal bride. The realization that I might never find another partner with Kathryn's attributes was at least in part causing my depression – along with the prospects of those boring day-care scripts, the apartment I didn't want, and the stewardess I dreaded to face.

The room felt sufficiently warm, and I jumped out of bed. *Quick, do your exercise;* a brisk ten minutes of deep-knee bends, push-ups and sit-ups, capped by running a foot-long rubber roller vigorously over my muscles for several minutes from head to toe. The roller had multiple rows of red suction cups and little rubber prongs, which made it look like something for internal use from a porno shop. Years ago, while living in the communal East Side brownstone in New York, the motherly maid who came in from Harlem had boiled my previous version of this device on one of her weekly visits, thinking it needed to be sterilized. On a subsequent trip to Europe, I had to make a special trip to Munich to buy a replacement in the only store which carried that line. Unlike the roller I had once bought in France, this one was perfectly machined with ball bearings that prevented it from snagging body hair. Maybe this unique instrument would help dispel the strange, forlorn feeling I hadn't been able to shake since waking up.

It was time for me to go to the kitchen. I could no longer hear Father's lunging and grunting as he shadow boxed. The inviting aroma of coffee was drifting up to my room. Mother, as usual, would already have eaten, but Father would be breakfasting now. I truly enjoyed my parents and didn't want to think of a time when they wouldn't be around. Yet, I knew how inevitable that was, and even this perennial reflection started to suffuse me with unusual grief.

Father was pouring his last cup of coffee. As I watched him add milk and stir in two spoonfuls of sugar, I noticed how vigorous and fresh he looked, with sparkles in his eyes. Born to a gentle existence, he had lost everything and was forced to learn how to fend for himself in the rough exposure to America's unprivileged ways. But he was reconciled with his lot, and his paramount aim now was to continue thwarting old age.

"Your face looks kind of crumpled," Father observed jovially. "What's the matter, didn't you sleep well?"

"I slept just fine, thank you."

"I'm sure it's something in your head again. If you made a nice son or two, like I always told you to, you wouldn't be having these troubles. You can't spend all of your life just ficking around and have nothing to show for it. At least I'm glad I did the right thing . . . that I made all of you kids and married Mother."

"Can't I please have my breakfast in peace?" I grumbled, as I finished squeezing two oranges and a grapefruit. I was feeling vulnerable to Father's familiar refrain, which served as a poignant reminder of what I had forfeited in losing Kathryn. I found myself blinking fast, remembering the night she had leaned over me in bed, and thinking I was asleep, whispered, "Oh darling, I love you so terribly and want to marry you and have your babies!" While a part of me had wanted to respond, I instinctively withdrew deeper into that feigned sleep. As much as I felt for her, how could I forever remove myself from all other inviting possibilities in the world, especially if my career were to start looking up again? Alas, it was only after she was irrevocably gone that I realized she had been the woman of my dreams.

I sat down across from Father and tried to concentrate on spooning out my two soft-boiled eggs and wolfing down several pieces of well-buttered toast. Although Father had finished eating, he put another piece of bread in the toaster.

"All that butter! I don't know how you do it without getting fat," he said with grudging admiration. "I get hungry just watching you. It's better when you have your zucchini. Then I'm not tempted at all. You know, in the old days, you would have made a great *Voresser*."

It wasn't the first time Father had ventured this opinion, and I knew what he meant. A Voresser was literally, *one who eats before*; usually a person of modest means hired by wealthy or noble families overstuffed with their five daily meals and in need of an example to work up their appetites. Gorging himself in the presence of this haughty company, the Voresser received both an ample meal and a nominal fee.

"That would have solved your job problem," Father laughed, while he sparingly buttered his toast. "As a Voresser, you would have really enjoyed your work."

Despite the way I felt, I managed a feeble smile. I didn't notice Mother, who had materialized seemingly from nowhere. A gray-haired elderly lady with deeply etched worry lines, she looked a bit hurt, as if Father-the-count had inadvertently slighted one of her plebeian children, for whom she had sacrificed so much and held such high hopes.

"Voresser?" she asked with a touch of irony. "And for that he went to Yale?"

I had come home just for the week between Christmas and New Year's, and my stay was drawing to a close. I was glad this happened to be the day I had promised to visit my sister Manya and spend the night at her house. Maybe the three-hour drive and change of scenery would help me find my old self again.

A year younger than I (she was the one whose pacifier I used to snatch from her mouth), my sister over the past dozen years could be categorized as a Jesus freak. A strikingly attractive but deliberately sedate mother of five in her mid-forties, she lived in a comfortable house on Cape Cod, where her husband was the manager of a large resort hotel. Manya welcomed my visits, despite her fear of the influence I might have on her children, especially on her pert ten-year-old who strutted around in her John Lennon T-shirt, dreaming of a chance for a tryout in film or on stage. But Manya was willing to take the risk for the opportunity to give me a personal pitch on how Jesus could change my life. She remained undeterred by my oft-repeated stance that I wasn't about to have Jesus cramp my style, especially as interpreted by some horny celibates in the Catholic Church. I invariably begged off Manya's invitations to her charismatic prayer meetings, which she said were the key to anyone's spiritual life. "I guess I'm not ready yet," I always said smugly, preferring to sit around with her husband for another glass of wine while she went off after dinner to meet with her group. "As you yourself say, Jesus will let me know when the right time comes."

It was early afternoon by the time I left for the drive to Manya's in my little hatchback car. Having felt distraught throughout the day, I was glad to be alone with my thoughts. At least I didn't have to worry about Mother or anyone else seeing me in this sorry state. And indeed, it wasn't long before I found myself wiping an occasional dribble off my cheeks as I again yielded to involuntary self-flagellation over Kathryn. I was anguishing over the time toward the end of our relationship when I had weaseled out of a promise that she could accompany me on a three-week skiing trip to the French Pyrenees. It wasn't a question of money, since she had offered to pay her way. But I wanted to include a weeklong visit to my aging aunt's château at the foot of the mountains where I planned to ski. This would have exposed Kathryn – or so I tried to convince her – to rats, bats, spiders and a whole array of other primitive living conditions, associated with fourteenth century dwellings. With a trace of sadness and a wan smile, she acquiesced. My real reason for wanting to travel alone was that I didn't want to be exposed to Kathryn's increasingly depressed moods. Her stress pimple was more prominent and she was seeing her psychiatrist twice a week. When I arrived at the Pyrenees skiing resort, I wrote her an exultant card, signing it, *Ever Singularly*. In our happier days, Kathryn had often joked how different I was; not only was I a civilian of fortune, *singular* is what she also called me. But seeing the word on my postcard, she took it the wrong way. When I returned a week later than she had expected, I could tell she was severely disturbed, despite being on Valium. That evening she haltingly confessed she had come close to turning on the gas, thinking I had left her for good. God, if I had only realized I was the source of her depression and could have lifted her out of it with a few well-chosen words! After several more days of gathering her strength, Kathryn gave me up like a noxious drug. We were mismatched from the start, she calmly observed, as she asked for my set of keys to her apartment and wished me well.

Remembering the parting scene in the solitude of my car, I clutched the steering wheel with both hands. God, how stupidly I had screwed myself! Kathryn had been willing to forgo a number of financially successful suitors for my sake, and I had balked at her proffered sacrifice. I suddenly recalled a remark by a casual friend who published ghoulish comic books featuring religious terror as their theme. "Being sorry for having screwed yourself is hardly a meaningful contrition," this self-proclaimed atheist had pointed out, with a mixture of sincerity and jest. "Nor is it enough to be contrite because you had screwed or offended somebody else. If you're to have any chance of being spared the fires of hell, you have to be sincerely and truly sorry for having offended God." I had tried at that time to dismiss those words as coming from a loon; now, as I continued the drive to Cape Cod, I was tormented with a distressing thought: *Had I indeed offended God – not only with Kathryn but throughout my life?*

By the time I arrived at Manya's, I felt emotionally drained. Fortunately, dinner was waiting, and I was able to camouflage my mood by concentrating on the food. I repeatedly complimented my sister on the evident care she had taken preparing the meal, if only for want of anything else to say. Then, as we were finishing dessert, Manya made her customary pitch. "There's a prayer meeting tonight," she said, with the caution of a child reaching out to a puppy that might bite. "Would you like to come?"

I was, in fact, anticipating her request. I had always been the type willing to try anything, the way I did with Dr. Bieler's zucchini cure for the breakdown of my health. Now, I was feeling on the verge of a breakdown of a different sort; so why not give Manya's salutary suggestion a chance?

The swiftness of my response took away my sister's breath. "Sure," I said, as casually as I could. "Let's go."

2/

A balding, chunky man was conducting the prayer meeting that night. He wore a shiny warm-up jacket over a heavy checkered shirt. He introduced himself as Al, in a thick Back Bay accent that made his every *a* sound as if it had been drawn out and pressed down. My sister told me he was the local plumber.

Attending the prayer meeting with Manya wasn't my first experience of this sort. A few years back, I had accompanied the shoe heiress from Saint Louis to her Manhattan Christian Science church in gratitude for being cured of my twenty-four-hour intestinal flu in one day. After enjoying an elegant dinner at the Cosmopolitan Club with her glamorous mother and the fashionable woman who had prayed for my healing over the phone, we crossed Park Avenue to the plush 65th Street church for the regular Wednesday evening show-and-tell service. There I heard perfectly coifed ladies in mink offer their personal testimonies how God had *demonstrated* his power; not only by healing their various ailments but by fulfilling their material aspirations, whether finding the right apartment or having their financial investments perform miraculously well. With this kind of personal information being divulged by so many single, rich women, no wonder I spotted in the comfortably upholstered pews a smattering of well-groomed single men in custom-tailored suits with four real buttonholes on each sleeve. While their motives may have been questionable, I was there solely to please my Christian Science friend. Thinking I would please her still more, I stood up on a sudden impulse during a lull between testimonies to deliver one of my own. "I'm not a Christian Scientist, but some of my best friends are," I started with appropriate gravity. "And because one of them happened to be with me at a critical moment in the middle of the night, I'm fortunate to have been saved from an unpleasant malady." I launched into a detailed but tactful explanation of my diarrhea, followed by general ruminations about God, life, and the human condition. Never for a moment did I think someone in the church might draw untoward conclusions from my testimony about the nature of my relationship with the shoe heiress at my side. But as soon as I sat down, she gave me an angry look. "You bastard, now everybody knows what we do," she whispered, clearly upset since sex outside of marriage was a fundamental no-no or *error* among Christian Science faithful. At the end of the service, however, when several of the older women congratulated me on my inspiring testimony, my intimate partner stood proudly at my side. Even the minister made the unprecedented move of stepping down from the podium to give me a personal pitch for joining the Christian Science Church. A few days later, I nevertheless realized my lovely friend was again doing a slow burn. All these years she had been hoping to gather enough courage to give a testimony of her own as a demonstration of her faith. Yet, there I was, a self-proclaimed fornicator who had done it as a lark, and all those old ladies fell for it.

The meeting where Manya had brought me was unlike the Park Avenue church. From a glimpse of the people filling several rows of the brown metal folding chairs in the auditorium of the local parochial school, I realized there would be no minks here, no four buttonholes on the sleeves – and thank God for that. This was the last place I wanted to be seen by any of those friends. I would find that no less embarrassing than for some of the occupants of these chairs to be caught at an X-rated film. I had too many answers about life to be entrusting myself to some simplistic approach geared to people who seemed to be foundering and in need of help.

Standing on a little podium in front of a provisional altar, Al paused to scan his somber-faced audience. "I know how happy all of you are to be here," said the plumber-turned-preacher with a touch of levity. "I only wish every now and then you'd let your faces know."

I felt the muscles of my jaws relax momentarily before resuming their grim set. Just because I was a sucker for corny jokes didn't mean that Al's observation applied to me. But since I wanted to make my sister happy, I figured I might as well play along. I held onto the hymnbook with Manya, I mouthed a few of the prayers I knew, and I listened impassively to individual attendees praise Jesus. If only they didn't always get so carried away in calling out to "Gee-zhus!" Some of them sounded as if they were mental patients on furlough, especially the rotund woman a few rows behind us who came forth with a torrent of gibberish, which I presumed was speaking in tongues.

"Appah, appah beezak, tooey hoo karrooh!" I heard her conclude with a flourish.

"Alleluia," responded several people around me, including my sister. "Alleluia."

"What was all that about," I muttered to Manya.

"She's talking directly to God," my sister whispered back. "It's her soul speaking. Only He understands."

I was trying to think of a clever repartee when my attention was distracted by a lithe twenty-year-old sitting in one of the front rows. Maybe there was something to being here after all, if people like her came! My gaze then traveled past her to a small band accompanying the singing of the hymns. Playing the tambourine was a girl with a dwarfish body and a grotesquely large head. She had been born with a pituitary gland tumor that took her sight — at least, that's what my sister whispered to me when she saw me watching this cruel parody of nature jiggle and strike her instrument so happily. As my eyes came to rest again and again on this girl's pitiful form, her cheerful radiance made me realize how little cause I had for gloom.

"Praise be . . ." somebody called out. Then from another part of the room, "Praise be, oh sweet Jesus!"

I tried to screw up my mouth into position so that I, too, could hurl forth expletives of praise. Yet even though my lips moved, no sound emerged. It would have made Manya so happy, especially if I could do it with that same *Gee-zhus* verve. What was embarrassing me was not just being here among so many self-avowed losers. Had I come as a curious outsider, I could have put on a creditable show. But instead, I was feeling uncomfortably close to being a participant; in fact, *needing* to be a participant.

"Let us pray," I heard Al, the group leader, intone. He paused to give everyone a chance to stand. "Our all-merciful Lord, put your loving arms around us. Heal us of the hurts we have suffered, forgive us for the sins we have committed . . . forgive us for whatever pain we may have caused others . . . for whatever we did that was wrong . . . for whatever we didn't do that we should have done."

The words continued to flow. I was no longer conscious of Al's brogue, which had a pacifying lilt. I was appreciating his low-key delivery and pauses, which let me think how his words might apply to me. I found it relaxing to close my eyes. I felt a certain comfort, a certain relief from the pressing nature of my cares.

"Thank you, Jesus . . ." Al was concluding, his eyes shut, his voice a whisper. "Thank you for guiding us and protecting us. Thank you for loving us. Thank you for being always there when we needed you the most."

"Thank you, Jesus," somebody interjected.

"Alleluia, Gee-zhus!" another voice chimed in.

As I watched Al link hands with the worshippers standing on either side of him, I felt one hand gently grasped by my sister and the other by a white-haired woman on the other side of me.

I felt my arms lifted upward, a crescendo of voices chanting in unison, "Praise be Jesus! Praise be! Praise be! Praise be Jesus our Lord!"

Once more, Al took the lead. "Oh Lord Jesus, hear our prayer. We ask for this moment of silence to bring before you our special requests. We entrust to you our most private thoughts so that thy will be done, and our burdens will be lighter to bear."

There was an extended pause. My eyes were pressed shut, and I was welcoming this moment of peace. It was like those five second silent prayers I had continued to offer since childhood to whoever was in charge in the yonder world: *Please keep me safe and sound, protect my parents whom I love, and spare me any personal calamities such as breaking a leg, or God forbid, some intimate disease.* Now, as I was about to run through a more pertinent version of this litany, I experienced an overwhelming surprise. Before I was able to make a single wish, I sensed a distinct but seamless shift, as if someone had gently turned a rheostatic switch. I felt a soothing, all-pervasive light illuminate the darkness within my brain and banish the somberness lurking there. I was filled with a lightheadedness, a liberation from worldly cares, and a sense of unabashed gratitude for this radiant moment. Any notion of embarrassment as to where I was and what I was doing here disappeared. I couldn't think of a problem I had or a request I wanted to make. All I could feel was a sense of inner strength, inner warmth, inner peace which couldn't be shaken. It was so sudden, so total that I couldn't question it or compare it to anything else. For the first time in my life I felt as if I needed nothing else. Oh, it felt so comforting and good. Oh, how thankful I was! *Yes, thank you, thank you, thank you, Jesus.*

The meeting was over. Around me people were embracing in that special, communal way. I released the hand of the old woman next to me and turned to look directly at her for the first time. She smiled, put her arms around me, and whispered, "Welcome back."

I didn't realize I had been that obvious. But I didn't mind. I was suffused by an outgoing warmth reinforcing the profound gratitude I was continuing to feel.

My sister also noticed the change. We didn't embrace since Manya had always been restrained about any show of physicality. But her eyes were shining and proud. I was her pupil whom she had been able to make see the light. All those prayers, all those persistent efforts I had spurned or ridiculed, had come to fruition before her eyes. It was proof that Jesus was real, that he was doing his work among us to this day. What greater miracle could anyone imagine than to witness what was happening to me just then?

With evident pride, Manya introduced me to several women who came by to say hello. They gave each other knowing looks, as if they were familiar with my case and had prayed on my behalf.

I didn't mind this public exposure. My lightheadedness verged on giddiness, and that nagging restlessness, which had been making me teary eyed, had vanished. I was free and without a problem. In my exuberance, I edged over to the attractive young woman I had been watching earlier, and we began to chat with a natural spontaneity. I felt the same loving communion toward her as I did when chatting with that elderly woman and my sister's other friends, who now seemed to be endowed with the same human worth. She told me she had come with her fiancé, a regular member of the group. This was her first time, too.

"You coming again?" I asked.

She glanced at her escort, and then nodded with a smile. "I suppose so."

"It kind of grows on you," I said, as if I were an old regular. "Maybe I'll see you around."

On the way back to my sister's house, my elation didn't abate.

"It's called being slain in the spirit," Manya explained. She recounted how it had happened to her years ago when her marriage was collapsing and she was in desperate straits. "I know how you feel," she concluded. "It put me on cloud nine, too."

We talked with a closeness we had never experienced before. There was a sense of being partners in something grand yet intensely personal, as we both bubbled over with unrestrained joy. Our sharing of happiness was akin to two people reverting to reality after making love for the first time and glimpsing a fantastic new dimension that promised to fill their lives with bliss. Feeling this way with my sister seemed almost indecent.

"So Jesus got to you, too," Manya's husband greeted us with good-natured humor. He wanted to have peace in the family and, over the years, accommodated my sister to the point of accompanying her to charismatic weekend retreats. "You don't know how happy you've made Manya. She's been praying for this, God only knows how long. As a matter of fact, she said a prayer for you today just before you came."

"Would you please keep quiet," Manya protested mildly.

"I might even get a little loving tonight," he said jovially, "thanks to you and Jesus."

My sister's nervous laugh reflected her embarrassment. "Not if you talk this way, you won't."

After bidding my hosts an especially cordial goodnight, I went upstairs to the guest room. I undressed, opened the window, and slid under the covers before the cold air could trail me in. But I wasn't about to fall asleep. I still felt as if I were riding one of those oxygen highs I had experienced on returning from a week of skiing in the Alps, with extra red blood cells coursing through my veins. I knew this could be a crucial point in my life. I had always suspected, in the back of my mind, that sooner or later I would return to religion. Probably later, much later; perhaps like my old friend Fuzzy Sedgwick, who had been a great bon vivant and philanderer until practically his next-to-last breath, despite a loving wife and a brood of children and grandchildren. But being also an avid historian, he had asked on his deathbed to be converted to the Roman Catholic faith just in case there was something to it after all, in view of its unparalleled two-thousand-year tradition. Certainly, no harm in touching all bases! Yes, I too had expected eventually to crawl back into the fold to play it safe. But never, never did I suspect I would accept Christ honestly, with no reservations, under no extreme duress. *Thank you, Jesus, thank you for sparing me from having to be a hypocrite in my final moments on earth.*

I lay there in bed in an alert trance. Rushing through my head, I could feel the miraculous truth of Christ continue to reveal itself. I could for the first time understand the unique opportunity inherent in bringing Christ into every aspect of my life. *Through Jesus Christ our Lord* . . . what a meaning in those words! No wonder my relationship with Kathryn had failed. How difficult it was to do anything without Jesus, yet how easy when you let him carry part of the load. What a sustaining force!

Lying in the warmth of my bed, I felt euphoric over this insight, which went beyond anything I had previously intuited or learned. How exciting to think of all the people I would be able to influence in this powerful new way! When it came to advising others on key issues in life, I enjoyed an implicit credibility among a wide circle of friends. What a heady feeling to think of the lives I would now be able to change in this incomparably more important way! *Thank you, Jesus; so this was your plan for me all along!* Indeed, I might become famous, and with more reason than those religious fakers and goody-goodies like Jim and Tammy Faye Bakker or even Billy Graham. What an unparalleled perspective I had, having been on the other side, one of the misguided for so many years. I would be able to show others how to take away the burdens of daily life . . . how much better they can live when everything is no longer of ultimate import . . . when there's something so much greater . . . when there's Jesus Christ.

Oh God! I was exulting to myself. *All my life I wanted to know what my role was. I was close for so long, yet I couldn't see it. I thought I was free before . . . but I was such a slave! Now I know . . . it's the scales falling from my eyes. If I've flipped, please let me stay flipped. Oh Jesus, don't ever go away from me . . . or withdraw from my life!*

I could hear the wind blowing outside, sending gusts of frigid air through the open window. I felt so warm and secure under the blankets, protected and looking forward to tomorrow morning, to starting my new life.

Is this what it meant to be born again?

When I awoke, I didn't want to face myself. I pulled the pillow over my head, trying to shut out the reality of the previous night. While I had none of the physical symptoms of a hangover, I felt as if I were coming out of a terrible drunk. I had slobbered all over myself with words, committed emotional excesses, and succumbed to embarrassing indiscretions of the mind. On top of that, I was again beginning to experience that strange restless feeling which I thought had left me for good.

How could I have allowed my judgment to become so impaired? I felt myself cringe within, remembering those extravagant details I spewed forth about Jesus, about my new life in Christ and converting the world on his behalf. Hadn't my experience really been a case of autosuggestion, a form of self-hypnosis? I had seen people turned on with equal rapture by Maharai-Ji, the Reverend Moon, the Hare Krishnas, Tim Leary, Baba Ram Das, and a variety of other gurus and prophets of our time.

Fortunately, the only person I had to face was my sister, and I hadn't been nearly as effusive with her as in my thoughts.

Manya was awaiting me in the kitchen. "How are you this morning?" she asked probingly. I could see in her expression the same joy she had shared with me the previous night, but which I could no longer reciprocate.

"I slept just fine," I said, deliberately noncommittal. "The bed in that room is really comfortable."

Manya insisted on preparing my breakfast. There was an uneasy silence as she hovered over the stove and then served me my food. I knew what she was thinking: After working on me all those years, had she lost me so soon?

She was delighted when I asked for a couple more pieces of toast, and would she mind making me some coffee after all? "I could really use a lift," I explained.

This seemed to be the opening Manya was waiting for. "I think I know how you feel. You shouldn't let it worry you if you're a little down today. That's not at all unusual."

"Now you tell me," I said, trying to keep it light. "Is there an antidote?"

Manya was measuring out the ground coffee for the percolator and paused to give me a reassuring look. "What you must do is trust the Lord. Don't be afraid. Trust the Lord."

I tried not to betray an instant of exasperation. It was this kind of an answer that had led me to conclude in recent years that my sister was compromising her intelligence. "Anything else?" I asked.

"You must pray. Whenever you can, you must pray and read the Bible. That's the way the Lord will speak to you."

"So that's what those priests and little old nuns are doing when I see them with their open Bibles on buses and trains! I always wondered what was the point of reading the same stuff over and over again."

"It's the only way to overcome your doubts and become strong in your faith."

"Sounds like brainwashing to me."

Manya glanced at me uneasily, as if I were blaspheming. "It's a great gift. I hope you take advantage of it." She brought me the toast and remained standing by my chair. "To pray, to read the word of the Lord . . . in fact, anything he inspired others to write . . . whether saints, humble priests, or everyday people . . ."

"And I suppose," I interjected a bit sarcastically, "I should also go to meetings and all that."

"By all means. As often as possible."

"But you always made it sound like a one-shot deal. I thought all I had to do was come to *a* meeting."

"I certainly didn't mean it that way. Don't you see, it's a commitment for a lifetime. There's no going back."

I crunched on my remaining piece of toast. "You sound like Dr. Bieler."

"Dr. Bieler?"

"An old medical doctor in California who also claimed there was no going back if I wanted to be saved. Two raw egg yolks and steamed zucchini for breakfast as long as I lived . . . if I wanted to live. Yet, look at me, here I am, almost ten years later, enjoying something quite different. Doesn't that tell you anything?"

My sister looked bewildered. "How can you compare the two!"

"Don't forget, Jesus was known primarily as a healer in his time. Making the blind see, casting out evil spirits . . ."

"That's different. Those were miracles."

"In many parts of the world, tribal priests still double as doctors. They know the importance of keeping body and soul together."

Manya seemed embarrassed for my sake. "But that's witchcraft. They're pagans. Just remember, Jesus loves you."

"Why can't I distill out of this Jesus stuff what's right for me . . . the way I did out of all that Bieler rigmarole?"

"Don't you see, you can't do it alone? None of us can do it alone." Manya paused to give me a telling look. "Besides, it's a mortal sin if you don't go to church."

The last phrase instantly made my dander rise. Obviously, she meant the Catholic Church; that whole authoritarian hierarchy with its spiteful internal politics and the nasty habit of arrogating to itself a monopoly of truth. Back in my intellectual history class at Yale, Professor Baumer alerted me to the perils of such a fallacious mindset. The evidence was certainly there, reflected in the horrors committed in Christ's name, whether the merciless slaughter perpetrated during the Crusades, the unimaginable tortures inflicted by the Inquisition, or the suppression of ideas to this day. If there indeed was any validity to my experience the previous night — to that liberating infusion of light which supposedly had been the visitation of Christ — I would stay open to exploring it on my own. But damn if I would do it through the Church! I hadn't been in thirty years, and I wasn't about to go now. Besides, if missing a single mass was a mortal sin, as Manya implied, I was already irredeemably lost.

Although this conclusion had started out as an attempt at being flip, it intensified the strange restlessness I felt within. Fleetingly I wondered, *what if Manya was right?*

The coffee was ready, and Manya poured me a cup. "Don't forget, it was through the Church that Jesus came to you last night. Oh, don't you see how blessed you are? Jesus has finally called you. It's a great honor."

It wasn't until driving home later that day that it suddenly hit me: Hadn't I always told my sister with such levity, in declining her previous invitations to prayer meetings, Jesus would let me know when the right time came?

3/

It was late afternoon by the time I returned to my parents' farm. I was hungry, but I figured a walk would do me good. An hour on the wooded trails beyond the fields adjoining our house would relax me after the long drive, and I could still be back in time to finish dinner before the evening news.

I walked out of the weatherworn green farmhouse and whistled to Blackie the dog. He was an affectionate mutt who loved to accompany me on my walks, even though it meant leaving the warmth of the furnace in the cellar where he slept. Blackie had a thick coat of curly hair to protect him against the winter cold, which was a hindrance when he relieved himself and heavy dried blobs accumulated around his tail. But the mutt seemed undeterred by this encumbrance from behind.

I set out for the woods several hundred yards from the farm, with Blackie leading the way. I turned up the collar of the battered sheepskin coat I had acquired years ago at the Antartex store in London, trying to keep out the biting late-afternoon frost. The crust of the knee-deep snow covering the field had softened earlier in the sun but was now solid again. The crepe rubber boots I wore didn't sink in or slip, allowing me to concentrate on my thoughts.

I had been in a strange turmoil all day. Whenever Kathryn intruded on my mind, a question I had never before asked myself presented itself with mounting insistence: *What sort of a person am I?* Several times I was on the verge of articulating the answer but at the last moment averted my thoughts. I also found myself repeatedly trying to recapture the enthusiasm of the previous night about becoming an influential spokesman for Christ. How remote that seemed now! What could I say to anyone? That higher theological understanding I possessed such a short time ago was inaccessible to me, like some special brilliance I had flaunted in a dream but was unable to recall on waking up. No matter how hard

I tried, I couldn't conjure up the spiritual conflagration that had been so real. Just enough residue remained to prompt a recurring thought: what if my life had indeed been based on a faulty premise, and I was in a state of mortal sin?

Blackie had by now disappeared into the woods. I was about to follow him and turned for a final look in the direction of the setting sun, a purple disc balancing itself on top of a distant hill. I paused on the firm snow to watch the last of the pulsating glow extinguished in the darkening crowns of the trees. Then I turned back to take the final few steps that would put me under the cover of the evergreens.

But I never made the move. The strange restlessness that had plagued me over the last couple of days suddenly intensified and became an immobilizing fear. In the darkening sky directly above, something invisible yet perceptible shifted, like two surfaces in an earthquake fault. It was a quick, abrupt move that appeared to open the sky and create a link like an endless umbilical cord, which made communication between me and the celestial rift instantly possible. And the first message was already coming through. Though without sound or words, it was unmistakably clear: *YOU HAVE SINNED!*

I stood there at the edge of the woods, mouth opened in a wordless gasp. The shock came not from being addressed this way; what was so oppressively squeezing my lungs was the idea of sin. Having always thought of sin as something to keep the simple-minded in line, I felt as if the most far-fetched of fairy tales were turning out to be true – as if all those transgressions I had heard spoken of as sins and dismissed with a smirk really were the rules of God. Perhaps I had a soul after all, the way I had imagined as a six-year-old, floating just above the area in my midsection where I now felt myself connected to that excoriating celestial source.

YES, YOU HAVE SINNED . . .

There it was again! I neither questioned nor doubted the message that was making me shake with fear. I remembered what it felt like years ago when I was being rebuked by my old headmaster for the indiscreet remark concerning Dr. Renny and Mr. Hale. People had often compared the Duke's infrequent but just outbursts to the wrath of God. Yet this was the real thing I was feeling now! I had always thought if the impossible did occur and God decided on this form of person-to-person call, it would be to commend me on the good and considerate life I had tried to lead, and what a capital and altruistic fellow I was. How evil did one have to be for God to single you out in this damning way?

Standing on the frozen snow, I felt a coldness spreading out from deep within. I had a sense of isolation, as if I no longer belonged or was a part of all that was familiar to me on earth.

I called out to Blackie roaming somewhere among the trees. What a relief to have him bound to my side, his steaming tongue hanging out as I gave him a few affectionate pats. I needed this contact with the living world to be reassured of its warmth, now that I had glimpsed a reality so chillingly strange.

LOOK HOW YOU HAVE SINNED!

The terrifying link continued to hold, with the messages conveyed in a distressing pattern I was learning to recognize. First there would be a stunned feeling in the gut, as if from a blow. The meaning then made itself instantly clear in images and unspoken words. With hardly a pause in between, one message crowded the next, each accompanied by that eviscerating thrust.

I was overwhelmed by what I recognized as an expanding catalogue of my sins. Most prominent were those deeds I had least wanted to face at the time of their occurrence and tried to tuck away in the back of my mind; like the suffering my affair with Stephanie might have inflicted on Albrecht, or the way my involvement with Avis must have affected her husband. How irrelevant that I had never been caught and always managed to cover my tracks! There was a tangle of other affairs where my pleasures had come at someone else's expense. Especially the scores of non-adulterous relationships, where I had evaded my partners' valid expectations. Poor Kathryn, how she must have suffered to have almost turned on the gas! How many of my former loves would have been better off had they never become involved with me? That statuesque stockbroker had been right in wanting me to parade my faults on a sandwich board. If only I could, as a way for making up for all of that now!

YES, *LOOK HOW YOU HAVE SINNED* . . .

Standing there as if stuck to the frozen snow, I felt stripped bare, fully exposed by this scroll of wrongs unraveling from a past I had rarely examined or recalled. I was now being forced to see how I had misused my life. I had received so much, including a privileged education with the expectation that I would use the knowledge to help others and make the world a better place. And indeed, while working at Scholastic and at the Institute and the Peace Corps, I had often told myself I was doing just that by contributing to international amity. Yet how clearly I now recognized that my primary goal had been to make the world as comfortable for myself as I could, even at the cost of compromising the truth. I could see the incident involving Eugene and the pencil sharpener replayed in detail that didn't spare me his mother's penetrating look. An array of other episodes flashed through my mind, highlighted by the agonized features of Bob Fitzgibbon at *Family Weekly*, wishing he could throw out the eight-million run of the article I had foisted on him. No amount of sophistry or rationalization could make me look one iota better than I was being shown to be. My frivolous attitude about life, which people had often found so charming and quaint, was being exposed as one continuous sin. How proud I had been of the sparkling beaches I had once enjoyed, the spectacular mountains I had skied, the vintage wines and delectable foods I had savored, and the wonderful places I had visited around the globe. Now, to my distress, I was being called to account for them all. *BY WHAT RIGHT DID YOU DO THOSE THINGS? SOMEBODY ELSE HAD TO SACRIFICE AND STRUGGLE MIGHTILY TO MAKE POSSIBLE YOUR INDULGENT LIFE. AND HOW ABOUT THOSE THIN-FACED MILLIONS WHO AT THIS MOMENT LACK THE NECESSITIES OF LIFE WHILE YOU'VE HAD MANY TIMES YOUR SHARE? WHAT MADE YOU THINK YOU COULD HAVE TWO ORANGES AND A PINK GRAPEFRUIT FOR BREAKFAST EACH DAY, WHEN EMACIATED CHILDREN ALL OVER THE WORLD ARE DYING FOR THE LACK OF A SINGLE WEDGE?*

Hoping to disrupt this distressing link, I ducked into the woods. I could barely make out the darkening sky through the heavy branches of the tall evergreens, but the messages continued to bombard me. *BY WHAT REASONING DID YOU THINK THAT ONE DAY YOU WOULDN'T BE HANDED A BILL?* My sudden awareness of its staggering size was making me wobble at the knees. No wonder the more luxurious stores discreetly hid the price tags on their most expensive goods! Only it was too late for me to suspend my shopping spree and slink away. Feverishly I searched for something with which I might be able to pay at least in part. I tried to recall the good deeds I had done, the sacrifices I had made, the occasions I had inconvenienced myself to do what was right. Oh sure, during my first Navy cruise, I had placed a bundle of discarded clothes in front of a refugee hovel in Hong Kong, after picking up my new suits at Mohan's custom tailors. More recently, I sent a fifty-dollar check to the Biafra hunger fund. I invariably gave handouts to derelicts in the streets and occasionally stopped for hitchhikers in the rain. But all of that added up to a paltry sum that made no difference on the bill. I was a beggar at Tiffany's, trying to pay off an overdue invoice with pennies in my hand.

INDEED, THERE WILL BE A PRICE TO PAY . . .

Surrounded by the pine-scented woods, I felt queasy from the relentless onslaught. Yet I now found myself having to contend also with a message of a different sort. I was beginning to see myself as a cassock-clad priest, praying on my knees and impervious in body and mind to anything impure. This new tableau puzzled me until it dawned on me: Is this what it felt like to be called? I had always considered the tales of receiving God's call and grappling with it as self-delusions of Catholic young men afraid of life, and especially, of sex. Yet that's what seemed to be happening to me now; yes, that was it, the only way to make amends was to become one of those porcine celibates. Oh, what a grotesque twist of fate! The thought constricted me within, tightening its painful grip around my churning innards and adding another dimension to my internal stress.

God, how screwed up could I be! I reflected. Lucky there was no mirror to see how terribly pale I must have turned, the last of my Florida tan neutralized. Maybe the best thing was to cut short my walk, go home, and make myself a good meal. Mother had bought me an excellent veal chop, which I would enhance with a superb bottle of 1969 Saint Estèphe. Maybe that would infuse my brain with some sense and clarify my muddled thoughts! I normally drank only half a bottle at a time, but I might want to make an exception today. A vintage Bordeaux such as this one, moreover, didn't keep well once uncorked, and it would be a sin to let it spoil.

Feeling myself grimace at this unwitting rationale, I called out into the darkness of the woods, "C'mon, Blackie, we're going home."

I hadn't eaten since breakfast. Despite abbreviating that distressing walk and returning early, I started making dinner right away. Mother usually fixed Sunday lunch, but the rest of the time I was on my own. I was especially glad she wasn't hovering near me now. She would know right away I was in some unspeakable fix.

And what could I say? She was a practical person who shared my religious apathy and had little patience for the fairy tales preached in church. Embarrassed that Manya had become a born-again Jesus devotee, Mother made her promise not to proselytize at the Christmas gatherings of our extended family. How could I now tell Mother that God had personally rebuked me a few minutes ago and was ordering that I become a priest?

I turned the oven to broil, determined to concentrate on the culinary task and forget, at least for now, what I had been through at the edge of the woods. I opened the refrigerator to take out the meat and placed it on a cutting board. Good veal was difficult to find. I still remembered the veal chop prepared by a chef in Italy at a hilltop restaurant over the Tyrrhenian Sea. I had sent back his first offering with precise criticism: The meat was from an inferior cut and leathery, and the pasta tasted stiff, about fifty-five seconds underdone. The chef must have realized I wasn't another tourist to be dispatched with scorn. He personally brought out his next attempt, a huge loin that looked juicy on the serving tray, and then stood by with pride as he waited for me to take the first bite. Of course, I deluged him with praise, which made him beam, as did the tip I bestowed on him in the kitchen afterwards.

The chop for tonight promised to be just as good. I could practically savor it already cooked, along with the yellow wax beans and the thin vermicelli spaghetti topped with melted butter and freshly grated Parmesan cheese. This would be preceded by a Bieler-sized green salad enhanced by my own dressing of vinegar, Maître Jacques Dijon mustard, olive oil, and a sprinkling of crumbled Gorgonzola. But what would truly make the meal was the bottle of Saint Estèphe, the last of a half-case I had discovered at the local package store.

I pulled the cork, sniffed it, and set it aside. I carefully poured a small amount of the wine into a large goblet of very thin glass. I swirled it around and brought it to my nose. Uhmm . . . how well the wine would go with the meal . . . especially the tannin which would balance the richness in the spaghetti and the meat. This was the sort of combination that might snap me back to life.

By now I had the chop laid out on aluminum foil, with dabs of butter and a little rosemary on top. It was time to turn on the burners under the beans and under the water for the spaghetti. The veal I would put in the oven when the beans began to boil, and the thin spaghetti would go in the boiling water last. That way everything would be done at about the same time — the secret of fine cuisine. In the meantime, I could sip from my exquisite glass, which held almost enough for the entire meal. The wine's continued exposure to the air would further enhance its bouquet.

I filled the glass and raised it for what was to be the first real sip. Uhmm, that dark ruby red Saint Estèphe . . . how it would mellow the brain and help me forget those messages for good!

The glass never reached my lips. With the force of an unexpected blow, I felt an implacable command coming through in nonnegotiable terms: *No dinner tonight. That's right, no dinner for you tonight!*

Incredulous, I shook my head. It was as if some deep-seated organic pain had just stabbed me anew. I couldn't believe this was happening to me here in the protective warmth of the kitchen at my parents' home.

I glanced around, wine glass poised at my lips. I mustn't give in! I have to fight this crazy thing. Just a few inches and then tilt a bit, and I shall be having a sip.

No, and again, no! That wordless message seemed to reverberate like an echo between a range of towering peaks. *No dinner means no wine. You've got a heavy price to pay . . . and you're going to start paying it now!*

It was a command that made the fear of the Almighty distressingly real.

I put aside the glass and slowly sat down. God, what was happening to me?

As I glanced toward the stove, the threat of no dinner intensified my hunger pangs. Seeing the water under the beans begin to boil, I realized it was time to start cooking the veal.

I stood up and opened the oven, turning my face away from the hot blast of air. The temperature felt about right. I took a step toward the cutting board and reached down to pick up the veal on the aluminum foil.

This time, the message came through with the intensity of a storm: *YOU HEARD, NO DINNER TONIGHT. TURN OFF THOSE FLAMES AND PUT AWAY THE FOOD!*

Petrified, I stood there holding the uncooked veal. Was this an ominous beginning to a pattern that would twist and tangle my life into an agonizing mess? Was this how Joan of Arc succumbed to her voices and ended up being burned at the stake?

For a few seconds I walked around the stove, abjectly miserable yet not daring to disobey. Acting as if in a trance, I put the veal back on the cutting board and turned off the stove. First the broiler, then the two burners on top. The water for the spaghetti I poured out next. Moving like an automaton and trying not to think, I drained off the yellow beans, wrapped the chop in aluminum foil, and corked up the wine. I hadn't felt this kind of emptiness in my stomach since the day I embarked on Dr. Bieler's draconian regimen. But that was necessary then. I had to recover from starch toxemia, or whatever I had. God, what in the world did I have now?

Dejected to the extreme, I opened the refrigerator door and started to put everything away, already imagining the long, empty evening ahead.

As I was about to finish the task, I suddenly felt another message coming through. And right away, I could tell its tone was dif-

ferent: *OKAY, YOU PASSED, YOU CAN HAVE YOUR DINNER NOW.
BUT WE'LL BE TALKING AGAIN . . . SOON.*

This was crazy! Nevertheless, I felt sufficiently relieved to
start taking everything out of the refrigerator again. But what did
it all mean? Especially this talking again soon? What surprise did
I have to steel myself for next? Was this what it meant to go out
of your mind? Surely, that's what an impartial observer would
have to conclude from the way I was behaving in the kitchen,
turning on the stove and redoing everything I had undone only
moments before. Yet I knew how terribly sane I felt, how overly
rational – which is what was scaring me the most.

This disconcerted state of mind didn't keep me from enjoying the
meal. The wine tasted even more delicious than I'd remembered,
though alas, it didn't particularly brighten my mood. Would I
never find peace again, I wondered, as I finished off the last of the
vermicelli and veal. How relatively predictable and straightforward my life used to be! What would Manya say about this inexplicable turn of events? Would she have some comforting words?
Trust the Lord, she said, pray to him and read his word . . .

I raised my glass for another prolonged sip; suddenly as if on
cue, I had a fortuitous thought that made me bolt from the kitch-
en to the living room. What I remembered was that over the past
ten years my sister had been bombarding every member of the
family with a barrage of religious books. Most were simplistic, not
much beyond the level of pulp fiction. But others were by writers
I had studied in Baumer's intellectual history – Saint Augustine,
Thomas à Kempis, Thomas Aquinas and the like. If I managed to
find one of those, perhaps the answer would become clear.

We didn't have a library, but on the long Renaissance table in
the living room where Father did his paperwork, stacks of books
were haphazardly piled, along with an accumulation of Exercycle
invoices and bills, back copies of various health magazines, and

political monographs from obscure Central European émigré groups. More of the same was piled along every window ledge as well as on the mantle over the large stone fireplace. Father favored biographies of powerful contemporaries, chronicles of World War II, and spy thrillers. Still, if I rummaged long enough through this assorted mess, I might find one of Manya's books that had somehow missed being thrown out.

I went to the first pile, intending to go through it book by book, then repeat the procedure with other piles. But I was startled by what happened next. The very first book I picked up had on its cover a prominent white cross and was titled *The Seven Storey Mountain* by someone called Thomas Merton. I glanced at the publisher's blurb: "The extraordinary autobiography that has become a modern spiritual classic — the testament of an intensely active and brilliant young man who decided to withdraw from the world only after he had fully immersed himself in it."

I shuddered. Could that part about withdrawing from the world after fully immersing himself in it apply to me? Merely coming across this work seemed eerily more than coincidental.

Merton's book in hand, I returned to the kitchen to clear the table and stack the dishes in the sink. As I was corking up what remained of the wine, I noted with momentary satisfaction that the bottle was still better than half-full. Why not take the Saint Estèphe up to my room? It might be just what I needed to accompany Merton's book and make his message go down more easily.

I glanced once more at the stove to make sure the burners were off. I tucked the promising tome under one arm and started to pick up the bottle and glass.

NOT SO FAST . . . I felt that implacable command stop me in my tracks. *FIRST, POUR OUT THAT WINE!*

I found myself struggling to reason. *Think of the labor that went into this vintage, think of the years it took to produce it. And to waste it all now?*

IN THE SINK!

If I leave it in the fridge, it'll keep . . .

IN THE SINK! It was a thunderous command that brooked no delay. Putting down the glass and Merton's book, I inverted the bottle and mournfully watched the tempting liquid hurtle out and disappear down the drain.

From behind I heard, "What are you doing that for?" It was Mother's voice. She had come into the kitchen in time to see me empty the last of the wine.

I resisted the impulse to face her. "I'm afraid this bottle has turned," I mumbled over the sink. Then, sensing Mother still there, I started to fidget with the dishes.

"Never mind those," she said. "I'll take care of them . . . as I always do."

"I think I'll go up to read and turn in early." I tried to sneak past Mother, thinking how ridiculous for a man in his mid-forties to be afraid of being found out.

She stepped in front of me. "Are you all right?"

I paused but didn't look up. "I guess I'm a bit tired."

She sized me up with a worried look. I could tell by her wrinkled brow that she sensed I was somehow unwell in a different way. I never believed my mother's warning that only after children grew up would they really cause you grief. Mother sighed, then gave me a sharp glance. "I hope you aren't coming down with something. Don't expect me to take care of you."

I managed to squeeze out a smile. I knew Mother would enjoy nothing more than taking care of me, provided, of course, it wasn't serious.

"By the way, Manya sends her love," I remarked offhandedly, giving in to Mother's gaze. I didn't want to cause my sister difficulties over her proselytizing zeal. But when Mother continued to look at me expectantly, I felt compelled to add, "Manya took me to one of her meetings."

"I knew it, she's been working on you again!"

"I went because I wanted to."

"You?"

"Well, I've been thinking during the last few days . . . I'm really not a good person."

"Nonsense," Mother said with unusual firmness. "You've always been kind and generous. Everybody says that about you."

I nodded. "But I've also been self-centered."

"Just like your father. You inherited that." Mother smiled at me reassuringly. "It goes to prove you really are our son, and they didn't make a mistake at the hospital."

"Except that Father always came through in the crunch."

"He's not like normal people," Mother said thoughtfully. "You're merely complaining of being human."

"That's how I always rationalized it, too. Unfortunately, it doesn't work anymore."

Mother flashed a look of anger. "What in the world did Manya do to you?"

"Please, don't blame her. Whatever is going to happen isn't her fault."

"And what is going to happen?"

I shrugged and made a grimace, then went upstairs with the Merton book.

I was glad to be in my room, which felt cozy and warm. The closed window was already covered with the intricate designs of frost, and the occasional rattle from the radiator had the reassuring effect of a crackling fire. Though it was only seven o'clock, I would do my reading in bed. I was feeling as if I were somehow ill. Was I perhaps undergoing the spiritual version of Dr. Bieler's surgery without knives, whereby the poisons accumulated in the body's tissues by years of physical excesses were purged through his rigid regimen? Did the long-term moral poisons I had accumulated over the years and kept carefully hidden in the back of my mind suddenly start pouring out in the form of that agonizing reckoning on the snowy field?

Shaking off this disturbing notion, I undressed and put on my winter sleeping attire, an old cashmere turtleneck with multiple holes that made it unsuitable for anything else. I spread out my worn-out sheepskin coat over the lower part of the bed, then fluffed the two pillows to prop up my back.

I was beginning to feel better. Surely, the crazy internal compulsions I had been experiencing would disappear, along with those irrational religious thoughts, and I would be able to reaffirm who I was. While my symptoms seemed strange, this sort of thing undoubtedly happened every day, especially to men around my age. If I were to seek psychiatric help, my case would most likely be viewed as nothing out of the ordinary.

I turned on the little lamp at the side of my bed and flicked off the overhead light. Then I opened Merton's book.

The very first paragraph riveted my attention: "I came into this world . . . the prisoner of my own violence and my own selfishness, in the image of the world into which I was born. That world was the picture of hell, full of men like myself, loving God and yet hating him; born to love him, living instead in fear and hopeless, self-contradictory hunger."

I had come across such sentences in Professor Baumer's class, and occasionally in other courses too. It was the kind of material I had studied in the abstract, so that I could draw appropriate comparisons between different modes of thought and do well in my exams. But as far as I was personally concerned, it added up to so many empty words, unrelated to anything I had experienced in life. More than once, I had disparaged such ideas as intellectual chaff.

Now, I found myself reading from a startlingly different perspective; from the perspective that *was* my life, and at a critical juncture at that. As I continued down the page and then further into Merton's book, his words not only spoke to me, just as my sister had predicted, but seemed specifically written to be seen by me at this particular moment in my life. Here was a worldly writer searching for an elusive goal, which had held him back from making a commitment either to a profession or a wife. Perhaps that was the reason for my own lack of commitment, as I had fleetingly recognized during my exuberant night at Manya's. Some of the lesser details of Merton's life also meshed to a remarkable degree with mine, though I did conclude that he had most likely never engaged in sex, perhaps never savored a kiss. If the sexual revolution I had enjoyed came a generation too late for Merton's youth, I doubted he would have indulged no matter what the social mores.

Merton's absorbing style continued to draw me in. Even without the half-bottle of wine, I was recovering my aplomb. Surely Merton would indicate a way out of my dilemma!

As he began to detail his disillusionment with life and search for new pathways and goals, I was no less eager to tag along. Alas, too late did I realize that the road he was traveling led to prayerful submission to God – precisely where I didn't want to go. Merton's graphic descriptions of his all-night vigils left me queasy and shocked. I had stayed up only two nights in my life, while serving as a young naval officer in the South China Sea. That had been an exciting time, as we steamed in formation with a dozen ships, launching aircraft and refueling underway at fifteen knots, while Filipino stewards brought hot coffee and scrambled eggs to the moonlit bridge. But praying all night? I had never prayed more than a few seconds at a time, even under the most favorable conditions. I shuddered at the thought of doing so for three, six, perhaps eight hours without a break; kneeling on a wooden bench in an unheated chapel, hands cold from the night's penetrating chill, fighting sleep and the urgent temptation to let my rear sag against my heels. My sole relief would come from clutching a rosary ever more intently and repeating my prayerful words ever more fervently; and after this seemingly endless ordeal, breakfasting on a bowl of tepid gruel, then returning to a dank cell-like room and not finding any warmth under the thin blanket covering a hard pallet. Yet that would be just another typical night of the rest of my life.

I groaned as I set aside Merton's book. I had never experienced such an adverse reaction from reading mere words. No wonder this book was making my illness worse! It was as if I had tried to put my mind at ease before heavy surgery by reading the most grisly descriptions of how they would cut me up and what agonies I would have to endure. Merton had sought to present an awful experience as near-orgasmic joy. He must have been a secret masochist. No, no, I wasn't like him after all!

Yet even as I sought to distance myself from this Cistercian monk, I was beginning to be possessed by another dimension of his life. I was coming to sense what it would be like to become celibate; not just to withdraw from engaging in sex for practical reasons for a given period, but to resort actively and deliberately to the permanent suppression of this elemental drive and become a different human being, with different thoughts, different smells, different movements and expressions. I could feel myself being enshrouded in long clerical robes that would protect my lower body from the sensuality of this world and help me be vigilant against dangerous thoughts.

God, what if Kathryn could see me in this state! I glanced at the little photo of her propped up on my dresser. I had snapped it when our relationship was already starting to turn but before she gave up hope. I could see the hurt in her eyes, yet the consuming physicality still evident in her expression brought back a poignant scene. I had fallen asleep prematurely after too much champagne and a few drags on an overpowering joint, and awoke some hours later to find Kathryn watching me mournfully. I couldn't at first get her to tell me what had upset her so. She hemmed and hawed about how distant and uncommunicative I was after smoking grass, how alone she felt with me asleep, how forlorn. Then she blurted it out: I had conked out after only ten minutes of making love. She sounded reproachful and hurt, as if I had inflicted on her a grievous wrong.

Now glancing at Kathryn's photo once more, I again noticed in her eyes an overpowering sensuality, which made me cower and withdraw further into my celibate mood.

It wasn't nine o'clock yet, but I would try to fall asleep. I quickly got out of bed to open the window, then jumped back in on a bound to outrace the blast of frigid air. I flipped off the table light and pulled the covers tightly around me, leaving only my head exposed. The cold against my face made me all the more aware of the secure warmth of my bed.

For a moment I lay there, trying to make my mind go blank. In the next moment, I was on my knees, as if compelled from within, muttering, "Oh, please God, give me the sense to make heads or tails of this mess. You've always helped make things turn out right. How about doing it for me again just this once?"

That ought to do it, I thought to myself as if to say, "Amen." Nevertheless, I remained kneeling ramrod straight. I could feel the protective layer of warmth being absorbed by the frigid air streaming in, and I was beginning to shiver. Is this what it felt like for Merton during his all-night vigils? Secure in the knowledge I could dart back under the covers whenever I chose, I remained kneeling a few seconds more to get a still more vivid idea of those sleepless vigils in the cold.

4/

My condition failed to improve over the next couple of days. I hadn't received any more of those unwelcome messages. But I slept fitfully both nights, finding myself frequently on my knees, praying with unrestrained fervor for help.

My sister was right. These sporadic bursts of devotion did bring momentary relief. But I wasn't about to call Manya for more of her well-meaning advice. That's how I had ended up with Merton's *Seven Story Mountain*. No wonder books like his left me unmoved in the past! The mind had to be appropriately predisposed and sick before these abnormal exhortations could strike a responsive nerve.

Then on Sunday morning, things got worse. Distraught and consummately sad, as if something of immense value was about to be taken away, I found myself also in the throes of a compulsion to go to church. Unlike the previous commands, which seemed to have originated in the beyond, this one felt like a self-generated apprehension about what might happen if I *didn't* go.

I was embarrassed by what was happening to me and didn't want to worry my parents in any way. Not so much Father; he was too absorbed enjoying himself to notice anything odd over the last couple of days. But Mother had already wondered aloud why I skipped my usual dinnertime wine twice in a row. She had often complained of having to be extra careful in washing my large goblet of thin glass; now, she missed that chore. If I told her I was on my way to church, she would know that only the most compelling personal distress could prompt me to such a drastic move.

As the internal pressure continued to mount, I felt I had no choice but to comply. Even if going to church wouldn't bring me the relief I sought, it might help propitiate the angry powers beyond. How well I was beginning to understand why worship was such a time-tested palliative against divine wrath!

Hoping to avoid any fuss, I would try to slip out quietly. But as I stood up and started to put on my jacket, Mother intervened. "Where're you going?" I heard her voice from her favorite chair in the far end of the living room. "You haven't finished the Sunday paper yet."

"Do I have to tell you everything?" I said peevishly. "I'm no longer eight years old."

Father looked up from the book review section he was reading on the couch. "To Mother, you'll always be about eight years old," he observed with a laugh.

I was already regretting having snapped at Mother. Mustering whatever equanimity I could, I tried to make light of my intent. "I thought I'd go to church and nullify my sins with a prayer or two."

Mother looked distressed. "It was your visit to Manya, I knew it."

"She had nothing to do with it."

"What I don't understand," Mother continued, "is how someone as intelligent as you could let yourself be influenced by Manya. I was always afraid she might confuse the grandchildren when they came for Christmas. I never imagined it would be you."

"You've always laughed at Manya's devotion," Father reminded me, without looking up from his reading. "Poor girl, she takes it a little too seriously."

Father shared Mother's apathy for the Church. As a teenager in a private Catholic gymnasium in Austria, he had been caught reading Emil Zola and was given a choice to blatantly lie or be kicked out, a deceitful ploy he would never forget.

"You don't know how disappointed I am in you," Mother said.

"I'm not exactly overjoyed with myself either."

"Maybe you should become a priest," Father proposed in his detached, lighthearted way. He lowered his paper to glance at me. "You've got no career, no commitments, and you're probably too old to make a child anyway. As a priest, you could enjoy your food and wine, and I'm sure you could have women on the side."

I laughed uneasily, trying not to yield to the desperation I felt. With Father once again absorbed in his reading and Mother maintaining a glum silence, I saw a chance to make my break. "Why don't I start this new career by saying a prayer for us all," I said as cheerfully as I could while heading for the door. "Whatever the case, I'm sure it can't hurt."

As best I could reconstruct from having gone as a child, I judged the mass to be about halfway through when I arrived. I remained standing in the back, partly obscured by one of the pillars in a spot where it was dark. I could see the goings on yet remain relatively unseen and hide that consummate sadness I felt since waking up.

The church was filled to capacity. The parishioners were from the area where we had our farm; mainly working families employed at the toilet seat factory and at the state epileptic hospital. Dressed in their Sunday best, the women at first glance looked the way I remembered them as my customers from the summers I had delivered milk. I thought I recognized Mrs. Womek, who used to take three homogenized and one heavy cream in the shade on the back porch. She had just married then, and now was surrounded by her grown children, in-laws, and grandchildren filling an entire pew.

I found myself irrationally beset by the scene. During my sporadic visits home over the past quarter century, I hadn't interacted with these people beyond exchanging polite greetings on the street. Now, as I watched their children fidgeting and being pacified by a gentle pat of a parental hand, I could feel the preciousness of their family ties. I was mournfully overwhelmed to realize they possessed something I could never have. I had to suppress an urge to rush up to them and individually congratulate them on being the most fortunate people in the world. If I'd had the chance, I would have at that moment willingly made a commitment to the homeliest of the women in those pews. They were hardly the types seen at Le Club or listed in The Book. Yet there wasn't a one of them who didn't look becoming in my eyes.

Blinking back an upwelling of tears, I felt I had forever forfeited my chance of having a family of my own. I knew it made no sense, and I tried to reason with myself, but to no avail. Was this what it meant to be condemned to hell? To see something that had for so long been freely offered suddenly taken away and forever removed from your reach?

Standing in the back of the church, I no longer cared if some of the parishioners happened to see me dab at the rivulets glistening on my cheeks. My sole relief throughout the remainder of the mass came while on my knees on the cold stone floor, shutting out reality with the anguished repetitious mumbling, "God, forgive me; forgive me, oh God. I've sinned, even if I didn't know what I was doing, I've so foolishly sinned!"

By the time I returned from church, Mother had finished preparing the usual roast duck for Sunday lunch. Also as usual, she had prevailed on Father to clear his papers off the Renaissance table for this one meal each week, and then set two place mats where he and I would sit. Mother herself preferred to eat from a tray in the adjoining living room, where she could sit in her favorite stuffed chair and be more alone with her thoughts. While she and Father depended on each other in the special way of people who had been together for almost half a century, the butcher's daughter never bridged the gulf between her and the illustrious nobleman she married. Even though Father was selling fitness equipment by making house calls, she still felt he belonged to a different world. She alone in the family never gave up hope that we would return home. She alone declined to become a U.S. citizen, at first claiming she would be depriving my underage younger brother Tom of his title, since he would automatically become a U.S. citizen along with her. She stoically ignored our mildly derisive arguments that all titles in Czechoslovakia had been abolished long ago, and we would never be going back anyway. After Tom turned eighteen and became a citizen on his own, Mother continued to balk as if becoming naturalized were tantamount to betraying the country of her birth. What finally prompted her to file for citizenship without delay was her first Social Security check. It was for more than three hundred dollars – an astronomical sum considering that she had been saving nickels, dimes and quarters from her household budget to add regularly to her savings in the bank. Such unexpected largesse, Mother felt, required a show of loyalty in return – though she never stopped mulling over this decision, along with most of the other decisions she had made throughout her life.

I had never protested Mother's desire for solitude, yet the notion of us being in any way separated now was causing me distress. The sense of impending loss I had felt earlier, I realized, entailed being deprived of my parents as well. I was desperate for us to be together, and a separation of even a few feet seemed unbearable.

"Why can't we for a change all eat at the dining room table," I said, trying to sound casual, "the way other people do?"

Father laughed. "Since when have you wanted to be like other people?"

Mother seemed more amenable to my request. "Always trying to change things," she fretted, "now that I've got everything on my tray."

"Please?" I said quietly, in an attempt to keep my voice from choking, "I'd really appreciate it."

Mother's worried expression deepened. She stood up, and without uttering a word, brought her tray to the table.

I tried not to betray the disproportionate gratitude I felt. As I watched Mother transfer her plates and utensils onto a place mat she had set at the other end of the table opposite Father, I could understand what it meant for someone to have a last meal with those he loved, be it a convicted businessman about to report for a stiff term in jail or a migrant laborer leaving his family to earn sustenance in places unknown. What a privilege to be sitting in the warmth of this home with the two people most precious to me in the world; what a memory to sustain me in whatever lay ahead . . .

I tried several times to put my emotions into words. But each time, I choked up before I could make a sound. Whatever my fate, I wanted to let my parents know what had always been implicit but I had never said outright: I loved them and was grateful for everything they had done for me in life.

"I don't understand what's happening to me," I finally blurted out, "or what is going to happen . . ."

"That's nothing to be dramatic about," Father said breezily. "You're now eating your lunch, and I think afterwards you'll go back to reading the Sunday paper."

I wanted to clutch him by the arm and feel his closeness for one last time. But he would have taken it as a symptom of my irrationality and shaken me off. In his life, Father had surmounted dramatic turns of fortune and made much harder choices than I — not only in crashing his car into an oncoming truck to avoid sharing a platform with a Nazi, but also in defying his rational instincts to marry Mother, and then choosing to face the uncertainties of bringing his family to the United States. No doubt, Father was made of sterner stuff than I. Had I perhaps been spoiled by my doting grandparents? Despite his incomparably more opulent childhood, Father had been brought up with cold showers, a habit he continued to this day.

I watched Father take a sip of his daily bottle of beer with his usual gusto. "I know I've never said this before . . ." I started once more, but failed to continue when I felt both of my parents suddenly glancing up. I could sense that such maudlin talk was the last thing they wanted to hear.

"I think the duck this time was a little dry," Mother interjected.

Father put down his knife and fork next to the bones on his plate. "I can't wait for Mother's cake," he announced, then turned to me. "Are you going to make the coffee?"

I realized the moment had come and gone. Having forfeited the chance to express what I had so desperately wanted to, I was at least determined to make the best cup of coffee I could, with exactly the amount of sugar and cream Father liked. As for Mother, maybe I could help her later with the dishes without being obvious about it.

Standing alone in the kitchen by the stove, I felt momentarily free to vent my grief.

It took all the self-control I had to make it through the rest of the day without openly breaking down. What a relief to be once more ensconced in my room for the night, where I didn't have to rein in my distress.

I continued to console myself by attributing my condition to some malfunction of the brain, whether a bona fide mental disorder, or the normally taciturn right side of the brain speaking its mind, as I knew could happen under extreme stress. Whatever the case, I had lost touch with reality as I had always perceived it in the past. The harsh new horizon looming before me was separating me from the world I knew and loved. With each passing moment, I felt myself drifting further and further away from familiar ground.

As I sat there in bed, leaning against the fluffed-up pillows, I was impervious to the softness of the old cashmere turtleneck against my chest and the feel of the fresh cotton sheets directly against my lower half. My body seemed to belong to somebody else, and the mere thought of any sensual stimulus was taboo to me now. I understood what Albrecht meant about the restrictions in the Perfect Universe and why priests might want to remain celibate. Far from seeing it as an extreme and unnecessary privation, I recognized it as an essential minimum for the priestly state. Only someone without a true calling might deign to question that. After all, how could anyone pursuing personal pleasures or caring for a family devote himself selflessly to serving God and his human flock? How essential it was to keep one's mind on God rather than focusing on some personal goal! There simply was no way to intertwine the two. From what I could remember about Saint Augustine, this church father hadn't gone far enough in merely requiring abstention from sex. Although it made me shudder in revulsion and fear, I could appreciate the more extreme of the saints; those who had retired to the desert to sit for decades on a little perch, famished and exposed to the elements, their bodies slowly rotting away. Why, even Saint Francis, with his terrible privations and bleeding stigmata was pursuing that inexorable path only in a moderate way.

As I continued to be subsumed by this alien frame of mind, I could understand why the Church had occasionally flirted with strictures against graven images, and why Moslems had in fact outlawed such materialistic fluff from their mosques and worshipping rituals. I could see how the most innocent pictorial renderings could escalate in dangerous ways. I only needed to glance at myself in those photos on the wall. They were all immoral and in one way or another led to sin. Especially that large color blowup on Elbow Beach, glorifying the human flesh which had so enslaved me and made me a puppet of my desires. To think of the effort I had expended to maintain and beautify this physical self, while it was gradually destroying the essence of who I was! Rather than living for me, my body had tricked me to live for it. How could I have considered taking some of these pictures to Florida to deco-

306

rate the walls of my new apartment in Coconut Grove? That would be blasphemy of the crassest sort, perpetuating my sinful ways from which I was being increasingly removed. If I ever did manage to resume a normal life and return to Florida, I would have to leave behind even the etchings of my ancestors with their arrogant airs, pretentious uniforms, and frilly, degenerate clothes. What a spectacle of pathetic pride! I would, of course, have to leave behind most of my magazines and books, with their immoral, seductive ideas; not just the few pornographic ones expressly designed to titillate, but also the informative ones, such as *Newsweek* and *Time,* so replete with suggestive attitudes, stories, and ads. First thing the next day I would have to get rid of them all, along with all the boxes of letters, pictures, and trinkets I had accumulated over the years. They were a reflection of a life that was no longer mine and were better discarded as so much waste.

Yes, I could see what terminal horrors the world was heading for with such blatant appeals to the eyes in films and on TV and everywhere you looked, promoting sex and virtually every physical desire, appetite, or want. The forthcoming conflagration loomed no less imminent than Albrecht had predicted on his most pessimistic days. It would turn out to be more terrible than the gruesome prophecies of the biblical fundamentalists. No wonder the ayatollahs in Iran were running wild, veiling their women in black, throwing suggestive music off the air, and otherwise purging their society of these evils of sensuality that inevitably led to disastrous ends. They were only doing what was right and shouldn't be vilified. I could understand why the horrors of the medieval inquisition chamber once had a constructive role, and indeed, had been designed to save the sinner from paying a more terrible price. Who knew what tortures I might have to undergo to pay for my sins? The threat of an inquisitor's rack between my sophomore and junior years at Yale might have spared me a lot. It all made sense, now that I was possessed by this primitive, righteous spirit that demanded a return to the most basic of laws; laws which were unmerciful yet so necessary and just, at least as they were being applied to me. Only my lifelong attitude of live-and-let-live and abhorrence of overt violence kept me from feeling obliged to sally forth and force on others the rigid standards that held me in their throes. They were for me alone to submit to, I repeated to myself.

Sitting there in bed, entranced by these thoughts, I was seized with a missionary zeal. If only there was a way to shout a warning to keep others from following my path! Whatever was happening to me could happen to millions of similarly unwitting souls. My transgressions had derived from merely following the popular mantra of our times, "You only go around once; so get all the pleasures you can!" If only somebody had warned me in a persuasive way, as the Duke had tried to do when he finally saw through me just before I graduated from his school. He was the one person who knew how to attack human flaws. The various churches and self-styled moralists, alas, always sounded self-righteous, pompous, and out-of-date. As for Albrecht, his homilies were more likely to amuse me than instill fear.

Before turning out my bedside light, I glanced at the photo of Kathryn on my dresser. There was the same diabolic flicker in her eyes that I had noticed several nights ago. Wasn't it possible Kathryn had been partly possessed, like the witches of old? After all, isn't that what witches were — super-sensuous women whose uncontrolled moans in the throes of passion had been overheard by vigilant neighbors?

I wasn't astonished at this bizarre thought that was helping me realize how much Kathryn and I had been alike. Her desire for the narcosis of pleasure must have been as strong as mine; indeed, perhaps stronger, making it doubly inevitable for our relationship to end up with nowhere to go.

Taking care to avoid eye contact with her demonic look, I forsook the warmth of my bed to turn Kathryn's photo face down on the dresser top. I opened the frost-covered window and switched off the table light. As I stood in the dark by my bed, arms upraised and begging God to help me in some way, I could feel the cold seeping around my body. I contemplated for a moment what it would be like if I remained praying all night, but then was back under the covers again. As soon as I began to feel their protective warmth, I jumped out of bed once more, and with arms upraised, continued to implore God for a few moments more in the penetrating cold.

Twice more I succumbed to this compulsive pattern before wrapping myself in the blankets and waiting for sleep to release me for the night.

5/

The next morning, I knew. It was well before daybreak when I suddenly sat up with a start. It was as if someone had passed through the room. The window was still open but the clarity of the message made me impervious to the cold.

How presumptuous to have thought God wanted me to become a priest or a monk! I had considered it a punishment to be a servant of God. Now, I could see what an honor it would have been; an honor for which I couldn't begin to qualify, certainly not before paying the price.

Now, I knew what I had to do. There was no mistaking the message. I understood why I had felt the way I did the day before; why I sensed I would never see my parents again; why during church I thought my chances for a married life had been forfeited for good. How right I had been, because all that was to be a part of the price.

Yes, it was so clear now! I was to leave home right away; not tomorrow, not this afternoon, but early this morning to get a good start. I had a long day ahead in the wintry cold. I was to pack a little suitcase, preferably an older one, with only the necessities that would keep me clothed. I was to take no more than two hundred dollars and leave everything else behind; leave behind the little hatchback car; the custom-made suits, whether from Sills or London's Savile Row; leave behind whatever money I had, the twenty thousand dollars or so, which had heretofore served as an insurance policy against having to indenture myself to some less-than-pleasant job. That option, obviously, I would no longer need.

My marching orders were to hitchhike the 150-odd-miles to New York, to wherever my ride would let me off. From there, I was to take a subway to the Bowery or a similar neighborhood frequented by old hoboes and drunks. I was to seek out the nearest shelter or charity home and volunteer my services. I was to work there with the derelicts, mopping up their puke, dressing their ulcerated skin, or just speaking to them a few kind words. I also was to get a job as a short-order cook in some cheap all-night eatery; maybe one of the White Towers, a chain I knew for the garish lights and starkly white decor of their franchises. Of the money I earned, I was to keep just enough to subsist. If it turned out I couldn't stay at the shelter and had to get a place of my own, it was to be one of those cold-water walk-up rooms I had occasionally seen in depressing movies with a filthy sink, a single-element hot plate, a bare electric bulb, and an army metal cot. The rest of the money from the White Tower job I was to spend on the derelicts.

I sat rigidly in bed, the icy blasts gusting in through the open window. What a terribly ingenious punishment! Even my culinary talents would be put to use. Not that there was anything in these orders I could modify or change. They had been delivered with the same uncompromising resolve as when I had first been told of my sins, and then commanded not to eat that meal. There was no bargaining possible, no questioning allowed. This was something that had to be done, an obligation to be discharged, the price to be paid. The purpose was not so much for me to help others at this stage. That was incidental to the far more personal mission I had to undertake: to learn to submit, to atone, to subjugate myself, to give up the self. I would be starting at the lowest rung among those aspiring to serve God. Only after years of this annealing process could I be ready for the honor of becoming a priest or a monk, or doing similar exclusive service to God. But I didn't need to worry about that. God would let me know in no uncertain way. He had the means, just as he was so clearly directing me what I had to do now.

Oh, no! I wailed half-aloud and slid deep under the covers. What had I gotten myself into? Was this God's answer to the uncertainty I had begged him to resolve? I pressed my eyes shut and tried to make my brain go blank. But there was that implacable command again: *BETTER GET GOING . . . REMEMBER, YOU NEED AN EARLY START.*

Outside, the darkness had softened and the first bluish wisps of dawn began to delineate sky from land. How I wished that light would never come and I could slip into the restfulness of a dark oblivion that would protect me until all of this went away. More so than on any day of my life, I dreaded getting up to face the world; the world that had always looked so inviting, full of welcome surprises and treats. How bleak and cold it now appeared through the still-open window, beneath the frosted panes of glass! The heavy, dark clouds seemed overstuffed with snow. What would I wear? What would I pack in the little suitcase that would be most useful for what I had to do? Thank God I had a lot of skiing things for blustery weather on the slopes. I could perhaps start out wearing my thermal underwear and woolen socks. The old sheepskin coat covering the lower part of my bed would come in handy, too. Lucky I hadn't thrown it away! It had rubbed through in several spots and I wore it only at home. Yet it had once kept me warm in the best of style. I remembered wrapping it around my head in the plush first-class compartment of the overnight Paris-Munich express to separate myself from other well-turned-out passengers gathered there for the night. Now, I might have to use it at night to separate myself in the derelict ward from what was to be my new world of drunks and other unfortunates of life. Maybe I would get a corner bed, where I might at least have the privacy of two walls.

I tried to bury my head beneath the two pillows on the bed. But that uncompromising command once more sprung me into a sitting position. *HURRY UP, HURRY UP . . . YOU'VE GOT NO TIME TO WASTE!*

I could smell the coffee aroma drifting in through the crack under the closed door. Mother was having her breakfast. Father would be up shortly to do his hour of exercises, and then have his breakfast about the same time as I normally would. God, what to tell my parents? Thanks for everything, I'm leaving, I won't ever see you again?

I felt myself whirl into a posture that was becoming familiar by now: on my knees, hands clasped over the chest, and head bowed. "God," I prayed, "if I have to do what I have to do . . . give me the strength to do it . . . give me the grace and the courage to go through with this test . . . just like you gave your son, Jesus Christ. Please, God, give me strength . . . strength which I never had . . . strength to follow the hard road. You know what a sucker I've been for the soft road. But I see it's your road I have to travel now. God, give me that special spirit . . . your spirit . . . to make it through. Protect me and don't leave me . . . hold my hand and help carry me through."

I had never prayed with such intensity before. I must have been on my knees only a few minutes, but by the time I finished I was strangely calm. I didn't feel happy, yet neither did I feel sad in the same way as before. I felt accepting of my fate, unafraid

312

and strong, almost serene. Somehow, I knew everything would be all right; that I would get a ride to New York; that I would find a homeless shelter with a spare bed. And right around the corner would be that White Tower with a HELP WANTED sign. I could start right away. Within twelve hours, I would be settled into a new life, irreversibly separated from my former world as if guillotined yet able to survive. I had a powerfully liberating feeling that my own well-being didn't matter, even my life didn't matter. I had only one purpose. To do what I had to do. To do the right thing, the will of God . . . and thereby earn salvation.

Despite this protective trance suffusing me with strength and resolve, I remained aware of what I was going through. "Hmm," I said to myself, from within that comforting cocoon, "so this is what's meant by the Spirit of the Lord descending on you from above. It really does work! Oh God, thank you, thank you, oh God!"

As I faced Mother across the table in the kitchen nook, I already had on my sheepskin coat. For a moment we sat in silence. She was finishing her second cup of coffee and lit her morning cigarette. Her solitary breakfast was perhaps the most consistent pleasure in her life over the past thirty years. Now, each of us was sizing up the situation.

It was Mother who spoke first, employing one of her standard lines as if nothing unusual was happening. "How can you walk around the house in such a heavy coat? I don't want to have to play nurse if you get sick."

"That's all right, Mother. I'll be leaving soon."

"So early?" she asked in a normal tone. "Where're you going this time?"

"Away," I said, with a finality that surprised me.

Mother took a puff on her cigarette. Exhaling slowly, she was momentarily obscured by billows of smoke.

"I'm going to New York," I continued. "To the Bowery. I've got to go there to work with hoboes and drunks."

Mother blew away the smoke and looked at me as if I had turned quietly insane.

"I know it sounds crazy," I said, feeling that strange calm within. "But look at me. Don't I look all right?"

She nodded. "But you *sound* crazy."

As best I could, I explained my plan for hitchhiking to New York and starting a new life.

"But you can't do that," she said, as if grasping at the most visible straw. "Hitchhiking is against the law in Massachusetts. You know that!"

I couldn't help an ironic smile. "I'll be doing God's will. He'll be watching out for me."

"God's will?" Mother asked bitterly.

"He told me this morning . . . around five. I thought I'd have more time to prepare myself. But I guess he's getting impatient. The message I got this morning was that there was to be no more fooling around."

Mother put down her cigarette. She looked as if she was about to go into shock. "What *is* happening to you!"

"I'm trying to work out my salvation," I said, surprised at my own answer.

Mother looked incredulous. "Your salvation?"

"I've broken many commandments," I continued. "You've often witnessed that yourself."

"So what? Even priests break them today. It's nothing unusual."

"That's their problem, don't you see? It's frightening how clearly I know what God wants me to do. At last I know. For the first time in my life, I know. And right now, he wants me to go to the Bowery to do that work. I have no choice."

314

"If you really feel you've got to do that," Mother said, making an effort to sound matter-of-fact, "you can do it right here at the state hospital. I'm sure working with the epileptics there is no picnic. But at least you won't have to go anywhere."

I shook my head. "I couldn't begin to do here what I have to do. It's far too comfortable . . . my nice bed, the fireplace, my wonderful meals, you and Dad. Don't you think I love it here? But as I said, I have no choice. Part of my mission is precisely to leave everything behind, never to return or in any way look back, and start a new life where my own comforts or preferences no longer matter."

Mother abruptly ground out her cigarette. "Well, don't come running to me when you get sick," she said, with feigned impatience. She paused, then in a calmer tone gave me the practical reasons why I couldn't leave: I had signed the apartment lease in Coconut Grove, and I had to write those day-care center scripts. "And don't forget, you have a ten o'clock appointment to have your car oil changed."

I felt a sad smile on my lips. When I didn't immediately respond, Mother continued, "Surely you can't be as irresponsible as all that. Surely you can't let all those people down."

"What if I suddenly died?" I asked gently.

"What if trees could fly?" Mother countered.

"I'm sure dying is more common than what's happening to me now."

"That doesn't mean you should tempt fate. Among those derelicts, you could get stabbed, who knows, perhaps even . . ."

"Don't you see, that's irrelevant?" I interrupted. "I'm not going there for my health. I'm going there to start the life of the spirit. As of now, forget my body."

"But that's wrong, wrong, wrong!" Mother wailed. "You're still young, you're good-looking, you've got everything to live for."

I nodded. "Above all, my salvation."

"What about your parents? Don't you have a responsibility to us?"

"That's what pains me the most," I said, feeling an upwelling of emotion, yet remaining calm on the outside. "Somehow, I knew yesterday I'd be saying a final good-bye. That's why I wanted us to eat together. I also wanted to tell you . . ."

I paused, struggling to say what I had left unsaid the day before. Despite my apparent fortitude, I could feel a tear worm its way down my cheek. "I just wanted you to know how much I love you and Dad . . . even if I didn't always show it."

The tears were now running down Mother's cheeks. I reached over and did something I had never done before. I took her aging, gnarled hand in mine and held it gently. "I realize you always knew what I was feeling," I said, "but this is so different. It's as if . . . as if it wasn't me speaking. Don't you see, we all live only by the grace of God. What if God took me from you in an automobile accident, and I was in the state I'm in now? Can you imagine what eternal damnation is all about? I know I'll never see you again, but you're not losing me. I'll be working for my salvation, for my next life."

For a moment, Mother didn't respond. She drew a paper napkin from a dispenser on the table and dried each of her cheeks in a single motion.

"I don't suppose you've told Father?" she asked.

"I won't leave before he gets up."

This seemed to make my departure more real, and after a moment of silence, fresh tears started to roll down Mother's cheeks.

"Don't you see," I resumed, "I'm gradually being called to enter the City of God. It's a great honor. But the road from the City of Man, with its temporary pleasures and concerns, isn't easy. We get so easily deceived . . ."

I paused, again surprised at what I was saying. Were these words coming from some ethereal source outside my brain, or was

my memory being nudged at this critical juncture in life to recall
some of what I had absorbed about Saint Augustine in Professor
Baumer's class more than a quarter century ago?

Mother's voice brought me out of my ruminations. "At least
have some breakfast," she said, in an effort to sound normal, and
crumpled up the paper napkin in her hand.

Gently, I released Mother's hand and stood up. "I think I need
to go to the bathroom," I said, and quickly headed upstairs. I was
still feeling that special spirit and strength which was continuing
to sustain me. But a part of me, the visceral part was taking its
toll.

The spiritual trance seemed to remain unimpaired as I flushed
the toilet, pulled up my long johns and pants, and started to wash
my hands. I held them under the pleasantly warm water, thinking
of the piercing weather outside in which I would have to hitch a
ride.

Just then I caught a glimpse of myself in the mirror above the
sink. I could barely recognize the waxen image. In the days of feeling great, looking in the mirror reinforced that positive feeling. At
the moment, I figured it was just as well I couldn't establish rap-
port with that sallow reflection; it kept me from recognizing the
desperate straits I was in.

I was about to turn off the hot water when I suddenly detected a familiar glimmer in the vacant eyes staring back at me. That
snapped the trancelike state, and I was looking at myself again. At
the same time, a new message was distinctly impressing itself on
my consciousness: *YOU DON'T HAVE TO GO! NOW THAT YOU'VE
PROVED YOUR INTENTION, YOU NO LONGER HAVE TO DO IT.*

I don't have to go! I don't have to go! I repeated to myself. The
words continued to echo within my mind like a crescendo of peeling church bells spreading the good news. *I don't have to go! I don't
have to go! I don't have to go!*

I remembered what had happened several days earlier, when I started to put away my meal. I no longer had to, once I had shown my intention to comply. Was it the same thing now? I had honestly forgotten about that unwitting ploy, which had served either to fool the psyche or get a dispensation from the powers beyond.

I kept the hot water running on my hands for an instant more, luxuriating in its warmth. For the first time, I noticed in the mirror how awful I looked. My face was sallow and I had deep hollows around the eyes, almost as if I had stepped out of a grave. Thank God the dispensation had come! I managed a little smirk at my image before bolting out of the bathroom and rushing downstairs with the good news.

Father was already doing his leg raises in his underwear on the living room floor. Nothing could normally interrupt his routine, but seeing me, he paused to give me a reproachful look. "What's this nonsense of yours that Mother's been telling me about?"

"I don't have to go," I said with excitement. "It's all right. I-don't-have-to-go."

"You shouldn't scare your poor mother that way," Father chided me, and then resumed his exercising as if nothing of consequence had happened.

In the kitchen, Mother was taking the unprecedented step of lighting her second cigarette. "Come on, have some breakfast," she said numbly. "I'm going upstairs. I've had it for the day."

6/

My peace of mind didn't last long. Shortly after breakfast, I started to have that unpleasant feeling again, as if somebody were forcibly kneading my guts, and an increasingly persistent message was beginning to get through. *BETTER GET GOING! BETTER GET*

GOING WHILE THERE'S TIME . . . OR FACE THE CONSEQUENCES FOR AS LONG AS ETERNITY LASTS.

Not again! My response this time was to protest, having just recalled a biblical precedent for what I was going through: how God had stayed Abraham's hand from sacrificing his only son after Abraham proved his willingness to do just that. God certainly didn't tell Abraham a few hours later that he had changed his mind. So why pick on me? Hadn't I made my willingness to obey amply clear?

That's what was beginning to worry me. Had I truly intended to go when I received that reprieve? The most objective proof was that I had put on the long johns in anticipation of my hitchhiking ordeal. I normally wore them only under skiing pants while riding chair lifts on freezing days. But I recalled putting them on for other occasions, too. Besides, I was an excellent dissimulator. I could have put them on just to pretend I intended to go.

I started to walk around the living room, sporadically rubbing my temples and crinkling my eyes. Would my salvation depend on exactly why I had decided to wear my thermal long johns that day? What was my life coming to?

BETTER GET GOING, IT'S GETTING LATE! YOU MUST LEAVE NOW TO GET TO NEW YORK BEFORE DARK . . .

The message wasn't hitting me with the swift, sharp blows as it had at dawn. It seemed to have been engraved on a heavy tablet of stone and dropped into my abdominal cavity, making me feel uncomfortably cramped and providing a constant reminder of its intrusive presence there.

I made an exaggerated grimace, and several times banged the bottom of my hand against the side of my head, as if trying to jar my memory.

"Aren't you ashamed of yourself?" Mother asked, after watching me for a while. She sensed that the danger of my leaving had passed, and firmness was the best approach. "Get ahold of yourself! I think what you're doing to yourself is a sin."

"Oh, you don't understand," I said, gritting my teeth. "Would you dare turn God down?"

"Why don't you stop this nonsense and go get your oil changed."

I couldn't keep the pain from showing on my face. Mother's reference served as a poignant reminder that I should have been on my way.

"It's all in your head," Father suggested, with an easy wave of the hand. He had promised Mother he would stay home to keep an eye on me. He was poking through some of the papers he had already dumped back on the Renaissance table since Sunday's lunch. "Maybe what you've got is a form of *Platzangst*," Father said, without interrupting his paperwork chores. "Just as I always predicted, but I never thought you'd get it this bad. You'll end up like my old uncle Serge, yet."

"I know, I know," I said impatiently. This wasn't the first time I had been given the example of Uncle Serge, an old bachelor who had been the laughingstock of the family when Father was growing up. Platzangst meant literally *fear of place* or agoraphobia, but the designation was used more as a fashionable catchall to explain the eccentricities of the noble rich. Poor people obviously couldn't indulge such symptoms as being terrified of throngs of other common folk. Platzangst sufferers had their carriages draped when traversing public squares, and if caught unawares, they might wrap themselves in horse blankets or pull up their coats or dresses as a shield. "I'd rather have Platzangst any day than what I've got."

"Tell me again," Father said with a total lack of seriousness, "what exactly is it that you've got? I'm afraid I still don't understand."

"Isn't it obvious?" I groaned. "I'm fighting the will of God. I've failed to carry out his commands."

"Maybe I'm dumb," Father said, "but what makes you so sure it's God telling you these things?"

"I know, I just know," I said, continuing my anxious pacing of the living room. Of course it was God! Who else but? Those messages sounded exactly like the Old Testament God I still remembered from our daily chapel readings during my four years at the Hotchkiss School; the just but angry Yahweh, inexorably stern with those who dared disobey his word.

Yet that's what was puzzling me now. How come the Jesus I had so briefly experienced at Manya's prayer meeting had been so gentle and comforting? Wasn't Jesus the same as God, an integral part of an indivisible Trinity? How could God then be so demanding and stern? You'd think that if the Trinity were to have credibility, the various entities would have gotten their act together by now. Maybe Father did have a point. Maybe my mind was playing dangerous tricks. From what I had read, I knew how implacable a guilty conscience could be; how it could demand even self-mutilation and suicide, or turn its vengeance on the world. Almost every week, there were stories in newspapers and on TV of individuals claiming that God had told them to do this and that, from grisly murders to hijacking of planes and countless other nonsensical acts. I had dismissed such people as deranged, acting under irrational impulses from the brain. Yet they must have been every bit as convinced of their divine inspiration as I – indeed, far more so to have carried out their acts.

The possibility that I was merely deranged seemed to have a calming effect. I stopped pacing and sat down on the living room couch. Yes, I needed to have additional proof; proof that it really was God ordering me around. Even in the Bible, God had occasionally given proof. Like when Saul of Tarsus had been blinded on his way to persecute Christians in Damascus, and then regained his sight as he started speaking out for Christ as St. Paul. Not that I needed anything so dramatic, or that I saw myself as a future saint. I was a miserable reprobate who had barely seen the light and wanted to be left alone.

I realized proof in this area wasn't easy to come by in our age of skepticism and doubt. If God in his familiar guise as the Creator on the Sistine Chapel ceiling appeared at a psychiatric convention, delivered the keynote address, and walked out through a closed door, those scientific-minded sophisticates could quickly figure out how to dismiss what they had witnessed as a subjective delusion. I needed something more substantial than my perception of those celestial messages; something that would stand up to hard, objective scrutiny.

But what, God, what?

Why not numbers? I suddenly thought. I didn't need Albrecht to remind me that numbers were our most reliable tool for ascertaining reality throughout the universe. Surely, if God could communicate to me his detailed message about hitchhiking to New York, taking a subway to the Bowery, and all the rest, he could communicate a few authenticating numbers as well.

I stood up and once more started to pace the living room floor.

Okay, so it's numbers, I said to myself, *but which ones? Where do I begin?*

Just then, I realized I was standing by the window sill, where more of Father's papers were messily stacked. I reached into the nearest pile and started to grope around. My intent was to pull out at random some document with a number on it and try to match it with a number in my head.

I was still trying to formulate that number when I heard Father say, "I'll thank you to stay out of my papers and not mess up everything."

I resumed my nervous pacing, trying to figure out what to do. But then Mother had a suggestion. "Why don't you do something useful," I heard her through my fog, "and get that oil changed? You're already late."

It was almost noon by the time I returned home, the car oil good for another 6,000 miles. While in town, I also took care of several errands at the library, hoping to ease the internal tension I felt. But that stern, nonnegotiable command continued to press heavily within. *GET GOING! SUBMIT TO MY WILL . . . OR FOREVER FACE MY WRATH.*

Lunch wasn't for another hour yet. Maybe a walk in the woods would help. I was leery about what had befallen me the last time I ventured there, but I figured the chances of anything of that sort happening again were about as unlikely as two consecutive aviation disasters on the same route. "Come on, Blackie," I said, opening the cellar door, "Let's go!"

Outside it was cold, with an unpleasant dampness in the air. A leaden sky looked as if it might drop of its own insupportable weight and smother everything below.

Blackie was oblivious of my depressed mood. Joyful to be outside with human company, he raced ahead on the narrow forest path as if he were a scout. After his exuberant foray, he settled down no more than a dozen yards ahead to lead the way. He was getting on in years and showed his affection in an occasional backward glance rather than jumping all over my sheepskin coat.

Absorbed in my distressing thoughts, I was surrounded by the forest's tall evergreens, a sliver of overcast sky making the enclosure complete. I shook my head sharply from side to side, checking on the strange pangs I had been sporadically feeling for several days. It wasn't a headache, but a pain deep within my brain, somewhere in the region of the pituitary. Maybe that's what I had, a pituitary gland tumor. It wasn't that uncommon a condition, I had recently read, and was operable now – a procedure in which the surgeon went in through the nose, boring his way to the base of the skull. Ugh, what people wouldn't do to stay alive, though I didn't really think I had anything surgery could fix. Maybe the pituitary was the means for receiving those messages from beyond, just as it was the center where tranquilizers and sleeping pills often did their work. I had, in fact, considered several times easing the tension this way. But the same warning had always come through: *KEEP YOURSELF OPEN TO MY WORD . . . REMEMBER, THERE ARE NO TRANQUILIZERS IN HELL!*

"Come on, Blackie, over here," I called, when I saw the old dog start on another path in the fork ahead instead of the one I wanted to take. But Blackie ignored me, as he often did. I merely shrugged and turned to follow him. Maybe this would prove to be another sign from beyond, I said to myself, with a mixture of despair and jest.

About a hundred yards farther on, I came across a rock in my path that I had never noticed before. Judging by the way it was embedded in the ground, it must have been there since the turn of the century, when the area had served as a granite quarry. It wasn't really an obstacle but jutted out enough to make me pause. I was puzzled how this rock could have escaped my attention on my occasional treks.

I looked around. For the first time in the years I had been walking here, I discerned an unused path leading off to the left. Trees and overgrown bushes were partly blocking it, but I could easily get through to the clearing I spotted ahead. Blackie had disappeared on another foray of his own, and I was left to press on alone.

I was in the clearing now. It was peacefully quiet here, except for a gentle hum in the crowns of the trees. Looking up, I saw the sky begin to take on an eerie glow, as if the sun was trying to break through. Oh God, I said to myself, give me a convincing sign in our world of disbelief and competing truths . . . let me know with certitude the meaning of what's been going on!

The conditions seemed ideal for some kind of a revelation or a miracle to occur. The setting reminded me of a film I had once seen about the peasant children in Portugal who had a vision of the Virgin Mary hovering on the outskirts of their hometown of Fatima. How lucky they had been! They hadn't been to college and had no liberal education to hinder them in matters of this sort. It was easy for them to believe what they had seen. Wasn't that what their eyes were for? How could someone as smart as I end up so helplessly cornered, no longer certain what was and wasn't real?

I was suddenly suffused with a sense of devotion. I felt as if I were standing in a cathedral, with the tall trees becoming the graceful ribs of a soaring medieval nave and the small patch of brightening sky fragmented by the many branches forming a stained glass window to God. I felt myself sink to the ground and kneel on the hard layer of frozen snow, then raise my arms in a prayerful way. Now, God, now! Please, the sign, now!

I was absorbed by the dramatic potential of the moment. All I needed was the sign. Or rather, *not* to get the sign. If I wasn't going to get the sign under these ideal conditions, I would probably never get it at all. I squinted my eyes to refract the light shimmering in the branches above. Maybe I could help those fragmented rays fall into a revealing pattern or shape; a cross, a face of Christ, or some kind of a symbol of divinity or God. Surely, in the absence of even such a contrived sign, I would be free to resume a normal life.

I was beginning to feel the cold wetness of the snow on my knees, soaking through my pants and long underwear. The sun was becoming obscured by the heavy clouds again, and the surrounding woods had reverted to their normal wintry look. The best time for a miracle had obviously passed, and it had failed to materialize.

I lowered my arms and was about to get to my feet, when seemingly from nowhere, Blackie appeared. He startled me by leaping up and putting his paws all over my sheepskin coat. As if that wasn't unusual enough for sedate old Blackie, he was acting in a weird non-dog way. He was nipping away at me and pawing me as if he didn't want me to move from this spot. When I finally struggled to my feet after repeatedly pushing him off, he again started to hurl himself at me to block my way. He took a firm bite of the hem of my sheepskin coat and tried to drag me back. He then bit into my gloves and almost pulled them off.

"Come on, Blackie, what's the matter?" I tried to reason. "Good dog, Blackie, good dog!" It was as if he didn't know who I was. Though neither angry nor affectionate, the mutt continued to charge with a single-minded purpose that he seemed not to understand but was determined to carry out. Never in the years I had been walking with Blackie had I seen him act this way. It just wasn't Blackie. He persisted for at least two minutes more, until I got out of that clearing where I had knelt. Then, as abruptly as he began, he trotted off nonchalantly, good old Blackie again.

I could feel my heart pounding; not from any exertion but because of what was inescapably clear. I felt as if I had blundered into the world of some spooky TV show. Only it was all so terribly real! I suspected all along what it was about, from the instant Blackie had come charging in. I wanted to get out of that clearing as quickly as I could, fearing what might happen if I stayed. Yet what more could have happened to dramatize the sign? The most frightening moment had come at the end, when in a trice, as if on command, Blackie became his old self again and sauntered off as if he no longer cared. That's when I knew what it meant beyond a shadow of doubt, no matter how much I tried to tell myself otherwise.

As I hurried home on the narrow forest path, illuminated by an eerie verdancy refracted from the evergreens, I was gripped by a primitive terror humans experience when face-to-face with the unknown. Yet I was also feeling a strange elation for having been singled out by the powers beyond. How many saints, from my limited knowledge of their lives, ever had to grapple with an experience of this sort? It certainly surpassed the miracle of Saint Augustine, who, asking for a divine sign in his own spiritual quandary, heard a child's voice sing, "Take up and read" – bringing him to a crucial section of the Holy Writ.

Rushing along the eerie path and thinking of Saint Augustine's ordeal, I was beset by a wild idea that nevertheless seemed more and more logical with each step. Was I perhaps seeing those trees and shrubs casting their ghostly shadows, as if illuminated by a light source in eclipse, through the eyes of Saint Augustine? Was I, in fact, Saint Augustine, reincarnated in a modern guise and chosen to follow the very path he had to endure as he wrestled with himself and begged, *God make me chaste, but not yet!* That's exactly how I would have described my condition now. Or was I the one who had been Saint Augustine fifteen hundred years ago, and Saint Augustine now was me?

As I continued along the forest path in the spectral light, engulfed in my mystical turmoil, I had an altogether different thought. Maybe I was just another megalomaniac taking his act to new heights on a different stage. The world was full of madmen thinking they were saints or Jesus Christ, singled out by God to fulfill some messianic mission on earth. Maybe Blackie's behavior had been nothing unusual, merely a dog bewildered at seeing me act so strange. Maybe I had been sending out in that prayerful position some special Alpha waves that altered dumb Blackie's behavior in such a dramatic way.

On three separate occasions while rushing home, I did a little test. I went down on my knees, and after a few moments of praying fervently I waited to see how Blackie would react. In each case Blackie stopped, and with evident patience but no special interest, watched me from where he was. When I finally called to him from my kneeling position, he merely trotted up. It took a torrent of encouraging words before he gave me a couple of affectionate sniffs. Then he sat down on his haunches a few feet away, again waiting patiently until I was through. In near desperation, I tried to get him worked up so he would jump up and play a little rough, or engage me in a tug-of-war for my sheepskin coat or gloves. But to no avail. Blackie continued in his same, apathetic way, without the slightest reminder of the way he had acted in the clearing only moments ago.

If only poor dumb Blackie, with the dry blobs hanging from the long hairs around his tail, could have realized how much had been at stake!

"I'm afraid I might have to leave after all," I informed my parents in a trembling voice when I returned.

I tried to explain what had just happened in the woods, but Father cut me short. "How can you talk so stupidly," he snapped, in an uncharacteristic departure from his lighthearted attitude to my ordeal. "Now you really are getting to be worse than old Uncle Serge. Poor Blackie's probably the dumbest dog in town, and you want to base your future on what he does?"

I was tempted to argue that Blackie being dumb was probably more of an asset than a liability for missions of this sort, offering a malleable psyche unhindered by a priori views. Yet, on further reflection, I did have to admit that Blackie's behavior couldn't be quantified into hard objective evidence. Trapped as I was between carrying out God's nonnegotiable demands and what I profoundly didn't want to do, my only alternative was to resume my search for evidentiary proof; proof that would either make me willingly submit or release me from my involuntary task.

This meant returning to the mathematical criteria I had set forth prior to the Blackie episode. And here, I intuitively hit on a new technique. I now recalled what I had never paid any attention to before: The afternoon newspaper listed every day ten Social Security numbers selected at random to receive a five-dollar prize each. These were nine-digit numbers, so the chances I would get one right were one in a billion.

On a little slip of paper, I composed a nine-digit number that gradually came into my head. If it turned out I hit the number right on, that would authenticate the source of those messages. I made a solemn pledge in such a case to leave home without delay.

Now, all I could do was wait.

By mid-afternoon, I was beginning to have second thoughts. The paper should have been delivered by then, and I realized I had miscalculated. Since I had written down only one number, and ten numbers would be printed in the paper today, this reduced the odds by a factor of ten — making it a far riskier gamble than I had assumed.

By four o'clock the paper still hadn't arrived, and I was becoming increasingly nervous. Who knew where the newspaper boy was; perhaps engaged in some romance of the ten-year-old set, smoking a joint behind the drugstore, or hanging around town with other kids until dark, waiting for something exciting to liven things up. If he only knew in what an agonized state of suspense he was keeping me!

Still no paper by five; and when it hadn't come at six, I was thinking of calling off my bets. After all, how could I be expected to start hitchhiking to New York at this hour? Maybe the fact that the paper hadn't come yet was in itself a sign that I was to refrain from any immediate moves.

Ten minutes later, I heard the click of the mailbox. The boy had stuffed the paper in, then was off on his bicycle before I could ask where the hell he'd been. In a way, I welcomed the delay; for no matter what the numbers, I couldn't possibly leave before the following day. I figured this wasn't a dishonorable modification of my pledge.

I laid the paper on the table in the kitchen nook, my anxiety holding me in a tremulous grip. It was like coming to the bulletin board in my student days and seeing the grades posted for a final exam on which I wasn't sure I had done well. There was nothing I could do — just brace myself.

Quickly, I scanned the numbers, printed in two columns of five, comparing each against the number on the slip in my hand. I got a series of little shocks as I came across several numbers that started with the 014 prefix I had written down, only to differ totally in the digits that remained. I also had a few breathless moments as I saw my number 56 crop up several times in the second group of digits. As for the final four-digit group, here is where my heart palpably paused. Not only did I instantly spot my number among the listed ten, but in writing down those four digits my hand had slipped twice and I ended up putting down a different number from the one I had originally had in mind. I remembered telling myself then, with a mixture of apprehension and jest, that God had been guiding my hand. And there, imprinted within that little box in the paper before me, were precisely those final four digits I had written down as a result of those slips.

I sat at the kitchen table in a daze. No, I hadn't hit the number right on. But wasn't it possible that this numerical freak, for which the chances must have been exceedingly remote — maybe thousands or even tens of thousands against one — had a special significance for me? Perhaps it was expecting too much of God to speak with absolute clarity. If God did that, what would be the purpose of faith? Maybe God was willing to go just so far to help a person like me.

I started to walk around the kitchen, rubbing my temples with the fingertips of both hands. I was trying to keep out the reality of what had just occurred.

I didn't hear my parents walk in. I wasn't aware how long they had remained silent before trying to bring me out of my self-induced trance.

"Do you have a headache?" I heard Mother ask cautiously.

I shook my head. "Unfortunately, that's not my problem, not by a long shot."

"Well, then?" Father joined in, an edge creeping into his voice.

"I'm afraid I'm going to have to leave," I said, now fully out of my oblivion and struggling not to succumb to a sudden wave of grief. "I guess I better get my suitcase packed tonight so I can get going first thing in the morning."

"What's all this nonsense again?" Father asked tartly. "I thought we already settled that."

"I'm afraid the picture has changed. I've been getting more messages.

"Stop this with your crazy messages," Mother said sharply. "I don't want to hear another word about these . . . these fantasies."

I shook my head. "This time I've got proof. Overwhelming evidence that my messages are real. Numbers unfortunately don't lie."

"First you hear voices like Joan of Arc . . ."

"No, no," I corrected Father. "I never said I heard anything."

"Then it was stupid Blackie," Father continued with evident forbearance. "Well, what about these numbers?"

I was ready, in fact, eager to present my proof. I had in my hand the newspaper as well as the slip of paper with the number I had written down. It was evidence that couldn't leave anyone unconvinced.

Father didn't let me finish. "Ach, your numbers are no good!" he exclaimed in utter disdain, as soon as he got the gist. "You'd never win a lottery that way. Any idiot knows that unless you get the exact number, it's no good. There's no such thing as being close." Father paused, then resumed cheerfully. "Now, if you really could become good at guessing numbers . . ."

I didn't hold it against my parents that they refused to understand. In their noncomprehending way, they were merely trying to help. "I'll miss you both," I muttered, in a tone which let me keep my voice under control. "I'll miss you terribly." I blinked several times to clear my eyes, and when I looked up, my parents were no longer there. They had withdrawn quietly to the living room, where I could hear them tuning in the evening news.

I propped up my chin in the palms of my hands and glanced through the frost-covered windows wrapped around the kitchen nook. The evening sky was heavily overcast; no doubt, it would snow all night. By first light, there might be more than a foot. I could see myself setting forth from the house, trudging through the drifts to the Massachusetts Turnpike three miles away, my small battered suitcase in hand. It wouldn't be right to have Mother or Father drop me off. I would have to make the final break at our front door and start walking without turning back.

But the more I thought about these details, the more I realized I never would leave. Not unless I was again imbued with the spirit of calm and otherworldly strength that I had experienced early that morning. Without it, I was too weak, too addicted to the comforts of my world, and far too unwilling to make a complete and permanent break. The chances of my doing so would further diminish with each passing day, moving salvation further and further from my grasp. Was it the decision to truly go that had of itself given me the special grace to be able to see it through? And was it because throughout the day I had never again decided to go that I didn't feel this special grace again?

That evening the relentless assault didn't let up: *BETTER GET GO-ING! YOU HAVE AN ENORMOUS PRICE TO PAY . . . START PAYING IT NOW OR FACE ETERNITY IN THE DARK.*

My desperate mood drove me to consider an approach I had previously ruled out. Why not phone my sister, I suddenly thought. Manya had served as an instrument to get me into this mess; so, why not see if she could get me out? If she had brought me this far on God's behalf, surely he wouldn't allow her to steer me wrong.

I dialed Manya's number from the kitchen phone, reluctant to compound my parents' worries after all I had already put them through. I listened to the phone ring several times, my apprehension mounting that Manya might not be home. With each additional ring, I somehow became more and more convinced she held the key to my fate.

What a relief to hear her voice!

"We were eating dinner," Manya explained.

"I can call later," I suggested.

"No, no," she countered, with the fervor of a salesperson who has a promising prospect on the line. "I've already finished."

This time, it was my sister who seemed ready to take the lead. "Well, how are you?" she asked. We hadn't talked since my fateful visit, and I could sense her eagerness to hear about the difference Jesus had made in my life.

"I'm afraid not well, Manya. Not well at all."

"Oh?" Her voice betrayed disappointment as well as curiosity.

As briefly as I could, I summarized what had been happening to me. I told her about the messages directing me to work in the Bowery, about Blackie's behavior, and the other proofs authenticating God's word.

Manya didn't say anything until I got to the part about the numbers. "Now stop right there," she said with authority. "You had me puzzled for a while. But now, it's all crystal clear."

I felt myself clutching the receiver. So it was clear to her too! That's what I had been afraid of. The proof was that obvious.

"Don't you see?" she continued. "It's the devil who's after you! God doesn't deal in numbers. That's the work of the devil. Always has been. The Lord doesn't work that way."

"The devil?" I asked hesitantly, caught off guard by hearing this mythical abstraction referred to as reality. Already as a child, I had merged the old village priest's fearful image of a furry creature wielding a pitchfork with the neighboring farmer's teenage son, who used to come to entertain us in that guise on Saint Nicholas's day, in expectation of a tip. In subsequent years, the devil had metamorphosed for me into an amalgam of portrayals by artists over the centuries as a sort of unrestrained, naughty, leering entity endowed with animalistic sensuality. This was in line with the popular expression, "The devil made me do it," which usually referred to something mischievous rather than evil. I had, in fact, often been called a devil in jest and took it as a compliment. Now, to hear my sister talk of the devil as if he were real simply failed to connect. "I'm afraid I don't understand," I said.

"There's nothing to understand. Numerology is the sign of the devil. Not only do I think so. The Church says so too."

"Why in the world would the devil try to get me to go to skid row and do charity work with a bunch of derelicts?"

"Because he knows you can't do it. He's trying to ruin you. Set you against yourself. Make you crack up."

"Well, he's doing a damn good job of it."

"The devil's probably jealous of your rebirth, of your new potential with Jesus."

"Why wouldn't he command me to do something wild? Hijack a plane, murder somebody . . . wouldn't that meet his goal better?"

"The devil is devious. He wants you to think it's God talking. Then he's got you where he wants . . . rejecting God when it really *is* God talking."

Despite my compelling desire to believe Manya, I was exasperated with her reasoning. "That is devious," I said trying not to sound sarcastic.

"Sometimes it's very difficult to tell the difference between the devil's voice and the voice of God. That's why we all need help. Somebody who's got experience, like a priest. It's dangerous for you to try and do it alone."

"It's no use, Manya. You're a dear for trying to help, but I'm afraid I know where those messages came from. And it's not the devil."

There was a pause. "I still think you should see a priest, especially on this numerology thing."

"How then do you explain Blackie going berserk? Just as I was praying for a sign?"

"Well," my sister said, now hesitating, "I don't know. That's why you should see a priest."

"You see, I'm afraid if I don't offer my life to those Bowery hoboes . . . that's it for my salvation."

"That you *don't* have to do," Manya interrupted decisively. "About that, I am sure."

"You are?" Her certainty on this crucial issue gave me fresh hope.

"Confession. That's all you need. Then a good act of contrition. I'm sure any priest will give you absolution."

"Oh, that!" I said with thinly veiled contempt. I had been hoping for something more original. I still remembered the last time I had gone to confession at fifteen, when the priest tried to ascertain whether I had experienced any *bodily changes* while kissing, which would help him determine if I had committed a sin. I had little confidence that mumbling a few Our Fathers and Hail Marys was an adequate substitute for the debt I had to discharge. How I only wished it were! I would have gladly done a thousand of each, especially if they weren't too bunched up. "Look Manya," I continued, "how can some old geezer who doesn't know me from Adam for-give me for the last thirty years?"

"Haven't you forgotten something?"

"I have?"

"The suffering of our Lord on the cross! He died for you. He died for your sins. You see, he already paid the price for you. That's why you don't need to go anywhere."

"I don't?"

"Don't you see? Our Lord knew people like you would need his help. None of us can pay for our sins alone. They're too immense. He came to save us from a fate such as yours. He is your savior."

"He is?" I countered feebly.

"All you have to do," I heard my sister continue, "is go to con-fession, and then receive the body of our Lord in holy commun-ion."

"Are you sure? It sounds too easy."

"Not when you think of how much our Lord suffered on the cross. For you. For me. For all of us. But right now, above all, for you. Just imagine, God's only son going through all that for you."

I never had occasion in the past to relate my fate to the ago-nies endured by Jesus Christ. In fact, I had often wondered, why all this ado about Christ? Others had died a still harsher death, and I vaguely resented any suggestion that Christ had died for me.

Now, I started to see it in a different light. Yes, yes, it made sense. Christ's blood was the way out of my personal mess! Hear-ing Manya reiterate her simple explanation over and over again, I felt myself engulfed by mounting waves of gratitude and relief. And maybe there was something to this two-thousand-year un-broken history of the Church. Who was I to dispute this enduring institution's word?

The intense emotions released a flow of tears. I now under-stood why only something so excruciating as the suffering endured by Jesus Christ could pay off my staggering debt. But I had a practical thought. "How can I confess thirty years of sins? I could be in that little booth till eternity begins."

"All you need is to make a general confession."

"Isn't it the details they want? Especially in transgressions having to do with sex?" I asked, perking up.

"Well, it might be better if we find someone who understands," my sister conceded, now herself in an upbeat mood, as if she had closed the deal and was merely negotiating the payment terms. "That old priest you've got up there might go into shock."

Manya had one more suggestion before hanging up. She wanted me to call Al, who had been the leader at the prayer meeting that started it all. She thought it wouldn't hurt if I double checked with him and received a second opinion on my case. "Give me a few minutes. I'll call him and explain who you are. I'm sure he'll tell you exactly the same as I."

That made me nervous. What if this Al character told me I had to go to the Bowery after all? Where would I be then? On the other hand, if he supported my sister's opinion, I would be truly in the clear.

When I returned to the living room, I was in a much better mood. "I just talked to Manya," I announced to my parents. "She said I don't have to go skid row after all."

Mother made a face indicating she wanted no further part in my inanity, but father smiled. "You see! Isn't that what I've been telling you?"

"All I have to do, Manya says, is to go to confession."

Mother looked up. "I don't care what you do. Only please, don't do it here."

"That's all right. Manya will arrange it for me somewhere near her. Right now she's talking about my case to the man who conducts her prayer meetings. I'm supposed to call him in a few minutes myself."

"What for?" Father wanted to know.

"Just to chat. Look, I'm not out of the woods yet."

"Is he a priest?"

"I think he's a plumber."

"A plumber?" Father repeated. "In that case, you'll probably get good, solid advice."

But Mother shook her head sadly. "Aren't you ashamed? A Yale graduate calling a plumber to find out what to do with his life!"

7/

Well before dawn the following day, I found myself being practically kicked out of bed. It couldn't have been more than five; yet, there I was, being forcibly ejected from beneath the warmth of my blankets into the frigid air coursing through the room. Though barely awake, I came to with lightning speed, as the old message made itself felt with the compelling force of a kick in the rear: *WHAT ARE YOU WAITING FOR? GET GOING, GET GOING WHILE YOU STILL HAVE A CHANCE! YOUR TIME IS RUNNING OUT . . .*

Oh no, not again! Wasn't this ever going to end? I stood on the ice-cold floor next to my bed, naked except for the old cashmere turtleneck. I looked up in reverent desperation. "Oh, Jesus, help me, Jesus, please help! I can't stand this much longer!"

I lowered my head for a moment of pious contemplation, then took a couple of steps to let the window down and bounded back to bed. At least until the room warms up, I thought to myself.

NO, RIGHT NOW!

I felt that inexorable command shaking me to the core. I burrowed deeper under the covers, as if I could evade that silent voice or pretend it didn't exist, the way I had done with Kathryn when she thought I was asleep and articulated her secret hopes over my slumbering form. There was no way I could do it now; no way to ignore or shut out God's insistent message. This led me to agonize: would I one day be infinitely sorrier for refusing to heed God's word than for having ignored Kathryn? How much sorrier I might be when the full truth about human existence was revealed and I realized what a chance I had missed! It perplexed me to reflect how, in barely a week I had come to adopt a medieval outlook, accepting afterlife as a reality and salvation as the paramount purpose of our sojourn on earth.

I was now alert again, focused on what was going on. Another message was beginning to make itself felt. It was a number. At first I wasn't sure if it was 423 or 432, but gradually I settled on 432. There was a deliberate pause after the four, making me visualize it as 4:32, which I couldn't help but conclude meant the time.

What was going to happen at 4:32 – whether to me or the world? Was I going to be struck down in some way, perhaps in an automobile accident or by something as ridiculous as slipping on the snow and breaking my neck? Or were the implications to be more universal, perhaps heralding the earthquake that would sink California beneath the waves of the Pacific or inundate the East Coast under a tidal wave surging over the top of the Empire State Building? In my condition, I wasn't ashamed to find relief in this abysmal thought, since a disaster of such magnitude would put me out of my misery as well. But almost instantly, I realized that would mean going from the proverbial frying pan into the fire. Because of the unredeemed state of my soul, I would merely be exchanging my temporal hell for an eternal one.

GET GOING, GET GOING . . .

As I continued to cower under the blankets, I had no doubt these messages would eventually make me crack; not in a way that would make me obey, but rather assure me a berth in a psychiatric ward. Since talking to my sister the previous evening on the phone, my condition had deteriorated. The reason was Al, the prayer leader whom I had called at Manya's behest. No, he didn't dispute or countermand what my sister said. If anything, he was more adamant that the messages were the devil's work and were to be ignored. I realized Al couldn't have possibly remembered who I was. I had the feeling he visualized me as a teenager, intent on running away from home to join some devilish sect, and he considered it his duty to try to stop me or thwart my plans. "Jesus doesn't work that way," Al explained. "He wouldn't want you to run off half-cocked to who knows where and get your parents all upset . . . " As much as I appreciated this reassurance, Al's rationale had given him away. If there was one thing I remembered about Jesus Christ, it was his attitude on this point. Forget your family, Jesus had repeatedly urged, and follow me. I had checked it out myself before going to bed. There it was, spelled out in Saint Matthew. "A man's worst enemies will be the members of his family. Whoever loves his father or mother more than me is not worthy of me. Whoever does not take up his cross and follow in my steps is not worthy of me. Whoever tries to gain his own life will lose it." There! What could be more plain? This passage cast doubt on everything else Al and my sister had said. Their prescription of confession and communion no longer seemed a convincing substitute for what God had commanded me to do.

The occasional rattle of the radiator disrupted my thoughts and made me aware that the room was gradually heating up. I could smell the aroma of freshly brewed coffee wafting up from Mother's breakfast. God, how could I tell her I was leaving again? The stark images of what lay ahead once more invaded my brain. I could see myself working the night shift in the White Tower as a short-order cook, when some glamorous people wander in after attending a charity play at an experimental theater nearby. Among them is the trendy shoe heiress from Saint Louis, who feared having to work in just such a place had she become my wife. Although I am a shadow of myself in a white T-shirt and a paper cap, she recognizes me right away, and nodding as if she understands, asks solicitously, "Are you all right?"

I tried to let my mind go blank. I didn't want to entertain these thoughts, or anything else pertaining to the reality closing in on me. I realized that my self-pitying act, coupled with my lack of determination and strength, was beginning to turn me into a self-parody.

Suddenly I found myself on my knees, imploring God with all the emotion at my command. "Oh, please let me know in a decisive way what to do. Let me know that it's you. I can't say I want to do your will, but if you give me the strength, I know I'll be ready to obey. Please don't ask me to do anything I won't have the strength to fulfill."

For a moment, there was no response. Then I got a message, crisp and clear, the way I had received the preceding ones. There was no doubt what it said: *THERE WILL BE NO NEW MESSAGES. IT'S YOUR LIFE . . . IT'S UP TO YOU TO DECIDE WHAT YOU WANT TO DO WITH IT. YOU'RE ON YOUR OWN. NO MORE NEW MESSAGES.*

And that was it, as if the line had suddenly gone dead or the other party had hung up. All I knew was that we had been disconnected for good.

While this last message came literally as God-sent relief, I had to cope with a new concern: Could it be that I had finally been abandoned by God? That he had finally become disgusted and had given up on me as Kathryn and the statuesque stockbroker had done? And others as well who had reached the point of *enough?* With my equivocation and mental gymnastics, I had given God ample cause. Not only did I suspect all along the messages were genuine; I had been offered persuasive proof. How could I ignore all those numbers staring me in the face? Perhaps most convincing – and deeply embedded in my mind – was the image of Blackie going berserk in the woods.

I had no idea what might happen at 4:32, but I was determined to follow normal routine. From Professor Bernard Knox's Classical Civilization at Yale, I still remembered the distressing saga of the Oedipus family – otherwise exemplary folk, who saw no alternative but to resort to criminal measures to thwart a horrendous prediction about their fate. Yet the prediction had come true only because of elaborate attempts to evade that fate. Had they left well enough alone, no portion of the perverse tragedy of a son killing his father and marrying his mother would have materialized. That lesson from history I had managed to learn.

I even risked venturing into the woods with Blackie, since this was the kind of day on which I would have done so in the past. As it turned out, I again found myself following Blackie on that alternate path toward the clearing where I had witnessed his deviant behavior. Only this time when I reached the crucial fork, where the large rock had been in the middle of the path and prompted me to change my course, I could only see a not-too-conspicuous stone. It certainly didn't look like anything that would even make me pause. I must have been seeing things differently on my previous trek, or this wasn't a good day for signs.

I decided to risk telling my parents of the latest communication from beyond, alerting them as dispassionately as I could to witness some final message at 4:32. If it proved sufficiently dramatic, perhaps they might take me seriously at last.

"I wonder what's going to happen," I asked myself within Father's hearing range, as the time approached.

"My hope is you'll start acting sensibly again," Father said. "That would be enough of a miracle."

"Remember, it's going to be at four-thirty-two. I want to go on record that I'm telling you well in advance."

"Yes, yes. Four thirty-two," Father repeated, as if trying to humor me.

At 4:15, I took a call from the producer in Miami who had hired me to write the day-care center scripts. I decided to talk to him normally, without hurrying the conversation to meet the 4:32 deadline. Maybe the message would be in something he might say. On the other hand, I wouldn't try to prolong the call.

As soon as I was off the phone, I glanced at my watch. It was the same Rolex Oyster Perpetual I had bought at the tax-free airport shop in Zurich some ten years ago. It originally had a tendency to gain or lose a minute a week, no matter how often I took it for a free adjustment at the Rolex office in New York. Then about two years ago on Long Island's Southampton beach, while changing the date on the calendar at the end of June to skip the 31st, I forgot to screw back the crown before plunging in the surf. I had to have the watch overhauled at considerable expense, and since then, it kept perfect time. Now, it was just a few seconds after 4:30.

"I think the paper just came," Mother said.

Normal pace, normal pace, I kept repeating to myself, as I went out to the mailbox to bring the paper in. Despite the snow, I didn't put on a coat, because I would never do so for the few steps. I avoided looking at my watch along the way, not wishing to be tempted to slow down or speed up, even if just a mite.

On returning to the house, I shook off the snow and headed for the living room. I plopped myself down on the couch next to where Father was sitting, and on an impulse, reached into my pocket for the Social Security number I had jotted down the previous day. I hadn't prepared any new numbers, having focused on the event that might occur at 4:32.

I opened the newspaper to the second page where the numbers were listed, and then looked at my watch. It was five seconds before 4:32. On a sudden impulse, I held out my arm in front of Father's face so that he could see the watch.

"Okay, the paper came at four thirty-two," he said nonchalantly. "It usually comes about this time. So what?"

My eyes were already scanning the numbers, comparing the
one on my slip with those on the printed page. Almost right away,
it caught me with the surprise of a haymaker punch, and even
though sitting down, I felt weak in the knees. There it was, the
same four-digit sequence repeated routinely from the day before;
the one on which my hand had slipped twice and made me write a
different number from the one I had intended.

In a flash I understood it all. Why of course, no *new* messages;
hence yesterday's number, written down with someone guiding my
hand. And despite what Father had said about the paper always
coming about now, it never did since we got the new delivery boy.
There was a three-hour window during which he might choose to
drop it off. I didn't even want to contemplate the odds against the
boy bringing it exactly when he did.

I was again witnessing something caused from beyond this
world, something controlled by forces I couldn't understand. I
couldn't escape what this meant for my life.

Father dismissed the coincidence with a wave of his hand.
"That's easy," he said. "As I told you before, the trick is to get the
whole number. Four digits still won't win you anything."

"But don't you think it's odd it happened at four thirty-two, at
exactly four-thirty-two?"

I could tell Father was uneasy for a moment. He thought of a
way to answer, then decided on a different tack. "Just as your
message told you this morning. You're on your own. I'm not going
to stop you."

"Neither am I," Mother chimed in.

"If you still want to leave," Father said, "go ahead. My God,
you're over forty years old. Don't expect us to tell you what to
do."

I could feel my innards tighten. My last buffer had crumpled. I was on my own.

Moments later, I was in my room. I normally never spent any time there during the day, but I had sneaked away from downstairs as soon as I discreetly could. Having that paper arrive at exactly 4:32, then finding the four-digit combination reprinted from the previous day, was making me lose all semblance of control.

I paced the little room back and forth, feeling as if my head might explode and splatter all over the place. Was this how Father had felt during his desperate wartime drive to the Sudetenland? I pulled at my hair, then banged the palms of my hands against the sides of my head – hardly an admirable way to react even with nobody around. But that was my least worry now. I could already see eternal life and perfect knowledge floating out of my reach, as if I were on an iceberg inexorably drifting from shore, where basking in a golden light I could discern everything and everybody I loved, and they couldn't hear my cries for a final comforting glance. As I entered into the frigid darkness of this infinite void, how trifling seemed the years I might have to put in with the derelicts!

God no, spare me that train of thought! I hit my head against the wall several times in rhythmic raps, then sat down on the edge of my bed. This calmed me down, as if I had truly knocked some sense through my skull. I rubbed my face with my hands, then cradled my chin in my palms, elbows propped up against my knees. I realized I had little choice but to turn to the alternative my sister had proposed. Considering how inextricably trapped I felt, it didn't take me long to evolve a new rationale to validate Manya's approach. Wouldn't it be a blatant lack of faith in Jesus and his confessional, I reasoned, if I decided to go to skid row and personally tried to atone? Who was I to take matters into my hands and determine how much penance I should do? That was up to the Church, which was uniquely qualified to adjudge matters of this sort with its millennia of experience. Why, for all of my misdeeds and sins, they probably wouldn't sock me with more than several Our Fathers and a number of Hail Marys to match.

How trivial! I started to smirk, but suddenly was caught up in an infinitely greater truth that for the first time pierced the gloom which had enveloped me for days.

I sat up on the bed, electrified by what I now realized. How stupid and blind I was, how ignorant of God's mysterious ways! The answer had been there all along. All I had to do was to add up the facts. Here I was, ready to return to the Church after thirty years and partake in confession and communion, the most basic of all the sacraments. Had anyone suggested a week ago I would be thinking along these lines, I might have responded, though in jest, that only God could bring such a miracle about. Yet that's precisely what he had done! God obviously never intended for me to take him at his word about those Bowery derelicts. That had been his way of making me aware of the punishment he could demand and the mercy he could exercise. Nothing less than the trauma of the previous week could have gotten me to accept the Church and all that it entailed. Without those messages and various proofs, there is no way I would have taken such a step. Even if I had, how long would I have kept this commitment without the fearful memory of what I had been through? Yes, I would have to stick to the straight and narrow, yet how infinitely more welcome that would be than what I had faced! And I wouldn't be altogether weaseling out on the debt I still so acutely felt. I now remembered another near-providential fact. Just a few hundred yards from where I was going to live in Miami's Coconut Grove was Mercy Hospital. I could put in several hours each week with terminal indigents, and then during the summer months, perhaps volunteer a couple of weeks in camps for underprivileged youth. Yes, I was going to be starting a new life, liberated from the unwitting misorientation of my previous one.

Had I just completed another stage of being born again?

Sitting at the edge of the bed, I felt suffused in a prayerful gratitude. *Oh, thank you God, thank you for being so persistent to make me see the light. You certainly work in astounding ways, and for a while, you sure gave me a scare. But thank you, God, for understanding me in your absolute wisdom and directing me in the only possible way. Nothing less extreme would have worked. You knew that all along. Now, I know it, too!*

8/

My sister arranged for me to confess the following day to a young charismatic priest not far from where she lived. Father Ted was his name, and Manya promised he would be understanding of my case.

"God does work in mysterious ways," she remarked joyfully, shortly after I arrived in the midst of a snow storm at her home and finished sharing with her my latest interpretation of God's intent. "I think you're absolutely right."

I couldn't resist reminding Manya of a crucial detail she seemed to be overlooking now. "But what if those messages had indeed come from the devil," I wanted to know, "as you and Al so confidently claimed? How could they have led to this providential result?"

My sister was hardly at a loss for words. "Well, the devil does overplay his hand every now and then," she said with a reassuring smile. "But I wouldn't give it another thought. Don't forget, Jesus was with you all the way, looking out for you and guiding you."

Manya left for the kitchen to phone Father Ted, while I remained seated on the living room couch. From the array of magazines on the coffee table at my feet, I picked up the first to catch my eye. It turned out to be a Catholic weekly, whose title I failed to notice in any memorable way. What did arrest my attention on about page three or five was a catchy ad for visiting the Holy Land. The tour was to be escorted by a priest named Father Carrigan, whose smiling, corpulent photo appeared above a headline: "THRILL to the Manger at Bethlehem! WEEP at the Via Dolorosa! CRUISE on the Sea of Galilee! CLIMB the Mount of Olives! ENJOY Cairo, Amman and Samaria!"

As I continued to peruse the ad, I had an empty feeling within. My God, it was no different from the enticing, mildly deceptive material I used to put out while working for the Institute. In its implicit self-indulgence and fun, how reminiscent was this ad of the life to which I had heretofore subscribed! Maybe it wasn't by chance I came across this magazine now, any more than I had picked out seemingly at random the book by Thomas Merton. Maybe it was God himself who had intended for me to see Father Carrigan's ad and make me realize how far I was straying from my designated path! After all, what could Father Carrigan and his ilk have in common with the austere mission I had been called to carry out? Comfort was imprinted on his face, as well as on the faces of other priests pictured in prosperous social settings on the pages of this diocesan magazine.

As I continued to leaf through the glossy periodical, I started to get my anticlerical dander up. Hell no, I didn't want to have anything to do with this hierarchical institution, whose dogmas had the potential for inflicting discord and suffering. I couldn't help but feel hypocritical about my acceptance of the Christ story and the confessional to save my skin. What was I getting myself into? After all, I had never received any message from God to go to confession and communion. Was it really in the nature of God to resort to such devious ways? Perhaps all that deviousness had originated solely in my human brain . . .

Just then, my sister came bustling into the room. "Father Ted is waiting," she said, with an undertone of excitement. "He'll see you as soon as you can get over there."

Outside the rectory, it was still snowing hard. The study where I found myself closeted with Father Ted was comfortable and warm. Several fresh logs were smoldering in the fireplace, quickly put there by an elderly domestic before she discreetly withdrew. Except for the sizable crucifix on one of the walls, this could have been a study or a den in any well-to-do home. Neat rows of books lined the other walls; there was an attractive carpet on the floor, and the comfortable furnishings had a New England antique look.

I felt curiously out of place. I came dressed as a penitent; as if I had, in fact, obeyed God's command and was on my way to skid row. I was wearing my battered sheepskin coat, my oldest Irish-knit white sweater which was yellowing around the neck, and a pair of thick whipcord pants from one of my Sills suits I had taken out of commission years ago, after a dish of chicken tandoori at an Indian restaurant in London accidentally landed in my lap. As I now looked around, my guess was that most of the parishioners came here in their Sunday best. Shouldn't I at least tip off Father Ted to my sartorial disguise? I hadn't really meant to feign poverty, the way people often did when having their taxes audited. Perhaps if I were to let Father Ted know I usually wore custom-made suits with four real buttonholes on each sleeve, he would be in a better position to visualize my sins. But it was just a fleeting thought. I figured my sins were overwhelming enough even in their attenuated form.

I liked Father Ted right away – and not only because he belied my stereotype of priests, which had just been reinforced by Manya's diocesan magazine. From the moment we met, Father Ted seemed to attune himself to my somber, remorseful mood. He was a thin, ascetic-looking man about ten years younger than I, who appeared impressed rather than overwhelmed by the worldly range of my sins. I must have been the classic case about which he had often preached but rarely encountered so full-blown in the flesh. During my two hours of often tearful outpouring, his attention never strayed as he listened with sympathy. I couldn't help but feel that my pathetically sorry state was validating for him the life of self-denial to which he had been called. He seemed almost surprised how readily the consequences of my freewheeling life confirmed the wisdom of the restricted path he advocated to his parishioners in church.

The only aspect of my outpouring that appeared to disturb Father Ted were my presumed communications with God. Normal people weren't supposed to have experiences of this sort unless, of course, proclaimed as saints or certified insane. With all of his church expertise, it wasn't anything Father Ted was prepared to comment on.

"The worst of it is, Father, I believe those communications more than what we're going through now."

"I don't think you'd be here if you didn't believe," he pointed out gently. "You believe enough to have come."

Maybe Father Ted was right, I tried to tell myself. Just to have driven there in the hazardous snow must have taken faith. Yet I felt I ought to be more forthright as to where I stood; to define the limits of my potential devotion – not unlike I had tried to do with that Fly Me! stewardess – prior to taking any irretrievable step. "What bothers me," I volunteered, as I shifted uneasily in my chair, "is that I don't really know to what extent I'm here as a substitute for what I was commanded to do."

"It's not unusual for human faith to begin when we're in dire need," Father Ted assured me, again showing no surprise at my admission. "This is how Jesus Christ brings us to him."

350

I managed a feeble smile. "I guess God knew how to whip me in line."

"This is only the first step, a chance for you to grow," Father Ted continued. "What's important is that you're sorry for your sins."

"I think that's embarrassingly obvious."

"Then I'm prepared to give you absolution."

I nodded uneasily. "Thank you, Father." My voice was subdued. Yes, of course, I wanted absolution. That's why I had come. Absolution gave Father Ted the power to do what no psychiatrist could. Instead of having to put me through extensive therapy to merely rationalize my sins, he had the authority to instantly wipe them out thanks, to a benefactor two thousand years ago.

Only I still couldn't quite get myself to believe that. My reservations were more fundamental than those I had shared with Father Ted. I wanted to shout that it wasn't the teachings of Jesus I objected to. It was the Church and the mumbo jumbo they had ritualized, including the confessional I was going through right now. I had often wondered what Christ would have thought of this Church which anathematized all other religions in his name.

Of course I didn't say any of this to Father Ted. Even in my distress, I retained sufficient PR savvy to know how far I could go. Father Ted would have been left with no choice but to withdraw his offer of absolution, at least until I had taken religious instructions to confirm my faith, a process that would probably have the opposite effect.

Father Ted began the prescribed rites, repeating whatever incantations were necessary to relieve me of my sins. He recognized how empty it would be to have me atone in any quantitative way; after all, how many prayers would I have to recite as a theoretical counterbalance for my sins? Seemingly unsure whether I remembered any prayers at all, Father Ted asked me to pray silently with him. While he merely closed his eyes and remained in his chair as he started to recite on my behalf, I tumbled to my knees, with tears streaming down my cheeks, as if to demonstrate my faith. Then during a pause in his supplications, I improvised a penitent prayer of my own, the likes of which I was sure Father Ted had never heard.

I was feeling increasingly grateful, as I continued to improvise my torrent of devotional words. It really was quite pleasant here, kneeling on the rug in this comfortable study protected from the outside snow, a crackling blaze in the fireplace. Was this why Jesus had died on the cross, so that people like me could be absolved in a matter of minutes for their years of transgressions? I had never considered the punishment to which I had been sentenced by God as excessive or unjust. But Jesus Christ, who had already suffered on my behalf, was making it unnecessary for me to serve any of that sentence at all.

When I paused momentarily in my prayerful outburst, Father Ted took the opportunity to punctuate my words with a brisk, "Amen!" I sensed that my outward zealotry was beginning to make him nervous. It obviously wouldn't be necessary to launch into any further spontaneous paeans.

"Thank you, Father Ted," I mumbled, getting back into my chair, grateful that this key requirement for salvation had been fulfilled. "I have one more favor to ask. I know it's supposed to be done only in conjunction with mass, but could you give me communion, too?"

Father Ted nodded. "I don't see why not. We'll just have to step next door to the church."

"I have to admit," I blurted out, "I was worried driving here in the snow. What if I had gotten killed before taking these sacraments? Would I have gone to hell?"

"The intent was there," Father Ted said calmly. He slipped on a pair of fur-lined rubber boots and was bundling up against the snow. "God doesn't condemn people on a technicality."

His remark once more triggered my doubts.

A technicality! I thought to myself. Isn't that what I was going through right now, trying to circumvent what I had been so sternly commanded to do? Indeed, wasn't the underlying function of organized religion to provide a structure for helping us find acceptable ways of making up for our repeated failures to submit to God's will? Wasn't religious ritual our own compensation or offering to God, not unlike human, animal, and material sacrifices of the past, for not doing what he really wanted us to do?

Outside the rectory, gusts of wind whipped the heavy snow. Walking the few steps to the adjoining church through the gathering drifts, I found myself wishing I could take off my shoes and have the soles of my feet iced until discomfort became pain. Was that what may have partly motivated Emperor Henry IV a thousand years ago at the gates of the papal residence at Canossa, where he exposed himself to the winter cold for three days while waiting to be absolved? Was I really that different from him or, for that matter, from the shivering derelict I had seen several winters ago kneeling penitently with his last strength on the icy sidewalk amid the chic crowds of New York's Fifth Avenue?

There was a momentary delay. Father Ted had to clear the church of several acolytes, diligently practicing various aspects of the holy mysteries. They had the air of apprentice magicians or medical students at a hospital. The way they so quickly withdrew, with hushed whispers and furtive glances at me, made me feel as if they were yielding to some grave emergency.

Father Ted started his incantations. As I knelt uncertainly before him at the altar, I kept reminding myself of his words that I wouldn't be here if I didn't believe. Yet, awaiting the thin wafer supposedly transubstantiated into the body of Christ, I was racked with the most intense doubts so far. Was this perhaps my ultimate hypocrisy? Wasn't I entering into as much of an ironclad commitment for the rest of my days as if I had gone to work with the Bowery derelicts? How long would I be able carry out my church-imposed obligations and chores? Perhaps God had understood me better than I thought. Perhaps I would have been able to adjust better had I submitted directly to his will rather than opting for the prerequisites of the Church. I might even have unexpectedly fallen in love in a strange and exciting way with that skid row ordeal.

But I had made my choice. As I now felt the wafer on my tongue, I kept repeating to myself it was Jesus Christ who was entering my body, fervently hoping I might again have that exultant feeling I had experienced at the prayer meeting conducted by Al. What a wonderful bond it would be for this shotgun marriage! It would prove I wasn't an opportunist and a fraud; that I wasn't resorting to this union merely for security and out of fear. *Please Jesus, give me that feeling now . . . yes, now!* But that feeling never came.

9/

I continued to carry out my obligatory chores, having already gone to mass two Sundays in a row. I even lined up with other parishioners to receive communion on both occasions, which I didn't have to do. But I wanted to show my good faith. As I inched closer to the altar, where the tasteless little wafer was placed on my tongue, I tried to reassure myself that this was, in fact, the body of Christ. I still remembered being strictly warned by the old village priest preparing our class for first communion, never, never to bite the wafer, but to let it slowly dissolve in the mouth. Otherwise, it might suddenly spurt blood, since what we would be biting or poking would be the body of Christ. Although none of us boys had dared to put that theory to a test, I was tempted to do so now. What more convincing proof to resolve my doubts? But as I saw other parishioners ahead of me in line openly and without undue concern chewing on theirs, I realized it wouldn't work. The rules must have changed, or this one had never been in force except with that old village priest.

I didn't mind so much going to church as I did the idea of feeling coerced by means of not-too-subtle threats. To think that for the rest of my days I would have to go; not only on Sundays, but on holy days of obligation too, or risk committing a mortal sin. As Manya had apprised me not so long ago, only one of those was sufficient to put me back in the peril of hell. In such a case, I could only hope not to die before having a chance to cleanse myself anew through the Church's sacraments – coupled, of course, with a sincere resolve not to miss mass again.

I also felt embarrassed, perhaps more so than by any misdeed or aberration that could be dredged up from my past. Being a fearful, lockstep churchgoer was an image grotesquely at odds with the one I had cultivated for years. How could I explain my behavior to friends, as their frequent guest at sumptuous country homes? I was the one they usually relied on to keep other guests entertained in a light, upbeat mood. For me to interrupt a leisurely Sunday brunch or a few sets of tennis to go to mass might cast a pall over everyone there, as if exposed to some contagious disease. My situation was harder to explain than lugging along a pressure cooker and supply of zucchini, as I had done for nearly two years while being faithful to Dr. Bieler's regimen. About that, my friends had at least been able to joke.

I was already having a problem at home. Again, not so much with Father, who was focused on those daily physical routines that kept him in buoyant health and helped him sell his exercise machines. When he noticed that attending mass had become part of my Sunday program, he shrugged it off as an expected aberration of a rootless bachelor of my age. "Thank God," he remarked several times after my session with Father Ted, "at least you've come back to your senses." Mother, however, interpreted my churchgoing as a continuation of an ominous pattern. It was as sure an indication I hadn't recovered from my malady as if I were still running a fever of a 104°. She worried and fretted that my condition could suddenly flare up with its former distressing symptoms. That's why I was glad I would be driving to Florida soon. At least there I would have a place of my own. Even having to face that Fly me! stewardess two doors down would be easier to finesse than Mother's constantly scrutinizing gaze.

Ah yes, what was I to do about sex, now that I felt inwardly released from that acute premonition of having forever forfeited my chances at permanent love? While I still wasn't interested in resuming this quest, the mere thought of having to subscribe to the Church's teachings in this area depressed me more than anything else. It was as if I would now have to cope with a highly unpleasant and chronic condition particular to people of the Roman Catholic faith, to which I had previously thought myself immune. It wasn't just the Church's position on abortion and birth control; it was the whole idea of Catholic sex. How could I ever accept that as long as I lived, I would never again be able to help myself here and there, in a carefree way, and savor whatever I liked? How could I ever accept that in my search for the ideal bride, I would never again be free to take an exploratory ride? The realization of how fettered I would be in this most vital endeavor was contributing to the all-consuming sadness that I had recently come to know: as if life could never again hold promise of any happiness or joy, as if earth was indeed a penal colony to which humanity had been condemned, and death was our only hope for parole.

Despite my tendency to make a scapegoat of the Church, I had to face the facts. I could no more blame the Church for my depression than I could have blamed Dr. Bieler years ago for the breakdown in my health. I felt no less grateful to Father Ted than to any doctor who had treated me in the past. Father Ted couldn't have been more effective had he prescribed the latest wonder drug against the disorder I had. I was still so intimidated by those messages that I felt the need to go to church without any doctrinal imperatives or threats of mortal sins. That's why I was voluntarily going to communion as well; to assuage my sorrow for having sinned and perhaps mollify God's wrath. I felt a need to remind myself of the true enormity of my transgressions and use them as a baseline from which to improve. If the Church hadn't been there, I would have had to invent some reasonable facsimile. I even found the ritual of mass comforting. The only part to which I took exception was the communal affirmation of faith: having to stand with the rest of the flock and proclaim my exclusive belief in the *One Holy, Catholic, Apostolic Church*. But by the second Sunday, I learned to anticipate this unacceptable oath in time to mentally stuff up my ears.

The harshest fact I had to face didn't relate to any doctrine of the Church. It simply was that my approach to life had failed. Aside from any fears of damnation in some hypothetical ethereal world, my behavior had sabotaged my best interests here on earth. By allowing the pursuit of immediate pleasure to dominate my life, I had harbored an unseen enemy. To think what I had endured in the guise of my romantic quest by just catering to the most demanding part of my physical self! Yet that arousable appendage had merely been acting in concert with the far larger body to which it was attached. Motivated primarily by the prolongation or repetition of what seemed most pleasurable at the moment, this physical self routinely imposed ultimatums on my behavior irrespective of broader considerations or interests. My whole life had been subservient to that seductive goal; my actions repeatedly distorted, the promises of pleasure driving me to do things I wouldn't have deigned to do otherwise. I always felt obliged to keep my options open in case still greater pleasures beckoned, whether to visit some fabulous new place or to woo a potential bride of unprecedented appeal.

And where did all that get me?

Clearly, I would have to change my act, if only to find some semblance of happiness in everyday life. Even without the restrictions imposed by the Church, I would need to adopt a new modus operandi. As with Dr. Bieler's diet, I had to recognize, if sadly and reluctantly, that there was no going back; otherwise, I would again start inflicting pain on myself and on others who crossed my path. Perhaps the Church's teachings were unnecessarily dogmatic and strict, but like Dr. Bieler's draconian diet, they contained principles that were far wiser than the ones by which I had previously lived.

These principles, moreover, were hardly unique to the religious tradition I had so recently embraced. I could just as easily have drawn on the precepts Gautama Buddha and his adherents had codified. How well I understood the Buddha's fundamental premise that our craving for pleasure was the cause of earthly suffering! He had at one time sounded to me like a loon; and, if I were to go out in the street and repeat to the first dozen people I met his conclusions, they would regard me as equally mad. Yet, how valid were the Buddha's words! – no doubt, far more applicable in our opulent times than in his day. Perhaps Albrecht was right. Perhaps humanity still was no different from Adam and Eve, and eating from that forbidden tree was no less perilous – to each of us individually, and when multiplied millions and millions of times, on a global scale as well. Whatever paradise we had so painstakingly built on earth could be lost in a trice.

II. A New Heaven and a New Earth

It was the end of January by the time I felt rational enough to leave home for the drive south, reasonably certain I wouldn't see God materialize on I-95 to block my way somewhere between North and South Carolina. "I hope you don't tell anyone what happened to you here," Mother admonished me, as I was about to pull out of the driveway. "They would have to think the same as I."

That was the least of my concerns. My mind was in a turmoil from having already caught myself backsliding from my resolve. In packing my belongings for the new apartment in Coconut Grove, I had filled my little hatchback car to the roof, leaving no room to pick up some shivering hitchhiker along the way. Although I off-loaded enough before starting out to free up the front seat – including those etchings of my ancestors I had vowed not to take – this didn't spare me from tormenting myself as I headed south. Wasn't what had just occurred ample proof I was resuming my former ways? Was that why God had so implacably insisted on dedicating my life to the derelicts and making the seemingly cruel break with my past? Was that the only way to truly change as required for salvation? I found myself drawing an unholy parallel with old Dr. Bieler's words, *You'll get well, if you're careful!* Had

Dr. Bieler been so rigid about his unpalatable diet because he knew that any pleasurable deviation would inevitably escalate? That an occasional sliver of cake or a glass of wine would eventually lead to indulging in *haute cuisine?*

What may have saved me from an accident while in this frame of mind was that I stopped for the night at my older brother's house in Philadelphia. A corporate lawyer and partner of one of the country's most respected firms, he understood the meaning of stress. He recognized my symptoms, and shortly before going to bed, handed me one of his Dalmane sleeping pills. "Don't argue, just take it," he said in the same tone he had used to boss me around in our youth.

It was the best sleep I'd had since this endless nightmare began. The next morning, I was still feeling pleasantly tranquilized — and remained that way for the rest of the fifteen-hundred-mile drive. Even in this mildly stupefied condition, I was able to concentrate on the road better than in my alert but agitated state. And tucked in my pocket was a small vial of those magic pills, which my brother had pressed on me prior to leaving. Practical considerations at this stage took precedence over any lingering worries about blunting my potential to receive further messages.

As soon as I arrived in Miami, I began working on the daycare scripts. I had originally signed the contract reluctantly through a seeming mental lapse. The daycare centers were for children primarily from deprived families and could hardly have provided the milieu to which I was partial at that time. Had God tipped my hand way back then, knowing how I would welcome this work now?

By the end of the week, I was also reporting to volunteer at Mercy Hospital, which was so significantly close to my apartment in Coconut Grove. Hoping to approximate my original calling, I asked to work with terminal indigents who had nobody else in the world.

My first assignment was at a nursing home, where the hospital warehoused cases of this sort. A glance down one of the bathroom-tiled corridors and a whiff of the stale urine smell confirmed the horror stories about places of this sort. Wherever I looked, I could see seemingly abandoned wheelchairs containing aged human flesh with vacuous eyes, sporadically groaning and aimlessly reaching out.

The one exception was ninety-three-year-old Fred. Though in a near-mummified state, he retained an optimistic gleam. "I don't know how old I am," he observed, as if pleasantly baffled, sitting in his cranked-up bed. "I think I must be at least fifty. They keep telling me here I'm sixty. I don't think I am. I was one of ten children, you know? My mother cooked for us, and it was excellent. Other mothers, maybe they also cook good. But our mother, she cooked really excellent . . . You know, I am one of ten children. I don't know how old I am. I must be at least sixty. They keep telling me I'm only fifty."

Old Fred was obviously feeling no pain. Besides, he already had visitors, a solicitous niece accompanied by her grumpy but understanding spouse.

I was politely bowing out when I spotted the type of case I had in mind. He was the other occupant of the room, stretched out on a bed at the foot of Fred's. He looked terribly alone, as he lay there fully clothed, eyes open, staring blankly into space. That he didn't seem especially old and had no visible ailment made his condition all the more compelling.

"How are you?" I asked, as jovially as I could.

"Rotten," he said, with deadly gloom.

"You'll get better."

"No, I won't. And I don't care."

"Is there anything you need?"

"Don't bother, Doc. It ain't worth it."

"Does anybody come to see you?"

"No, nobody comes to see me. My wife died eighteen years ago." He glanced at Fred across the room, then eyed me carefully. "Are you a relative of Fred's?"

"No, no. I just stopped by to say hello."

"Well, I say it because you look a lot like Fred."

"Do you talk much to Fred?"

"Naw, nothing much worth talking about."

There was a pause. I walked around to the foot of the bed and looked at his medical chart. "I see your name is Mr. Brady."

"Yeah, Phil Brady."

"Well, you're going to be just fine, Phil. I'll come back to see you again soon."

"Whatever you say, Doc."

"You're sure there isn't anything I can bring?"

Phil seemed hesitant, then shook his head. "Naw, I don't want to be no trouble."

"It won't be, really it won't."

"Well, I always liked tangerines. They don't give you none here. But as I said, I don't want to be no trouble."

A couple of days later I was back, a brown paper bag of tangerines in hand. I again found Phil fully dressed in bed, staring off into space. But he seemed to have taken a turn for the worse. He was deep under the covers, and despite the fetid mugginess in the room, he was shivering and looked fearfully withdrawn.

"How are you, Phil?" I asked with evident concern.

"Oh God," he moaned, trying to burrow deeper under the covers. "You'd have to see me this way!"

"Is there anything I can do?"

"Would you please get out? Can't you see, I don't want to be bothered!"

I stood there, stung by the venom of his words.

"And don't come back no more!"

I felt flushed, as if hit on the nose. I deposited the bag of tangerines on a chair by Phil's bed and beat a hasty retreat.

Driving home, I was struggling to control my pride. Was this my reward for having gone to all this trouble on his behalf? I quickly had to remind myself: I wasn't doing this for fun and praise. How easy it would be to take Phil at his word, a handy excuse never to return. But I knew he had acted this way because he was depressed. Yes, I would try again, I repeated to myself. And again and again until I was able to get through to Phil and help him in some way, if only with another bag of tangerines.

By the time I returned home, I had forgotten the harshness of Phil's words. I was feeling a new resolve, a buoyancy of spirit that came from sensing that I was pursuing the right path.

An altogether different case involved one of the hospital's outpatients, Nikos, whom I first met in the nephrology ward. Reclining in a contraption similar to a dentist's chair, he was covered to his chest with a white sheet, and from a permanently implanted shunt in his arm which bulged like a huge vein, his blood circulated through clear plastic tubing into a whirring dialysis machine. At seventy-five, Nikos was a tall, emaciated, olive-skinned former short-order cook born in Greece. He had labored his entire life, often twelve hours a day, and once went for three years without having even a Sunday off. The reason he was destitute was because of his wife, a homely, rotund woman whose tinted photo in an antique silver frame Nikos carried wherever he went. It took the entire seventeen thousand dollars he had saved from his lifetime of work to keep his wife alive a few extra weeks after she was diagnosed with terminal cancer of the brain.

"And I'm grateful for every day," Nikos unhesitatingly told me, as I helped him mow the lawn behind the neat little house he owned in a marginal neighborhood of similar homes. "We had been married for thirty-five years. She knew me so well! After I retired, I liked to go fishing. I'd lose track of time and come home a couple of hours late. Ever so gently, she would shout, 'Where were you this time, you tramp?' And I'd say, 'Did you miss me, you hag?' Oh, we had such fun."

Of my various charges, Nikos alone questioned the motives for my work. "The first time I see you," he confided, as soon as he began to feel comfortable with me, "I say to myself, hey wait a minute, what's this guy doing here? I mean, you were dressed so elegant. Why would someone like him be wanting to waste time on someone like me? He must be troubled or something. There must be more to it than meets the eye." Nikos shook his head. "And you shouldn't be wasting your time on me. You should be married, have a family, find a partner for life . . ."

Nikos seemed to appreciate my visits but became vague whenever I suggested a date to see him again. "I can't promise anything," he would say. "It's better if you call first." I knew he refused to contact his only son, an executive in Texas with an electronics firm, whom he had sent to college on his minimum wage. "He's got a family of his own," Nikos quietly explained. "I don't want to bother him. He has enough worries already." As calm as Nikos remained, I knew how much it hurt to have been abandoned by his own flesh and blood.

Nikos's one regret was that he had never made it back to the fishing village in Greece where he had been born. "I was eight when I come to America. I have four brothers and five sisters still live there. For each sister I sent money for her wedding. All my life I hope to see them once more. My two eyes next to their two eyes, understand? Then my wife, she get sick." Nikos glanced at the small tinted photo in the silvery frame propped up on the kitchen table where we were sitting. "And I don't regret it, not one cent. She deserve every penny." Nikos rubbed his face, then looked at me intently across the Formica tabletop. "Oh, you're so lucky! You've been everywhere. You've done everything. You've seen everything. Me? I spent my whole life with pots and pans and cook hamburgers to go. Oh, you don't know, you're so very lucky."

I sat there, uncertain what to say. Nikos had just congratulated me for having experienced a thousand times my share of pleasure in life – exactly as I used to congratulate myself.

Nikos seemed to read my mind. "When you die, you go to sleep. There's nothing. No heaven, no hell. I remember in the little village, when there was a rainbow, the old women said, 'God is happy.' Lightning and thunder, 'God is mad.' I have no education. I leave school after five years. But I read. All the time, read, read, read. I know about the Inquisition. I know about the Reformation. Nobody agree on anything and everybody say, 'I am right.' What is religion? I'll tell you what it is: Be good! I don't have to give you my shoes. But if your feet are cold, maybe I have an extra pair of socks."

I could see Nikos growing progressively weak. "I think they're taking too much water out of my blood," he explained, unable to keep up alongside of me as I slowly mowed his lawn. "You may think I'm crazy, but you know my pigeon Taki? A few weeks before my wife die, he start to bite her like crazy. He never bite me before. Lately, he's been at me pretty steady. But that's all right."

I wasn't surprised a couple of weeks later to reach a recorded disconnect message on Nikos's phone. It was just like him to want to go quietly, not to be any bother.

My sojourn in Miami didn't consist entirely of ministering to terminal indigents. I did that only as much as I had promised – no more than several hours a week. Neither did I go to church beyond Sundays and holy days of obligation, though I did attend Wednesday evening prayer meetings of a nearby charismatic group that Manya had tracked down through her network of religious friends. Some in the group seemed blithely carefree, filled with a consuming joy they said they felt from having Jesus at their side, walking with them through life. Especially Sol, whom I first spotted among this shirt-sleeved group because of his custom-made suits with four buttonholes on each sleeve. This elegant sixty-year-old businessman born in Minsk unabashedly explained during one meeting how he had lost his Miami-based multi-million-dollar plastics business, and coming out of a three-day drunk with a prostitute, was bent on suicide. He was about to gulp down several hundred aspirins after the pistol he had with him failed to work, when he suddenly felt Christ's comforting grace. It seemed to descend on him spontaneously, with no prodding on his part, although it may have come through the influence of his equally elegant Cuban wife. She had been praying for years that Sol would stop his gallivanting and be converted to Christ. Now, she felt a trifle miffed to see her husband vaulted to a plane beyond hers. "I did all the praying, and he gets all the grace," I heard her say with a sigh. Composing his poems to Christ, Sol appeared to be traipsing in a heavenly world. Week after week I saw him filled with the same carefree joy, whether working as a night watchman at a warehouse or negotiating trades in truckloads of plastic scraps. As he gradually returned to affluence, nothing mattered to Sol provided he felt Christ was at his side. Of course, there were others in that prayer group who looked depressed as if hopelessly mired in life. I could understand how the praying and singing and the pervasive communal spirit soothed the internal anguish they felt. That's basically why I went – and to see my friend Sol.

Otherwise I led a fairly normal life. I worked on the day-care center scripts and socialized in a subdued way with my younger brother, Tom, and a few friends. I knew I had to remain vigilant against any and all licentious thoughts. That Fly Me! stewardess two doors down was no temptation at all, although I did make various gestures at merely being friends, which she frostily rebuffed. The most formidable threat I faced was on the beach, where I spent a couple of hours every day, if only to stay in shape and keep my brain alert. It was an ordeal to rivet my eyes straight ahead, as if I had blinders on – even to cup my hands along the sides of my face to keep my vision from straying right and left, and God forbid, come to rest between some pretty girl's legs. I realized how an East Block Communist must have felt on being exposed to the consumer goods in our capitalist world. If I unavoidably did glimpse an especially alluring female part – a pretty rear, a shining mane of hair – I was determined not to break my stride, though I might be passing up the most beautiful woman in the world. I tried to rationalize that if I backtracked to double-check, the rear might belong to a not-so-attractive face, the shining mane to a not-so-attractive rear. Yet, it was precisely this sort of checking out I would have to learn to avoid; to stop reducing human personalities and lives to such superficial once-overs. Considering my past, this was a monumental task; in effect, a do-it-yourself deprogramming course. But whenever I managed to hold firm, I ended up with a sense of victory over my baser self. And if I happened to overcome several temptations in a row, I would feel a surge of confidence that promised to make the next temptation easier to surmount.

It nevertheless remained a struggle not to succumb, not to sneak more than an occasional peek out of the corner of my eye day after day. And I made it through several months relatively unscathed, having necked only once with another resident in the apartment complex, and very briefly at that. What terminated the relationship was when I tried to confide to her the details of the ethereal experience from which I had so recently emerged. She shrank from me as if I were a dangerous crank.

Then I had an accident of sorts, probably because I had relaxed my guard. Having already decided to move to Laguna Beach as soon as I finished the day-care scripts, the remaining weeks in Coconut Grove were hardly adequate to initiate a lasting liaison, and God forbid I should consider anything else.

She seemed to materialize out of nowhere; a buxom twenty-year-old radiating an enticing smile as she approached me with a civic-minded petition to sign. I was impressed that already at her age, she was volunteering so selflessly. Nor could I completely ignore the way she fit into her short-short cut-off dungarees, and how her knit polo shirt displayed her athletic build.

My ostensible intent was to play Cupid, to talk to her on behalf of my younger brother, who was out of town on a film shoot for several days. Although Tom had an astonishing supply of candidates in his own search for the ideal bride, he wasn't likely to turn down additional interviewees.

Yet she somehow ended up at my place. Her name was Sallie, and she had her heart set on a career in costume design. She appeared to be exceptionally intelligent and slightly crude in an exciting way. She was from a suburb of Peoria, Illinois, where her parents owned a third-generation haberdashery, and Sallie had for a time carried on with the local fire chief. Now, just the way she positioned herself on the couch made me realize I was in for a siege. The more I tried to shrink away and protest, the more aggressive she became. "You sure play harder to get than my man back home," she laughed, deftly negotiating the buttons on the front of my shirt. "He had the same cute silvery hairs on his chest, but you're in better shape, and he was married."

"How about my brother?" I reminded her.

She ran her hand down to my waist. "How do I know I'll even like him?"

"He's younger and better looking."

"You're good enough for . . . "

"But I told you, I'm leaving in a few weeks."

"That gives us lots of time."

I was beginning to experience the mixed feelings of an alcoholic confronted with a drink. She had somehow managed to get me to stretch out on the couch and was squeezing herself next to my extended form. "I promise I won't do anything you don't want me to," I heard her mutter in a strangely reminiscent way, as if borrowing a line from my past. "Let me just lie here next to you."

For a moment, she kept her word. But just then, I felt her slip out of her clothes, and most deftly disencumber me of my own. My God, I moaned, how did I get into this? I could already feel her moist warmth, and before I knew it, it was too late. God no, no! I tried to protest as she reassured me with another line I recognized so well: "Why not slip it in just a little," she whispered. "I promise, if you don't like it, you can take it out."

This incident confirmed what I had already suspected: there was no such thing as being careful enough. Only if I had gone to work with the Bowery derelicts would I have been safe. Not that I had anything against the physical aspects of what Sallie put me through. It was the lingering psychological trauma of this casual onetime encounter I couldn't countenance, an unpleasant feeling deep within as if I had mangled or torn something that was meant to remain whole. Was this the result of trying to uncouple a momentary pleasure from what had been coupled over eons of human evolution by nature, if not by the hand of God?

One of the aftereffects of that carnal tumble was to rededicate myself to volunteer efforts. The case of Rosalie and Annie, which the hospital authorities offered me next, provided its own peculiar twist. Rosalie wasn't at all sick but a hardy sixty-year-old black woman who had recently moved in to take care of Annie, her ninety-year old aunt bedridden with arthritis. Annie owned a two-room shack surrounded by a high iron fence to keep in a mangy Doberman and several fleas-infested cats. Recently widowed,

Rosalie had no other home. Moving in to help her crippled aunt appeared to solve two problems at once.

Her hair streaked with gray but unbowed by life, Rosalie seemed to possess the wisdom of the world. "Something is either wrong or it's right," she told me with total conviction in the mess of Annie's shack. Half-empty cans of beans and spaghetti were strewn here and there, and on the peeling walls hung numerous renditions of Christ. "I mean it's either right or it's wrong. The young ones nowadays don't know the difference. Or they don't care. All they want is money and to have a good time."

Absorbed with Rosalie's homilies — and helping her with such tasks as applying for Supplemental Social Security of thirty-three dollars a month — I didn't meet Annie during my first several visits. The door to her room had been closed, and I figured I would be ushered in at the appropriate time. If it hadn't been for the huge, ugly Doberman eyeing me ferociously whenever I approached the gate, this case could have been as rewarding as tending the Greek short-order cook.

Then came an urgent call from Rosalie. "You've got to come over. You've got to come over right now."

It was early afternoon, and I was about to leave my apartment for the beach. "What's the matter, Rosalie, can't it wait?"

"You've got to come right now. It's Annie!"

"Is Annie all right?"

"She won't let me out of the house. You know that big iron gate? It's locked and she won't give me the key. I can't get out. You've got to come right now."

God, what next!

Rosalie had temporarily tethered the dog, and I vaulted the fence. Annie was sitting up in bed. Her long, milk-white hair was combed into a single braid, and she looked as dignified as any human being I'd ever met. On a rudimentary dresser in her tiny room was a large framed likeness of Christ. Other icons and pictures of Jesus were affixed to the walls.

"I don't really know my niece Rosalie," Annie explained in a slow, deliberate way, as if measuring her words. "Rosalie's been with me only six weeks, and she's getting more and more to drinking whiskey and entertaining men at night. I don't like it. I don't like it one bit. Also, she don't take care of me, and won't clean up, like she said she would. You can see for yourself. And so far, she ain't paid me no rent. I reckon she's waiting to leave without paying nothing at all. That's why I locked the gate and hid the key."

"You see, she's old and greedy," Rosalie interjected, then turned to sneer at her aunt. "Where you're going, you ain't gonna need no rent. And you're going there soon, you better believe it! You hear me? Soon, soon, soon!" Stepping momentarily out of the room, Rosalie dragged in a torn mattress. "See what I have to sleep on? Yesterday she wouldn't give me no twelve dollars and fifty cents. They was having a sale. I could of gotten a brand new mattress, nice and soft."

"What's she saying, what's she saying?" Annie kept asking in those precise, measured tones, cupping a hand to her ear. "What's she saying?"

"You see, she don't want to hear nothing!" Rosalie shouted back. "She don't want to hear nothing. Only what she wants to hear."

I eased myself out of the cramped, strife-riven room and plopped down on the bald velvet sofa just outside Annie's open door. I heard more and still more of the same as I remained sitting there, trying to keep away the cats with their fleas and shaking off an occasional roach scurrying over my shoe. And, of course, I was ever-watchful for that mangy Doberman, eyeing me from across the cluttered room for a chance to savor human flesh. I was fleetingly reminded of the conditions at my aunt's château, if on a vastly diminished scale.

Hearing the argument between Rosalie and Annie reaching a new peak, I glanced around the room at the pictures and icons of Jesus everywhere, and on a sudden impulse, knelt in front of the icon nearest the door. "Oh Jesus, bring these two ladies together because they need each other so much," I intoned, in a clearly audible voice. "One has a home and cannot walk. The other can walk but has no home. Cast out, oh Jesus, the evil between them and fill them with understanding and love."

There was a stunned silence. Then I heard both women utter haltingly but almost in unison, "Amen!" When I got to my feet, the talk was only about what a good Christian person I was. On that they both seemed to agree, at least until the next time I came. That's when Rosalie touched me for a fifty-dollar loan to buy the mattress that was no longer on sale. Although her aunt's door was closed, Annie soon appeared in the living room, leaning heavily on two wooden canes. "I'm sorry to have to tell you," Annie warned me, in her grandiloquent way as if addressing posterity, "you'll never see your money again. My niece Rosalie will only spend it on whiskey and men."

But that was all right by me, too.

2/

My stay in the Coconut Grove apartment was drawing to a close. I had finished those day-care center scripts, and management was eager to release me from my lease. They had a waiting list and wanted to raise the rent. Eight months had passed since that searing conflagration at my parents' home, for which I had no explanation yet. Some days had been better than others; a few, much worse. That's when the flames would suddenly flare and remind me of the burning question that remained: was it really God who had singed my soul? I had yet to come across someone who had heard of a similar case. Was I some sort of a loon, destined never to know the truth?

All in all, I thought I was handling the problem well. From the dozen or so sleeping pills my older brother had given me, I still had several left. I was also benefiting from having discovered how to use coffee as an euphoric drug. The secret was to drink it no more than once a week. A five-hundred-milligram jolt would then provide more of a rise than I imagined any amphetamine could; especially when taken in an aesthetic dosage form, a triple-sized broad-rimmed cup of Limoges porcelain, hand-painted in France. A couple of sluggish withdrawal days would invariably follow; perhaps a low-grade headache, a touch more depression than at other times. But that was a price I was prepared to pay for an exhilarating day that reminded me how I used to feel, which helped carry me until another fix the following week.

I didn't go directly to Laguna Beach. One of the celebrated producers of large-screen documentary films in New York, Francis Thompson, commissioned me to do a short script for Southern Railroad. This would add several thousand dollars to my freedom buffer in the bank, and make it easy to visit my parents in Massachusetts. Mother had looked so glum when she waved good-bye, and I wanted to take this opportunity to reassure her about my mental state. I also wanted to pick up some of the knickknacks I had left behind, especially those etchings of my ancestors. I missed them in my apartment in Florida, and I no longer saw anything wrong with taking them out West. Surely, Father Ted would have said they were no peril to my soul.

While working on the railroad script in New York, I ran into that statuesque stockbroker, Annette, who had sent me off with her verdict that I should wear a sandwich board, warning unsuspecting girls I was a fraud. This time it was Annette who had spotted me in the street and hugged me like a dear old friend. She was eager to let me know that she was happily married to a real estate developer, and before we parted, she invited me to join her and her husband for dinner at their Manhattan coop.

Over cocktails, Annette confided she was shocked how depressed I looked. "You should be out there doing your thing, picking up girls and having fun!" she exclaimed after several glasses of wine, as the three of us sat down to eat. "That would blow away the little cloud I see hovering over your head. Remember, we have a right to be happy."

"Yes, but maybe not the way everyone tells us to."

"I think you're missing out on life."

When I tried to explain during the meal some of what I had been through, Annette nodded sympathetically but kept coming back to the same theme. "You need to cheer up, to be your old self," she observed in a well-meaning way. "If you're a little out of touch, I'm sure I could find one or two of my friends who'd be glad to help. I promise, you won't have to marry them. How long did you say you're staying?"

Remembering how Annette had wailed about my irresponsible ways, I couldn't help but smile. She had at that time urged me to see a psychiatrist to set me straight; now she seemed genuinely concerned I wasn't having non-committal fun. When I tried to point this out, she affectionately grasped my hand. "Ah, but you weren't happy then, either."

"I don't think I'll solve anything by regressing."

She smiled. "But you were happier."

"My view of happiness is changing."

"That's why you should see a therapist." She glanced at her husband. "Ours is terrific. We've been seeing her . . . well, since before we got married. She could really help."

"I don't want to waste the money," I said.

She shook her head. "I think you're afraid of the truth."

"I would welcome the truth. Believe me, it would be a relief."

"Then why don't you see her?"

"What can she tell me that I haven't figured out on my own? As for the rest, the messages, Blackie, God . . ." I shrugged helplessly.

Annette remained unconvinced. "I still think you're afraid to find out."

The therapist turned out to be an attractive, well-groomed woman of youthful middle age. Her office was in the same building off Park Avenue as Big Stick Beneventi's, whom I used to frequent for those agonizing treatments with the J-shaped rod. I didn't feel the same desire to unburden myself as I had with Father Ted, but the realization that I was paying more than a dollar a minute made me no less forthcoming.

The therapist took copious notes while I tried to convey to her the salient points of my case. Whenever I mentioned God, she nodded significantly, as if I wasn't completely sane. And she seemed to regard the details of my sexual restraint as gravely as if I were an anorexic refusing to eat.

"Do I understand it correctly," she interjected in an artificially detached way, "you don't now masturbate?"

"Only when absolutely necessary," I explained. "Usually no more than once a week."

"Do you think you're depressed?"

"Obviously, I'm not elated, but I really don't mind," I said, unable to resist launching into a broader perspective. "If the ancient Greeks were right that from suffering comes wisdom, maybe I'll become moderately wise."

"I see," the therapist said, as if I were further confirming that I was mentally ill.

"Surely, Aeschylus wasn't demented," I persisted, "but merely insightful into our human lot. That's why his dramas are as fresh today as twenty-five hundred years ago."

This observation drew a momentary blank. But in the next instant the therapist regained her aplomb and gave me a patronizing smile. "Don't you think you're being a little hard on yourself?"

The hackneyed query made me laugh. "The last thing I need is help in rationalizing away my misdeeds."

"Misdeeds?" she repeated. "From what you've told me, your behavior seems to have been well within the norm."

"Yeah, I know. Everybody else does it, too. Especially here in New York."

"Remember, you have a right to be happy," she assured me with the same certitude as Annette.

"Unfortunately, that's a recent assumption. Maybe it's no coincidence our civilization seems to be collapsing."

She pursed her lips and shook her head as she busied herself making more notes, while glancing not so discreetly at her watch. She charged me seventy-five dollars and had no qualms in expressing her preference to be paid right away. Later, she confided to Annette over the phone that on a scale of one to ten – ten being suicidal and requiring immediate hospitalization – I was a solid eight, possibly a nine. What if the therapist had seen me several months earlier in the midst of my divine throes?

"She's convinced she can help," Annette announced, when I stopped by to say good-bye. "If you ask me, I think you should stay right here in New York. Get a job you can handle easily. I mean in your condition. Selling books at Brentano's or something. That will keep you occupied and give you enough to live on modestly. You can use the money you've set aside for California to see her at least twice a week. She has a special long-term rate. You'd normally be eligible after several months, but I think I could talk her into giving it to you from the start."

God, I would really have to be insane to do that; to totally disorient my life to help this unremarkable therapist fill her appointment book. It would make far less sense than if I had gone to work with the derelicts in the first place.

"It's too late to change my plans," I told Annette, who I knew had my best interests at heart. "I can't wait to get out to California. You know how I've always talked about Laguna Beach."

"Then promise me," she said with heartfelt concern, "you'll find a therapist the minute you get there."

I sort of nodded, just as I did a week later when I briefly saw my sister Manya, and she urged me with equal concern to find a charismatic prayer group.

It was the only way, they both had said.

In Laguna Beach, I found almost right away what I was looking for – a tiny, furnished A-frame house that was indefinitely for rent. Perched on a rocky bluff some sixty feet above a little crescent beach, this one-room dwelling was only a few hundred yards from the more sumptuous quarters I had occupied a decade earlier while undergoing Dr. Bieler's cure. I hoped to be no less successful in finding an answer for whatever was disturbing me now.

Within a month in this exotic place, I felt settled down to a routine that included attending weekly mass at a nearby Catholic church. But I had yet to make an effort to connect with a charismatic group or find a psychiatrist, though I was about to see a doctor of a different stripe. He had been my classmate for four years at the Hotchkiss School and now was a prominent surgeon on the West Coast. Known affectionately as *Buzzy*, Francis G. (he didn't like to be called Frank, for whatever reason) had been a scholarship boy like me, and although one of the big wheels in our class, he had always been friendly in returning my greetings in the corridors. I hadn't seen him since graduation, but when I chanced in the local bookstore on a thoughtful collection of poetry he had published through a San Diego press, I called the alumni office for his address. I was delighted to learn he lived in LaJolla, just an hour's drive down the coast.

Francis greeted me by the arched, double front door of his sprawling, Spanish style hillside home. He had obviously done well. Starting from the same baseline as I, he appeared to be yet another example of how far I had fallen behind in life. The years had been kind to Francis physically, and he still had the type of tall, pretty-boy looks other men often resent and women adore. Wearing jeans and no shoes, he was relaxed and tanned as if he no longer worked. He was the one who had suggested on the phone that we meet in midmorning of a weekday for a long walk. He seemed in no rush as he introduced me to his wife and showed me through his tastefully furnished house, pausing in front of the photos of two modish, college-age students. Our tour ended by the pool, where I was astounded to see a five-meter diving board. Francis explained he had installed it several years ago for his son, who was then on the Colgate diving team and had hopes of making the Olympics. "Didn't quite make it," my host concluded, "but he still uses it when he visits." By the time Francis finally suggested we start our walk, I was again wondering: was this the schedule of one of the most prominent surgeons in the state?

Trekking along a narrow trail on a rocky bluff high above La-Jolla's shore, we exchanged pleasantries at first; what classmates each of us had seen, who was where and doing what. I had been preparing to question Francis about some of the more challenging aspects of his life as a surgeon. But in no time and without deliberately intending to do so, I found myself broaching the subject of my traumatic rebuke by God. I felt an immediate trust for this contemporary of mine, as if the schoolboy experience we had shared predisposed him to understand. I had never come forth so readily with anyone except Father Ted (to whom I had since sent a hundred-dollar check) and that New York shrink who had the clock running.

Francis appeared intent on hearing me out, as he walked a step ahead on the rugged coastal path winding through heavy brush and past several eucalyptus trees. "That voiceless source sounded just like the Duke at his terrifying best," I said, in a lighthearted reference to our one-time headmaster.

My companion abruptly stopped. We had reached a clearing high on a bluff, and I thought he wanted to rhapsodize over the expansive ocean view. Instead, he turned to face me. "You won't believe this," he said, with a faint smile. "You're the third person to come to me this month. Just last week, a friend I hadn't seen in fifteen years called from Pittsburgh and insisted on flying out to talk. I must have listened to a half-dozen people in the past couple of years. The details are different, but the gist of what they're so anxious to share is the same." Francis's disarming smile broadened. "You know, already when you phoned the other day I had a feeling this is what you wanted to talk about."

My heart perked up. He sounded like Dr. Bieler telling me he had diagnosed my ailment the moment I walked in. Maybe it wasn't entirely by chance I had come across my former classmate's little book, and that he happened to live so near.

"You could say these experiences reflect a form of borderline schizophrenia," he explained. "That, of course, doesn't make them any less real. The strange dimension or reality was there all along. You and the others just needed to be in a special frame of mind to perceive it."

"I sure was perceiving more than I wanted to," I said, eager to provide my doctor-friend with more details. "You'll probably think me completely loco, but I had a compulsion to give up everything and go off to the Bowery. I wanted to dedicate the rest of my life to helping derelicts and drunks. I know it sounds crazy, a guilt neurosis or whatever . . . "

Francis was now signaling with an upraised arm to let him speak. "That appears to be the common factor. A seemingly irrational drive to do something you absolutely don't want to do, and your better judgment warns you against. It can be as trivial as crossing a street at a certain point or as critical as breaking with your past. It's only after you have given in to it that bingo, you're free. You no longer feel you have to do it."

I stood there astonished. I hadn't said a word about how I had put away that dinner only to be told I could eat; or how I had looked into the mirror at the point I thought I was ready to go, and suddenly felt I no longer had to.

"You mean like Abraham no longer having to kill his son?" I asked.

Francis nodded. "Something like that."

So he really did understand my case! I felt an outflowing of warmth for my friend, standing there with me on the bluff over-looking the sun-glazed Pacific. "You don't realize what you've just done for me," I said, and bestowed on him a grateful hug.

My former classmate reciprocated, then resumed in the same low-key, instructive tone: "Unless your submission is genuine, you won't get that release. Whoever or whatever is involved isn't easy to fool."

"That's what I'm afraid of," I sighed. "My release lasted only about twenty minutes before that irrational urge returned."

"I suppose you want to know if it was genuine." Francis shrugged. "I'm afraid nobody is in a position to tell."

"I guess not until it's too late to redeem yourself from whatev-er damnation might be in store," I said, with put-on joviality. "Anyway, thanks for giving it to me straight, *doctor*."

My lighthearted appellation triggered an unexpected response. "In case you've wondered," Francis casually rejoined, "I don't practice conventional medicine any more. Only enough to keep my hospital privileges. I used to be very good at cutting up my pa-tients and giving them a bag for this, a bag for that, an artificial what-have-you. I was saving my patients' lives, but I wasn't improving their lives. Now, I'm more interested in teaching them how to make the most of the time they have left. My practice consists more and more of just talking to patients."

"You mean the way you're talking to me?"

Looking out at the brilliance of the ocean reflecting the afternoon rays, Francis nodded.

"So I really am here more as a patient than a friend?"

"What's the difference? Friend, patient, doctor. Doctor, patient, friend. That's what you are. That's what I am." He paused, then laughed. "This time around, let's just say you're here as a friend."

We resumed our walk, in silence for a while. We had to concentrate on our footing as we scampered single file down a steep, uneven path from the top of the bluff to the ocean's edge. But once we started on the hard, wet sand along the beach, Francis launched into a saga of his own. Yes, he also had been through an experience of this sort. As a doctor with scientific training, he had been especially skeptical as to what was going on. Yet he could clearly recognize being temporarily endowed with precognition powers, such as the ability to tell who was behind a door or know when a phone was about to ring. Most astounding were episodes when he started burning up, with smoke coming out of his shoes and curling out from beneath the collar of his shirt. He would sometimes have to interrupt his consultation with a patient and run off to soak his feet.

God, I thought to myself, no wonder he understood my case! This guy is further gone than I. While I might have merely tried to humor him a few years back, I was now listening as if what he himself had experienced held the key to my life.

"At one stage," Francis explained, as we neared the frontage of the LaJolla Beach and Tennis Club, "when things got heavy and I felt I was losing touch, I tried to turn it into a joke. I said, 'Hey God, I'm having a vision, aren't I?' You should have heard God bark me back in line. You're right, just like the old headmaster when he was mad at some poor slob! For a while, I also thought I was Saint Francis. This puzzled me because my parents were Jewish. My St. Francis delusion certainly didn't happen because I was named after a spinster aunt from Italy."

I laughed. "I thought I was Saint Augustine. Yet he's the one I always blamed for trying to screw up the world with his anti-sex legacy." I stepped around a patch of foam deposited by the surf, then stopped. "We really sound like a couple of middle-aged nuts."

My former schoolmate also stopped. "I'll never be the same, if that's what you mean. Talking to patients about how to live and how to die is hardly as remunerative as wielding a scalpel. I may have to sell the big house and cut back in other ways, too." Francis shook his head and smiled as if amused at himself. "When we were at Hotchkiss, my old man owned a bar in Queens where his profits came from customers getting drunk. I really don't feel I can any more justify making a whole lot of money from my patients' maladies."

I couldn't resist. "Hey Buzzy," I exclaimed, "it seems we've ended up on parallel paths after all . . . and not too far apart!"

Now it was Francis who gave me a hug. Despite his assured exterior, I sensed Francis shared with me a certain fragility. His gesture gave added meaning to his words, *Doctor, patient, friend, what's the difference?*

We had passed the main complex of the club and were standing in front of the panoramic window of the Marine Room. The sandy beach ended abruptly against a steep cliff, and we could go no further. How ironic! We were just a few feet from where my original paramour and I had renewed our relationship in the cocktail lounge on the other side of the huge window. That was more than twenty years ago. I could see the table where Avis and I sat, while she opined mournfully over margaritas that life was nothing but a dirty trick.

"I wouldn't want to change what I went through for anything in the world," Francis observed, as we turned to go back to his house. "I hope you'll eventually be grateful for what happened to you, too. Remember, we're merely reflecting a reality that others are afraid to recognize. Once we get enough people to acknowledge it exists, it will become the accepted reality, a new paradigm. What we need is a critical mass to get this transformation going in an irreversible way; the sooner the better."

3/

What I liked best about my Laguna Beach cottage was the feeling of openness and space. Extending across the front of this little house was a set of sliding glass doors that opened onto a spacious balcony about sixty feet above the Pacific. It was as if everything beyond that glass was an extension of where I lived, removing any barriers between me and the endless ocean and sky. From my balcony I could watch the way the surf would splinter against the rocks a few hundred yards beyond the beach, or survey the ever-changing texture of the distant horizon. And I never tired of observing the human activity on the crescent strip of sand below. This happened to be the same secluded beach I had considered such an ideal repository of potential brides just after leaving the Navy. They were still there, a new generation basking in the sun, their attributes intimately revealed by the latest in swimsuit wear. It was interesting to watch the subtle shift of who happened to be pairing up with whom on the towels for two. If only to keep the record straight, I myself paired up shortly after arriving from Coconut Grove. As in that misadventure with Sallie, it happened without premeditation and more or less by accident, and the subsequent feeling served as enough of a deterrent to have protected me since.

"Poor Onkel!" Stephanie sighed, sipping a glass of Chardonnay in the sun of the open terrace of my Laguna Beach abode. "You're worse than Pappi. He at least *had* to give it up on account of prostate cancer, though who knows? His relationship with Elizabeth seems to have survived the surgery."

Stephanie and I hadn't exchanged letters in weeks, and I was delighted when she surprised me at the door. She was on her way to San Francisco for a one-person show of her paintings, an avocation that was becoming a financial success. There was a mystical quality to her work, depicting fairy tale scenes with unicorns and princesses in a childlike, naive style. She had sold her Chelsea flat, and with the proceeds bought an airy, hillside villa on the island of Hydra, Greece. Though single now, she had committed in the intervening years what she considered life's biggest mistake number three. She had married an intensely serious, bearded Swiss Red Cross worker approximately her age, whom she met while sipping a *cassis au vin blanc* at an outdoor café across from the Cornavin railroad station in Geneva. It didn't take long before she discovered his penchant for violent jealousy. After seeing her Hydra home wrecked once too often, Stephanie filed for divorce.

"In the five years we were married, I'll have you know, I never betrayed him once," Stephanie said with mock outrage. A little smile played on her sensuous lips. Though almost forty, she still could turn on the dazzle of youth. "All I had to do for him to go berserk was to look at somebody."

"You do have a way of looking," I pointed out. "Another family flaw."

"Well, the judge took my side. Thank God it was in Switzerland. In Greece, only the husbands are allowed to look. Not that the Swiss are particularly advanced, either. But I did get custody of little Paulus. I'm teaching him English and German, and he's picking up Greek on his own. He's becoming fluent in all three, and he's only five."

"How is little Hansi?"

"Not so little. He's over six feet. He's got a one-track mind when it comes to girls. Girls and ouzo." Stephanie reached over to touch my hand. "Maybe he's a chip off the old block after all."

"He'll probably make all the mistakes I did."

"Was I a mistake?"

"A rather special one."

"I would hope at least that!" Stephanie sniffed the Chardonnay in her glass, then took another sip. "I'm glad you haven't given up good wines. There may be hope for you yet."

I held up my hand. "Normally, I buy it only by the jug. That way I don't want more than a couple of glasses."

Stephanie shook her head. "You really are turning into an old fuddy-duddy like Pappi."

"You should have seen me a couple of years ago."

"I can imagine."

"I'm not so sure you can," I said, and poured myself another glass. In my occasional letters to Stephanie, I had never detailed what happened on the snow-covered field, and I wasn't sure I could recreate the scene for her now. As I sat there next to her in the sun at the round metal patio table, the aftermath to that chastisement from beyond seemed remote. This was partly due to what I had recently heard described as "the dynamics of becoming dulled," whereby an unacceptable reality is slowly pushed out of the mind. But my perspective was also changing. Perhaps I wasn't so unfortunate after all to have received that devastating call. Wasn't what I had experienced merely a preview of the ultimate call all of us would one day have to take? Wouldn't we all one day be similarly exposed, with no rug under which to sweep the debris of our imperfect lives? Maybe hell was nothing else than having to contemplate eternally how we had failed to measure up, eternally saddled with the sorrowful awareness of our sins. Yet I was given a chance to amend my life and pursue a different path. Was that also why my former schoolmate in LaJolla wouldn't have exchanged his own disorienting experience for anything in the world?

"I can, too, imagine what you went through," Stephanie interrupted my thoughts. "How do you think I felt when Angelina was killed? I used to think that having a child was the most life-changing experience. But imagine seeing that child grow up until she's almost as big as you, seeing her right in front of you so alive . . . then seeing her as a corpse. Aside from everything else, it made me realize my day of reckoning, too, would come."

"Is that when you started painting?"

"Unfortunately, that's when I married into life's biggest mistake number three." Stephanie nodded, as if to acknowledge her stupidity. She refilled her glass and turned to watch the surf crash against the rocks a few hundred yards beyond the crescent beach. Her eyes traveled along the silvery trail of the reflected afternoon sun to the bluish hills of Catalina Island on the distant horizon. "I think Pappi is about to hand over the Schloss to Andreas for good," she resumed in a detached way. "What a mealworm, that Andreas! Here I am, having to support a child alone, and he's going to inherit everything." Stephanie's gaze returned to our patio table. "What do you think of his new bride? I understand you played the gracious host when they visited you on their honeymoon."

Indeed, they had stayed with me a couple of days, and I tried to do my best to make up for what I had once perpetrated on Andreas. "Karina certainly has a taste for the better things in life," I said.

"Why do you think she married him? It was a setup, not too different from the way it happened with pristine Tasha. Karina's mother once had a fling with Uncle Ferdinand in Vienna."

"I'm sure this marriage isn't going to turn out the same. Karina seems much too practical for that."

"If you ask me," Stephanie continued, "the girl who really loved Andreas was the one he dropped so fast when he met Tasha. They'd been going together way before Pappi chose him to become rich."

"Andreas obviously paid the price with Tasha."

The unfortunate details were publicly known. The marriage of the future heir had been annulled after less than two years by the same austere monsignor with two front teeth of gold who had found it difficult to render a verdict in Hansi's case. This time the situation was clear. Not only were there no children from the Andreas-Tasha union, but neither party contested the monsignor's suggestion that the marriage had never been consummated in the marital bed. The whole procedure had been for Andreas's benefit, and Tasha couldn't have cared less. She moved to Munich, where she took up law and dated actively. She was beautiful and a countess, die Gräfin, and had her hand obsequiously kissed. Eventually, she had a baby boy with the man who was subsidizing her legal studies at the university, a paunchy, middle-aged Hochstapler frequently in the headlines on suspicion of criminal activities. Only because Elizabeth had remained Albrecht's consort at the Schloss did the Fürst manage to ignore this blatant besmirching of his historic family name.

"What I most resent," Stephanie now observed, "is the way Andreas pretends . . . as if he were morally superior and I was some kind of a whore."

"He's hardly had the opportunities you've had, my dear. There's little virtue in obeying the speed limit when your car won't go any faster."

"God, and what a yes-man! Every time Pappi says something, Andreas turns red as a beet and does it. He obviously isn't about to do anything to jeopardize getting the Schloss."

I had to smile. "That's what I used to call good PR, remember? Only what I was covering up was more serious. Andreas is merely trying to keep your father from finding out he's normal."

"At least you didn't have to pretend you liked Pappi. The way Pappi watches him, Andreas must be ready to scream." Stephanie looked out over the shimmering ocean again, then smirked. "Did you see the huge portrait in *Town and Country* of silly old Hansi and his new Brazilian bride?"

"She reminds me of my favorite niece . . . about fifteen years ago."

"Thanks a lot! I found it nauseating."

"Hansi always claimed Brazilian ladies were duly appreciative of his talents."

"Well, she's welcome to him, hairnet and all!"

"They must have tied the knot without the blessing of the Church."

"I've certainly tried to annul him out of my thoughts."

I knew I shouldn't be engaging in a conversation of this sort. It was idle gossip, an unworthy endeavor, a form of backsliding. Besides, I always had a warm, friendly feeling for Hansi as well as for Andreas. As for Tasha, I was increasingly appropriating to myself much of the blame for that collusion with her as a fifteen-year-old. But Stephanie had a way of bringing out this baser aspect of myself, though I certainly didn't worry this could now lead to anything more serious. I knew Stephanie too well for such an entanglement to occur by accident or without premeditation. Besides, that aspect of our relationship had been reactivated but once, now almost ten years ago, and only because both of us thought it might help me recover from what ailed me then.

Yet something unexpected did happen that night. Glancing at my second cousin once removed asleep on the cot next to my little bed, I gained a graphic appreciation for the traditional taboo concerning sex between relatives. As close as she and I had always been in the way we thought and the physiognomy we shared, I perceived also something else. What kept coming back was the image I had formed of Stephanie earlier that day when she thought I wasn't looking and had slumped into a pronounced stoop. It was an image I could never again separate from the one I had of Albrecht and Issten contorted in an identical way. It made me feel even closer to Stephanie than before, but wholly in an unphysical way.

The next morning, as I carried her suitcase to the waiting airport limousine, Stephanie said, "I hope it won't be ages before I see my favorite Onkel again."

"I hope in the meantime you won't commit life's biggest mistake number four."

"I'll never be that stupid again."

We were standing in front of the van that had several other passengers inside. The chauffeur took her bag, and Stephanie gave me a tender hug. "Well, good-bye, Onkel dear." She paused to look at me somberly. "The only person I ever would marry . . . if I were to do so again . . . quite frankly is you."

"I'm afraid I wouldn't be much good to you," I said, trying to keep it light. "For years I subscribed to sex without commitment. I'm not sure that commitment without sex would be any better."

"Don't you see, it's enough that you understand me," she said quietly. For a moment, she looked forlorn. Her eyes misted over, and I could feel the same happening to me. Then she abruptly brightened up. "Besides, I don't think you're going to keep up this foolishness forever. I know my Onkel. I know you wouldn't want to lose your special touch."

Losing whatever *special touch* I may have once possessed was something I didn't worry about any more than that I could forget how to swim or ride a bicycle. While my *foolishness* didn't exactly coincide with the philosophy of Catholic sex I once bemoaned, I had come to appreciate the practical side in self-restraint of this sort. Not to be minimized in this era of still unpublicized AIDS was the freedom from worry about any of the nonlethal pathologies associated with sex, which were an ever-present and increasing threat. Yet if I ever were to become active again, I had learned from my few aberrant encounters that a reluctant stance was the most seductive technique of all. At the same time, I had a polite excuse for keeping any relationship at the cheek-kissing stage if the requisite inspiration wasn't there. Another benefit not to be overlooked was that I was gradually gaining the trust of husbands, too. Especially of white-haired Peter, the swinging developer-entrepreneur across the street, who was married to an alluring woman half his age. On the discreet advice of a fat Indian guru who claimed wiry old Peter was dangerously toxic from his materialistic thoughts, his wife made him wear a prophylactic whenever they made love. During my first months as their neighbor, I was repeatedly surprised to find the sixty-year-old husband at my door, anxiously peering over my shoulder as he inquired if I hadn't seen his wife. Now, Peter frequently confided to me his version of their marital woes, while generously overlooking whatever implicit affection his wife's friendship for me entailed. Moreover, I was free to use the washing machine in his garage even when nobody was home.

Best of all, I was able to remain single-minded in my quest to share with others what I had so dramatically learned. How to reach the likes of sixteen-year-old Hansi, whether or not he was my son, who seemed to have such a one-track, pleasure-oriented mind? (From the latest photograph Stephanie had sent, he was developing an astonishing resemblance to his original namesake in both expression and size.) How could I make Andreas aware he was as flawed as anyone else? I had come to recognize that our family predispositions were idiosyncratic only in the way they were acted out, but were no more unusual or rare than our susceptibility to Sodbrennen. After all, Sodbrennen was merely that most common of conditions touted endlessly in TV commercials as acid indigestion and heartburn. If only there were a way to make the bigots of the world realize that the differences between people – between races, religions, nationalities, and whatever – were insignificant when compared to the flawed tendencies we all shared. Whether or not labeled as original sin, how clearly I understood the consequences of this misdirected human orientation. Or as Albrecht had once put it, how we already *were* making a difference, but a negative one, simply by being who we were. Despite our technological strides, we were traveling along the wrong path toward a dead end. It was a situation in which the ante was constantly being raised, as I had discovered firsthand. The more you had the more you wanted and the less it meant, making you want still more. That was the pathology of pleasure, whose cumulative lethal effects reached beyond any physical dimension. I still remembered Albrecht's pithy remark, "With that, morality goes out of the window." I now understood at least symbolically what my cousin was trying to do before it was too late, working so feverishly on those lined yellow sheets to reorient the axis of the universe. And I wondered, would Albrecht countenance me now if I showed up in lederhosen at the Schloss?

4/

I hadn't forgotten my commitment to good works. I would be reminded of this long-ago pledge on seeing a busload of inner city children disgorged on our crescent beach. Shouldn't I be one of those harried counselors watching over these exuberant eight-year-olds? As it was, I settled for trying to pacify some of the beach-going regulars over this noisy invasion of their turf.

My volunteer efforts had come to a logical end with Rosalie and Annie in Miami, and I no longer felt the internal press to resume that aspect of my commitment in Laguna Beach. But I tried to incorporate the spirit of the Florida endeavors into my daily life. This took no willful effort on my part, and more often than not, turned out to be fun. Like the time I loaned Susanne, a German divorcee struggling to bring up her two boys, a thousand dollars to cover a cash-and-carry grocery bill at her quaint but badly managed restaurant. Susanne was unfortunately becoming more interested in learning how to read past lives than in planning a menu for Saturday brunch, and eventually she lost the place. Then there was Dorothy, a frail old woman with terminal liver cancer who lived alone across the street next door to white-haired Peter and his young wife. Puttering in her garden, Dorothy always knew what I was up to, whether sitting at my typewriter, talking on the phone, or defrosting my refrigerator. She even kept an eye on me during my regular early morning swims, when nobody else was on the beach. "Don't you dare die!" I told Dorothy several times. "I'd feel insecure without you." She would laugh but shake her head. Her husband had passed away years ago and she was ready, in fact eager, to go. In no time, she wasted to eighty pounds, was bedridden, and had round-the-clock nursing care. That's when the doctors put her on methadone, and suddenly Dorothy wasn't quite so ready to depart. "I want to smell the roses, I want to listen to the sea," she told me wistfully, as she reappeared to putter around her garden again. When I told Peter, who enjoyed an occasional line or a joint, about this amazing turn in her condition, he exclaimed, "Man, I want to be on whatever she's on! Do you suppose you could get her to leave me the prescription?" For six more months, Dorothy miraculously hung on, reduced beyond skin-and-bones to a mummy-like state. Yet, until the day before she died, I could discern a smile on her fissured lips as she listened to my stories about the neighbors on our street.

Then there was my friend Kenny, who felt inexplicably connected to the image in the Shroud of Turin, which supposedly covered the body of the crucified Christ. Known as *the Skipper*, Kenny performed a unique hop throughout Laguna Beach in tattered sneakers and frayed designer shorts, imploring the prosperous local citizenry to help him create a new heaven and a new earth. "Earth, earth, hear the word of truth! Only the truth will set you free!" he would begin in sync with his fast-paced skipping, rhythmically jarring his beard and undulating his shoulder-length hair like cresting waves of reflecting spray. Kenny's compulsive gait and intense gaze made me think that his skipping was no more voluntary than the holy gyrations of medieval victims of Saint Vitus's dance. "I need your vote!" he would yell, as if addressing the world. "I'm running for the office of life consciousness . . . my only opponent is death."

The Skipper's recurring theme was that eight or ten years hence a critical period in human history would begin, when humanity would have a final chance to create a new heaven and new earth – or face the consequences. Listening to Kenny's disjointed but urgent pleas for this transformation, I wondered if it didn't parallel the new paradigm so impatiently awaited by my former classmate, Francis G.

There he was again, an overwrought Jesus look-alike hopping along the boardwalk at almost a run, shouting his message at beach-goers dozing off in the afternoon sun. "I'm free, I'm free, praise the Lord I'm free, this crazy mixed-up world ain't got no hold on me!" How indifferent this high school dropout and Vietnam vet seemed to be to the materialistic world while preaching his truth! Skipping without a shirt even on the chilliest winter days, he appeared unconcerned about the food he ate or the depressing shoe-box-sized room in which he lived. He had spent most of the previous eight years on a steep, thousand-foot peak of rocks and scrub bushes behind the town's gentler residential hills. He was the only one to have evaded the police and fire department raids that cleared out the hippie commune occupying the hill in the late sixties and early seventies.

"Anybody who's ever come up here with me has been chosen by the spirit," Kenny ceremoniously announced, as we finished our ascent and waded several yards through thick shrubs to a small clump of bushes. "That's where I used to sleep. I used to kind of fold everything up so they wouldn't see me. I had this old sleeping bag, and I really loved it under the stars. Every morning when I woke up, I'd see this beautiful hummingbird hovering over my head. I know it was the same one, not just because of the way he looked . . . or she, or whatever . . . but because I felt like I got to know him . . . know him like a fellow being . . . like I know you. And there he'd be, hovering over me, sort of greeting me and letting me know the universe didn't forget me. I called him my God-bird. He would always hover and flutter his wings, but one day he landed on the ground, only inches from my face where I lay in my sleeping bag. He stopped fluttering his wings and just looked at me to let me know he loved me and trusted me. Then this God-hummingbird began to dip his head from side to side, from one side to the other . . . and every time he'd dip his head, he would take me to a higher and higher awareness. . . . Left, right . . . left, right . . . left, right . . . left, right . . . I couldn't count the numbers of dimensions where this bird was taking me. I was in another world, and every time he'd dip his head, he'd take me to a still different realm not attached to this world . . . a realm of harmony and connection of all life. I was aware of everything that was in the past, of everything in the present, of everything in the future. It lasted no more than a few minutes, but it seemed like eternity."

Kenny paused and shook his head, as if trying to snap out of a trance. "So the highest plane I ever experienced wasn't through drugs or alcohol, not through readin' the Bible, not through praying . . . but through this hummingbird. I had read the Word, but this bird was the Word. The Bible says all creatures shall bear witness to the creative force. Well, we were both bearing witness to each other. And the hummingbird was saying, 'I leave you now.' I knew he was going to leave that day and never return. But he left me with an illumination, with a new understanding of life and that we were surely one."

Within days of showing me his former hilltop retreat, the Skipper stopped skipping and began to wilt, as if drained of some energizing force within. At first I attributed his condition to the apparent lack of public response; yet his transformation was more profound. It was as if the Skipper had come to an abrupt awakening in an alien world and found himself saddled with the concerns of a materialistic life. He started to worry about his diet and increasingly resented the hovel in which he discovered himself to be living. His sleek, trained body began to stink, and no matter what measures he took, it continued to degenerate into a sickly mess. I drove him fifteen miles for free therapy to a chiropractor he had once met, and then helped him get to Georgia, where his widowed mother lived on Social Security.

"That's the power of the spirit for you," Kenny sighed, as I waited with him at the Los Angeles airport for his flight while fellow passengers cast nervous glances at this haunting Jesus look-alike who would be boarding their plane. "No, I didn't stop skipping because I got discouraged, and I didn't get sick because I stopped skipping. The spirit left me first. I felt it in my bones, in every ounce of me. The spirit left me first! Only then did I get discouraged. And only after that did I get sick. Man, without that darn spirit that comes to you from out in the cosmos, you ain't nothing."

In trying to fathom the essence of Kenny's life, I could discern far better the shortcomings in mine; imperfections which it was too inconvenient to change and delights I was too unwilling to forego, whether compensating on my own for my celibate state or going daily to the beach or making sure my diet was tasty as well as good for my health. Occasionally, I also indulged in too much wine, and once in a while, puffed on a joint at white-haired Peter's house. This combination led to uncontrollable munchies, driving me to consume every delectable tidbit on hand, including once a jar of homemade fig jam Peter had been saving for years. I also yielded to inexcusable pride, implying subtly that it was self-restraint on my part rather than the lure of Peter's money, as he claimed in his equally inebriated state, that kept his young wife from straying across the street. I apologized profusely to my neighbor the next day, even though he greeted me with an affectionate hug and repeatedly assured me I had nothing to apologize for.

Then something far worse happened which I wish I didn't have to reveal. It was after a sumptuous Thanksgiving dinner, when I left the festivities at Peter's house in a disoriented state and walked to another neighbor's where I had been invited. The jovial group on hand included the host's lively seven-year-old playing grown-up with one of her precocious first-grade friends, putting on lipstick and nail polish and wrapping herself in mommy's silk brocade. In my semi-daze, I didn't notice she had been standing in front of me until her father said, "She wants you to pick her up." This was something I normally was careful about when sitting down, since I knew this particular girl was likely to straddle my leg and energetically rock back and forth. That is precisely what happened now. But instead of immediately putting her down, I obliged her for several moments more, until she was the one who asked me to put her down.

When I awoke a few hours later at home, the significance of what had transpired made me sit up with a groan. Despite a dozen plausible excuses and rationalizations crowding my head, none ultimately worked. Was total perdition due to a ten-second aberration during a life span of twenty-five thousand days?

God, what did it take to truly change?

5/

During my two years in Laguna Beach, I had yet to miss Sunday mass; more accurately, Saturday evening mass, which had been officially approved in Rome as a substitute, leaving my Sundays free. Combined with the time in Miami, this devotional commitment was already lasting about as long as I had lugged around the pressure cooker for Dr. Bieler's zucchini diet. I was no less eager to recover from what I felt was still ailing me now. I even went to communion regularly, hoping it might speed up the process, though I didn't know exactly what the process was that needed speeding up.

What brought about the astounding event I am about to relate would be difficult to say. It could have come from my twice-weekly sessions with Michael Wu Quinto, a Los Angeles acupuncturist I had befriended, who offered a special toning treatment for augmenting the potential of the brain. With the needles positioned just right in both ears, the procedure could leave a person feeling euphorically smart. At least that's how it sometimes worked for me – though the event which would affect me so could just as easily have been caused by the kind of life I had been trying to lead. Over the previous two weeks, I had deliberately refrained from any manual release of sexual tension as I concentrated on transcribing as faithfully as I could what I had learned firsthand about the role of pleasure in life. And only the evening before, during communion at Saturday mass, I received a message of sorts. Trying to remain unobtrusive in the crowded church, I was the last of more than a hundred people lining up to receive the holy host.

Just as I reached the altar for my turn, the priest ran out of the consecrated wafers he had been dispensing from the gilded chalice in his hand. Now, I alone remained kneeling in front of the entire church as I waited for a fresh batch of the little round wafers to be transformed into the body of Christ. How embarrassed I would have been if some of my trendy friends from the beach wandered in just then! They might have mistaken me for another of those Christians unable to resist hinting at the superiority of their denomination over other denominations, religions, or sects. In that interminable minute or two on my knees, I also had a momentary shock. Perhaps this was God's way of telling me he didn't want me to engage in this charade anymore; that I was a phony at heart, unworthy of his gifts. But in the next instant I was filled with a lighthearted pride, a feeling that perhaps this was God's way of singling me out and letting me know I was indeed on the right track.

The following day, whatever euphoria I still felt I augmented with an exceptionally powerful coffee fix. It was a Sunday afternoon late in spring, a sunny day with persistent patches of fog hugging the coast. Sitting in the warm sand at the secluded end of Main Beach, I shifted my gaze from the pelicans perched on the rocky ledge beyond the breaking surf to the hilly skyline of houses and shrubs looming over the town. Amid the silhouetted greenery, a window glittered here and there, bright pinkish reflectors penetrating the obscuring mist. I was feeling detached, absorbing the sound of the ocean and the cool seaweed texture of the air, just as my friend Cliff broke his stride in his five-mile jog and paused to chat. "Hey man, the guys are hassling me again on account of their women giving me the eye," he complained. Cliff's six-foot-two, 220-pound body of gracefully muscled ebony tapered to a thirty-two-inch waist had placed him in a predicament I could appreciate. "You don't seem too upset," I countered with a laugh, and then watched him saunter off toward the crowds.

As I stood up to start down the beach, I was feeling more and more as an observer in this human drama that I was still trying to comprehend. I was experiencing an overwhelming gratitude for finding myself in such a special place. No matter what the future might hold, I wanted to remember the magnificence of being here and have no subsequent regrets for having failed to realize that.

It was while walking along this partly fogged-in beach that I felt an enlightenment slowly but palpably permeating my consciousness. It was an inspiration I sensed descending from above, not unlike what had preceded my harrowing excoriation by God; something shifting directly overhead to create an opening in the sky. I had the vibrant feeling of being in the path of a radiant beam focused directly on my brain. Only this time the news was good; I was endowed with a fathomless serenity, surrounded by an aura that made me immune to the concerns of this world. It was a sensuous emotion, crowding out all competing desires and thoughts. It was reminiscent of the way I had felt years ago, after that furthermost run on Jones Beach, when I helped an injured horseshoe crab back into the surf, everything within me in perfect harmony. Yes, it was virtually a repeat of the rapturous experience at Manya's prayer meeting. My sole desire now was to share this feeling with others, to reveal to them this comforting news. I felt capable of extraordinary communication with the human race, free of any barriers or bounds, totally accepting of people in whatever guise they came. Moreover, the good news I had to share was unburdened by any theological prerequisites. It made little difference whether Jesus was the Son of God, or a part alien endowed with some supergene from outer space, or whether he was an all-too-human rabbi inspired in a uniquely exemplary way. It seemed immaterial whether Jesus had continued to exist as some disembodied spirit in our midst, or his verbal legacy had the power to activate this joyfully pervasive emotion in the brain. Those were the kinds of details beyond the grasp of the human mind over which people had tortured and killed each other in the past. What I could exultantly vouch for was that this Jesus-emotion had the power to mediate on our behalf with the stern and uncompromising God I remembered so well, whether he happened to be the inexorable Yahweh of the Old Testament and Hebrew Scriptures, or still another emotive force within the brain. This Jesus-emotion was the antidote to primitive human wrath bent on enforcing God's will, whether embodied in an Inquisition torturer in medieval times or a member of a militant Moslem sect crazed by an Ayatollah's retributive words. This Jesus-emotion was a liberating force of which we could avail ourselves to find forgiveness for our most troubling frailties and sins.

I continued down the beach in my exuberant mood and thought, how could I have been ashamed of uttering Jesus's name? He was the trendiest of all and incomparably more! I felt a triumphant inkling of a privileged truth. Whoever or whatever he was, Jesus was the essential factor without which humanity could never make it out of that materialistic dead end envisioned by Albrecht and other doomsayers of his ilk. Jesus had the power to guide and sustain us along a lengthy, demanding trail to an incomparably more satisfying goal. Perhaps earth really was a training ground for a higher universal role, a place where incarnated souls – those individual packages of evolving human consciousness – had to learn to correct basic flaws inherent in their design. I was beginning to understand how God, whether a personified supreme being or a non-corporeal force or some superhuman intelligence on a planet spinning around an unknown star, might have sent a special signal, an emissary, or even a speck of his essence to become incorporated in a human *son* who would show us how to overcome that array of flaws to which he also was heir.

Strolling down the crowded beach, I couldn't help but smile at this scenario invading my mind. It seemed so convincingly clear! Sensing this bond with Jesus, I felt myself straighten up from the familial stoop. Better step on it, I thought, and hurry home. I realized these revelations came in waves, and I wanted to write everything down while I still felt engulfed. Once the wave was spent, I might remember its overall shape but have little recall of its multitude of eddies and swirls.

Within six months of that enlightening day, I stopped entirely going to church. For I had come to a curious realization. The Jesus I was ashamed of wasn't the uplifting, resurrected one I had so vividly experienced myself, but the depressing dead one on the cross, so often used for man's purposes and misdeeds. The Jesus I had experienced was truly one of universal love, laying down no doctrinal prerequisites and holding forth an all-encompassing embrace.

I now arrived at my own understanding of the Trinity — not as an abstract theological construct, but based on what I had come to know firsthand: God the Father, who had so sternly rebuked me; God the Spirit, who had given me the necessary strength the one and only time I was prepared to submit — and whose abandonment of my friend the Skipper had left him stricken; and God the Son, whose euphoric grace had twice set me aglow. This personal perception seemed to be significantly at odds with the declaration of the Council of Nicaea about the Trinity being *Three-in-One* and *One-in-Three*, separate but coequal, yet one. Accepted by the Church since the fourth century and known as the Nicene Creed, this definition admittedly reflected a mystery beyond the comprehension of the human mind. Alas, it also left such devotees as my sister Manya blithely using the coequal God-the-Father and Christ-the-Son interchangeably. No wonder she and her cohorts as born again followers of Jesus identified the stern commands I had received as the work of the devil, just as they would have dismissed any modern-day version of God's demand that Abraham prove his faith by sacrificing his son. And with good cause, for surely Jesus didn't work that way!

Yes, the Church had been a logical and welcome place for me to seek refuge in a storm. But it was too stultifying when the weather was fine, just as Dr. Bieler's diet became intolerably rigid, even a hindrance to good health once I was again feeling well. I did suspect that if another storm blew in, I might again seek shelter in the Church, just as I might return to those rigid basics of Dr. Bieler's regimen if I became truly sick. This was the kind of human frailty Jesus would have understood only too well. For that reason he may indeed have countenanced his namesake faith with its multiplicity of denominations and sects, knowing that his saving grace could eventually transcend all divisions and faiths, rendering irrelevant who had it right or wrong, even more or less.

6/

Toward the end of my third year in Laguna Beach, I left for a short trip to the tiny village nestled at the foot of the snow-covered Pyrenees, where my aunt was being laid to rest. "I would like to be buried in a shroud or a simple pine box," Issten had told me on a sunny spring day when everything around the yellowing stone of her crumbling château was beginning to bloom in great splashes of morning-glory blue. "Yes, a pine box," she had said, with a bursting emphasis on the *p* and the *b*. "I want to return to nature as quickly as I can . . . dust to dust!" Too bad it was winter now, the ground too cold to reabsorb my aunt swiftly into that ethereal whole.

I'd often wondered what this day would be like. Although Issten had forfeited the château years ago, she staved off eviction to the end. The lender wasn't from the area, and no local official or gendarme was ready to enforce the law. They shrugged in their typically Gallic way, as if it weren't within their jurisdiction to act, then muttered with a mixture of exasperation and awe, *"Ah oui, la comtesse!"* That was supposed to explain everything. A compromise was finally reached whereby Issten agreed to restrict herself and her retinue to the château's third and most dilapidated floor.

"She was fine until her ninetieth birthday, then she suddenly stopped eating," explained Maya, after greeting me with a heart-felt hug. Maya was now almost completely gray, and the protruding cheekbones of her rounded face made her look drawn. "I should have known something was wrong when she lost interest in her apiserum. I only wish we could have done more."

I wasn't surprised that Stephanie didn't come. She had phoned from Hydra to let me know she was out of funds and couldn't travel until after her next one-person show a few months hence. Now I learned that Albrecht also wouldn't attend. At the last moment he had decided to remain in Austria to undergo intensive hydrotherapy for his shooting arm that was progressively going numb.

This was particularly disappointing news. I had been looking forward to seeing my cousin after all these years and being exposed to his views from my changed perspective. But I was also miffed. What a lame excuse for Albrecht not to come! Now that Mammi was dead, he couldn't wait to put the château out of his mind. He obviously didn't want to risk establishing future ties by personally showing up, the coward.

Then Albrecht's younger brother, Ferdinand, arrived. Wearing an elegantly tailored blue pinstriped suit, he was a seventy-year-old gentleman with thin, graying hair gracing a likable cherubic face. He bore a striking resemblance to his half-sister, though his pinkish white features still looked fresh while Maya's velvety brown visage appeared sadly worn. According to Ferdinand, Albrecht's illness was far more serious than anyone had originally thought and would require surgery to clear the arteries to his brain.

Sitting at an old, rough-hewn table in the center of the once-stately third-floor drawing room, Ferdinand appeared mindful of the château's retinue standing attentively at a discreet distance. On his right at the huge wooden table — and separated by a few feet — sat Maya, whom he repeatedly addressed with the formal *vous* as they conversed. Raising his voice, Ferdinand announced that Albrecht would continue the pension, which produced a perceptible feeling of communal relief. But when he quickly added with ominous emphasis, *"Mais, au tarif reduit!"* a silent tension permeated the room. This was followed by an audible groan as he disclosed what it meant: Instead of two thousand Swiss francs per month, only five hundred. I realized even this token amount represented a concession over which Albrecht must have agonized. Yet it was an unfortunate compromise; for it would neither sustain the château nor bring my elderly cousin the peace he had sought.

Ferdinand moved from the center of the chilly drawing room to the massive stone fireplace. That's where I had found a warm retreat, along with Maya's shivering old black-and-white Great Dane, from the icy winds whipping in through several cracked windowpanes. Ferdinand held a glass of cheap red wine in one hand and a cigar in the other. "This is a sad day," he said to me in a friendly way, with genuine feeling in his voice. "We always knew it would come, like some inevitable calamity. But thank God it's over. My mother was a destructive force, a totally selfish person. Never in her life did she do something she didn't want to do. As much as we all loved her, we've suffered because of her. She ruined my father's life . . . and look at the disaster she's leaving here. More victims of my mother's crackpot schemes to save the world." Ferdinand glanced at Maya, who had remained sitting at the table, bundled up in a heavy black shawl. Her head was bowed and there was a new dimension to the perpetual sadness in her eyes for failing to be the boy my aunt had counted on. Ferdinand glanced at several of the younger children, now in their teens, looking as if they had spent the night in tears; at Yura, the self-effacing father of the twins, who appeared to be as stunned as he must have been when Issten slapped him in the barn for making her daughter *enceinte*. Albrecht's brother turned toward the Rumanian diviner who kept promising the golden Madonna to the end in return for soup. Clutching under his arm the Havana cigar box containing his magic rod, he was surrounded by other hangers-on of many years. Everyone seemed distraught, as if on a rudderless ship. "You see," Ferdinand concluded, "she left nothing. Absolutely nothing. And we've had to foot the bill."

I heard the bells begin to toll. It was time to walk to the village church, at the foot of the steep hill beneath the château. Most of the mourners were gathered outside in their Sunday best, waiting in silent little groups for the coffin to arrive.

Suddenly there was a burst of deafening sound as a jet helicopter swooped down on a small meadow alongside the church. It was piloted by two dusky young men with an identical exotic look. Beneath their silvery flight suits, they were nattily dressed in black, as were their stylish female companions who could have graced the cover of a fashion magazine. It was the twins, in whom Issten had placed her hopes; her grandsons, Igor and Grichka Bogdanov, who would one day do great things. They were already proving her faith that one plus one could indeed be more than two. Together, they had published a well-received science fiction book and were about to launch a weekly one-hour futuristic series on French TV. While they could hardly afford renting that helicopter yet, they must have decided to splurge, perhaps because Issten had always insisted on their flying lessons even when there was no money for bread.

And there was Issten, arriving at practically the same time. As I watched the simple wooden coffin solemnly borne toward the entrance of the church, I could almost hear her whispering in my ear, *But of course it was all worth it, this so terrible thing I did! I always knew it would work out, I always had faith. One day the twins will be as proud of who they are as of what they have attained. And even if nothing at all had worked out, it would still have been worth it. What is life if not to do what one absolutely must?*

I heard her words reverberating with the church bells in the peaceful valley beneath the snowbound peaks. Was this the ultimate message my aunt had once promised to send?

Later, I sat next to Albrecht's brother in the second pew of the packed village church, listening to the eulogies. "*Elle était une grande dame,*" the old village priest intoned, with a drama only the French language could convey. "Yes, she was a great lady . . . never was there any suffering when the countess wasn't there to help, to do whatever she could . . . and always, always to bring solace. During the war, those difficult days under Nazi rule, she took in Jews. She saved lives at the risk of her own. Never, never did she give a thought to herself. *Oui, mes amis, elle était une grande dame* . . . She was a great lady, and above all, she was our friend."

I glanced at Albrecht's brother next to me in the pew, but he continued to stare fixedly ahead.

The obsequies for my aunt were recorded on a roll of color film I snapped during my brief visit. As soon as I returned to Laguna Beach and had the film processed, I sent a set of prints to Maya at the château, with a note about an amazing enlargement that would soon follow. It would show an eerie, brilliant glow over the top of Issten's coffin as it was being lowered into the ground.

Two weeks later, I received the following reply from Issten's daughter with Roland Hayes:

My dearest:

The pictures are wonderful and recall vividly the great, sad, and un-
forgettable time we lived together. We had all expected the end, but
when the moment really is there and you stand before it, then you get
an idea of what eternity is and how little a being counts on earth. You
have caught time just in time to stop it forever. Snapping people in a
graveyard is one thing, but catching a heartbeat at the second it is beat-
ing is what I think is a godsend. Bless you, my dear!

I'm looking forward to the "truly amazing" picture you write
about. Have you also one where my beloved Great Dane is seen? He
died on Wednesday last. I'm very sad and upset about it, and would
like to have a picture of him. He was old and ill, but he died because I
wasn't there to nurse him as I ought to have been. And I wasn't there
because I broke down after the funeral when everybody had gone, and
decided to go to the hospital and have a thorough rest. I guess the reali-
zation is finally sinking in. When Mamma was alive, I felt I was a
planet trapped in a strange orbit I didn't like. Now, I feel as if the sun
has gone out. I'm here in the hospital since a week and expect to leave
on next Tuesday or Wednesday. So I shall probably be home again
when you get this letter.

When will we meet again? I know California isn't next door, and
I wish it were. You're not far from the land of Winnetou which I
would give anything one day to visit. If we go on seeing each other eve-
ry ten years, I'm afraid there won't be much time left for me. Thank
you again for the pictures, thank you for having been here, thank you
for being you and do write soon.

Hugs and kisses and lots of love from all of us.

I finished rereading Maya's letter only moments before the
phone rang. The somber voice at the other end of the line was that
of the twins in Paris. Their mother had passed away earlier that
day without leaving the hospital.

Was Maya now a part of the eternity she had so poignantly described? Was she at last at peace, riding off into the sunset with Winnetou?

7/

According to the letters I received in Laguna Beach from Stephanie, Albrecht had surgery on both sides of the brain, with six weeks of respite between each side. The operations turned out well. Within two months of the second one, my cousin was not only able to resume hunting but succeeded in bringing down the most majestic stag on his property. It was the only animal to have evaded Albrecht for two years after he had decreed its doom – two years of unauthorized gallivanting among Albrecht's does. In a triumphant and uncharacteristic frenzy, Albrecht waved away the Forstmeister and pounced on the still-twitching deer to disembowel and decapitate him. There was vengeance in the way Albrecht wielded the hunting knife, as if striking at some taunting demon within. It was at the instant of cutting off the stag's head that Albrecht began to feel faint. When he tried to stand, he staggered as if his spinal cord had been cut, then collapsed on top of the bloody carcass. A medical helicopter airlifted the unconscious Fürst from the remote slope, and for a while, it looked as if he wouldn't survive. Yet when he did come to, his most immediate concern was the cost of the private hospital suite where he had been placed. Such extravagance surely bordered on sin! Albrecht insisted on being moved to the hospital's most public ward, much to the chagrin of the attending physicians. The problem was finally resolved by moving my cousin into a room with only three other beds and telling him it was the indigent ward.

"He's past that stage now," Stephanie wrote in her next letter from the Schloss, where she was on an extended visit. "All Pappi cares about is his therapy. He's on some experimental drug that's supposed to scour his veins. Lucky he's got Elizabeth. I never particularly liked her, though I suppose I can't blame her for those comparisons I had to endure with pristine Tasha. Elizabeth practically lives in the kitchen, keeping an eye on Frau Kunst. You know how Frau Kunst cooks. Delicious, but all that salt and fat and sugar would finish off Pappi in a week. I think Frau Kunst is finally ready to call it quits, go into *Ruhestand,* as she said, retire. Can you imagine, Pappi insisted on a warmer setting for the refrigerator, and some meat spoiled. When he tried to enlighten Frau Kunst about dead electrons, she said, *'Ja, ja, wunderbar!'* It was the first time I saw her give Pappi a scornful look."

Frau Kunst wanting to quit? That wise mainstay of the Schloss? The situation must have been critical. The incident was being whispered about as evidence that Albrecht was turning senile. Yet what had changed? I still remembered my cousin as a young man almost half a century ago at our home in Prague, when I spied him turning out the lights that had been left on in the halls for the night. Adjusting the refrigerator setting in his old age was merely a continuation of his life's most consistent theme. I couldn't vouch for Albrecht's theory of dead electrons, but how clearly he perceived the peril in humanity's boundless desire for more!

Over the coming months, I received additional news reflecting on Albrecht's mental state. Depending on whose letters I had in hand, my cousin had either lost his mind or finally came to his senses. For he was now insisting that Andreas renounce half of the estate Albrecht had signed over to him only weeks before. The once-reliable heir was no longer living up to the image he had projected while waiting for his benefactor to act. Within days of the formal property transfer, Andreas traded in his drab, six-year-old Ford Taunus for a sporty Alfa Romeo. It was far more expensive than any car on which Stephanie had splurged. Soon after, Albrecht discovered Andreas was drawing up plans to increase his revenues by cutting down more trees. Most disturbing was that the new owner took out a hefty mortgage on the land to construct a small hydroelectric plant to harness the power of the many mountain streams on the property – and thus personally cater to humanity's wastrel ways in a most blatant way.

Always loath to criticize, Albrecht issued an ultimatum: either Andreas came to his senses or there would be consequences. But now that his benefactor had signed over all rights, Andreas proved to be of an independent mind. Although he still turned beet red when speaking or spoken to, the new owner refused to budge. He speeded up refurbishing the spacious living quarters adjoining the Forstamt in the center of the village, which had been vacated by the head forester whose duties Andreas assumed. Whatever peace between benefactor and heir remained was shattered when Karina deliberately shot the wrong stag to have a more impressive trophy on the wall. That to Albrecht was tantamount to homicide. "Ach, I told you it was the other one," he despaired in their pine tree perch, as he saw the robust animal drop to the ground while the feeble companion bounded away. "This one I was counting on for another ten years!" Thereafter, Albrecht icily ignored Karina, and the situation continued to deteriorate. By the time Andreas and his wife moved to the Forstamt residence refurbished to palatial standards, they didn't even invite Albrecht to celebrate the christening of their first child.

That's when Albrecht had decided he wanted half of the property to go to Stephanie after all. She, at least, was his own flesh and blood, and he was fond of her boys. Hansi was apprenticing as a carpenter and could eventually switch to forestry. Little Paulus had the same captivating liveliness as his departed half-sister, for whom Albrecht still mourned. The photo I had taken of Angelina clutching Opapa's hair remained on his desk in a simple leather frame next to that of his wife.

Albrecht and Andreas were now barely on speaking terms, with Elizabeth consoling Albrecht, and at the same time, discreetly agitating against her former son-in-law and his present wife. Ferdinand, not surprisingly, stood by his son to the point of cutting off all communications with Albrecht – or so he had written me, concluding, "In his old age my brother is proving he can mess things up no less horribly than our dear mother." The matter was headed for a scandalous resolution in the Austrian courts. It was an ordeal to which my aging cousin was prepared to submit, if only to uphold a principle that was becoming less and less clear.

With Albrecht finally ready to fulfill Elizabeth's yearning to legalize her status, made all the more urgent by the prospective groom's deteriorating health, the bride-to-be made a tearful plea for a considerably greater lifelong annuity than Issten and her entire household had drawn – and far greater than Albrecht had proposed. Wouldn't it also be nice, the about-to-be Fürstin suggested to the Fürst, if they adopted her Tasha's little boy so he could have a name? That was at least something to think about; what she wanted right after the wedding was a suitable party to announce her noble status to her friends.

Finally, I heard from Albrecht. He started the letter with a brief mention of the marriage, adding dutifully, "I probably should have done it a long time ago." That he avoided getting more personal didn't surprise me. It was almost a decade since I had last seen him, and we were practically strangers again. "Despite some genuine disappointments in my old age, which I suppose we should all expect, I am feeling physically better; at times, quite normal," he wrote, in a barely legible hand. "But I never forget that after a stroke you aren't the same as before. I've put away my calculations for now, although I remain convinced that the solution to the universe exists. It means that man one day will *know*, whereas until then he has to *believe*. But only theoretically, I'm afraid, because the dead end is approaching fast. Never mind whether it shall come next year or some years later. We will finally learn the lesson that in the last resort there are no problems other than moral ones. A million years hence, should anyone care for a brief explanation of our inevitable demise, the Biblical tale of the Fall would say perfectly well just about all that needed to be said. *Yes, they too had everything and wanted more.* "

8/

There was panic on my little crescent beach, a sudden scampering and yelling as men, women and children in unruly little groups tried to evade the unexpected wave. As I watched the bedlam while treading water just beyond the turbulence of the cresting waves, I wondered: Is this what the end was going to be like? The way those people screamed and scurried around as if about to be smothered by that *ultimate* wave – the towering wall of swirling green water that supposedly would one day engulf California and wrench it from the United States. Yet these beachgoers had merely been trying to keep from getting wet; to move their towels, picnic baskets, and tanning oils out of the path of a wave surging unexpectedly far. They were now back in their little groups, beyond the water's reach, enjoying the sun. That they were somehow being given a second chance surely didn't cross their minds.

I was grateful for being able to continue living in this exotic, festive place. Even the personalized automobile plates here along Pacific Coast Highway seemed to have a certain flair, whether CRE8INK, ENLITND, or ATTITUD. Not surprisingly, there also was B42LATE. And what an ideal time to be alive! For only a dollar thirty-five, I could buy a loaf of still-warm-from-the-oven Dutch whole wheat bread at Stadelman's bakery on South Coast Highway, a few blocks from where I lived. This bread was as good as any in the world, especially if it didn't completely rise and wouldn't be quite so full of air. Ironically, that's when it was on sale at one third off. And for four dollars, I could have a five-gallon jug of water, fresh from a mountain spring, delivered to my door. A mere quarter a day would plop two hundred pages of the *Los Angeles Times* into my driveway at dawn.

How easy it was to have these things, how hard not to take them for granted! Still, I had moments of the same sort of vivid appreciation as I had years ago for those eight-dollar Bordeaux wines that I suspected would one day sell in the five-hundred-dollar range. And I wondered, what would that newspaper, the water, and the bread be worth tomorrow if we were to sustain some catastrophe before the end of the day?

I recalled with a sense of nostalgia the era of a few decades ago, when THE END IS NEAR was touted almost exclusively by a few scraggly characters, holding up crudely lettered placards or parading their message on sandwich boards. They preferred to position themselves in places where they could best confront the people most addicted to the luxuries of modern life, be it on Fifth Avenue in New York in front of the sparkling displays of Tiffany's and Cartier's, or near the George V Hotel in Paris, where the message was *La Fin S'Approche*. They tried to catch your eye with their flimsy signs and perhaps rivet you with a fleeting glance, hoping it would remain stored deep within your mind and from time to time pop disturbingly into your consciousness. No wonder most passersby wanted to avoid these scruffy sign toters, perhaps crossing the street or inwardly laughing them off, or even having some compliant *portier* shoo them away as so much vermin.

The possibility of the human experience winding down was no longer a crackpot thought or peculiar to such pessimists as Professor Baumer at Yale or my cousin the Fürst, whose latest letter about the approaching dead end I couldn't easily dismiss. All anyone had to do was to pick up the morning newspaper. President Reagan was finishing his first term, and the vast military buildup to confront the "Evil Empire" was in full swing. A MIG fighter plane had shot down a Korean airliner with U.S. citizens aboard, and Soviet troops were locked in hot combat with our surrogates in Afghanistan. The arsenals of each side were stocked with more than ten thousand nuclear weapons targeted at each other's cities and sensitive sites. From my days as a young naval officer, I could graphically recall what just one of those so-called devices could do! Would the end come as abruptly as that unexpected wave I had witnessed on the beach, or more poignantly, as John F. Kennedy's death – cheering and carefree smiles transformed in an eye-blink into incredulous, agonized gasps? Or would it be more gradual, perhaps a global economic collapse caused by the spending and borrowing frenzy that ignored the basic premise that if you take out a loan, you have to pay it back? Of course, the end could also come through some sort of an ecological disaster from having un-wisely tampered with nature too long to satisfy our multiplicity of appetites.

Was there truly no alternative? Was such a human-caused Armageddon as inevitable as had been predicted since earliest times? Were we powerless victims and culprits both, destined to succumb to our flaws? To rephrase the question: Were we doomed always to live in a world where we suffered and died because there wasn't enough – or in a world where we suffered and died because we didn't know how to handle plenitude? Were we forever caught between the scourge of scarcity on the one hand, and on the other, the debilitating excesses to which we were driven by our Survival Overcompensation Trauma – by our enduring SOT? Were we for-ever doomed to share the fate of Sisyphus working his rocky bur-den to the mountain's peak, only to have it come crashing back?

RESTITUTION

"Why don't you go to Prague," I occasionally suggested to Mother, when the situation throughout Eastern Europe began to ease in the late 1980s. "That's one place you might feel comfortable."

Her answer was always the same. "Do you think I'm going to let people see me as an old wreck?" Mother also had a secret fear that on deplaning at the airport in Prague, some Czech official would say to her, "How do you do?" and she would freeze and forget her English. Mother's trauma dated back to when she had first taken up with Father and he bemoaned her lack of languages. Intensely proud, Mother sought to remedy the situation throughout her years on the farm by finding time to study on her own. Until recently, she had been subscribing to magazines from Spain, France, Germany, and the USSR.

Now, macular degeneration robbed her of all but her peripheral vision, and arthritis deformed her back. She was so frail that even if she could see she would have lacked the strength to drive. Her main enjoyment came when I took her once or twice a week to some cut-rate department store in the nearest shopping center. Over the past forty years she hadn't bought anything for herself beyond the essentials; now, she suddenly seemed intent on refurbishing her wardrobe. Leaning forward in her decades-old Harris tweed overcoat to examine a rack of cheap dresses with her thick, gilded lorgnon, she truly looked like some aging, eccentric countess. Yet no matter how careful she was in her selection, the following week she would return whatever she had bought.

Her other diversion came shortly after the first of each month, when her Social Security check was credited to her savings account. She insisted that I promptly take her three passbooks to be updated at her bank. (She had been able to collect a blanket and a clock as premiums for opening the two additional accounts.) She repeatedly made me total up the passbooks and go over the results. She was disheartened by the low interest rates of Reagan's second term in comparison with the era of Presidents Carter and Ford. Part of her will to live seemed to derive from being able to add yet another monthly check to her account.

Despite knowing that I would be Mother's primary beneficiary, I wasn't always as patient with her accounting and other endeavors as I should have been. To think how I had yearned for just this sort of opportunity during that nightmarish week when I thought I would never see my parents again! On the other hand, had I shown such devotion now, Mother might have worried I had relapsed to that inexplicable disease of which she had long since considered me cured.

The beginning of the end for Mother came when she again fractured her hip. Unlike the successful first operation, this one left her legs paralyzed, while the medication she was given for pain disoriented her mind. She wailed about an old geezer with a wicker basket on his back tracking her down, and begged me not to let him throw her into some cold, dank cellar. But then on one visit to the hospital, Mother greeted me with a strange alertness. "Come on, you're late!" she said with obvious impatience. "Don't you know the show must continue? Quickly, we must go back on stage."

"On stage?"

"You fool! How do you think anyone could make it through life if it wasn't only a play?"

When Mother died shortly thereafter, I discovered for the first time how actively she had vied for her role in that play. From what Manya now revealed, Mother had confided to her that the encounter on the tram with Father had been no accident. Having learned through the rumor mill of Father's frustrated yearning to have children, Mother had carefully researched the habits of this high-profile nobleman, and as the prettiest girl in Prague, she was confident she could devise a lure he couldn't resist. The reason she then made Father wait for five years was to solidify his intent. And to keep his romantic illusions thereafter intact, Mother had floated to us children the version that she thought the strange-looking man who had followed her onto a tram was an unemployed professor with extraordinary nerve.

Mother had certainly played out her lifelong role; yet had she known what it would entail, would she have chosen to audition for it in the first place?

2/

Within a month of Mother's death, Father had sold his exercise business and was leaving Massachusetts to return permanently to Prague. In the three years since the Velvet Revolution of 1989 brought down the Communist regime, he had gone back several times to file for restitution of his properties. Each time, he was greeted with a mixture of incredulity and awe as if he were a modern-day Odysseus returning home. One of those visits had been courtesy of the Czech government, when President Vaclav Havel bestowed on him the nation's highest honor, the Order of T. G. Masaryk. At that ceremony, Father was seated next to another recipient, Alexander Dubcek, who led the country in 1968 into the liberalization of the Prague Spring. On being introduced to this heroic figure, whose attempts to give Communism a human face were crushed by invading Soviet troops, Father poked him in the stomach and said, "Ach, you really screwed it up! I could have been home twenty years sooner."

Father wasn't returning merely to expire in the country of his birth. As I drove him to the Boston airport, this ninety-five-year-old talked incessantly about refurbishing his properties and helping his native country regain its self-confidence. As we approached the terminal, Father turned to me and sighed, "Ah, just think what I could do if I was only eighty-five!"

Two months later, I followed Father to Prague. In my carry-on flight bag was a box containing Mother's ashes, which were to be given a permanent place of repose in the family tomb. I had a vivid sense that Mother was finally coming home. By the time I arrived, a graceful marble urn had been inscribed and arrangements for the ceremony were under way.

This wasn't my first time back since leaving Prague as a child. Unlike Father, for whom it had been impossible to return throughout the four decades of Communist rule, I had visited several times since the early 1960s, usually as a side trip from Albrecht's Schloss. Still, it was a different feeling now to be able to walk past our Renaissance palace or the Chicago office building not as another gawking tourist but with the confidence of ownership. As I watched the throngs troop festively along Wenceslaus Square, it was as if the sun had finally broken through after an interminable depressing spell. To see the neglected drab buildings being spruced up in pastel shades, and placards glorifying Communism being replaced by brightly lit marquees, promoting Lanvin and Benetton as well as K-Mart and McDonald's, was beyond anything I could have imagined. And more than once I wondered: with the end of the Cold War, were we entering that critical period in history my friend the Skipper in Laguna Beach had predicted, when humanity would have one final chance to get things right or forever face the consequences?

I found Father comfortably settled in the wooden villa he had built in the 1930s on the outskirts of the city in the Barrandov section of Prague. Overlooking the Moldau River from a tree-filled hillside parcel, it was a brown chalet structure with green wooden shutters. Father had located it in this highly desirable neighborhood to disabuse Czech citizens of substance of their traditional contempt for anyone whose primary residence was made of wood. Father's villa had served as a demonstration model for the prefabricated houses he was manufacturing before the war at his sawmill in the Sudetenland. Rather than being inspired, Father's neighbors at that time felt aggrieved by this intrusion into their stylish milieu of Bauhaus-type brick-and- mortar buildings. If he hadn't been Mr. Count, Father might not have been allowed to put such a structure there in the first place. The wooden construction was also the reason why the villa had never been taken over as a residence by any high Communist functionary, but served as a refuge for Ministry of Interior officials prior to the Velvet Revolution. Added to this former family residence during their tenure was a space with an impressive array of bulky porcelain urinals, which were apparently used for conferences, with the participants standing and the water running to neutralize any possible listening devices. Since only a top-level operative and his mistress – rather than some family – had to be moved out from what had been their hideaway, restitution caused relatively little emotional distress.

Within days of my arrival in the Czech capital, I came to appreciate how much of a national hero the former Exercycle salesman from New England had become. He had captured the hearts of the populace by handing over that Renaissance palace to the National Theater for the next twenty years at a symbolic rent of one crown per year. (The Communist regime had spent the equivalent of three million dollars to eliminate the ice cream store on the ground floor and otherwise restore this neglected edifice to its sixteenth-century splendor.) Father stipulated a similar arrangement for his ivy-covered castle in the Bohemian woods, so that it could continue to serve as a retirement home for the mentally afflicted. The generosity of these gestures appeared all the more pronounced in a country where the nobility had been vilified over the previous four decades as incorrigible exploiters, and where former émigrés now rushing back to Prague to make their claims were often depicted as gold diggers.

What undoubtedly burnished Father's laudable deeds with an untarnishable sheen was his record of progressive social views as a young entrepreneur, and then by his staunch opposition to both the Nazi and Communist regimes. He was the living symbol of the country's golden years of democracy and independence. Moreover, he had avoided entanglement in the United States with any of the contentious émigré groups, though only because he had been too busy shoveling manure and delivering milk. This unimpeachable background lent authority to Father's optimism about the future of the new democratic state, which he exuded to the procession of newspaper interviewers and television crews coming to his green-shuttered villa. Expecting to be received in a rigid, august setting, these visitors usually found Father in worn slippers and an open-necked shirt, surrounded by piles of newspapers, letters and books spilling over a coffee table and inundating the floor around his chair. Unable to conceive of Mr. Count's lifelong messiness, they cited this as evidence of his unassuming ways.

Father's age was also a great asset. The media never tired of quizzing him about his diet or photographing him doing his daily fifteen kilometers on the stationary bicycle he had brought with him from the United States. Indeed, Father was proud of his continued vigorous health. While he could still read a telephone directory without glasses, he compensated for his partial loss of hearing by telling everyone, including the country's president, that they mumbled. "I didn't understand a word you said," Father interrupted Vaclav Havel in their initial meeting. "Why don't you speak clearly the way I've heard you on television." When the nervous president took out a pack of cigarettes, Father instantly groaned, "Ach, Jesus Maria!" The former playwright-dissident looked exasperated and may well have been reminded of his years as a political prisoner. But Father pressed on: "You know, in America intelligent people don't smoke any more. My father smoked five packs a day and died of lung cancer at fifty-seven." When the president tried to defend himself by saying he'd recently had a physical and his lungs were found to be in order, Father dismissed his words with an abrupt wave of the arm. "When they do find something, it will be too late. The country needs you too much."

Never one to mince his words, Father was apt to be even more personally forthright with me. "You really look good," he said, as he eyed me across the dinner table toward the end of my first week in Prague. "I think you still have it in you to make a son or two."

"In that case," I shot back, "the credit goes to Barbara for resurrecting my life."

"Oh Barbara, Barbara!" Father retorted.

"Listen, if she had asked you in for a cup of tea when you were selling Exercycles and she was at Wellesley, you would have taken it as a great personal success."

"Hah!" Father exclaimed scornfully. "Barbara would have never bought an Exercycle. She's a Yankee. She wouldn't want to spend the money."

"That's probably true," I admitted. "But look how she has improved my life."

"The point is, she's too old to have children."

"So?"

"Just because you sleep with her doesn't mean you have to marry her. And even if you do, that's no reason why you can't make a son or two on the side."

"Sometimes I don't think you realize what you're saying."

Father was undeterred. "If you made some heirs, I could sign over to you one of the office buildings right away."

I shook my head and stared back. "Aren't you ashamed of yourself?"

Despite my words, I wasn't angry at this not-so-subtle bribery attempt. I realized Father was merely being consistent with what he had always urged me to do, and he wasn't about to change at ninety-five. To have children, especially male heirs, was his life-long ultimate aim, and fulfilling it justified whatever means had to be employed. I knew Father was in the process of transferring his properties to my younger brother Tom, which he wanted to accomplish for tax purposes before he died. Tom had forsaken his Miami Beach oceanfront condo — along with his carefree, well-paid gigs as cameraman-director — and was helping Father in such tasks as cutting through the Kafkaesque bureaucratic maze to get permits for refurbishing our long-neglected office buildings, freeing Chicago office tenants trapped in the stalled sixty-year-old elevator, or going to buy Father a piece of scrod at the French store, the only place such items as fresh seafood, Romaine lettuce, and Honeydew melons were for the first time after forty years again available, trucked in daily from Paris.

"I'm perfectly happy if Tom runs everything," I said as an afterthought. "Mother always believed his day would come." Although Tom had often worked for me as a cameraman, ours had been a warm, brotherly relationship, and I would defer to him just as often as he would to me. Athletic, personable, and conversant in a half-dozen languages, he was the one with star power in the family.

For a moment, Father looked glum. "I'm no longer so sure he's going to produce either."

Indeed, Father's sole reservation about Tom was that at fifty, he was still looking for the ideal bride, just as I had been for so

426

many years before meeting Barbara. What redeemed Tom in Father's eyes was that he had already busied himself interviewing an array of candidates in Prague, all of whom appeared to be in the early part of their childbearing years.

3/

Several days prior to the memorial mass for Mother, Tom drove Father and me to check on the preparations at the family tomb. It was located beyond the city of Pilsen, in a tiny village about 120 kilometers from Prague. Father had been born there, in a massive baroque castle that he gleefully exchanged in the 1930s for what he then owed the architect of the Chicago building. The castle was now a hulking wreck, abandoned after forty years as a barracks for the People's Red Army. Although Father was in the process of repossessing some forests and fields in the area, it was the restoration of the family tomb that brought him on regular visits. Even if the Communist regime hadn't collapsed and he had remained in the United States, Father had intended to have his body shipped back and be laid to rest here alongside his forebears. Topped by a small, rotund chapel with whitewashed stucco walls, the tomb was at the edge of a hilltop graveyard dominated by a rustic, seventeenth-century church with a weatherworn reddish onion spire. Father's first allocation from the rentals of his office buildings in Prague, which were the only moneys coming in so far, was for this long-neglected site.

We arrived as several workmen, using block and tackle, pulled back a rectangular stone slab inside the chapel's entrance, revealing the steps leading to the tomb below. The last time this stone had been removed was more than half a century ago as part of a similar check on the conditions inside. Some hooligans had apparently sneaked in after working hours to see if there was anything of value to spirit away. The story has it that when they came face-to-face with the glass-topped coffin of my great-grandfather, the hapless field marshal, his bemedaled remains looked so ferocious that the would-be thieves ran away.

I couldn't resist this opportunity to take a peek, if only to check out the field marshal. As I descended the few steps into the semidarkness, I felt enveloped by the cold dankness of the cellar-like room. Lying every which way on the stone floor were a dozen or so austere metal caskets. They could have been old steamer trunks strewn in a ship's hold. Even here the family disorder pre-vailed! On closer inspection, I realized these were not coffins but locked metal containers into which the ornate coffins had been placed. Finding the field marshal's container open is what had tipped off the local officials to the robbery attempt fifty years ago.

Now, as I stretched out my arm, I was acutely aware that just beyond my fingertips might be the remains of my grandfather Le-opold, survivor of the last fatal duel of the Austro-Hungarian Empire; his wife, the daughter of an international tobacco mag-nate, whose wealth enabled my grandfather to reclaim the family estates; their son, my uncle Sascha, entombed here shortly after Marlene Dietrich had obliged him in his hospital room and lifted her skirts. Somewhere here was also Sascha's wife, the Russian princess, who claimed her husband's philandering had been the cause of their childlessness, and then failed to produce an heir af-ter she seduced Father into marrying her. And of course, some-where here was the field marshal, whose distinctive features had been passed down to me. Unfortunately, with all the metal en-casements looking the same, it was impossible to tell which rela-tive was which, except for two violin-sized cases that must have held Father's twin brothers who had died shortly after birth, and another viola-sized case undoubtedly containing the brother who died at two. Seeing these little boxes before my eyes, I could ap-preciate Father's obsession about the family line dying out.

The cold mustiness was beginning to have an oppressive effect. Could this be the dank cellar Mother had wailed about? During the last years of her life, while still in possession of her faculties, she had been explicit about not wanting to be interred in the family tomb. That's why she had insisted on being cremated in the United States. Having spent a lifetime with a Turner-of-the-Wheel, she didn't want to be locked up for eternity with the entire crew, perhaps even ending up next to the Russian princess.

Mother would have her wish. Upstairs in the chapel above this cellar of final repose, the workmen were busily carving out a prominent niche in the wall. That's where the marble urn with Mother's ashes was going to be placed, illuminated by a permanent light, in dominion over the nobility below.

4/

Father's outlandish offer had been welcomed in one respect: Having turned down this opportunity to acquire great wealth, no one could say that this casual civilian of fortune had paired up with such an accomplished woman for questionable goals. The decision hadn't been at all difficult, and I never had second thoughts. Not only was I daily acknowledging my gratitude for this relationship that was fulfilling my life, I had yet to meet somebody, already well off, whose joie de vivre was augmented by sudden great wealth, be it Andreas or some of my Hotchkiss classmates marking time until they could tap into their trust funds. My younger brother's life certainly didn't improve in Prague as heir apparent to the entire family estate. Even in his favorite pursuit, he had a far richer variety of options in the carefree atmosphere of Miami Beach than under the watchful scrutiny of his life in Prague.

Despite his determination to behave correctly during Barbara's visits for my sake, Father's frustration at seeing his son involved in what he considered a sterile relationship showed through. "Why do you always have to mumble?" he would reproach her at the start of virtually every conversation. And indeed, Barbara did speak in measured tones, having been accustomed in her various professional roles to have her listeners' attention. Raising her voice to compensate for Father's hearing loss was for her a strain, and I tried to minimize the conversations between Father and her in whatever ways I could. A climax of sorts came at breakfast one morning when Father seemed to be particularly hard of hearing. He had just posed a question to Barbara about her work with the Carnegie Endowment for International Peace, and as usual, she paused to think over her answer while finishing her mouthful of muesli. When I seized this opportunity to jump in with an answer in Barbara's stead, Father immediately cut me off. "Can't a big shot like Barbara speak for herself?"

"I'm afraid not," I said, shaking my head. Seeing Father's attention suddenly piqued, I paused before adding significantly, "You see, she has a problem. She mumbles."

By the time Barbara and I left Prague, I solidified another conclusion: not only did sudden great wealth — especially when augmented by an enviable title — rarely improve the quality of one's life, it failed even more consistently to improve character. This was increasingly evident in the way Father was beginning to take for granted being deferred to obsequiously at every turn. While he had remained notably outspoken in the United States, the imperatives of having to earn a living had placed restraints on how far he might let some of his more peremptory instincts reign. I didn't blame Father now any more than I blamed my younger brother Tom, who was also becoming less willing to negotiate his views. In fact, the proliferation in my direction of *Mr. Count this* and *Mr. Count that* during the three weeks I was there didn't leave me entirely unscathed.

My frequent sojourns in Prague over the next couple of years were at least partly on business. Already on that first trip with Mother's ashes, I had explored the possibility of taking advantage of our name recognition and publishing the story of my involvement with Albrecht, Issten, and Stephanie. An editor with a reading knowledge of English eventually managed to convince a leading publisher to take on the manuscript under the title loosely translated as *Confessions of a Frivolous Nobleman*.

In those early years following the Velvet Revolution, translators still occupied an enviable niche. Over the previous four decades behind the Iron Curtain, they represented a vaunted window on the outside world. In promoting a Shakespearean play, the translator's name was liable to appear more prominently on the marquee than that of the director and leading man. My translator was an elderly lady whose intent was to follow the accepted practice of imposing her voice over the author's and making the book her own. She also took it on herself to try to improve my prose whenever she didn't consider it dignified enough for a count. With hardly anyone over the years in a position to question a translator's work, the most she had come to expect were a few stylistic adjustments from the supervising editor. But loyal to the Duke's admonition to keep up my Czech, I was in a position to propose literally hundreds of changes. This was a brash affront, and I had to take full advantage of being Mr. Count in exploiting the patience of my beleaguered translator.

I nevertheless ended up being grateful – and not only for the resulting quality of my translator's work. Our give-and-take enabled me to improve my command of the language to the extent that I could answer questions in hour-long radio interviews without seriously messing up. And while on the air, I never missed an opportunity to further utilize what I had learned from my old headmaster. "Don't think that because you're going to be richer and more powerful or perhaps have more education than most people," I often cited him in the press as telling his elite Hotchkiss boys, "you will also somehow be better than they. The only way you can do that is by being less selfish and more humble than they." In a country recently under the impression that a TV episode of Dallas reflected the sum total of the United States, the Duke's words came as quite a surprise.

With my book soon topping the best-seller list, Father didn't disguise his pride, and more than once, renewed his offer of a substantial portion of the properties, which by then had been restituted to him.

"I'm sorry you can't accept things the way they are," I replied on one such occasion. "You're depriving yourself of a chance to get to know a person I think you'd really like."

"What has that to do with it?" Father said, and made a circular motion with his arm as if to wave me off. "Your first responsibility is to have children."

"As I've told you before, I may have already produced . . . "

Father again interrupted, making a similar motion with his arm. "You mean Hansi? He's a nice boy, but the prices he offers to buy my wood are no good. He also speaks German with that terrible Austrian village accent, which my grandson would never do. But the final test is, did you or did you not intend to make a child with Stephanie?" He gave me a quick scrutinizing glance. "With Mother, I intended to make every one of you. If you don't intend to make a child, then you have nothing to do with it."

This wasn't the first time I heard Father articulate such a view, which must have been a part of the standard educational curriculum of teen-age nobility under the Austro-Hungarian Empire. Was this also the reason Kristina's first husband, Hansi the prince, never truly embraced his illegitimate child as his own? Rather than any legal or ecclesiastical bond, this question of intent at a crucial moment during an extra marital liaison would determine who might or might not be accepted. However, when it came to inheritance, Father didn't feel bound by tradition and considered himself free to leave the property to whichever of his children he wished.

"You could still have a wonderful life ahead of you," Father interrupted my thoughts. "You wouldn't have to worry about money, you're now famous in your own right, and everyone loves to see you in Prague whenever you come." Father gave me a significant look. "I think you could have any woman here you want!"

I realized Father was trying to pay me a compliment. "I'm doing just fine, thanks," I said, and left it at that.

5/

How improbable that I would become closely involved in investigating the murder/suicide of the country's foreign minister, who had made that cup of hot chocolate for my brother and me in his London flat, only weeks before his unexplained death some forty-five years ago.

The wispy, aging man who approached me in 1994, while visiting my father at our restituted villa, was Dr. Antonin Sum, one of Jan Masaryk's three personal secretaries at the foreign ministry. From his well-worn satchel, Dr. Sum took out a sheaf of documents. "Here's a copy of the autopsy report," he said, handing it to me. He could vouch for its accuracy, he said, because he had been present in the morgue until he fainted when the coroner sawed off the top of the Minister's skull.

"Of course, it was a suicide, but unfortunately, other versions have cropped up that are pure fiction," Dr. Sum explained. "With your literary success here and the respect for your family name, you have the credibility to write an authoritative version that will put this matter to rest."

The unprepossessing, almost jovial demeanor of this thin, be-spectacled oldster, who had at one time assisted at conferences with world leaders, belied what he had been through. Imprisoned and facing the death sentence for conspiracy and high treason in the 1950s political show trials, he felt relieved to receive only twenty-two years. The first ten of those he spent in the country's Jachymov uranium mines. His jailers singled him out for especial-ly harsh treatment, with several of them periodically growling that *the underground latrine detail was too good for that rogue Sum.* Then, as Communist orthodoxy began to relax in the early 1960s and Dr. Sum was granted amnesty, this former multilingual dip-lomat with a doctorate from Charles University earned certifica-tion as a chimney sweep. It took another seven years of scaling Prague's gothic rooftops in blackened togs before he was able to return to a modicum of normal life in various low-profile adminis-trative posts. In a novel departure from his routine tasks, he was occasionally dispatched to international conferences, where he would act as translator for the Communist government's delega-tion and implicitly set the standard for acceptable behavior.

Now, Dr. Sum was offering to extend his full cooperation and provide the necessary documentation that would enable me to ex-plain how Jan Masaryk's broken body had ended up on the stone pavement beneath the open window of his third-floor apartment in the Foreign Ministry office building in the early morning hours of March 10, 1948.

Intriguing as I found Dr. Sum's offer, I had reservations about accepting. My fond memories of Father's deceased friend notwithstanding, did the Czech people really need someone who had spent virtually all of his life in the United States butting into their affairs? What could this sporadic visitor to Prague add to what had already been uncovered by countless writers, criminolo-gists, psychiatrists and other individuals with incomparably more background know-ledge of the case, not to mention the ongoing

434

governmental effort by the Office for the Documentation and In-vestigation of Communist Crimes? An earlier official investigation initiated during the Prague Spring had been aborted when Soviet tanks rolled in in 1968, though not before an investigative reporter from the United States, Claire Sterling, was able to gather enough new material for her well-documented book, *The Masaryk Case.*

Sensing my hesitation, Dr. Sum once more repeated his man-tra: that the Minister's suicide was not some spur-of-the-moment decision; that the Minister had gradually come to the conclusion that he must do this to alert the West about the danger of trying to deal with Stalin – and that his deliberate personal sacrifice led to the creation of NATO. "The Minister deserves to have the prop-er historic perspective," our visitor concluded.

"Let me think about it," I said. "I'll keep an open mind."

In the coming months merging into years, I would monopolize more of Dr. Sum's precious time than any other reporter or foreign dignitary. The venue for our two-to-three-hour meetings soon shifted from our restituted villa in Barrandov to his cramped, fifth-floor walk-up in an old apartment building near the center of Prague that his family had once owned but that had not yet been restituted. Dr. Sum was pleased to have Barbara joining us, since he regarded her as an esteemed foreign policy colleague due to her previous posting at UNESCO. And it wasn't long before Dr. Sum became for me *Tonik,* and when we occasionally reverted to Czech, we both used the familiar *thou* form of address. The relationship nevertheless remained on a handshake, matter-of-fact basis, as if a protective barrier was shielding Tonik's innermost self. Was this perhaps a leftover from his decade in the uranium mines?

Tonik never tired of repeating that the Minister's suicide was a deliberate act of self-sacrifice to rouse the West. Yet from my own preliminary reading, I had come to realize it was clearly the West that had been trying to rouse Jan Masaryk over the three years since the end of the war, when his country fell under Soviet sway. In fact, at the very time that Masaryk was making hot chocolate at his London flat for my brother and me, he was sharing with my father the disastrous results of his trip to the United States. President Truman had refused to receive him, and Secretary of State Marshall had chastised him for knuckling under to Stalin, and refused to provide the assistance Masaryk had desperately sought. Reading Masaryk's personal report of that encounter made it appear as if Marshall had personally written off this lifelong friend of the West.

While I remained unconvinced of Tonik's self-sacrifice rationale, I became increasingly aware that the Minister had ample cause for taking that fatal leap. The crisis leading to his demise had started when the country's democratic-leaning ministers resigned en masse in February 1948, hoping to precipitate new elections and inflict a decisive defeat on the Communists. But Jan Masaryk, on whom they had been counting, declined for whatever reason to join the group that had resigned, leaving them one vote short. Backed by nationwide agitation, the Communists were thus left free to form a government of their own, in which Jan Masaryk would remain the foreign minister. To provide the appearance of legitimacy for what in the West was widely condemned as a coup d'état, the Communist prime minister, Gottwald, sent word to his internationally respected foreign minister to show up in parliament on March 10th for the introduction of the new government. For Masaryk to appear with this band of Stalin's lackeys would have been even more of a shaming than for Father to have appeared during the war with Henlein in the Sudetenland. Jan Masaryk was the son of the republic's revered first president, whose world-wide repute was noted even by my old head-master, the Duke, in awarding my older brother and me nearly full scholarships.

Not everyone was entirely saddened by the violent outcome of Jan Masaryk's predicament. "We mourn his loss – it is a heavy loss," declared Winston Churchill in Parliement shortly after noon of that fateful day, "but one cannot help rejoicing . . . that the esteemed name to which Masaryk was heir will remain an inspiration to the people of Czechoslovakia."

Father, of course, refused to believe that his jovial, fun-loving friend would ever do something so stupid as jump out of a third story window. However, without ruling out the possibility that the Minister may have indeed jumped in a post-midnight fit of depression at the thought of appearing that day at Gottwald's side, the more realistic alternative seemed to be that he had been pushed or thrown out; that is, murdered. In the Western World, including in Claire Sterling's book, the blame for who could have been behind such a deed fell exclusively on the Communists – be they local operatives or henchmen dispatched by Stalin. For me the most viable scenario within this context was that it had been a case of a *house inspection* gone awry. Suspecting that Masaryk was about to flee to England, a group of men led by a certain Major Schramm had been deputized to sufficiently scare the Minister to insure he would show up the next day at Gottwald's side. However, in trying desperately to escape the clutches of his nighttime invaders, the Minister happened to tumble out of his bathroom window.

In listening to my friend Tonik dispassionately recount the details of this theory, my suspicion was that Masaryk's alleged defenestration had not been a *house inspection* gone awry, but that this Major Schramm was a double agent, carrying out orders from the West, which he had artfully grafted onto orders from his Communist superiors. *A most regrettable turn of events,* he might have afterwards ruefully reported to those superiors. According to Sterling's information from an unassailable witness, both Prime Minister Gottwald and Interior Minister Nosek were not only surprised but visibly shaken by Masaryk's death, and "there were tears in M. Nosek's eyes." Although Schramm had impressive Communist and USSR credentials, he had at various times shared a house with his brother, who was a member of the YMCA and had spent the war years in England. Moreover, in Tonik's telling, within days of Masaryk's demise, Schramm's three alleged accomplices had turned up in West Germany at the Regensburg refugee center that served as a U.S. counterintelligence facility.

This was the first time Barbara and I had heard of any possible connection with the West, and we glanced at each other as if simultaneously electrified. Tonik's revelation dovetailed with what had been previously publicly documented: that another recent escapee to the West by the name of Choc had been sent back from his Regensburg asylum to kill Schramm, ostensibly in revenge for murdering Masaryk but more likely to silence him.

"No, no, Choc did not kill Schramm," Tonik corrected me, eager to weigh in on another publicly unresolved issue. He had firsthand evidence, since he happened to be in the same prison bloc awaiting trial the night before Choc was to be hanged. The authorities had allowed the condemned man's girlfriend to visit him, Tonik explained, and Choc swore to her he didn't kill Schramm. "He certainly had no reason to lie," Tonik concluded. At his trial, Choc had claimed that Schramm was already dead when he arrived at his house; moreover, his mission had never been to kill anyone but to abduct Schramm to face justice in Regensburg.

Had Schramm perhaps been quietly eliminated by his own operatives who had figured out his duplicity?

"These may indeed be facts," Tonik mused, "but we have no proof of their relevance to the Minister's death. Schramm's murder most likely was the result of some internal dispute. What you have here is another of those theories that keep cropping up. There's even a theory," Tonik continued with an impish smile, as if to further disparage the previous facts, "that the Minister may have been resting in the middle of the night in the middle of the winter on his bathroom window sill, and fell."

I often challenged Tonik's assertions, didn't defer to him and questioned him sharply. Tonik nevertheless responded with patience and good humor, leaving me feeling guilty about my unsparing treatment of this elderly gentleman who had been through so much. Tonik's incarceration had been a relief after the endless interrogations to which he had been subjected, culminating on the day of his trial, when the prosecutor opened the courtroom door and pointing to the witness chair, snarled, "Repeat exactly what we've rehearsed, or it's the noose . . ." When I tried to apologize if I was beginning to sound like those inquisitors of the 1950s, Tonik merely smiled, as if to say that I was hardly in the same league, his courtly, innocuous façade obscuring a steely constitution developed during his ordeal.

Tonik was a modest man, reluctant to talk about himself; yet the most relevant information I gleaned from him was as an aside to his own life. On more than one occasion he informed Barbara and me that he had been regularly reporting during this period to the U. S. embassy, and one of his colleague-secretaries, who had spent the war years in England, had been regularly reporting to the British and the French. More than once Tonik mentioned with evident satisfaction that within hours of the Minister's death, he was at the American embassy reporting, "It was a suicide." This revelation takes on new significance in light of Sterling's theory that the countless cigarette stubs of diverse brands found in Masaryk's bedroom suggest that the perpetrators had tried to talk the Minister into taking the fatal leap of his own volition, before resorting to violence. This begs the question: would Stalin's henchmen have bothered with such niceties? His own countrymen might have, considering Masaryk's cherished persona, as also might have perpetrators deputized by his former allies from the West.

Was Tonik's hasty trip to the U.S. embassy a case of reporting *mission accomplished?* As Tonik often pointed out, "There are circumstances when you cannot always act the way you would normally act." Single-minded though Tonik was in adhering to his mantra of the Minister's self-sacrifice, he allowed that he couldn't be more than ninety-nine percent certain, since he wasn't a witness to the deed. Reflecting on his personal experience in jail, he was ready to concede that "the Russians in those days were capable of doing their work without leaving traces, as also were the Americans."

Considering Tonik's uncompromising orientation toward the West and his loyalty to Masaryk, I ventured to ask at one point how he had personally felt about Masaryk's failure to resign.

Tonik didn't hesitate. "Awful," he almost wailed, as if feeling the pain of his untenable situation to this day. "But my colleagues and I had been hoping the Minister would remove himself from the scene by going into exile."

Beyond any supportive evidence gleaned from Tonik, the unavoidable conclusion Barbara and I had to draw was that while the Communists were counting on Masaryk to appear in parliament on March 10th, the Western powers had a strategic interest in keeping Masaryk from showing up. Did the world have it wrong? If there had been a murder, had it been perpetrated by operatives acting on behalf of Britain or the United States? Was that the meaning of Churchill's eulogy over Masaryk's apparent suicide in saying, "We cannot be unhappy . . . ?"

Hoping to find more information to confirm or refute these unpalatable implications, I turned to the CIA, invoking the Freedom of Information Act. But my request was repeatedly denied on the exception that such information could compromise sources or adversely affect international relations. "By this action," read the CIA rejections, "we are neither confirming nor denying the existence or nonexistence of such information." British authorities were no more forthcoming.

[The Czech police would formally close the Masaryk case in 2004, designating the Minister's death as murder, but still unable to name any perpetrator.]

The most startling revelation during these interviews was not anything about Masaryk in 1948 but what had happened to Tonik shortly after the Velvet Revolution. That's when rumors surfaced that he, yes, Tonik, had killed Jan Masaryk. Tonik mournfully came forth with this shocker only after I had forced myself to inquire, with profuse apologies for merely pursuing unhampered objectivity, whether Tonik and his Western-oriented colleagues had taken any measures for relieving their untenable situation? In making his emotional revelation, Tonik deviated for the second time from his dispassionate demeanor. Both Barbara and I had by then come to entertain the possibility that he and his colleague may have indeed, wittingly or unwittingly, provided the crucial intelligence to their Western embassy contacts that set into motion the fatal process of removing the Minister from the scene. Was Tonik's single-minded quest to credit the Minister for his sacrificial deed and restore the reputation of the Masaryk name a form of expiation for his guilty conscience? Was Tonik's revelation another classic case of the perpetrator's need to confess? Perhaps more speculative: could Tonik's especially harsh treatment in the uranium mines have been partly related to his guards' suspicion that he had been complicit in depriving the country of its universally most beloved public figure? How else would this slight, self-effacing young prisoner, who had fainted at Masaryk's autopsy, be viewed as *that rogue Sum?* While Tonik never specifically denied to us that *he had killed Jan Masaryk* – and I never had the gumption to ask him directly – he attributed these rumors to some of President Havel's political operatives, who were overly eager to scuttle any possibility of Tonik's own candidacy in the June 1990 presidential election. Despite having received for several years thereafter numerous threatening telephone calls and letters, Tonik had decided not to fight these rumors. As he explained, "That would only have given the whole affair greater visibility."

I kept up with Tonik until the end. Shortly after the publication of the last of his own books on the Masaryk family, he complained that his legs were giving out. My next visit coincided with the delivery from his publisher of a package of those books, and I was glad to be able to run down the five flights and bring the package to him. Suspecting that this might be the last time I would see Tonik, Barbara had suggested I visit him on my own. As usual, Tonik made us some tea, but instead of waiting for me to pose the questions, he launched into reminiscing, with unusual feeling, about his years as chimney sweep; how he loved being alone on the rooftops and the unique perspective his work gave him on the world below. I was by now reconciled that whatever secrets Tonik may have held, he would take with him to the grave. I tried to convey how much the chance to interact with him over the years had meant to Barbara and me, and on leaving, I unexpectedly felt free to give him a quick hug. His friendship at the moment had become more important than learning the truth about Jan Masaryk's demise.

Although I never wrote the book Tonik had been hoping for — nor came close to accepting Tonik's narrative about the selfless circumstances of Jan Masaryk's death — the resulting twenty-or-so hours of microcassette tapes would definitively confirm what I myself by then firmly believed: that Tonik himself had always acted in a selfless way, regardless of personal risk, to preserve for future generations the democratic ideals associated with the Masaryk name.

6/

The series of improbable coincidences I am about to relate occurred on my next trip to Prague; this time, to launch the publication of my second book, *Confessions of a Czech American*, and also to deliver in manuscript form *Confessions of an Unwitting Sinner*, the final part of what was becoming a trilogy.

I had an appointment to meet in the National Library with a seasoned observer of the Czech literary scene, Milena Nyklova. Several days earlier, she had interviewed me about the forthcoming book and related themes, just as she had done after the publication of the first confessional volume. Now, having negotiated my way through the vast baroque library complex, I had in my hands Milena Nyklova's typed version of our conversation for *authorization*.

I was particularly grateful for this opportunity to look over what I had said, which was standard practice harking back to the Communist regime. My intent wasn't to strike out anything stupid or politically embarrassing but to ensure I had expressed myself in Czech approximately the way I would have if the interview had been conducted in English. While my command of the language had continued to improve, I relied on my interviewers for the occasional mot juste or the unstilting of a phrase.

Milena Nyklova seemed to have done a remarkable job. As I sat next to this erudite, grandmotherly woman at one of the long tables perusing her single-spaced pages in the quiet of the library's main reading room, only once did I feel constrained to lean toward her and point to a sentence. That's where she had me quoting the seventeenth century philosopher, Jan Amos Komensky, about something called *eyeglasses of general deception*.

"I've never quoted Komensky in my life," I whispered.

She smiled and nodded. "But the idea you express here is exactly the same as his."

I felt no urgency to press the issue in the hushed nave-like room. But later that day, as I went about my errands in the city, I felt increasingly uneasy about the Komensky quote. After all, I had neither the inclination nor the academic wherewithal to cite Komensky. In Baumer's intellectual history class, Komensky – or Comenius, as he was known outside his country – rated no more than part of one lecture, and on the few occasions I had noted his name in my various readings in subsequent years, it was only because of his Czech origin rather than any kinship I felt for his ideas.

When I returned home to our restituted wooden villa, I phoned Milena Nyklova. "As much as I appreciate the honor," I explained, determined to make my position clear about the Komensky quote, "I don't want to appear smarter than I am."

"But it's such a trifle," she rejoined. "It's perfectly normal to make far greater enhancements."

"Believe me, I'm grateful for any enhancement, as long as it's consistent with my capabilities. But quoting Komensky is not one of them. Whether regrettably or otherwise, I know almost nothing about him."

"Even so, I was astonished how often you sounded like him." She paused. "But that's all right. I'll put it in an editorial note instead."

Later that same week at my *autogramiada* at one of the largest bookstores in Prague, I was being assisted by Mila Tuzarova, a diminutive, energetic woman with short bleached hair, who had played a similar role at the signing of my first book. Standing alongside my table amid the floor-to-ceiling stacks, she handed me each of the books and helped me spell some of the trickier Czech names. She kept the line moving and enabled me to devote myself momentarily to each recipient of a signed book.

Because of Mila's size, her head remained close to mine as we bantered back and forth, reflecting an evident concordance between us. That seemed to encourage some of the shyer readers to speak up while having their copy of the book inscribed.

The signing had started at 3:30, a half hour ahead of time, and continued for another half hour past the store's six o'clock closing. As Mila and I relaxed and sipped champagne brought by one of the patrons, she suddenly reached down to a nearby lower shelf and retrieved a glossy black volume. "I think this will interest you," she said, placing the heavy book on the table in front of me. "It's a wonderfully lively study of the work of Jan Amos Komensky. It was published in nineteen-eighty-seven . . . one of those remarkable books that every now and then made it through some crack past the officialdom."

"It must have caused a sensation," I ventured.

Mila pursed her lips and gave me a level stare. "Remember, that was two years before our Velvet Revolution. People usually ignored books published officially. The underground presses, the *samizdat*, that's where the action was. The publisher in this case printed twenty-five thousand, and five years later, most of them were still unsold. They were going to be shredded, but my boss loves books, and he managed to save several hundred."

I glanced at the main title, *Pictorial Atonement*. The smaller print explained it was a book of photographs on the theme of one of Komensky's works, *General Consultation about the Improvement of Human Affairs*.

My interest was piqued. It was only days ago that Milena Niklova had alerted me to my intellectual kinship with Komensky. Shouldn't I at least try to find out a bit more about this obviously wise, seventeenth-century itinerant Czech?

I opened the heavy cloth binding and started to turn the glossy pages of the oversized book. Interspersed with the promised photographs was one quote my eye immediately seized on: "If we are destined to wise up eventually, why not wise up now?" My God, that could have been uttered by the Duke!

"Would you like to have it?" Mila asked.

"I think I've just enough money for the taxi home."

"For you, Mr. Count, it's a gift." Then she quickly added, "A small token for helping us sell so many books."

In perusing Mila's gift, I savored the pervasive common sense reflected in Comenius's words. Among his writings was counsel I could have offered to my fundamentalist sister Manya. "Let your religion consist in serving me quietly, and in freedom from ceremonies, for I do not require them of you," Comenius cited the enlightener of his soul as advising him. "When you serve me as I teach you, in spirit and in truth, do not quarrel about your religion with anyone, even if they should call you a hypocrite, a heretic or what not."

Comenius was putting his thoughts on paper amid great economic chaos and personal tragedy. *His Labyrinth of the World and the Paradise of the Heart* was written shortly after his home in Bohemia had been plundered and burned by invading troops, and his wife and two children succumbed to the ensuing pestilence. No wonder that when Comenius's enlightenment about the true state of human affairs came, his redemptive prescription entailed a complete withdrawal into that *Paradise of the Heart*.

"I have wandered about not knowing where to go," Comenius wrote in the book's concluding paean to his enlightener and redeemer, "but Thou hast overtaken me and hast returned me to myself as well as to Thee."

This didn't stop Comenius from trying to improve conditions on earth. He dedicated the remaining four decades of his life to reforming education, espousing the radical idea that schools should be made available to girls as well as boys – and that learning should be fun. His other focus was trying to find the best way to redirect those human proclivities that led to the sort of wrenching disasters he had experienced. That's what caused him to lament, "If we're meant to wise up eventually, why not wise up now?" Three centuries later, Comenius's precepts for maintaining peace among nations influenced the writing of the charter of the United Nations.

I saw no conflict in Comenius's endeavors to straddle the spiritual and materialistic realms. Despite the grateful optimism with which I approached daily life, his overarching pessimism about our human condition was something to which I could relate. How vividly I still recalled my own bleak outlook on the world following that unexpected excoriation from beyond, when my glasses of deception had been summarily removed! Nothing in my life had been more real and influenced me more than that experience on the snow-covered field, except of course, for the joyous enlightenment that had unexpectedly enveloped me in Laguna Beach.

7/

COUNTRY'S OLDEST ARISTOCRAT DIES AT 98 – that was the headline for the story in the *Prague Post*, illustrated with a photograph of Father astride one of his machines in his prime as Mr. Exercycle in the United States.

I returned to Prague as promptly as I could to help with the funeral arrangements. I was grateful that only two months earlier, I had been able to spend several weeks with Father in connection with the publication of the final part of my trilogy. On my last evening there, when I looked in on him in his bedroom, he asked me to feel his hands and feet and tell him if I didn't think they were unusually cold. Indeed they were, but since I didn't want to say anything that could upset him, I made no comment. "Oh, that's all right, I know I'm coming to the end of the road," Father rejoined in a dramatically calm voice. "Yes, the end of a long, long road. But there's no reason to be sad. I'm satisfied I've done all I can."

Now, two black-suited attendants wheeled the refrigerated body into the tiny hospital room reeking of formaldehyde, and silently took their leave. Father was lying fully clad on a canvas stretcher on top of what had once been an operating table. It was strange to behold so irrevocably stiff those ever-expressive Turner-of-the-Wheel features that I had so noticeably shared — the sloping forehead and the prominent nose with a slight cleft at the tip. Nothing could reanimate them now. As I placed my hand on Father's ice-cold forehead, the realization that this also was the end of the long, long road he and I had traveled together gripped me with the anguish of an irreversible loss.

As was the case with Mother's funeral, I accompanied my younger brother to check on the preparations at the family tomb in the village where Father had been born. Tom had inherited Father's chauffeur, Vladimir, whose lingering fame as the country's top automobile racer a quarter century ago was as much of an advantage when blundering into a speed trap as volunteering that his passenger was Mr. Count. Watching Tom from the back seat chatting with Vladimir, I had to remind myself that my brother was now one of the country's wealthiest residents. No longer the carefree camera director from Miami Beach, he was a gaunt, graying man with Mother's worried mien, who had aged markedly over the past three years. I had reluctantly come to realize that our lifelong relationship no longer felt the same because he had become afraid I might grasp the property offer Father was periodically dangling before me.

The final detail to be resolved was the matter of eulogies: whom to select, without slighting anyone, from among the country's cultural leaders, politicians of various stripes, and Father's leading employees vying to eulogize Mr. Count. The fact that the January weather had converted the unheated church into a freezer box, combined with the custom of seemingly endless oratory, could have turned the service into an ordeal. Our solution was that only my brother and I would speak, and very briefly at that. But the evening before the funeral, Tom ate something at the family banquet that didn't agree with him and spent much of the night throwing up. The following morning, after dozing off on the front seat next to Vladimir, he awoke about twenty kilometers from our destination, turned to me, and said, "You can have my time."

Although we arrived at the village church with a half-hour to spare, we had to wend our way through the crowded aisles to the apse where our family members were gathering. That put us only a few steps from Father's simple wooden coffin, flanked by an honor guard of a half dozen of his foresters dressed in green, and a dozen local firemen in blue, their breath condensing into individual puffs of mist. Behind them at attention were four senior members of a national athletic organization, proudly braving the penetrating cold in the tan shorts and short-sleeved shirts Father had financed.

Everyone in the church remained standing. It may have been because they were enthralled by the pervasive sense of history, which seemed to meld them into a single entity; a more practical reason was that if those who had managed to secure a place in the pews sat down, their view would have been obliterated by the standees. As it was, the bishop serving the mass and his four assisting priests had barely enough room in front of the baroque altar to carry out the rites.

Standing slightly apart from everyone else next to Tom at the edge of the elevated part of the apse, I listened sporadically to the bishop's homily exhorting the people who filled the church to pray that God quickly admit Father's departed soul to heaven. I was mentally trying to go over my unwritten text and impress on my memory the Czech words I intended to use. The one phrase I would repeat in English for our relatives and friends who didn't speak Czech was Father's farewell, "I'm coming to the end of the road, yes, the end of a long, long road. But there's no reason to be sad. I'm satisfied I've done all I can." And that he had done, including putting his life on the line to do what he felt he absolutely must, and having worked selflessly to insure the future of his children. Perhaps Father had done God's will when it really counted, and whatever transgressions he might have committed amounted to barely visible blemishes on an otherwise sparkling soul. Was that why Father seemed to have been so miraculously at peace? Yes indeed, I kept repeating to myself, there's no reason to be sad.

By the time I positioned myself behind Father's coffin, I felt composed. "Some ninety-eight years ago, in this church, just about in the area where I'm standing now," I began, "a small group of people gathered to christen a newborn. The mayor assures me they used the same pewter christening urn a few steps to my left behind some of our guests. The year was eighteen-ninety-seven, the times were more orderly, and one could pretty much predict the course of life for a newborn, especially for a child coming into the privileged circumstances of a Turner-of-the-Wheel."

I paused to scan the surrounding array of faces and register momentary acknowledgment in the eyes of the people I personally knew. They were letting me know that they recognized the incredible turn of fate that had twisted and enriched my father's life from the course it had been meant to take. I raised my arms to encompass everyone in the church and pose a collective query: "Who could then have imagined what journey lay ahead for this newborn before he would return to be here with us today!" With that I placed both hands on Father's casket, as if to enfold his life and the century it had spanned.

EPILOGUE

Within two months of Father's passing in 1996, Barbara and I were married — and have been fortunate to benefit from marital concord to this day. The role of husband to my wife provides the indispensable balm when struggling with past regrets and tussling with daily shortcomings.

My younger brother Tom survived his tenure as one of the country's wealthiest men for eight years. By the time he died in 2004, he had fulfilled Father's wish, having sired two children with a woman nearly half his age, whom he never married and who brought him increasing grief. But as had been Tom's intent in leaving no will, his underage children under Czech law inherited the entire estate, with their mother appointed as executor. In this capacity, she terminated the Theater's twenty-year gifting lease, despite the ten-year extension my brother had provided on his deathbed in a written note. Moreover, using the power of her new wealth, she has consistently sought to portray her two children as my father's sole legitimate successors in the centuries-old Turner-of-the-Wheel tradition.

Sic transit gloria mundi — or as Walter Cronkite used to sign off, *that's the way it is.*

45141693R00281

Made in the USA
Columbia, SC
20 December 2018